POLITICAL PROTEST AND SOCIAL CONTROL IN PRE-WAR JAPAN
The Origins of *Buraku* Liberation

Ian Neary

Department of Politics
University of Newcastle upon Tyne

Studies on East Asia

HUMANITIES PRESS INTERNATIONAL, INC.
Atlantic Highlands, NJ

First published in 1989 by

HUMANITIES PRESS INTERNATIONAL, INC., Atlantic Highlands, NJ 07716

Not for sale outside North America

Editorial responsibility for *Studies on East Asia* rests with the East Asia Centre,
University of Newcastle upon Tyne, England, which promotes publications
on the individual countries and culture of East Asia,
as well as on the region as a whole.

Library of Congress Cataloguing-in-Publication Data

Neary, Ian
Political protest and social control in prewar Japan.

(Studies on East Asia)
Bibliography: p.
1. Buraku people. 2. Zenkoku Suiheisha (Japan)
3. Buraku people—Government policy—Japan.
4. Japan—Social policy. 5. Japan—Politics and government—1912-1945
I. Title   II. Series
Studies on East Asia (Atlantic Highlands, N.J.)
HT725.J3N4 **1989**   305.5'68   87-4209
ISBN 0-391-03495-2

PRINTED IN GREAT BRITAIN

Contents

List of Illustrations

Preface

Many have assisted in the process of translating the idea for a dissertation about the *Burakumin* into a completed thesis about the *Suiheisha* and shaping a D.Phil. thesis into publishable form. My debt to those scholars who have written on this and similar issues will become apparent from a brief glance at the bibliography. But, over the thirteen years which it has taken to get from the initial proposal to the printing press, special encouragement to persevere with the project has come from several sources which I would like to acknowledge here. First, at Kyushu University, Professors S Hidemura and A Shigyo have shown me round libraries, introduced me to fellow scholars and helped to track down articles. Then, at Sussex University, Dr J W M Chapman guided me through the process of enrolling for and later completing the doctoral programme while Professor R P Dore provided stimulating criticism and otherwise inaccessible documents. Later, colleagues at Huddersfield Polytechnic and Newcastle University have read all or part of the revised chapters, helping to improve both style and content. Throughout much of this period S Anai has provided invaluable support and insights on the nature of Japanese society.

I am particularly grateful for all the time generously given by the residents of the many *Buraku* communities I have visited over the years and the assistance and advice provided by the activists in both wings of the liberation movement. Nevertheless, I am aware that many of these people to whom I owe much will not agree with some of the opinions and interpretations of *Buraku* history for which I alone am responsible.

July 1986

Introduction

To the distant observer Japan presents an image of homogeneity and harmony. Indeed, policy makers across the world look at Japan's cultural homogeneity and social harmony with some envy and have sought to reproduce some aspects of it within their own societies. But it was not always so. In the middle of the nineteenth century the small élite which made policy was faced with a country divided into some three hundred semi-autonomous political units and a society split into four main classes each of which was further sub-divided. It is true that many of the class barriers were beginning to break down and that feelings of national unity were emerging in the face of the threat from the West. Nevertheless, the task which consumed the energies of the political élite in the first years of the Meiji era was to break down the barriers to social and geographic mobility and generate a consciousness of nationhood within the minds of the residents of the Japanese archipelago. So successful was this and later generations of policy makers that Japan is not usually perceived as a society in which there is social protest or political conflict. Yet a closer examination of the historical record reveals that beneath the patina of social stability there has, throughout the modern era, been a pattern of protest against social injustice by many of the less advantaged sectors of society who were not benefiting from the political, economic and social changes which were engineered by the élite. The sector of society which most conspicuously failed to receive its share of the increased economic activity has been that which descended from the outcast communities of the pre-modern period now usually referred to as the *Burakumin*.

In 1922 a group of young *Burakumin* held a conference in Kyoto to launch the *Suiheisha* as a movement which would fight against the prejudice and discrimination which they encountered in their daily lives. Very quickly this grew into a major social movement organisation which allied itself with the left wing peasants and labour federations. As has been well documented, the government, alarmed by the radicalisation of significant sections of the population, adopted a series of measures to win back the allegiance of the citizenry and to prevent any further challenges to its authority. There was devised a specific policy – known as the *Yuwa* policy – which was addressed to the *Buraku* problem and to the threat posed by the *Suiheisha*.

The main concern of the chapters which follow is to describe and explain the emergence of this social protest movement and the dialectical relationship between it and the policy which aimed to control and replace it. A small but growing body of literature exists in English about social and political change in pre-war Japan and this present volume is intended as a further contribution to this pool of knowledge.[1]

But it is hoped that this work will be read not only by existing specialists on Japan interested in this as yet undeveloped corner of Japanese studies but also by others within the academic community and beyond. Political historians seeking a different perspective on the formation of social policy in Japan, social historians interested in the formation and development of social movement groups and social anthropologists looking for new examples of minority groups and social protest will all find items of interest in the pages that follow.

Such specialists and, indeed, the general reader will bring with them different skills and seek answers to different sets of questions, and it is unlikely that a single work will be able to provide answers which will satisfy every reader. Broadly speaking, we will be concerned to cover four main areas; firstly, to provide a narrative account of developments in the *Buraku* communities which led to the formation of the *Suiheisha* and its growth over the next two decades; secondly, to relate the events of *Buraku* history to concurrent events in the wider political and social context; thirdly, to consider the interaction between this social movement and the formulation of one aspect of the social policy – the *Yuwa* policy – in the period 1900-1940; and finally, without seeking to test one single or series of social theories about minorities or social movement organisations, reference will be made to the work of writers who have examined similar social phenomena in other social structures. In particular the work of Barrington Moore Jnr. will be referred to frequently throughout the text. His discussion of how individuals come to be conscious of their inequality and how they respond to suggestions that they themselves can do something about their hardship provided me with a useful perspective from which to assess the activities of *Burakumin* in the late nineteenth and twentieth centuries.[2] Overt comparisons are, for the most part, avoided but it is hoped that the material is presented in such a way as to enable readers interested in comparative perspectives to draw their own conclusions.

But, who were these *Burakumin*? How many of them were there? What were their living conditions like? What kind of discrimination did they endure? Before embarking on a detailed discussion of the historical origins of the communities, a brief description of some aspects of the *Buraku* problem in the early twentieth century may be useful.

Prejudice and Discrimination against Burakumin[3]

Discrimination against *Burakumin* was (and indeed still is) common everywhere in Japan but was particularly virulent in the south west, where a majority of the *Buraku* communities were located. It was based on deeply-rooted prejudices, some of which derived from concepts found in the *Shinto* or Buddhist religions but included other, more bizarre aspects. One writer gives the following as example of popular notions about *Burakumin* current in the first decades of this century,

One rib is lacking; they have a dog's bone in them; they have distorted
sexual organs; they have defective excretory systems; if they walk in the
moonlight their necks will not cast shadows, and, they being animals, dirt
does not stick to their feet when they walk barefoot.[4]

Most of these beliefs about *Burakumin* stressed that not only were they not
entirely human but that contact with them would pollute human beings. These
prejudices were not confined to the largely uneducated mass of the population
but were to be found among the highest civil servants. A report issued in 1880,
several years after the formal abolition of status distinctions, described *eta:hinin*
as,

the lowliest of all the people, almost resembling the animals.[5]

The attitude which lay behind the actions of many government officials,
including those charged with the duty of assisting *Burakumin* to improve their
environment, was expressed with unusual candour by one local government
officer in Shiga prefecture who is reported to have said,

If the government, instead of issuing the emancipation ordinance in 1871,
had exterminated the *eta*, all this trouble would not have ensued.[6]

Perhaps this was an extreme case, but one gets the impression that many of the
bureaucrats who became involved in programmes to give aid to *Burakumin*, even
if they were not hostile to them, would have preferred to ignore their existence.

It was possible for most bureaucrats and many Japanese to ignore the
problem. *Burakumin* themselves, however, were constantly faced by examples of
discrimination in their daily lives. Because *Burakumin* were believed to be
carriers of pollution many practices had developed to minimise contact between
them and the majority population. In most areas *Burakumin* were not permitted
to cross the threshold of the house of a majority Japanese. Shopkeepers would
refuse to accept money directly from them and would insist that the coins be
placed in a water-filled box. Thus, the chance of physical contact would be
avoided and any 'dirt' washed off. *Buraku* day-labourers in rural areas were
provided with separate and inferior eating utensils and toilet facilities. In towns,
factory owners would avoid offering employment to *Burakumin*, and only by
concealing their origins was it possible for them to rent housing outside *Buraku*
areas.

Discrimination was particularly evident in schools. Until the early Taisho
period (1912-13), it was usual in many areas for *Burakumin* children to attend
separate primary schools and to find that they were prevented from entering
secondary schools. Even when institutional segregation was forbidden,
Burakumin children would still be seated away from the others at the back or side
of the classroom. Play groups would be arranged so that non-*Buraku* children
did not come into physical contact with *Burakumin* pupils, and toilets and eating
equipment were usually kept separate. Indeed, it seems that most *Burakumin*

first experienced the full force of discrimination at school and many recall their school-days with special bitterness.

However, what was most instrumental in keeping *Buraku* and non-*Buraku* communities apart was that, in addition to the fear of possible defilement by physical or social contact, there developed the 'modern' belief that,

> . . . they are inescapably carriers who can transmit to any offspring their blemished nature and hence contaminate a blood lineage into which they may marry.[7]

Until the late nineteenth century, status distinctions and communal separation kept *Burakumin* apart from the majority community and it seems unlikely that any inter-communal marriages took place. But, migration to the urban areas and increased inter-communal contact resulting from changes in the rural social structure produced circumstances in which liaisons and marriages which crossed the 'caste-barrier' could take place. Such relationships were regarded with distaste by the majority community and, in fact, *Buraku* endogamy remained the norm throughout the period we shall be examining. Official support for this feeling was provided in 1904 when the Hiroshima District Court approved the divorce of a non-*Buraku* wife from her *Burakumin* husband on the grounds that,

> according to tradition, it is still normal for those who are not *eta* to abhor marriage with one.[8]

In urban areas migrant workers would take care to avoid the company of men or women suspected to be of *Buraku* origin and careful investigations would be made of a potential spouse's background.[9] Where there was suspicion that he or she came from a *Buraku* community strong family pressure would be applied to prevent the marriage taking place. Ideas about the genetic transmission of 'pollution' have persisted into the modern period and have been the major single factor in encouraging the continuance of discrimination.

Population – its size

The Home Ministry conducted two surveys in the pre-war period to ascertain the size of the *Buraku* population; the results appear in the table below:

	1921	1935
Total Population	56,787,000	68,665,000
Buraku Population	830,000	1,003,000
	1.46%	1.46%

The *Suiheisha*, however, claimed to speak on behalf of 3,000,000 *Burakumin*. Can these very different figures be reconciled? Sometimes the difference is explained away simply by saying that they were a result of the hyperbolic rhetoric of the *Suiheisha* leaders. This may, in part, be true, but it is not a completely adequate explanation. To begin with, even the supporters of the government policy recognised that the official figures underestimated the size of the *Buraku* population. But the main problem lay with the definition of *Buraku* or *Burakumin*. The liberation movement has always included in its estimates all those who were (or are) actually exposed to discrimination or would be if their status origins were known. So, their estimates include all those who live in areas known to be *Buraku* communities and those who are trying to 'pass' as majority Japanese by hiding their background and living in the majority community.

The definition adopted by the Home Ministry survey only included those who lived within the boundaries of *Buraku* communities as defined by local government officials and who were descendants of those classed as *eta:hinin* in the *Tokugawa* period (1600-1867). But many *Buraku* communities, especially in urban areas, had expanded beyond their traditional boundaries; migration into *Buraku* communities by those who were not descendants of *eta:hinin* was not uncommon and, despite the risks, emigration into the majority society was fairly frequent. The Home Ministry would include neither immigrants nor emigrants in its estimates, the *Suiheisha* would include both. To anticipate a theme which will be developed later, we may note here that this typifies the contrasting approach taken by the two organisations: government policy aimed at improving the *Buraku* communities, the *Suiheisha* sought to make former feudal status irrelevant.

Population – its distribution

The *Buraku* population is not distributed evenly across the country. As can be seen from the map (p 6), the heaviest concentrations of *Burakumin* and *Buraku* communities were to be found in prefectures bordering the Inland Sea, Fukuoka prefecture, the Kinki area and the Kanto region.[10] There are very few *Buraku* in the north-east of Japan and none in Hokkaido. Various explanations of this peculiar population distribution have been suggested although none seems wholly satisfactory. However, as will be argued later, *Buraku* communities developed mainly in the *Tokugawa* era and it can be no coincidence that relatively high proportions of *Burakumin* are to be found in areas which were the most economically developed in that period. It seems reasonable to suppose that if a pariah caste is to develop, there has to be a substantial economic margin within which it can exist.

Buraku living conditions

One can get an idea of the living conditions in urban *Buraku* by briefly considering the results of two surveys of conditions in *Buraku* communities in Kyoto, the former imperial capital. In 1886 it was found that in one large *Buraku*, of the 1,100 households surveyed 840 survived by relying on odd jobs, and of these 750 lived on the edge of dire poverty; 400 of them were selling off their possessions in order to survive and 350, having nothing to sell, only survived thanks to the charity of others.[11]

Number of *Burakumin* per 1000 majority population in 1935.

Japanese towns referred to in the text.

The situation had barely improved some 50 years later. A survey of the six *Buraku* of the city of Kyoto revealed that one-fifth of their population were officially classed as destitute while more than half of the total number of families had an income for the whole family which was less than 40 yen a month, at a time when the average wage for a single labourer was 40–50 yen. The population density was six times greater than in the rest of the city; over 90% of the houses in these areas were officially described as unfit for habitation; half the households used communal toilets; 60% of the houses were not connected to public sewers. Not surprisingly, there were serious health problems: the infant mortality rate, for example, was two and a half times that of the rest of the city, 40% of their children suffered from trachoma compared to 3% in the majority population.[12]

Conditions were no better in the rural *Buraku*. A national survey carried out in 1931 found that the average income of a *Burakumin* peasant household was about one quarter of the national average.[13] *Burakumin* had always farmed smaller plots of the least fertile land and relied on other sources of income, part-time work and day labour, to make ends meet. This dependence on external income is demonstrated in the following figures:

Farmers Income 1930[14]

	Buraku	*Non*-Buraku
Incomes from farming		
(land either owned or rented)	151 yen	499 yen
Other income	153 yen	226 yen
Total	304 yen	725 yen

So, despite the formal commitment of the government to equality of treatment for all its citizens, more than fifty years after the Emancipation Declaration of 1871 most *Burakumin* still lived in poverty in separate communities, were subject to discrimination from the majority Japanese and were conscious of their own inferiority.

Burakumin Protest

During the *Tokugawa* period political protest was severely dealt with; the leaders of protest groups were invariably executed. However, in the relatively liberal atmosphere of the Meiji era there emerged demands for social justice from a wide variety of groups in society including the *Burakumin*. By 1922 these demands for equality of treatment had culminated in the formation of the *Suiheisha*, which within a few years had established branches across the country. In the first section we will be concerned to answer such questions as: How were the *Buraku* formed and how did discrimination against them develop? How did *Burakumin* cope with the rapid economic and social change of the second half of the nineteenth century? and How did they acquire the consciousness of belonging to an unjustly oppressed minority?

But the *Suiheisha* was not the only social movement to be launched and prosper in the early 1920s, the high water mark in the era of *Taisho* democracy. In urban areas semi-legal trade unions were emerging to demand improved wages and conditions for their members. In the countryside, tenants unions were becoming involved in campaigns to demand rent reductions. Those active in the *Suiheisha* often had close links with or were actually members of such workers, or peasants, organisations and the *Suiheisha* was strongly influenced by the left wing ideas current in the social movement in Japan in the 1920s. Indeed, a major theme in the debates which raged within the *Suiheisha* was how closely the movement should ally itself with other groups and how far their ideas should guide its search for a theory.

Both the peasant and worker organisations were perceived by the state as a threat to national stability and the government soon took steps to try to minimise the influence of these subversive elements. Just as the government had supported the formation of the *Kyochokai* (Harmonisation Society) in 1919 to promote industrial harmony at a time when labour unions were first displaying a potential for disruption, so, in the same year, did the state sponsor two conferences to discuss the *Buraku* problem. And in the following year the first central government money was provided to establish a *Yuwa* programme. This, it was hoped, would prevent the radicalisation of opinion in the *Buraku* communities. However, if the general intentions of the policy makers were clear from the start of the 1920s there was little agreement even among those involved in the *Yuwa* activities on what tactics would best achieve these aims. Within the *Suiheisha* this problem was even more acute. All of them sought to establish a state of affairs in which there was no discrimination against *Burakumin*, but whether this could be achieved by gradual reform or required a social and political revolution was an issue which more than once was to threaten the movement's very existence. In the second section we shall be concerned to trace the development of the *Suiheisha* movement and *Yuwa* policy through the 1920s. However, the reader is warned that this was a rather messy process. There were numerous false starts and frequent examples of duplication of effort, especially in the attempts to create a *Yuwa* movement which might have been able to replace the *Suiheisha*.

In the 1930s, however, the picture becomes clearer. To begin with, the government provided the *Yuwa* movement with more money at the same time as placing it under closer central control. *Yuwa* policy becomes part of the Home Ministry's programme of social control which from 1936 aims at the mobilisation of the entire nation behind the war effort. Weakened by the arrests of its leading activists in the late 1920s, it seemed unlikely that the *Suiheisha* would be able to survive in the face of competition from its well funded rival. Moreover, despite its weakness, factional rivalry and political argument continued to consume much of its members' energies. The gradual decline in its influence and support reached a nadir in 1932, but then, perhaps surprisingly, the movement regained and indeed expanded its organisational strength and influence within the *Buraku* communities. In the final section we shall explain how the movement was able to achieve this regeneration by examining its revitalised theory and practice and the official response. Finally, in the last chapter, we will discuss the response of both the radicals within the *Suiheisha* and the *Yuwa* bureaucrats to the onset of total war following the intensification of the war in China and the outbreak of the war in the Pacific.

So far I have been concerned to map out the territory which will be explored in the body of the work and to describe some of the themes that will be pursued. Most emphasis has been and will be placed on the development of policy at central levels, whether in the Home Ministry in Tokyo or in the central committee of the *Suiheisha*, but, quite obviously, most of those who were involved in either movement never had direct contact with the central institutions. Any study of a social movement is bound to be to a great extent a study of its central leadership. Documents of committee meetings and conferences, the articles and editorials of the journals are written by and about them. But in order to try to give some impression of the experience of *Burakumin* within the local groups two complementary strategies have been adopted. Firstly, every so often the discussion of developments at the national level will break off in order to consider how the concerns of the central institutions were reflected in the activities of *Burakumin* in Mie and Hiroshima prefectures. In each of these areas there was a substantial *Buraku* population which generated a well documented *Suiheisha* movement which was outside the orbit of influence of the movement's most prominent leaders. Secondly, what most *Burakumin* did as members of a *Suiheisha* group was to take part in *kyudan* campaigns – campaigns of protest against those who discriminated against *Burakumin*. *Kyudan* campaigns were to the *Suiheisha* what strikes and rent struggles were to the labour and peasant organisations. Changes in the tactics employed in these campaigns reflect developments in the movement's overall strategy.

So, the principal concern in what follows will be to explain the emergence of *Suiheisha* movement and *Yuwa* policy in the 1920s and to discuss the relation between them as they developed over the next 20 years. However, the process which led to the formation of these outcast communities has received little attention by Western historians and must be our point of departure.

Notes:

1.   I am thinking in particular of such work as: S L Large, *Organised Workers and Socialist Politics in Interwar in Japan* (Cambridge University Press, 1981); R H Mitchell, *Thought Control in Pre-War Japan* (Cornell University Press, 1976); R J Smethurst, *A Social Basis for Pre-War Japanese Militarism* (University of California Press, 1974); B A Shillony, *Politics and Culture in Wartime Japan* (Oxford University Press, 1981); although there are several others.

2.   B Moore Jnr, *Injustice: the Social Bases of Obedience and Revolt* (Macmillan, 1978).

3.   The problem of how to refer to the inhabitants of these communities is one that has taxed analysts both in Japan and in the West. Early Western analysts referred to

them as *eta* but this has been discarded as being as insulting as trying to analyse the race problem in the USA in terms of 'niggers'. In Japan, a variety of euphemisms has been adopted by the government and the liberation movements: *Saimin Buraku* (Poor People's *Buraku*), *Tokushu Buraku* (Special *Buraku*), *Hiappaku Buraku* (Oppressed *Buraku*), *Mikaiho Buraku* (Unliberated *Buraku*) and *Hisabetsu Buraku* (Discriminated *Buraku*). This latter term is most commonly used by Japanese writers, but in this thesis, in common with most Western work, the communities will be referred to as *Buraku*, their inhabitants as *Burakumin* and the overall issue as the *Buraku* problem. Where it is necessary to refer to that sub-unit of the village usually translated as 'hamlet' we will use the lower case *buraku*.

4. Kikuchi Sanya, *Etazoku ni Kansuru Kenkyu* (Research on the *Eta* race) (Tokyo, Sanseisha, 1923), pp 72-3. Also quoted by Shigeaki Ninomiya, 'An Enquiry Concerning the Development and Present Situation of the *Eta* in Relation to the History of Social Classes in Japan', *Transactions of the Asian Society of Japan (1933)*, p 56.

5. Quoted in G O Totten and H Wagatsuma, 'Emancipation: Growth and Transformation of a Political Movement', in *Japan's Invisible Race* ed G deVos and H Wagatsuma (University of California Press, 1973), p 38.

6. Ninomiya, p 116.

7. DeVos, p 297.

8. DeVos, p 38.

9. It might be objected that in the big cities it would not be possible to identify immigrant *Burakumin*. However, especially in the west of Japan where awareness of the *Buraku* problem was strong, it was usual and relatively easy to check on the origin of a worker or workmate. When, shortly after the Meiji Restoration, commoners were allowed to adopt surnames in some areas the local government officials would insist that former *eta:hinin* adopt a surname which would be avoided by others so that *eta* would continue to be easy to identify. So a person whose name was (say) Hirooka and came from Hiroshima would be suspected of being of *Buraku* origin. Such suspicions would be sufficient to terminate a friendship or employment.

10. Although this map was drawn using data from the Home Ministry survey which probably underestimates the total size of the *Buraku* population, it is thought that the figures reflect the distribution of the population fairly accurately.

11. Harada Tomohiko Hisabetsu Buraku no Rekishi (History of the Discriminated *Buraku*) (Tokyo, Asahi Shimbunsha, 1975), pp 202-3.

12. Harada, pp 328-9.

13. Harada, p 328.

14. DeVos, pp 122-3.

CHAPTER ONE

Genesis of the *Buraku* Communities

Prejudice and discrimination against *Burakumin* in the nineteenth century and for much of the twentieth century were thought to be a natural part of the Japanese tradition. Such attitudes were regarded as part of the heritage whose origins could be traced back hundreds, if not thousands of years. Many *Burakumin* themselves accepted this, regarded themselves as different and their separate and unequal treatment as justified. Before the *Suiheisha* movement could develop, these basic attitudes had to change. Moreover, there had to be a change in the approach of the government which insisted that it was not responsible for the existence of discrimination or prejudice, and that these were problems that the people had to sort out among themselves.

However, research which began in the 1920s and which has advanced rapidly in recent years has demonstrated that the formation of *Buraku* communities and the development of discrimination against them are, historically speaking, relatively recent phenomena. Certainly, there existed a cultural or religious tradition which defined some activities as polluting, and this tradition can be traced back to the time of the formation of the Japanese nation itself. But it was not until the seventeenth century that distinct communities of leather workers or groups pursuing occupations defined as outcast were set up on the marginal lands outside the town or village proper and it was only in the early eighteenth century that policies were pursued which insisted on making legal distinctions between these groups and other commoners. Indeed, the evidence indicates that central and local government policy in the mid to late *Tokugawa* period (1700–1868) was to institute measures which separated the newly formed outcast groups from the majority community and which sought to heighten an awareness of difference between them. Thus, despite its later disclaimers, there is a sense in which the government was (and therefore still is) responsible for creating the prejudice and discrimination against *Burakumin*. As we shall see, realisation of this spread among the *Buraku* community and it inspired some to demand that the government accept its responsibility and make improvements in *Buraku* living conditions as a first step towards eliminating discrimination. In most of this study we will be concerned to explain how such protest emerged and how the government responded to it. However, it is important to begin with a brief description of the process which led to the formation of *Buraku* communities and discrimination against them.

The Ancient Period

The belief that contact with death is polluting is rooted in Japan's earliest religious traditions. Prior to the *Nara* period (AD 645-794) the location of the imperial capital would frequently change following the death of an Emperor, which is thought to reflect the desire of the court and nobles to avoid the pollution of death. From at least the early eighth century one of the major duties of the Emperor was *Oharai* – the Great Purification – to ensure his court was free of pollution, and no doubt those in the rest of society would take care to avoid such defilement too.[1]

As Buddhism permeated its way through Japanese society, the notion of pollution came to include the idea that it could be caused by contact with the bodies of dead animals, and thus it came to be associated with leather work and even the eating of meat. Gradually the *Shinto* concepts of *imi* (taboo) and *kegare* (pollution) which were associated with human death became linked to Buddhist prohibitions on the taking of any life. First government proclamations which outlawed the eating of the flesh of certain domestic animals occurred in AD 676.[2] In part this was inspired by a mixture of Buddhist and *Shinto* ideas, but it may also have been intended to deter peasants from killing horses and cattle that otherwise might have been used to increase the productivity of the fields.[3] The first edicts banning those who had eaten meat from entering Buddhist temples appear in the middle of the eighth century, but Buddhist dietary laws were not strictly observed.[4] Nevertheless, thereafter until the *Tokugawa* period every so often edicts would be issued warning against the consumption of meat. On the one hand, this was a religious issue: people were warned that the consumption of (say) beef or chicken would result in pollution for a certain period of time during which time they were not to enter temples or shrines.[5] At the same time, the issue was related to military or economic considerations as the government wished to discourage the eating of draft animals or beasts of burden. Contact with the dead was officially discouraged and morally disapproved of. Those who had regular contact with dead humans or dead animals came from the margins of society and were avoided by others.

Meanwhile there developed in Japan a social system of considerable complexity. The formation and subsequent collapse of the status systems in the *Nara* (645-794) and *Heian* (794-1185) periods have been described in detail elsewhere and need not detain us here. The key issue is the emergence of a social definition – a line – which separated the good from the base. Within the complex hierarchical structure that developed in the *Nara* era the crucial distinction was between those who were ranked close to the top, and thus were close to the Emperor, who were considered good (*ryomin*), and those on the lower rungs of society who were considered base (*senmin*). The upper and lower aristocracy and the peasantry belonged to the former category while the rest of society, who were mainly slaves and other marginal groups, were classed in the latter category. Though changes occurred in this class structure during the *Heian* period this distinction remained and the two groups were kept apart by regulations which absolutely forbade intermarriage.[6]

So, in the earliest period of Japan's recorded history there were ideas about ritual pollution associated with certain occupations and some social customs and there was a complex status system which included a distinction between good and base. However, the notions of ritual pollution and definitions of social class were not to converge until considerably later.

The Middle Ages

The relative stability of the *Kamakura* era (1185-1333) gave way to a period in which the authority of the central government was gradually eroded by the rise of the *daimyo*. The *Ashikaga* Shogunate was characterised by almost continuous violence culminating in the *Onin* war (1467-1478) and the *Sengoku Jidai* (Period of warring states, 1482-1558). This latter period, often referred to as the 'age of overthrow of the higher by the lower', was one in which in many areas conditions were so chaotic that there was a total breakdown in law and order. Mobility both up and down the social hierarchy was possible and frequent; great houses were overthrown, members of outcast groups rose to positions of authority.[7] In this time of social confusion, the class hierarchy and the notions of pollution ceased to operate to prevent the advancement of those from outcast communities.

This is not to say that ideas about the defiling nature of contact with dead animals disappeared, but they do seem to have become quite weak. In a time of almost continuous warfare there was increased demand for such leather goods as armour, equipment for horses and bowstrings. Local warlords began to encourage leather workers to settle in or near their castles by offering them special privileges such as reduction of or exemption from taxation. As the leather trade thrived the number of workers increased, attracting not only those on the margins of society but also those previously unconnected with *senmin* occupations. Working with leather was still an occupation which caused the pollution of the worker, but the period of defilement was finite and it did not necessarily affect the other members of his family. A document dated 1558 warned:

> To witness the death of a cow or horse and then to dispose of the carcass brings one day's pollution. To skin the hide of the carcass brings five days pollution on oneself.[8]

Connection with the leather trade was not, yet, the basis for defining a social group. If a family severed its links with the trade they would lose all traces of defilement. Towards the end of the sixteenth century *daimyo* began to exert stronger control over the leather workers' communities to ensure the uninterrupted provision of this essential material. They were provided with land which was usually unfit for farming, often prone to flooding and located on the outskirts of town. Being on the edge of town and under the direct control of the lord, members of these settlements were sometimes used as a front line defensive force and from this developed police and penal duties. No specific discriminatory laws existed at this time, but there is evidence of ill feeling towards these groups; by the mid-sixteenth century they were being referred to as *kawata* – leather workers – or *eta* – a name with much clearer derogatory implications, an approximate translation being 'defilement abundant'.[9] Those in charge of this leather trade became quite wealthy, but most of those living in these communities were poor and their settlements became areas in which beggars, day labourers and dispossessed peasants would gather.

Leather production was found principally in those areas of east and central Japan which were comparatively well-developed economically and able to provide sufficient surplus in the form of taxes to enable the lord to maintain a fighting force which would use the leather goods. It was in these same areas that an extensive road system was first established. A reliable network of communication not only encouraged the development of trade but also increased the ability of the lord to control his domain. Particularly during this period of constant warfare, it was important to ensure that the roads were both well maintained and safe. Research on the location of *Buraku* communities in the Yamato (Nara) area and the rest of the Kinki region has concluded that most of the communities are to be found spaced at regular intervals along the major thoroughfares. The regular distribution along these roads and their location, often perched on a hillside commanding a good view of the road, suggest that they were deliberately positioned to carry out a variety of functions. They ensured the roads were kept in a good state of repair, they hired out horses and certainly from the early *Tokugawa* period, and in some areas before this, they were used by the authorities to control peasant unrest.[10]

In other areas, for reasons which remain unclear, makers of bamboo articles – called *sasara* or *chasen* – were also considered to be *senmin*. In some places in and around Kyoto a group known as *aoya* who specialised in the craft of indigo dyeing were considered to have low, polluted status. Apart from these trade associated groups, there was a quite substantial population of itinerants, beggars, diviners, entertainers and prostitutes who during the middle ages became known as *kawaramono* (riverside folk) because they too settled on river banks near towns. Those living in these communities held no formal status and became known as *hinin* (non-people). The term *eta:hinin* is used in the middle ages and the *Tokugawa* period to refer to those groups who were not peasants (even though they might cultivate some land) nor were part of the formal ruling structure but who carried out various occupations in the interstices of the social framework. Some, though not all, of these occupations were associated with tasks regarded as ritually polluting, but until the *Tokugawa* period mobility out of these lowly social groups was quite possible. The line which separated the socially and ritually acceptable from the unacceptable was ill-defined.[11]

The Tokugawa Period

Only with the advent of the *Tokugawa* administration is it possible to identify any systematic policy aimed at separating groups like the *eta:hinin* from the rest of society. Although the four class model of society – soldier, peasant, artisan and merchant – was adopted as an ideal from the start of the seventeenth century, in the early years of the *Edo* era there were few regulations which were intended to create a high degree of status consciousness. As Halliday has remarked:

> The *Tokugawa* shogunate cannot be characterised as a centralised autocracy, at least not in its initial stages. It was more like a nationwide truce. . . But by the end of the seventeenth century, after about one hundred years of *Tokugawa* rule, Japanese society had been formally immobilised.[12]

Even this statement tends to underestimate the changes which took place in the latter century and a half of *Tokugawa* rule despite, or perhaps because of, the rigid regulation of most spheres of society. In general, during the seventeenth century, discrimination which existed against the *eta:hinin* groups was of a customary nature and was not backed by formal statutes, moreover there were relatively few *eta:hinin* communities scattered throughout the country, and those that did exist were very small. But by the end of the *Tokugawa* era there were large numbers of *Buraku* communities. In Chikuzen han (Fukuoka), for example, the number of *kawata Buraku* increased from 26 to 130 in the period between 1602 and 1867.[13] These communities were subject to a large number of detailed regulations which prescribed the type of clothes to be worn, the accommodation which was permitted and which greatly restricted their social behaviour. First we shall look at the development of controls over the *eta:hinin* groups, then consider their role within society and the reasons for their increase in size.

Control of the Outcast Communities

Until the end of the sixteenth century it had been possible for *senmin* to be absorbed into the peasant class by developing new land or claiming abandoned fields. But following the land survey carried out between 1585 and 1598 on the orders of Toyotomi Hideyoshi, the peasant was tied to his plot of land and nearly all existing arable land was apportioned to a peasant farmer. With land rights fixed, it was no longer possible for *senmin* to be absorbed into the main communities. Those who worked in the leather trade continued to prosper for a while and their communities grew as other low status workers settled alongside them. Not all these outcast groups were connected with leather; in some regions other occupations were regarded as *eta* monopolies, in Takayama fishmongering became an *eta* trade, elsewhere stone cutting was an outcast monopoly. Rural society in the north of Japan was economically and socially backward and therefore did not experience the class division and division of labour witnessed in more prosperous areas. In the north peasants, even in the *Tokugawa* period, continued to do trades which elsewhere were outcast specialities, in some places even the leather trade was operated without legal or customary restrictions. Moreover, there was land available for the use of any immigrant who, thus, could be absorbed into the peasantry with relative ease. In the rest of Japan there is no single pattern, an occupation which was an *eta* monopoly in one area might be a normal pursuit elsewhere and *vice versa*.[14] Even where the outcast community was regarded as specialising in a defiling occupation, there might be only a few of the households who were actually engaged in the trade full time. As for the rest, they worked as day labourers, would make and sell straw, or bamboo goods, or even scrape a living from untilled and barely fertile waste land.

The *daimyo* and *Shogun* tried to regulate the leather industry in order to divert some of the profits into their coffers, but until the early eighteenth century there were no measures which were aimed specifically at the outcast groups. However, between 1715 and 1730 a series of reforms was implemented by the central and local authorities which has become known as the *Kyoho Kaikaku*. These measures were designed to heighten an awareness of status distinctions between the major social groups by strengthening the regulations which circumscribed the day-to-day activities of their members. One aspect of this policy was to institutionalise the isolation of the *eta:hinin* groups from the mainstream of Japanese society.

In Kyoto (1715) and Tokyo (1719) surveys of the *eta:hinin* population were carried out and the registers drawn up were ordered to be kept separate from the other registers. Henceforth, *ashiarai* – the process by which they could be formally accepted into the peasant or urban population – became impossible for all *eta* and all but a tiny group of *hinin*. At the same time, the authorities introduced a taxation system which placed burdens on the *eta* who were under the direct control of the *Tokugawa* and placed restrictions on the type of clothes that *hinin* were permitted to wear.[15] In Tokyo, from the mid 1720s, *hinin* were regarded as being of lower status than *eta*, they were all (apart from their chiefs) forbidden to wear any kind of headgear even when it was raining, the men were to keep their hair cut short, the women were not to shave their eyebrows or blacken their teeth.[16] Within the next two decades similar measures were implemented in most other regions to ensure that the *eta:hinin* groups were clearly distinguishable from other sections of the population and to discourage social contact with them.

At the end of the eighteenth century, a new round of restrictive regulations was introduced by the central government to deepen division between the *eta:hinin* and other town dwellers. In 1774, regulations were issued which, amongst other things, forbade *eta:hinin* from entering public places such as shrines or temples, and in 1796 another series of detailed regulations was introduced which was specifically aimed at *hinin*.[17] This later set seems to have been designed to further separate *hinin* groups from the other social classes so that they would be more reliable when required to police the local society; the way stations established in the middle ages had occasionally been used in this way and now the central authorities were giving positive support to such developments.

The final phase of *Bakufu* legislation which had grave importance for the *eta:hinin* groups was enacted in the period between the late 1830s and the end of the *Edo* era as part of the last desperate attempts to shore up the class system on which the *Shogun*'s power depended. After the widespread riots of 1836-7 following the Great Famine (1832-6), the government feared the emergence of the united action of the poorer urban dwellers and discontented peasants. The *Tempo* reforms (1830-44) were introduced in an attempt to prevent the emergence of such solidarity by trying to encourage status consciousness. Further, more restrictive regulations were imposed detailing the type of clothing and hairstyles which were to be worn, and, for example, prohibiting *eta:hinin* from crossing the threshold of a peasant's home. Searches were made of the larger cities like Kyoto to capture *eta:hinin* who had illegally left their home communities for the towns.[18] Those who were caught were returned to be dealt with by the local *senmin* leader. It seems to have been thought that the rebelliousness of the peasants and urban dwellers would be reduced with the reminder that there was a group which was even worse off than they were. On the other hand, by further dividing the *eta:hinin* from the rest of society, they became reliable as soldiers to be used to suppress the peasant riots.

The measures passed by the *Tokugawa* government were applicable only within those areas over which it had direct control, but they were also intended to serve as encouragement for similar measures to be taken in other areas. For example, following the initial set of measures initiated by central government, the leaders in Hiroshima in 1726 and in Kokura in 1728 issued their own set of detailed regulations, and it seems that similar rules were issued in most other areas throughout the country at this time. In Edo, Kyoto and Kokura where, in the early eighteenth century, a legal distinction was made between *eta* and *hinin*, the former were always ranked above the latter.[19] There were, however, regional variations: in Tosa (modern Kochi) the *senmin* were divided into three groups: *chori*, *hinin* and *eta* in descending order of status rank.[20] In Hiroshima there was only a tiny group of *hinin*, all other *senmin* were referred to as *kawata*, while in neighbouring Fukuyama there were three groups, *hinin*, *chasen* and *eta*, ranked in descending order.[21]

There was little or no organised opposition to this imposition of duties and restrictions, at least not until the mid-nineteenth century, but this should not be taken to indicate that the *eta:hinin* groups accepted the new regulations. For the most part, however, their protest seems to have taken the form of attempting to ignore or find ways round the regulations. The very fact that new regulations needed to be issued at regular intervals would seem to indicate that at least some *eta:hinin* were challenging the way they were being socially defined. A set of regulations issued in Kokura in 1770 noted with alarm the growing influence of *eta:hinin* and referred to signs that they might begin to demand higher status. In the same area regulations introduced in 1830 and 1853 forbade *eta* to work with or for peasant farmers or to sell firewood or vegetables in a way which suggests that they had been doing precisely these things.[22] The regulations of the 1770s and 1830s included measures to prevent *eta* from leaving their areas of residence, measures which were presumably connected with the surveys made in urban areas to locate vagrant *eta:hinin* and to send them back home.

Outcast Leadership

Following Hideyoshi's land survey it was not possible, in theory at least, for peasants to buy or sell land or to move from their village. The basic unit of administration was the village (*mura*), which paid its taxes as a collective, it being left to the village leaders to ensure each household contributed its due. Each village, then, became a closed corporate unit into which the government rarely intervened as long as taxes were paid. The *eta:hinin* communities across the country were also permitted to exercise a considerable degree of control over their own affairs.[23]

In Edo all *eta:hinin* belonged to one of the guild-like bodies which were under the overall control of Danzaemon, the head of the Iyano family. The Iyano family lived in Nerima from 1590, but in 1657 they were ordered to move to Asakusa, an area which became known as Shinmachi. The *eta* population of Shinmachi was quite small, less than 250 households, most of whom pursued one of the outcast specialities related to leather, but by the middle of the seventeenth century Danzaemon controlled all the city's *eta:hinin* population.[24] However, the ascendancy of the Iyano family was not secured until the early eighteenth century. In 1722 one of the *hinin* chiefs in Edo (Kuruma Zenhichi) challenged the authority of Danzaemon and in the course of the subsequent legal proceedings Danzaemon presented a charter as proof of his right to rule over both *eta* and *hinin* groups in the city. Kuruma lost his case. Though the *Bakufu* officials must have been aware that the document was a fake, the case gave them an opportunity to rationalise their system of control over this section of the city's population.[25] The extent of Danzaemon's authority fluctuated during the late *Tokugawa* period, but for most of the time he had overall control over the *eta:hinin* living in Edo, the *eta* in the eight provinces of Kanto plus those living in Kai, Suruga and Izu as well as indirect control over the *hinin* in most of these areas.[26] At the height of his power, Danzaemon had authority over as many as 9,805 households with over 5,000 of these being outside Edo. He led a life like that of a small feudal lord with an income in 1847 of 4,300 *koku*.[27] This income was derived from his control over the leather trade of the region. He was the official supplier of leather goods to the *Bakufu* military government and was the sole supplier of hides to all the leather workers in the Kanto area. All finished leather goods had to be sold through one of his four warehouses. Infringement of the rules he imposed was sometimes punishable by death.[28]

Control of the affairs of the *eta:hinin* communities in the rest of the country varied greatly according to locality. Between 1624 and 1707 the six *eta* settlements in Kyoto were under the control of the Shimomura family for which duties they received a small stipend. Thereafter, the *eta* were placed under the control of the city magistrates, who decided, for example, how many guards were required for the prisons, although it was left to a committee of elders to decide which *eta* village should supply how many individuals.[29] In general, the policy of the central and local governments was to respect the customary bodies of self-government which existed or were created within the *eta:hinin* communities.

There was no single *eta:hinin* leadership and the élite groups which existed largely co-operated with government officials to maintain status barriers. It is reported that in 1777 Danzaemon demanded of the *Bakufu* government that *eta:hinin* be no longer treated as outcasts, but his request was turned down. When, a few years later, proposals were put forward to send the entire *eta:hinin* population to establish colonies in Hokkaido, negotiations took place with Danzaemon, but the plan came to nothing. In some areas the outcast chief had considerable prestige, was permitted to dress like a *samurai* and even wear a sword; elsewhere the local administration controlled individual *eta* communities directly through the village leader.

The absence of consolidated leadership partly explains the lack of organised resistance to the imposition of increasingly onerous restrictions. Indeed, there is only one known case of mass resistance to the imposition of regulations and this occurred in Bizen (Okayama) in 1855. Here the *eta* chiefs refused to submit to the new set of regulations, objecting in particular to the rule that their clothing should be a plain dark brown or indigo colour, as this would cause undue hardship since most of them wore second-hand peasants' clothing. The revolt reached its peak with a demonstration held in June 1856 at which 3,000 *eta:hinin* gathered to present a petition to the *daimyo* in which they threatened to leave their communities, desert their feudal obligations and seek the patronage of another *daimyo* if the regulations were not removed. The crowd was dispersed, the *daimyo* launched an investigation into the uprising and the eight who had presented the petition plus four others were arrested and imprisoned.[30] In the final years of the *Tokugawa* era there are reports of formal protests about new regulations in Matsuhiro (Nagano) and Tamba (near Osaka), and it is possible that there were similar protests elsewhere.[31] It should be noticed that none of these demonstrations were protests against the status system itself or the place of the *eta:hinin* within this system but rather complaints that the lord was demanding more from his *eta:hinin* subjects than he had the right to.

Irrespective of local variations and despite active and passive opposition to the increased regulation, the overall pattern is clear. The *Bakufu* government took the lead in implementing measures which divided the *eta:hinin* from the rest of the Japanese population in a way that both enabled the poor peasant to take consolation from the fact that there were groups in society of lower status than himself and provided the authorities with a group that could be relied on to put down peasant uprisings. At the beginning of the period there was little formal discrimination and, though towards the end of the seventeenth century there seems to have been a trend for patterns of discrimination to become more overt, it was not until the various decrees passed in the period 1715 to 1730 that rigid legal distinctions were made between the *ryomin* and *senmin* populations and between the groups within the *senmin* communities. These measures firmly established a line which separated the majority from the minority outcast group and the measures enacted in subsequent years confirmed this division in society and widened the gap between the two sections of it. In the final years of the *Tokugawa* period further measures were implemented, partly to try to stem the spread of peasant discontent and partly as a means of strengthening the domestic social structure as a preliminary step to resisting any threat of the kind that seemed to be impending after the arrival of Commodore Perry's Black ships in 1853.

Population Growth and Occupational Structure of the Eta:hinin Communities

The population of Japan as a whole remained quite stable in the later *Tokugawa* period: a census in 1726 recorded a population of 26.5 million; by 1852 the population was estimated at 27.2 million and in 1872 a perhaps more accurate survey put the total population at 33 million.[32] There are no comparable comprehensive surveys of the *eta:hinin* communities; being non-people they were ignored for census purposes, but an estimate made in 1715 put the national *eta* population at 145,000 and the first national census to include *eta* taken in 1872 estimated their population to be 280,000.[33] Even though these figures are unreliable there would appear to have been a substantial overall increase in the size of the *eta:hinin* communities against a background of population stability. An examination of the research carried out in specific areas confirms this pattern and even suggests that these overall estimates may understate the nature of the problem. Although prototypes of *eta:hinin* communities certainly existed in the middle ages, surveys of temple records and tombstones seem to indicate that very few communities existed before 1610 and references to them in public documents from most areas do not occur for another fifty years. Documentary evidence of *eta:hinin* communities may simply reflect the fact that customary discrimination was being replaced by institutional discrimination, but equally the need to register the communities would only arise if they were economically or socially significant. One study of *kawata* communities in the Osaka area shows that the first registers of *kawata* were made between 1660 and 1680 and most *eta:hinin buraku* seem to have been first recorded at this time.[34] When these two communities were first surveyed they were found to be composed of 28 households each, but by 1869 they were made up of 220 and 395 households. Put another way, the population of one of these increased over 700% in the period 1644-1872 compared to a 34% increase in the size of the neighbouring village.[35] In Hiroshima detailed studies indicate that in one economically and historically more important region *kawata* made up 5% of the population in 1825 compared to 2% a hundred years earlier.[36] These and similar studies of other regions indicate that the *eta:hinin* groups were increasing in size both absolutely and relative to the surrounding population. In many areas, the *eta:hinin* groups were no longer tiny, more or less isolated groups, but had become substantial minorities.[37]

The ritual defilement which was said to pollute those who had contact with dead bodies, whether animal or human, was not an absolute phenomenon; after a few days an individual would be considered clean once more. Of course, those who regularly dealt with animal skins would, when they were busy, be polluted for 365 days of the year, but outside the castle towns there was rarely the supply of hides nor the demand for the expensive leather goods to occupy more than a handful of families full-time. Furthermore, the demand for leather goods declined during the peaceful years of *Tokugawa* rule. So this increase in population did not result from a larger number of people becoming involved in polluting trades. What appears to have happened is that the increased regulations which began in the late seventeenth century resulted in a greater number of people being formally classified as *eta:hinin* and at the same time new opportunities arose for their employment.

In the middle ages and during the early years of *Tokugawa* rule only those in the family who were actually involved in polluting activities were considered to be defiled; the defilement did not necessarily attach to his relatives or his descendants. But concurrent with the re-issue of regulations prohibiting meat eating and the formation of separate *eta* temple registers, the definition of *eta*, *kawata* or its local equivalent was expanded to embrace the whole family, often including branch families even though they may not have been engaged in any defiling activity. This trend towards a stricter definition of *eta:hinin* was confirmed, consolidated and encouraged by the regulations issued by the *Bakufu* government in the 1720s which prevented any social, geographical or occupational mobility.

Shortly after these rigid regulations had been imposed, in 1732, there was a severe drought which caused the failure of the harvest throughout western Japan and resulted in the starvation of up to one-third of the peasant population. In Chikuzen (Fukuoka), for example, 96,720 out of a total peasant population of 367,100 are reported to have died.[38] Apart from the misery and hardship caused to all sections of the peasant population, it also posed a problem for the local authorities since they still needed to exact the same amount in taxes to support the local lord. The decimated labour force meant reduced yields over the next few years. In order to make fullest use of the land as soon as possible, under-employed *kawata* were moved to the badly affected villages to take up work on the land. There was some opposition to this influx of *kawata* from the surviving villagers, but it will be remembered that taxes were imposed on the village as a unit and so it was in the interests of all the individual families that the use of all the available land should be maximised so as to reduce the burden on each family. In fact, the formation of *kawata hyakusho* (polluted peasants) had begun in the middle of the seventeenth century when *kawata* were sent to villages to develop previously untilled land.

After 1732 the *kawata* farmers were usually established on the orders of the local government, but there are occasions documented when village leaders petitioned the local authorities to allow *kawata hyakusho* communities to be established. These new peasants carried out the same work as their neighbours, paid similar, if not higher, taxes but were prevented from having normal relations with the nearby communities. They were established as farming communities after the legal definitions of *eta:hinin* status had been imposed, separate registers formed, and restriction imposed on their dress and lifestyle. Further, having been established late, often on new land, they were excluded (or not included) in the established irrigation system. The fertility of the land, whether taken over from others or newly developed, was low and after a brief period in the early eighteenth century they were unable to extend their land-holdings as discriminatory customs and practices became firmly entrenched.[39]

Nevertheless, the *kawata* population continued to grow relative to that of the surrounding peasant communities. This growth was the result of a number of factors. In some areas *eta:hinin* were more reluctant than others to practise abortion or *mabiki* to control the size of their families because of their pious devotion to Buddhist teaching.[40] That they ate meat meant they consumed more protein than other peasants, enabling them to produce healthier children. Perhaps of greatest importance, though, is that they were better able than most to survive the periodic droughts and famines. Leather merchants made greatest profit when poor harvests resulted in the starvation of draft animals, providing tanners and other leather workers with normally scarce hides. The tanners would eat the carcass and the leather goods could be sold in areas not affected by the drought. Even where the *eta:hinin* were not associated with leather, the cash they earned from the production of handicraft goods or from serving as prison guards, executioners, etc., made them less dependent on the fluctuating harvest. In addition to the natural increase of the population, these communities also grew due to their recruitment of peasants who had been forced to leave their villages after misfortune had left them destitute or misbehaviour had caused them to be expelled. It was quite easy to move into these settlements, but exit from them was difficult after the regulations of 1720 and thereafter.

In the castle towns, the *eta:hinin* groups served the local lord by providing him with leather goods either for military use or for sale on the Osaka market.[42] As leather production became of lesser importance, members of these groups were allocated functions like guard duty at the entrance to the towns or, particularly in the case of *hinin*, were charged with the obligation of carrying out executions and other penalties imposed by the courts. Gradually they were given more police duties. In the countryside, too, the *eta:hinin* communities that had developed around the way stations found alongside the major roads had their duties extended from being road minders and hirers of horses and, under the control of the local authority, were employed to keep the highways safe and in emergencies were used to quell peasant unrest. In Fukuyama there was extensive rioting in the years 1717, 1753, 1770 and 1786, and on each occasion *eta* were mobilised to put down the unrest.[43] Cornell writes:

> . . . in Fukuyama during a general famine three *eta* villages adjacent to the lord's castle were mobilised for defence during a peasant attack. Again,

large numbers of *eta:hinin* were called upon to defend the castle of Takasaki (Gumma prefecture) during a peasant onslaught in 1871; and in 1823 more than 500 *eta* were ordered to garrison a fortress during an uprising of some 70,000 peasants in northern Kii (modern Mie/ Wakayama).[44]

Although only *samurai* were permitted to carry swords some *eta:hinin* were issued with weapons such as spears or pikes to use in their role as emergency militiamen. At a time when literacy among the peasant population was generally low there was often a high level of literacy in these communities because of their need to communicate in writing with the local authority. Even today there are many *Buraku* which bear the name *Yakuinmura* (roughly translated, official village), testifying to their grass roots role of representing the local feudal authority. Formally ranked at the bottom of the social hierarchy and cut off from the surrounding population, these *eta:hinin* groups were relied upon increasingly by the feudal governments to defend the social system against disruption. Arming the *eta:hinin* for this purpose was permitted by a measure passed in 1853 and a local ordinance which set up an *eta* militia was issued in Choshu (Yamaguchi) in 1863.[45]

The sale of handicraft goods made of leather, bamboo or whatever and the provision of services as police or militia made the *eta:hinin* groups better able to survive hard times than the ordinary peasant even if they were scarcely prosperous. Yet outside the castle towns most *eta:hinin* depended on agriculture as their major source of income. In the early eighteenth century most families would farm their own plot of land, but in the outcast communities, just as in the majority villages, land gradually passed into the hands of landlords, sometimes within the community, sometimes outside it. Typically a small group would be able to dominate the agrarian outcast community because of its control over land just as an élite group monopolised control of leather or bamboo production in the castle towns. Having lost their land, many *eta:hinin* had no choice but to sell their labour power. In the region surrounding Kyoto *eta* entrepreneurs organised the production of hemp-soled sandals as a cottage industry, using the cheap labour of families who had lost their land through debt.[46]

Elsewhere they would sell their labour power to farmers in their settlement or in a neighbouring village. There they would work, not directly with the produce, for this would pollute it, but engaged in menial work such as carrying crates. They would be subjected to harsh treatment, not permitted to mix with others, and they would be provided with food which would be thrown to them.[47] So, on the one hand, there was a large section of the outcast population which was landless, possessed no capital and thus was forced to find work where it could. Meanwhile, there was a small group forming perhaps 10% of the population which was able to accumulate wealth and control the public offices in the community. The wealth and authority of this élite grew in the final years of the *Tokugawa* period and many of them were able to continue to dominate their communities well into the twentieth century.

Summary

Prejudice against certain groups and certain trades existed prior to the *Tokugawa* period, as did a body of ideas which could be used to defend or rationalise these prejudices. The *Tokugawa* shogunate adopted Confucianism as the state ideology and soon the Confucian values supported the *Shinto* and Buddhist ideas in defining as socially unacceptable those who did not fit into the four class status hierarchy. The four class model was not completely suitable for the reality of Japanese society; those who dropped or were forced out of their allotted role, who carried out roles such as gaoler which were not allowed for in the framework, or who were involved in activities defined as polluting by social custom, all these found themselves beyond the pale of civilised society. The Confucian obsession with completeness and wholeness complemented the Buddhist and *Shinto* ideas that ritual impurity was associated with those who performed pariah tasks on the margin of society. Those who held ill-defined, imperfect social status came to be regarded as imperfect human beings. It has been remarked in another context that:

> . . . people living in the interstices of the power structure (are) felt to be a threat to those who have better defined status. Since they are credited with dangerous, uncontrollable powers an excuse is given for suppressing them.[48]

This seems appropriate for the Japanese context too.

The *eta:hinin* groups performed tasks essential for the smooth operation of society and became increasingly important for the ruling class, but they did not fit into the ordered Confucian framework and were associated with various notions of defilement connected with their occupations. However, it was in the interests of the ruling class to perpetuate these beliefs to make the *eta:hinin* more reliable as a police group and in order to stabilise the whole social structure. The series of regulations which insisted they adopt specific styles of clothing and behaviour which prevented normal social contact with the surrounding communities confirmed existing beliefs that they were different and encouraged superstitions to develop. Moral justification for the retention and strengthening of the status distinctions was provided by the kept scholars of the ruling class, but support for the regulation of the *eta:hinin* among the mass of the peasantry was based on the ideas of pollution and 'difference' that the ruling class policy carefully fostered. The disruptive potential of this group was minimised by labelling them as non-human and their isolated social position used to ensure their reliability as a militia.

Myrdal explains the increase of prejudice in terms of a 'hypothesis of dynamic causation' (or principle of accumulation) in which generalised prejudice in the majority leads to low standards of living, health and morals among the minority which supports increased prejudice and discrimination.[49] This downward spiral of cumulative causation was set in motion in the early years of the *Tokugawa* shogunate and the process was supported by all the institutions of social legitimation, whether they were tied to Confucian, Buddhist or *Shinto* ideals. Further, it was seen to be in the interests of the ruling class to give additional momentum to this process, and successive waves of legislation were introduced imposing still further restrictions. Moreover, this process reached a peak in the years which immediately preceded the fall of the *Tokugawa* government as the *Bakufu* régime frantically tried to shore up the status system on which its power depended and became more reliant on the *eta:hinin* militia groups to suppress peasant rebellion. Thus in the period immediately before the start of Japan's modern era, prejudice and discrimination were at their height.

We have noted that there was little or no collective resistance to these restrictive regulations and no demands from the *eta:hinin* themselves for the end of status discrimination. Before moving on to consider developments in the *Meiji* period, it may be useful to suggest some reasons for this acceptance of gross inequality. One obvious reason is that the *eta:hinin* were just one part, albeit at the bottom end, of a status hierarchy within which all members of society were subject to sumptuary rules which restricted their movement, choice of clothing and dwelling place. Secondly, some of the regulations which granted *eta:hinin* monopolies in leather production and other handicraft trades ensured the prosperity of at least a section of these communities. The authorities which imposed the restrictions also enforced regulations which benefited the *eta:hinin* élites economically and guaranteed their social status within their communities. Little wonder, then, that apart from the occasional protest, the *eta* and *hinin* chiefs sought to co-operate with the local élites. As has already been indicated, there was no unified leadership of the outcast groups. Even within one *daimyo*'s domains the outcast community was fragmented into various groups such that consolidated action was impossible. Just as there was no leadership, so there was no outcast culture. All that existed within the *eta:hinin* groups was simply a deviant reflection of the majority culture of the locality. With neither leadership nor culture there was no sense of identity. Indeed, the development of a set of religious beliefs which supported the regulations systematically imposed from the eighteenth century, effectively prevented the emergence of any kind of self-esteem which could provide a basis from which to challenge superior bodies. The *eta:hinin* regarded themselves as impure, not quite human, not deserving equal treatment.

Notes:

1. Nagahara Keiji, The Medieval Origins of the Eta:hinin, *Journal of Japanese Studies*, vol 5, part 2 (1979), pp 387-8.
2. Ninomiya, p 78.
3. For discussion of this point see W L Brooks, *Outcaste Society in Early Modern Japan* (PhD, Columbia University, 1976).
4. Ninomiya, p 79.
5. Brooks, p 14.
6. Ninomiya, chapters 1-3, discusses the social hierarchy of *Nara* and *Heian* Japan in considerable detail.

7. Hachisuka Masakatsu (1525-1585), a general who served both Oda Nobunaga and Toyotomi Hideyoshi, is reputed to have risen to his position from birth into a *kawaramono* family. Other *daimyo* of this time are also said to have been descended from families which pursued *senmin* occupations. Brooks p 50f.

8. Brooks, p 26.

9. The word *eta* is said to be a corruption of the word *etori* which, according to the most widely accepted explanation, was the name given to a group which was attached to the Department of Falconry at the *Nara* court whose duty it was to butcher horses and cattle in order to feed the hawks and dogs of the Imperial household. Possibly due to the spread of Buddhism, this department was abolished in 860 and this, now unemployed, group is said to have drifted into the ranks of cattle herders, butchers and disposers of the dead, still somehow keeping the same name. By the thirteenth century, *etori* had been corrupted to *eta* or *etta*. Although no acceptable alternative to this theory has been proposed, it presents several problems. In the first place, *etori* as employees of the court would have had high status, almost certainly being *ryomin* and even in the twelfth century do not seem to have been involved in defiling occupations as at this time they are recorded as being those who dug wells and carried portable shrines, etc. Secondly, the number of people involved in such occupations would have been very small and even after losing their employment would not have settled outside the Kyoto area. Thirdly, there is no obvious linguistic progression from *etori* to *eta*. While the theory may give an explanation of the origins and derivation of the word *eta*, it tells us little about the social group that came to bear the name. Kita Teikichi (ed) *Minzoku to Rekishi*, vol II, no 1 (July) pp 118-123. This was a special issue of the journal which was devoted to essays on the origin and current condition of the *eta:hinin*. It was the main source used by many Japanese writing on the problem in the 1920s and 1930s.

10. Along the old Ise road *Buraku* communities are to be found an average of 5.43 km apart, and along the road between south Yamato and Yoshino they are found at distances of between 3.5-5.5 km. Such evidence seems to confirm the truth of the saying '*ichi ri no eta, ni ri no shuku*' *ri ri* ('every ri an eta community, every two ri a relay station'). Ryoke Minoru, The Nature of the Distribution of Outcaste Communities, *Kwansai Gakuin University Annual Studies* no 14 (1965), pp 93-105. Higashi Yoshikazu, Yamato no Hisabetsu Buraku (The *Buraku* of the Yamato area), *Buraku Kaiho Kenkyu* no 4 (March 1974), pp 12-37.

11. Brooks, p 86f.

12. Jon Halliday, *A Political History of Japanese Capitalism* (Pantheon Books, 1975), pp 4-5.

13. Matsuzaki Taketoshi, Edo jidai ni okeru Fukuoka chiho no Buraku to Nogyo I (*Buraku* and Agriculture in the Fukuoka area during the Edo period), *Buraku Kaihoshi*, Fukuoka, no 6 (January 1977), pp 24-43.

14. Brooks, pp 63, 107-8.

15. Kita, p 256.

16. Ninomiya, p 99.

17. Goto Masato, Bakuhan Horei ni arawareta Senmin no Shihai no Shoso to Tenkai (Various aspects and developments in the control of *senmin* as shown in the statutes of the Bakufu and han administrations), *Hosei Kenkyu* no 23 (1973), pp 159-160.

18. Kobayashi Shigeru, Kinsei ni okeru Buraku Kaiho Toso (The *Buraku* Liberation Struggle in the Edo Period), *Rekishi Koron*, no 6 (June 1977), pp 88-95.

19. For a comprehensive list and analysis of the regulations passed in Kokura han, see Nakamura Masao and Matsuzaki Taketoshi, Chikuzen Kokura han no Buraku Seisaku (The *Buraku* Policies of Kokura han), *Buraku Kaihoshi*, Fukuoka, no 2 (October 1975), pp 30-55.

20. Kita, p 290.
21. *Hiroshima-ken: Hisabetsu Buraku no Rekishi* (Hiroshima prefecture: history of the discriminated *Buraku*) Ed *Hiroshima Buraku Kenkyujo* (Tokyo, Akishobo, 1975), pp 46-52.
22. Nakamura and Matsuzaki, pp 22, 42-51.
23. Koyabashi, p 93.
24. A detailed discussion of Danzaemon's economic and political role can be found in Brooks, pp 220-235.
25. Although the name Danzaemon was not adopted by the Iyano family until 1868, it is used to refer to the head of their family in both the *Tokugawa* and *Meiji* periods. The Iyano family claim to have come originally from Ikeda, Settsu (modern Hyogo), and to have acquired a charter from the Emperor in September 1180 which gave them control over the *eta:hinin* guilds. It would appear that the family did indeed come from Settsu but close scrutiny of the charter has revealed it to be a fake, probably produced between 1570 and 1585. Arai Kojiro, Edo jidai ni okeru senmin shihai no ikkosatsu (A consideration of the control of *senmin* in the Edo period), *Tokyo Buraku Kaiho Kenkyu*, no 3 (November 1974), pp 94-113.
26. Kita, p 255.
27. John A Price, The Economic Organisation of the Outcasts of Feudal Tokyo, *Anthropological Quarterly*, no 47 (October 1968), pp 215-6.
28. Brooks, p 78f.
29. Brooks, p 100.
30. J B Cornell, From Caste Patron to Entrepreneur and Political Ideologue, *Modern Japanese Leadership* Ed B S Silberman and H Harootunian (University of Arizona Press, 1966), pp 60-62.
31. Kobayashi p 95. See also Shibata Michiko, *Hisabetsu Buraku no Densho to Seikatsu* (Tradition and Life in a Discriminated *Buraku*), (Tokyo, Sanichi Shobo, 1972), pp 137-8.
32. I Taeuber, *The Population of Japan* (Princeton University Press, 1958), pp 21, 45.
33. Kita, p 155.
34. Further details of these two *kawata Buraku* may be found in Teraki Nobuaki, Edo Jidai ni okeru Hisabetsu Buraku Nominso no Bunkai (An analysis of the *Buraku* peasant class in the Edo period), *Buraku Kaiho Kenkyu* no 4 (March 1975), pp 38-53. In Mie prefecture the large Amagawa *Buraku* of Matsuzaka was established some time between 1661 and 1672. *Buraku no Jotai 1. Toshi Buraku*, Ed *Buraku Mondai Kenkyujo* (Kyoto, 1964) p 37. Goto (*op cit*) notes the first record of a *eta:kojiki:hinin* community does not appear until 1667, p 157. Kitahara found the first reference to his *Buraku* in Gifu prefecture in a document dated 1666. Kitahara Daisaku, *Senmin no Koei* (Tokyo, Chikuma Shobo, 1974), p 12. No doubt a thorough survey of the literature would reveal similar dates.
35. Teraki, p 42. In the other *Buraku* examined there was a ninefold increase in population between 1679 and 1861 during which time the neighbouring village grew only 1.9 times.
36. *Hiroshima-ken: Hisabetsu Buraku no Rekishi*, pp 46-47.
37. In the Kii area (Wakayama) the outcast population saw a 5- to 15-fold increase. In the eighteenth century there were 5,000 registered *hinin* in Edo, by the early nineteenth century this had increased to between 10 and 13,000. Brooks, pp 100, 165.
38. Matsuzaki Taketoshi, Edo jidai ni okeru Fukuoka Chiho no Buraku to Nogyo II, *Buraku Kaihoshi*, Fukuoka, no 7 (March 1977), pp 13-21.
39. Matsuzaki Taketoshi, Buraku to Nogyo, I, p 38. See also his essay, 'Hinkon to Sabetsu' no rekishi kara 'Seisan to Rodo' no rekishi e (From histories of poverty and

discrimination to histories of production and labour), *Buraku Kaihoshi*, Fukuoka, no 18 (December 1979), pp 7- 17.

40. Kita, pp 156-8, Brooks, p 110. *Mabiki* is a form of infanticide where the child was killed immediately after birth as a form of population control.
41. Brooks, p 70.
42. For a detailed description of the organisation of leather production, see Brooks, pp 65-78.
43. *Hiroshima-ken: Hisabetsu Buraku no Rekishi*, p 72.
44. Cornell, p 63.
45. Goto, pp 159-160.
46. Cornell, p 71.
47. Brooks, p 140.
48. Mary Douglas, *Purity and Danger* (Pelican, 1970), p 125.
49. G Myrdal, *An American Dilemma* (New York, Harper Bros, 1944). For a discussion of the 'principle of cumulation' see pp 75-80 and Appendix 3, pp 1065-1070.

CHAPTER TWO

Burakumin in Modernising Japan

The years covered by the *Meiji* and early *Taisho* eras saw profound changes taking place within Japanese society such that Japan ceased to be regarded as a feudal state and had, by 1918, been accepted as one of the Great Powers. The social changes which had been engineered by the Meiji oligarchs to bring about this change in the international image of Japan were diverse and far reaching. Most of the measures taken in the early years were devised to dismantle the feudal political and social structures which hindered the formation of a strong, centralised nation-state and the development of industrial capitalist institutions. One major part of these reforms was the abolition of the formal status distinctions of the four-class hierarchy; within a generation, consciousness of such status divisions had virtually disappeared. The *eta:hinin* were freed from feudal restriction by the Emancipation Declaration of 1871, but, despite this, discrimination against *Burakumin* remained severe throughout the nineteenth and into the twentieth century. In this chapter we shall look at the circumstances which surrounded the promulgation of the Emancipation Declaration, the social and economic changes in the *Buraku* communities, the emergence of protest against the continuation of discriminatory practices and the development of government policy to cope with this and similar protest movements.

The Emancipation Declaration

In the previous chapter we indicated how discrimination continued to be strengthened and enforced right up until news of the emancipation reached the towns and villages. There had been, however, from around 1860 isolated articles written which recommended that *eta:hinin* be treated as human beings. Senju Junnosuke, an advocate of the reform of Japan's political and social structure, in a treatise written in 1864 urged that status discrimination be ended and that *eta:hinin* be regarded as equal citizens before the Emperor.[1] There were also demands for the abolition of status discrimination from the *eta:hinin* themselves; in 1867 an *eta* village in what is now Hyogo (then Watanabe-mura, Settsu) protested to the local authority that it was illogical to discriminate against them on the grounds that they ate meat at a time when government officials were frequently meeting foreigners who were known to be carnivores.[2] Similar arguments were later developed by those who advised the young *Meiji* leaders, notably Hoashi Banri and Yano Gendo. In January 1868, Danzaemon and his immediate followers were formally liberated by the *Bakufu* government although his petition asking for the liberation of all *eta* under his jurisdiction was not successful.[3]

In spring 1869, an 'Assembly of Peers' (*Kogisho*) was formed of 227 nobles to debate issues and advise the government. On 18 April, Kato Hiroyuki, then an advocate of the theory of natural rights of man, presented 'A Proposition to Abolish the *Eta:hinin* system' to this body and his proposal was followed by several similar from other nobles who sought the legal abolition of the appellation *eta:hinin* and equal treatment for them.[4] Most of the debate was concerned with the need for such changes in order to ensure complete national unity and the motions were approved by a large majority.[5] Other bodies sought to encourage the new government to abolish formal discrimination against the *eta:hinin*. Kyoto-fu presented a petition to the government in December 1870 pointing out that the principle of universal brotherhood (*isshi dojin*) as proposed by the Emperor required the equal treatment of the outcast groups and indicated the practical need to integrate these groups into the web of state control so that members of these communities could be set to work on such projects as the construction of railroads and land reclamation.[6] In January and March of the following year, detailed proposals on the problem of the *eta:hinin* were drawn up and presented to the government by Oe Taku. Born in Tosa in 1848, Oe absorbed Western ideas in Shanghai and Nagasaki before living in Kobe. There, he came across and visited several *eta buraku* and found the existence of such groups a particular embarrassment in a town where there were so many foreigners. He became convinced that the pronouncements of the Emperor on the equality of all classes and the need to sweep aside all 'evil customs of the past' should be applied to the *eta:hinin* problem. Consequently he drew up a series of proposals which he presented to the *Minbusho* (Ministry for Popular Affairs). In the second, more comprehensive petition he advocated not only equality before the law but also positive economic aid of several thousand *ryo* per year for at least five years to be given to assist the *eta:hinin* overcome their poverty and enter the modern era economically equal to other groups.[7] Shortly after he had presented the second petition, he was recruited into the *Minbusho* and sent off to Kanagawa, where he learnt about the Emancipation Declaration only after it was issued on 28 August 1871. It stated:

> The titles *eta* and *hinin* shall be abolished and henceforth the people belonging to these classes shall be treated in the same manner both in occupation and social standing as common people.[8]

Henceforth all commoners would be enrolled on the same register. No reasons for the 'emancipation' were given and it seems to have been just one of a series of decrees which ended formal status distinctions, for example a few days earlier, on the 23rd, a decree had been issued permitting marriages between nobles (*kazoku*) and commoners (*heimin*).[9] It is hard to assess what effect (if any) the various petitions had on the *Meiji* rulers, but there were perhaps three major arguments which persuaded the new government to include the emancipation of the *eta:hinin* in the series of measures passed in the régime's early years. First was the need to unite all Japan into one political system, a system which had to include *eta:hinin.* Secondly, the *Meiji* government rapidly adopted an ideology of anti-feudalism, and the thorough pursuit of this attack on feudal values and structures necessarily involved the removal of all formal status restrictions. Thirdly, there was the economic need to establish a free labour market and the freedom to develop industries, which meant that the monopolies granted to certain *eta:hinin* communities had to be abolished along with the other restrictions on occupational freedom. These three arguments could be applied in principle to many of the reforms introduced by the *Meiji* government, but there were particular arguments which related specifically to the demands for *eta:hinin* emancipation. One pragmatic consideration was the need to recognise formally the existence of *eta:hinin* communities to enable accurate maps to be drawn; in some areas the part of a road which passed through an *eta* village was not included in the overall distance between two places, which made mileage estimates unreliable. Another recurrent theme which no doubt impressed the *Meiji* government was that the continued existence of formal discrimination against such groups was a source of national shame.

Discrimination in Meiji Japan

In many parts of the country the news of the emancipation aroused hostility amongst the peasantry, who feared that it meant they were being reduced to the same low status as *eta*. However, the extent of the 'anti-*eta* liberation rioting' should not be exaggerated. Between 1868 and 1878, 548 peasant riots were recorded and only eleven of them included anti-*eta* statements in their list of complaints. Even then, in most cases the peasant uprising was mainly a protest against the disruption caused by the new government policy with resentment against '*eta* arrogance' in the assertion of their rights being of secondary importance. Nevertheless, where riots did include anti-*Burakumin* sentiments the wrath of the peasants would frequently be directed at the *Buraku* population and their houses would be destroyed and people killed.[10] Where *eta*-hunts did develop, the destruction and personal injury caused a deep scar in the collective memories of many *Buraku* communities. In other areas, the peasantry resisted *Burakumin* attempts to claim equal treatment more passively. Often, the main village would ignore the news of the decree so that the *Buraku* would only learn of their emancipation directly from the prefectural authorities many months after its promulgation. Many rural villages refused to allow them to participate in village affairs and in village festivities. In reaction to this, some *Buraku* began to demand complete independence from the main village. It is reported that in the period 1873-9 over one-third of the *Buraku* in Shiga became involved in such struggles.[11]

The *Meiji* ruling class was formally committed to the idea of the equality of all citizens before the Emperor. As the reforms of the early years swept aside the old status system so the neo-Confucian ideas which had been used to defend it had to be abandoned, or at least shelved until they would be revamped ready to be used to legitimise the *Meiji* régime. However, the Buddhist-*Shinto* ideas which had been used to support the discrimination against *eta:hinin* remained and, indeed, in the next few years, as part of the process of strengthening the Emperor-centred state, organised religion was revived. Strong prejudice continued to exist within the government hierarchy. A government publication produced in 1880, referring to former *eta:hinin*, implied that they were scarcely more than animals.[12] Government policy, to the extent that there was any considered policy about the *eta:hinin* problem, was confused. As early as 1783 a plan had been formulated to send Danzaemon and 70,000 *eta:hinin* to colonise Hokkaido at a time when Japan's northern frontier was threatened by *Ainu* unrest and the offshore presence of Russian ships. The plan came to nothing at that time, but was revived during the debates in the *Kogisho*.[13] In nearly all the writing on the *Buraku* problem during the *Meiji* era, emigration of the *Burakumin* either to Asia or to countries more distant is the only solution suggested.[14] To a certain degree, these ideas reflect the imperialist obsessions of the *Meiji* ruling class who may well have considered encouraging such emigration, especially to the Asian continent, as a prelude to annexation. On the other hand, it may simply demonstrate the fact that prejudice and discrimination were so deeply rooted and widely practised throughout *Meiji* Japan that there seemed little or no possibility of a domestic solution being found.

Certainly prejudice against the former *eta:hinin* remained fixed in the minds of the bureaucrats who served the new *Meiji* government. In 1872 the first modern family register was compiled. On this new register there was a space in which the clerk would record the family's status; either *kazoku* – member of the peerage – , *shizoku* – descendants of *samurai* – , or *heimin* – commoners. However, in many areas the officials would also, where appropriate, note on the form that the family were former *eta:hinin* or would insert the character *shin* (new) before the word *heimin*. This phrase, '*shinheimin*', became the new term of abuse in the *Meiji* era. During the twentieth century the family register system was reformed and reorganised, but access to all the family registers was open to anyone who cared to examine them. This meant it was fairly easy to check on an individual's status background whether he was an applicant for a job or a prospective spouse for one's child. The existence of and easy access to these registers greatly facilitated status discrimination in the twentieth century. As we shall see, both *Suiheisha* and *Yuwa* activists requested the government to restrict access to the records, but in fact no such action was taken until 1968.

A majority of *eta:hinin*, whatever monopoly they held or profession they pursued, depended on either part time tenant farming or seasonal day labour to make ends meet, even if they were not full time farmers. The land they farmed was often that on river banks prone to flooding, of low fertility and frequently not served by the local irrigation systems. Having lost their traditional monopolies, they were forced to rely entirely on agriculture but, though formally emancipated, they received little assistance from the main villages. As we have seen, most villages were reluctant to grant them full access to communal facilities or equal participation in village events. A new land tax was introduced in 1873 which altered the tax system from one which was assessed as a proportion of the produce of the land, thus protecting the régime against the possibility of a fall in revenue in the case of a bad harvest. The survey taken as the new tax system was introduced resulted in a 48% increase in the total amount of agricultural and residential land registered and liable for tax.[15] It seems likely that some of the land farmed by *eta:hinin* communities would have been brought within the taxation system for the first time. In addition, the new principle on which the land tax was based made the position of the farmer of marginal lands even more precarious. Major problems arose in the 1880s when the deflationary policy caused a drop in the price of rice from 9.28 yen per *koku* in 1880 to 4.71 yen in 1884. This forced many peasants to take up a cottage industry or to dispose of their land in default of tax payment; between 1883 and 1890 some 368,000 peasant proprietors lost their land.[16] It seems likely that a substantial proportion of these were *Burakumin*, and probably many who did not possess land felt the squeeze of the land tax.

Those who left the land to work in the city tended to live in newly created slums often in or near former *eta:hinin* settlements, doing whatever work was available such as day labour, collecting rubbish or rag picking. As Taira has pointed out:

> After the *Meiji* government emancipated all classes of people from the feudal restrictions, the traditional poor quarters were used by the poor in general, regardless of their social origins.[17]

Bancho, a large *Buraku* in Kobe, grew rapidly during the *Meiji* period; it had a population of 388 in 1867, 2,208 in 1887, 3,489 in 1907 and 4,452 in 1915.[18] A report indicating dire poverty in the Yanagihara *Buraku* in Kyoto made in 1886 showed that fewer than one-third of the residents had been born there and over half regarded themselves as temporary residents.[19] Rapid growth of the population resident in urban *Buraku* seems to have been a common phenomenon in the *Meiji* period and, although many of the poor farmer peasants may have regarded themselves as only temporary migrant workers, one suspects that many of them became regarded as permanent residents and subject to various forms of discrimination even if they were not formerly of *eta:hinin* status.

In other, more rural, areas *Buraku* were established in the middle to late nineteenth century. Half the *Buraku* in Tottori *ken* were formed during or after the *Bakumatsu* period, some being set up to farm new land, others to provide labour for building projects such as the construction of a harbour in 1897-8. In the Matsuzaka area of Mie prefecture, only 6 of the 18 *Buraku* existed before the Tempo period (1830-1834).[20] In Tagawa *gun*, Fukuoka, the first *Buraku* communities seem to have been formed around 1840 at the same time as coal mining started to be developed. In 1852, 10% of the population of the area were *Burakumin*; this rose to over 20% by 1875 and was estimated at around 40% by the mid twentieth century.[21]

Moreover, while all the explanations of the formation of these *Buraku* talk in terms of *Burakumin* moving as a group from one area to another, it seems quite likely that not a few impoverished peasants came to live in these communities only to find themselves henceforth regarded as *Burakumin*. Thus, the number and size of the *Buraku* communities continued to grow even after emancipation, and where individuals of families from a *Buraku* moved from a rural to urban community they tended to move to settlements performing marginal roles or doing temporary work. Where *Burakumin* worked in 'factories' it was generally in those which were set up inside the *Buraku*; rarely did they work alongside 'ordinary' workers. Fujitani quotes an example of women working in Osaka Tenman Boseki (a cotton spinning company) who refused to work with women from a *Buraku* village in Ishikawa.[22] It was hard for *Burakumin* to hide their status origin and the penalty upon discovery of their subterfuge was almost certain dismissal. The conditions experienced by the inhabitants of *Buraku* communities ensured another generation of poverty which justified existing prejudice.

Equal access to educational facilities would not have solved the problem of discrimination overnight but it might have reduced prejudice among the majority population and enabled a greater degree of social mobility among certain sectors of the *Burakumin* population. Compulsory primary education was introduced in 1872, but many *Buraku* communities could not afford to set up the schools and there was little money provided to assist them to do so. Even where schools did exist many *Buraku* children were unable to take advantage of them either because they were unable to afford the nominal fees or because they were not permitted to share the facilities used by the other children. In some regions of Japan where discrimination was most blatant, for most of the *Meiji* era what little education *Buraku* children did receive was to be had either in small schools set up (say) in the local temple where the teacher would be someone educated but with no formal qualifications or it would be in a branch school formally linked to the local primary school but whose pupils (and sometimes teacher) would be all of *Buraku* origin. The system of *Buraku* schools was not ended in Hiroshima until 1908 and in Nara the separate school system was not abolished until 1912.[23] Where *Buraku* children were permitted to attend the usual school they would be segregated from the others; seated at the back or side of the classroom, provided with separate (and often inferior) eating and toilet facilities and majority children would be encouraged not to play with them.

Industries with which the *Buraku* had traditionally been associated grew rapidly following the *Meiji* restoration although this did not necessarily mean that *Burakumin* benefited. Meat became part of the diet of those Japanese who could afford it, but the slaughter houses, no longer a *Buraku* monopoly, were taken out of the hands of private individuals and came under the control of local government organisations. Nevertheless, the majority of those who were employed in such trades continued to be *Burakumin*.[24] The leather industry expanded rapidly too; between 1884 and 1918 total leather production in Japan increased seventy-fold.[25] But much of this increased production was leather shoes made in modern factories outside the *Buraku*. Even as early as 1872, shoes made up 86% of leather goods produced and only 24% of the total production came from *Buraku* communities.

Some attempts were made to import modern production techniques into the *Buraku*. Danzaemon hired some American advisers to help establish a training factory in Tokyo to teach Western leather working techniques.[26] The factory proved to be a failure, but the arrival of the foreign technicians had unforeseen consequences. Firstly, it made at least some *Burakumin* in Tokyo aware that leather workers in other countries were not subject to discrimination. Secondly, these foreigners brought with them knowledge of Christianity, a religion which unlike Buddhism did not support discrimination against leather workers or butchers. Christianity won many converts in the Tokyo *Buraku* communities in the 1870s and 1880s and stimulated an interest in other Western ideas.

Elsewhere in Japan élite groups were able to adapt successfully to the changing times. Large landowners in the Nara region were able to increase their wealth by introducing new cash crops. Others established enterprises to produce new items such as matches or artificial mother of pearl or found new uses for leather or bamboo. Whether related or not to the low status occupations of the feudal era, these new industries nearly always required large amounts of cheap labour which the chronic labour surplus of the *Buraku* communities could easily supply.[27] When they were not working in industries traditionally considered polluted, the work was usually dirty or dangerous or both. So, while the number of the poor in urban *Buraku* grew there was also a sector of the former outcast population which was able to avoid poverty and ensure that at least its male children acquired some sort of education.

People's Rights Movement and the Appearance of Buraku Improvement Groups

Agitation for democratic rights in Japan first emerged in the form of the People's Rights Movement (*Jiyu Minken Undo*). Led by Itagaki Taisuke, the movement tried to utilise the popular opposition to many of the *Meiji* régime's policies to gain support for its demands for limited democracy at home and more aggressive policies abroad. Although it is probably true that at the national level it was 'little more than one wing of *samurai* opposition to a specific form of oligarchic government'[28], nevertheless the influence of liberal ideas spread beyond the metropolis. The Liberal Party (*Jiyuto*), formed in 1881, was, in Tokyo, little more than a political club with limited political importance, but at the local level it attracted the support of many middle to large scale landowners. In some areas the local Liberal Party found support among the wealthiest *Buraku* leaders who no doubt were fascinated by these ideas which were critical of the remaining feudal privilege. In Hyogo, Kanagawa and Osaka, for example, a substantial proportion of the members of the Liberal Party were *Burakumin*.[29]

In Fukuoka, the visit of one of the leading People's Rights activists – Ueki Emori – in 1878 stimulated young *Burakumin* to take an interest in liberal ideas. The Liberal Party itself broke up in 1884 after peasant discontent with its landlord-imposed policies had led to division,[30] then, three years later, the government invoked the *Hoan Jorai* (Preservation of Peace Regulations) which it used to expel 600 anti-government activists from Tokyo, most of whom had been associated with the People's Rights Movement.[31] While on the one hand, this marked the end of the movement's influence on national policy making, many of those forced to live outside Tokyo found work on local newspapers, or set up local newspapers through which they spread their liberal ideas. Nakae Chomin's *Shinonome Shimbun* was the best known of such newspapers, but in Fukuoka, for example, the *Fukuoka Nichi Nichi Shimbun* was founded in 1888 by Okada Koroku, a former People's Rights activist. Such newspapers kept 'liberal' ideas in circulation and perhaps were the most lasting contribution of the People's Rights Movement to the development of democratic thought in Japan.

In 1881 a group of young *Burakumin* liberals formed the *Fukken Domei* (Restoration of Rights League), probably the first organisation to be formed for and by *Burakumin*. It had four constituent groups in Hakata, Kumamoto, Kurume and Hita and had plans to create a national movement, though no such organisation emerged mainly as a result of the general drop in enthusiasm for the liberal movement in the late 1880s.[32] In the wake of this group another band of *Burakumin* formed the *Kyushu Heiminkai* (Kyushu Commoners Association) in November 1890. Little is known about the activities of this group, but it seems to have provoked a strong reaction from the prefectural governor. In a newspaper article issued the following year, he argued that responsibility for discrimination lay not with the Emperor nor his government, whose wishes had been clearly expressed in the Charter Oath and Emancipation Declaration, but rather lay with the common people who should solve the problem among themselves. Rather than try to organise a group like the *Heiminkai*, the governor recommended that they expend their energies perfecting the understanding of the Emperor's will among the people.[33] In other parts of the country, too, groups with similar aims emerged; there are documented cases of groups being formed in Yamaguchi, Wakayama, Shizuoka, Nara and Osaka and probably they existed in other places too.[34]

The most sustained activity of all these improvement groups was that which developed under the leadership of Miyoshi Iheiji in Okayama prefecture. The first group was formed in 1896 by Miyoshi and 45 other young men who sought to change the living conditions and morals of those living in the *Buraku* in order to enable *Burakumin* to succeed in the world outside. In 1898, Miyoshi and the others drew up a programme of action and paid visits to each *Buraku* in the prefecture urging the leaders in every community to form their own improvement group. In August 1902, the *Bisaku Heiminkai* was formed by Miyoshi and his followers in order to co-ordinate the activities of the groups which had been set up in Okayama since 1896.[35] Miyoshi had worked closely with the reformed *Jiyuto* (Liberal Party) activists and had urged *Buraku* leaders to become more involved in *Jiyuto* activities.[36] In the course of meetings with other *Buraku* leaders, he seems to have become convinced that the time was ripe to launch a national organisation. Three events, all of which took place in 1902, seem to have drawn him towards this conclusion. In May of that year, a *Jodo Shinshu* priest had made various derogatory remarks about *eta:hinin*. In particular, he defended the decision to have a separate branch of temples for the *eta:hinin* communities and was heard to say that since even *eta* donate money to the temples, humans should contribute even more. Then, on 16 December, Ozaki Yukio, later to become well known for his leadership of campaigns to defend democratic rights, made a gratuitously insulting remark about *eta*. Protests were made both to Ozaki, demanding an apology, and to Prince Ito, the president of his party, calling for his expulsion. A provincial newspaper, the *Kii Nichi Nichi Shimbun*, took up the campaign, but both demands were ignored. During the same month, the district court in Hiroshima approved the divorce of a non-*Buraku* wife from her *Buraku* husband on the grounds that lack of disclosure of *Buraku* origin was a valid reason for divorce since 'according to tradition, it is still normal for those who are not *eta* to abhor marriage with one'.[37] In their own ways these religious, political and legal opinion leaders had all given evidence to the fact that prejudice was still widely held, and by expressing their prejudice had tacitly encouraged its expression by others. In order to organise to oppose this formally approved prejudice and discrimination the young *Buraku* leaders began to try to co-ordinate their efforts.

Twenty-four representatives of improvement groups from the Kinki area under the leadership of Miyoshi and Nakano Mitsomori met on 24 June 1903 to discuss the formation of the *Dai Nippon Doho Yuwa kai* (Greater Japan Fraternal Conciliation Society). Their plans received the active support of many of the local newspapers throughout western Japan, where the influence of the liberal movement remained strong. On 26 July three hundred representatives from groups as distant as Tokyo in the east and Fukuoka in the west met in Osaka to form this organisation which they hoped would work 'to guarantee total freedom, independence and rights of all society's citizens'. The conference unanimously approved as its objectives the improvement of *Buraku* moral training, customs and manners, general education, sanitary conditions, leadership, frugality and saving and overall economic conditions.[38] However, in spite of the high hopes held by Miyoshi and Nakano, this conference did not develop into a sustained movement, though it may have helped to spread the ideas of the self-improvement movement (*kaizen undo*) to groups throughout the country.

Most of the support for these groups came from the sons of the wealthier, middle class landowners or owners of small businesses within the *Buraku* who had been born after the *Meiji* Restoration. Most of them will have attended at least primary school, where they will probably have been subject to some form of discriminatory treatment but will have been exposed to enough education to make them aware of the differences between the theoretical equality of all citizens and the reality of discrimination against them and other members of their communities. Whereas previous generations had been able to shield their children from the cruel reality of discrimination till they were older, the primary school system exposed many young *Burakumin* to prejudice from a very early age. Similarly, just as the education reforms increased contact between *Buraku* and non-*Buraku* children, so the local government reforms increased contact between the *Buraku* and non-*Buraku* communities in general. Previously, it had been possible for those living in *Burakumin* communities to organise their lives so as to minimise their relations with outsiders, but the re-organisation of local government which took place between 1888 and 1890 ensured increased intercourse between *Buraku* and adjacent non-*Buraku* communities which gave more chance for prejudice to take its concrete form as discrimination. Some acts ranged from the petty, though personally humiliating, ways in which people avoided contact with them to refusals of the main village to permit *Burakumin* to participate in local festivities or the decision-making processes, to have access to common land or to take part in common irrigation projects. Moreover, as contact between the two communities increased so would the younger, better educated men become more aware of the disparity in living standards.

Meanwhile, there was a growing social awareness among dissenting Japanese intellectuals of the problems of poverty both in rural and urban areas, problems caused by the development of industrial capitalism in Japan. Yokoyama's important pioneering study of Japan's lower class life which examined in detail the daily life in Tokyo's ghettoes was published in 1898.[39] Nakae Chomin was warning whoever cared to read his newspaper of the danger of neglecting the problems of the *eta*, or *shinheimin* (new commoners) as they were now called. Articles which appeared in magazines like *Nihonjin* and Yanase's pamphlet pointed out that the condition in the *Buraku* groups could be improved only if assistance was given to improve religious and political knowledge and economic facilities, but there were no demands that the state should take on these responsibilities.[40] One of Nakae's pupils, Maeda Sanyu, had an article about the *shinheimin* printed in the prestigious *Chuo Koron* in 1903. Gradually more attention was being given to the problems of this underprivileged sector of Japanese society by the liberal scholars and activists; attention which seems to have encouraged the *Burakumin* activists.

The socialist movement, which was critical of most aspects of the social structure, also had an interest in the problems faced by *Burakumin*. Sakai Toshihiko had attended the meeting of the *Dai Nippon Doho Yuwa kai* in 1903, hiding his true identity by using an alias, and later he wrote an article for the *Yorozu Choho* in which he equated discrimination against *Burakumin* and *Ainu* with racial discrimination as practised in the West.[41] Maeda Sanyu wrote articles on the problems being faced by the *shinheimin* for the left wing newspaper *Heimin Shimbun* and several Christian socialists began to take a serious interest in the problem.[42] Few of the *kaizen* activists, though, were involved with the tiny socialist movement. Miyoshi and Nakano may have had some flirtation with socialist ideas from around 1904 and may even have been members of the short-lived *Nihon Shakaito* (Japan Socialist Party) which was formed in 1906, but they do not seem to have supported these ideas for long. Both they and the *kaizen* movement remained firmly within the liberal tradition.[43]

In the latter part of the nineteenth century then, we find that *Buraku* communities were proliferating and, especially in urban areas, were increasing in size, but they did not benefit from the economic expansion which was taking place, if anything they were becoming poorer. However, within the *Buraku* community there was emerging a propertied class which sought acceptance by the majority society but was unable to leave the *Buraku* without losing its economic base either on the land or in the craft industry or production/ distribution network. Those who made up this sector of society identified closely with the liberal reformers who persistently criticised the vestiges of feudal privileges and at the same time encouraged the self-improvement of the *Buraku*; both an amelioration of the material conditions and the rectification of the coarse and unruly habits of their inhabitants. Overt discrimination became worse as the introduction of the compulsory primary school system and the incorporation of the *Buraku* into larger administrative units resulted in more interaction. But, as a consequence of this process, there arose groups of young men in different parts of the country who sought a way of changing this state of affairs. The process of the modernisation of Japan exacerbated the material and social discrimination for most *Burakumin* but produced a reaction in a section of the community which led them to seek ways of overcoming or removing discrimination.

Gradually then, scattered across the country there were emerging small groups of young *Burakumin* who were not prepared to accept discrimination and poor living conditions; who sought change. They had even taken the first faltering steps towards organising a national movement to put their ideas into operation. There was a feeling that *Burakumin* across the nation suffered common problems which could be solved by collective action; the hitherto isolated communities were communicating with each other. In other spheres of life in Japan at this time there were groups being formed which sought social change and at the national level there were signs that political change was taking place albeit at a glacial pace. In fact there were few contacts between the growing social movement in the wider society and the *Buraku* communities, but changes of attitudes within them and the formation of groups which aimed at social change ran parallel to developments which could be observed in other sectors of society. The development of critical groups, independent of the state structure, posed a potential threat to the legitimacy of the *Meiji* oligarchy. It was in this context that a social policy was devised to contain the expansion of such subversive movements. Policy towards the *Buraku* movements – the *Yuwa* policy – was an integral part of the machinery of state which aimed at the repression of social movements.

Government Social Policy 1900-1915

From the first years of the twentieth century, especially after the Russo-Japanese war, there was a feeling of unease and vulnerability among those in the upper echelons of the *Meiji* oligarchy. There was a general belief that social problems would inevitably arise as a result of the programme of modernisation and rapid industrialisation which was under way. This was expected to cause social disruption of the kind witnessed in Western societies – a view which was shared by both socialists and bureaucrats. The latter group, however, believed that able statesmen such as themselves could direct and control what they saw as the 'forces of history' so as to minimise social unrest.[44] As they saw it, the major problem was the break-down of traditional village harmony, its traditional forms and structure. The solution was to integrate local administration with that at the national level to create a national village, strengthen patriotism among the masses to preserve the essence of Japanese culture and protect the nation from the influence of individualistic Western ideas. Over the next few years four major policy initiatives were launched which together made up the 'social policy'.

It was believed that the decay of village harmony and erosion of traditional values had not yet developed very far, and that by rapid action its worst aspects could be avoided. The Town and Village code introduced in 1888 and implemented over the next two years changed the basis of local administration from 76,000 *buraku* units to 12,000 town and village (*cho*, *son*) units. Here too, the prejudices of officialdom were quite apparent. Only two reasons were accepted for the retention of small local government units (that is, less than 300 households); that the community was wealthy and thus able to look after its own affairs or that a former *eta* community would be unable to co-exist peaceably with its majority neighbours. There is also evidence from Shiga prefecture of villages petitioning the prefectural authorities asking not to be merged with *Buraku* settlements.[45] In some cases, resistance to the merger of common resources and shrines arose from opposition to moves which would allow *Burakumin* equal access to common land and the *Shinto* shrines. *Burakumin* rarely benefited from these mergers; what little communal land or entry rights they had would frequently be administered by the village, but they would not be permitted full access to the communal facilities of the larger units.

When conscription was introduced in 1873, it was regarded not simply as a way of recruiting soldiers for war but as a means of building unity and commitment to national goals through the dissemination of the military ethos. After military service the soldier would return to civilian society and act as an example to the community. However, although all males aged 20 took the military medical examination, until 1937 only 12-16% of them went to barracks.[46] Worried by the progress of the socialist movement before and after the Russo-Japanese war, Yamagata Aritomo, together with his followers Tanaka Giichi and Katsura Taro, began to develop plans for an organisation which would place the remaining male population under some kind of military discipline and encourage those who had served in the Army to continue to uphold the values learnt there. To fulfil this dual function, from around 1908 steps were taken to launch the Imperial Military Reserve Association, which would 'protect the *kokutai* (national polity) and keep evil and materialistic foreign ideas from flowing into Japan'.[47] The organisation was established with branches throughout the nation in 1910. By 1912 there was a group set up in

nearly every community, and by 1918 there were 13,000 branches composed of
2.3 million men. Later, youth groups and women's groups were established so
that by 1935 11-12 million people belonged to an organisation which was directly
under military control. By spreading the notion that all citizens were soldiers,
Yamagata and his followers were hoping not merely to facilitate rapid
mobilisation of personnel at a time of crisis but to create a society which was as
disciplined and well ordered as an army. Both the reservist association and the
local improvement movement successfully mobilised the local leadership and
united them in support of the national mission.

Education was seen by the *Meiji* leaders as yet another means of orienting
citizens towards supporting the national polity; one of the first Education
ministers defined the role of school teachers as '. . . not independent scholar
educators, . . . but rather public officers, official guardians of morality
responsible to the state'.[48] *Shushin* (ethics) had been a compulsory part of the
school curriculum since 1880 and it defined the officially accepted morality. In
1903 a new set of ethics text books was produced for use in schools which
outlined the 'ethics for a modern citizens' society' and, reflecting the general
confidence about domestic conditions, little stress was placed on nationalism.[49]
However, strikes and the spread of socialist, anarchist and liberal ideas in the
period 1903-1908 were the source of grave concern among the ruling class, so
much so that in 1908 a special rescript was issued (the *Boshin Sho sho*) in which
the Emperor appealed for social harmony and self-sacrificial toil for the good of
the nation. Patriotic ceremonies were held in towns and villages all over the
country to spread the spirit of the imperial message. In the same year a
committee to revise the ethics textbooks was established under the chairmanship
of Hozumi Yatsuka, dean of Tokyo University Law School and a staunch
conservative. By 1910 a new series of textbooks had been produced in which the
modern ethics of the 1903 texts were modified in order to give greater
prominence to the virtues of what was called the 'Japanese family system'. The
Emperor was now defined as not merely the repository of the authority of the
state but he was that authority in his own person. Confucian familialism was
revived; the nation was not like a family, it was a family in which all the units were
distantly related to the imperial line. *Shinto* beliefs were re-animated and used to
sanctify the political authority of the State/Emperor by an appeal to its
transcendent symbols. In the words of Kosaka Masaaki '. . . by the revival of
ancient ethics the state was to be revered; it had become something to be obeyed
submissively. One no longer explained the state, one believed in it'.[50]

Despite all these measures, there were still some who found subversive foreign
ideas attractive. In 1904 the Home Ministry organised the *Koto Keisatsu* (Higher
Police) in order to 'investigate and control social movements and to suppress
radicals spreading dangerous foreign ideas'.[51] This special police system was
strengthened in 1911-1912 with the formation of the *Tokubetsu Koto Keisatsu*
(Special Higher Police). Through these agencies the Home Ministry was able to
keep a check on the nascent socialist movement.

However, this repressive policy was regarded as being a last resort and most emphasis was placed on the creation of social mechanisms and the propagation of ideas of national unity which would prevent divisive ideas from ever taking root. In 1908 Prime Minister Katsura explained the reasons behind the late *Meiji* social policy:

> Development of machine industry and intensification of competition create a gap between rich and poor and this becomes greater and greater; and according to Western history this is an inevitable pattern. Socialism today is accepted by a few, but if it is ignored it will some day spread. Obviously therefore, it is necessary to propagate public morals. What we call social policy will prevent socialism from taking root.[52]

Origins of the Yuwa Policy

Government policy towards the *Burakumin* was developed in line with this social policy and in the context of the other measures designed to bolster national loyalties. Previously, the central government had taken an attitude similar to that expressed by the governor of Fukuoka in 1891; the *Buraku* problem had been solved with the promulgation of the Emancipation Declaration and so it was simply a matter of making the masses aware of the Emperor's will. This basic policy did not change, the *Meiji* bureaucrats did not consider that the state had an obligation to alleviate poverty or to reduce discrimination, but they did regard the presence of impoverished groups as presenting a potential security problem. First steps towards establishing a government policy were taken in September 1900 when the *Himmin Kenkyukai* (Poor People's Research Council) was formed by government officers to advise on policy towards the poor, whether of *Buraku* origin or not.[53] Three years later the committee changed its name and became the *Zenkoku Jizen Domeikai* (National Charity League) which aimed at forming a national organisation which could supervise policies to assist the poor. The *Meiji* government 'discovered' the problems of poverty at the same time as liberal intellectuals were giving the issue publicity and at a time when groups were emerging which sought ways to alleviate the problems of discrimination and poverty.

The first central government policy which was specifically directed at *Burakumin* was associated with the Local Improvement project and consisted of a survey made to assess the number of *Buraku*, the size of the *Burakumin* population and the conditions in which they lived. The second Katsura Cabinet in 1908 established a policy to encourage *Burakumin* to emigrate and to develop the improvement projects, but no funds were allocated for this purpose.[54] Prefectural bodies were urged to set up *kaizen* (improvement) groups. In Nara, a branch of the *Kyofu Chiho Iinkai* (Regional Moral Reform Committee) was established in each *gun* and made responsible to the central prefectural group. Similar groups were established in other prefectures in what seems to have been a consolidated attempt to place all the groups associated with the improvement movement under government supervision.[55]

The circumstances of the *kaizen* groups varied greatly according to prefecture. In Mie, the governor, who had been a member of the *Himmin Kenkyukai*, took a special interest in the problems of the *Burakumin* and as early as 1905 he initiated a survey of all the *Buraku* communities in the prefecture to assess the size of the population, the occupational structure, the standards of health and education and the amount of crime.[56] In the next few years, nearly every *Buraku* in the prefecture was to form its own improvement group, usually organised in conjunction with the local police and local government officers. Although some public baths or clinics were established, these groups made few improvements to the communities; they exhorted the *Burakumin* to improve their moral standards and enabled the police to keep a close watch on former or suspected criminals.[57]

In Hiroshima prefecture, the first *kaizen* group was formed in Fuchu-shi in July 1904. Little is known about its activities, but it adopted a quite detailed programme which included improving customs, fulfilling the three duties of a citizen (payment of taxes, service in the army, attendance at school) and forming consumers' and producers' organisations.[58] In the city of Hiroshima, the *Itchi Kyokai* (Co-operation Association) was formed in June 1907, a month after a major fire had destroyed 200 of the 700 houses in the major *Buraku* community, Fukushima-cho. The 34 founding members of this group were the wealthier inhabitants of the community, sympathetic journalists like Maeda Sanyu and representatives of the local authorities, including teachers and police.[59] The group sponsored a large number of activities between 1907 and 1911, assisting with sanitation improvements, medical and night classes. Gradually, small *kaizen* groups were established throughout Hiroshima prefecture. Amano has found evidence of the existence of twenty-four groups and it is possible that many others were formed and dissolved without leaving any trace.[60] Here too, though, control of the groups' activities seems invariably to have been in the hands of local bureaucrats.

Formation of Independent Groups

After the conviction and subsequent execution of Kotoku Shusui and twelve other leading socialist and anarchist activists in 1911 which effectively suppressed the revolutionary movement, the government distributed 1.5 million yen for the building of hospitals and general relief of poverty and also initiated a survey to enquire into the nature and extent of urban and rural poverty.[61] Also in 1911 the Home Ministry distributed its first financial assistance for *Buraku* improvement schemes and tried to encourage the formation of a national *kaizen* movement and the development of *kaizen* groups in every prefecture.[62] Two years later, the Home Ministry sponsored a national conference of a new organisation called the *Saimin Buraku Kyogikai* (*Saimin Buraku* was a new euphemism for *Burakumin*). It was attended by representatives of the *Buraku* middle classes, teachers, bureaucrats and religious leaders and the conference had as its major theme how the *Buraku* could be 'improved in order to make the state more prosperous'.[63] The movement had been launched the previous year to try to consolidate the activities of the various *kaizen* groups, but little seems to have come of this conference and the group was not to hold another meeting until 1919. Nonetheless, in these two years the first tentative moves were made towards formulating government policy towards the *Buraku* problem.

Oe Taku had been one of the major advocates of the emancipation of *eta:hinin* at the time of the *Meiji* restoration, and at the beginning of the *Taisho* period he renewed his active support for the *Burakumin* cause.

The *Teikoku Kodokai* (Imperial Path of Justice Association) had been founded in June 1912 by a Buddhist priest from Yamaguchi, but Oe, now retired, began to take an interest in the group and soon became the organisation's driving force. Though he lived in Kamakura he went to the association's office in Tokyo every day after it was set up in 1913.[64] He was particularly concerned that improvements be made in the conditions in the *Buraku*, feeling that otherwise they would turn to support the radical movements.[65] In this there was little difference between his approach and that of the government or between the new movement and the improvement groups of the *Meiji* period. In the group's prospectus, after noting that 'the most benevolent Emperor' had issued orders to sweep away all evil customs, it is pointed out that:

> not a few Japanese are still ignorant, stubborn and old-fashioned. In their daily intercourse, they unashamedly forget the Imperial will and ignore the law of justice and humanity . . . The reason for our establishing this Association is no other than our wish to observe the holy Imperial will of the late Emperor Meiji and carry it out in practice . . . [66]

Its first conference was held in Tokyo in June 1914, at which the speakers developed the two themes of the necessity to accept reverently and carry out the Imperial will and the need to prevent 'dangerous thought' spreading to the *Buraku* communities. The leaders of this organisation were nearly all members of the House of Peers and its 450 listed members were all wealthy local notables. Nevertheless, its magazine – *Kodo* – which was published regularly between 1914 and 1917, often carried articles which were strongly critical of the government's lack of interest in the *Buraku* problem and made demands that the government should provide more funds to alleviate poverty and eradicate discrimination.[67]

Concurrent with the formation of this group based in Tokyo, there was renewed activity of groups at local level. New *kaizen* groups appeared in Nara, Fukuoka, Okayama, Shimane and Mie; the *Itchi Kyokai* in Hiroshima began to produce its own magazine as did the groups in Nara and Fukuoka.[68] The most influential of these groups was the *Yamato Doshikai*, formed in Nara in 1912. Through its magazine – *Meiji no Hikari* – it consistently urged the *kaizen* groups to form a national organisation which would be able to lobby the government more effectively to persuade it to provide financial assistance to the improvement projects. However, these groups were not really part of a protest movement; indeed, as we have seen, most of them accepted the government's assertion that there was little it could do. Their activities were still based on the assumption that there was something wrong with the *Buraku* communities which they had to put right before society would accept them. In 1914 there were signs that in some areas youth groups attached to the *kaizen* groups were beginning to question these basic assumptions, but, for the time being, the government was able to control the actions and ideas of the members of these groups.

However, if it was not yet a protest movement, the developments within the groups had encouraged even the most patriotic of them to become critical of government policy. Moreover, by assisting with the formation of a network of *kaizen* groups and indirectly encouraging the production of magazines, the government had helped to create a generalised feeling of solidarity among at least the wealthier sections of the *Buraku* communities and established a system of communication between them which facilitated the spread of ideas. Government policy had undergone subtle changes in the face of the emergence of these groups. As yet the government accepted no responsibility for conditions in the *Buraku* and would do little to help with improvements, but the potential threat to internal security which they apparently posed forced the government to adopt a policy which could control developments within the *Buraku* communities. As during the nineteenth century, the *kaizen* groups derived little or none of their inspiration from foreign sources, the influence of socialism was negligible and most of the liberal ideas had been interpreted by those like Oe Taku so that 'human equality' had less to do with inalienable rights of the individual and more connection with the concept of the equality of all Japanese subjects before the Emperor. Still, even this latter viewpoint provided the younger *Buraku* leaders with a yardstick which they could use to measure the effectiveness of government policy, or lack of it. Criticism of the policy was being found in the pages of the official group magazines, more strident criticism of the nature of the policy was emerging in scattered youth groups. Furthermore, the policy of the government in all spheres was no longer automatically accepted by the parties in the Diet; there were demands for the introduction of more 'democracy'. Protest and criticism of the government accelerated rapidly in the next few years and heralded the start of the period of *Taisho* democracy in the midst of which the *Suiheisha* was created.

Notes:

1. Ikeda Takamasa, 'Kaihorei Zengo' (Circumstances surrounding the Emancipation Declaration), *Kindai Nihon to Buraku Mondai* (Kyoto, Buraku Mondai Kenkyujo, 1974), p 47. The treatise referred to is entitled 'Eta o Osameru gi'. See also Ninomiya, p 106.
2. Fujitani Toshio, *Buraku Mondai no Rekishiteki Kenkyu* (Historical Research on the *Buraku* Problem) (Kyoto, Buraku Mondai Kenkyujo, 1973), p 30.
3. Ninomiya, p 106.
4. Ninomiya, p 107.
5. Mahara Tetsuo, *Nihon Shihonshugi to Buraku mondai* (Japanese Capitalism and the

Buraku Problem) (Kyoto, Buraku Mondai Kenkyujo, 1973), pp 11-13. The main motion was passed: 172 in favour, 7 against, 6 abstentions, 13 no opinion.

6. Ikeda, pp 49-50; Mahara, *Nihon*, pp 18-19 (full text).

7. Mahara, *Nihon*, pp 21-22; for Oe's own account of the process see Kita, pp 227-235. The full text of the two proposals can be found in *Buraku Mondai Seminar, No IV* (Kyoto, Sekibunsha, 1969), pp 5-8.

8. Ninomiya, p 109.

9. Nakayama Taisho (ed) *Shimbun Shusei: Meiji Hennenshi vol I* (Tokyo, 1940), p 295. Although all the references to the Emancipation Declaration state it was issued on 28 August, this compilation of reports from early Meiji newspapers refers to a measure permitting *hinin* etc. to be entered on the normal registers (*hinin nado minseki ni hennyu*) in an article dated 27 August.

10. Ikeda, pp 58-62; Mahara, Nihon, p 28, for a full list of the riots see pp 29-30.

11. Ikeda, p 56; Mahara, Nihon, pp 26-7.

12. ... *eta hinin wa jinmin chusai senzoku ni shite hotondo kinju ni chikaki mononari* ... (*eta:hinin* are the lowest group of human beings almost like birds and animals). *Zenkoku Minji Kanrei Ruishu*, published by the Shihosho (Ministry of Justice), Tokyo, 1880, p 2. This is only a slight improvement on an official report of 1826 which stated that *eta:hinin* existed on 'a level even lower than animals'. (*Dobutsu yorimo motto hikui teido*) quoted by Koyabashi Shigeru, p 91.

13. Akisada Yoshikazu, 'Hisabetsu Buraku to Kindai' (Discriminated *Buraku* and the Meiji period), *Dento to Gendai*, no 40 (July 1976), pp 103-111. See also Mahara, *Nihon*, p 15.

14. Sugiura Shigetake, tutor of the future *Taisho* Emperor, suggested in an article published in 1886 that the young men of the *Buraku* communities form an army and colonise an island in the South Seas, Hankai Yume Monogatari, *Buraku Mondai Seminar no IV*, pp 10-19. Yanase Keisuke, writing some ten years later, recommended both the introduction of public relief measures to assist *Burakumin* and their migration to recently acquired Taiwan or to relatively unpopulated areas like Mexico, Peru or Siberia; see his *Eta:hinin: Shakaigai no Shakai*, which was written circa 1896, published in Tokyo in 1901. Nambu Roan, in an article written in 1902, suggested *Burakumin* migrate to Manchuria or Korea, *Buraku Mondai Seminar no IV*, pp 48-53. Even Shimazaki Toson's hero in Hakai only escapes discrimination in Japan by migrating to America, see Shimazaki Toson, *Hakai* (The Broken Commandment), trans K Strong (University of Tokyo Press, 1974).

15. R P Dore, *Land Reform in Japan* (Oxford University Press, 1959).

16. Halliday, p 44.

17. Taira Koji, '*Urban Poverty, Ragpickers and the Ants' Villa in Tokyo*', *Economic Development and Cultural Change*, vol 17, no 2 (January 1969), pp 155-177.

18. Mahara, *Nihon*, p 46.

19. Quoted by Fujitani, pp 80-81.

20. Mahara, *Nihon*, p 264.

21. Ikeda, pp 63-4; Mahara, *Nihon*, pp 68-70.

22. Fujitani, p 213, who is quoting an example given in Yokohama Gen'nosuke's *Nihon no Kaso Shakai* (Japan's Lower Class Society) (Tokyo, 1898).

23. *Hiroshima-ken Hisabetsu Buraku no Rekishi* pp 19-20, 147-157. Also Mahara, *Nihon*, p 260. Yoneda Tomi attended one of these separate schools until his second year of primary school (1913) when the branch school was merged with the main school. *Buraku Kaiho Undo to Yoneda Tomi* (The *Buraku* liberation movement and Yoneda Tomi) (Nara-ken, Buraku Kaiho Kenkyujo, 1977), p 11.

24. Akisada Yoshikazu, Nihon Teikokushugi to Buraku Sangyo (Japanese Imperialism and *Buraku* Industries) *Buraku* (No 213, 1967), pp 32-3.

25. Akisada, 1976, p 108.
26. Ogushi Natsumi, *Hisabetsu Burakushi Kenkyu* (Research on Modern Buraku History) (Tokyo, 1980), pp 34-5.
27. Cornell, pp 73-4.
28. Halliday, p 30.
29. Fujitani, p 68. See also Mahara Tetsuo, *Suihei Undo no Rekishi* (A history of the *Suihei* movement) (Kyoto, Buraku Mondai Kenkyujo, 1973), p 30.
30. Halliday, p 105.
31. This law was the predecessor of the Peace Preservation Laws of the twentieth century and was modelled on a law passed in Bismarck's Germany in 1878 to control the left wing groups. R H Mitchell, *Thought Control in Pre-War Japan* (Cornell University Press, 1976), p 24.
32. For further details about the *Fukken Domei* see Mahara, *Suihei*, pp 30-34 or Moriyama Senichi et al. Fukken Domei no Kaimei (An explanation of the *Fukken Domei*), Buraku Kaiho shi, Fukuoka, no 1 (March 1975), pp 133-141.
33. The full text of this article can be found in *Buraku Mondai Seminar, No IV*, pp 26-9.
34. Yamaguchi group formed in 1886, see Narisawa Eichi, 'Yuwa Undo to Seisaku' (*Yuwa* movement and Policy) in *Suihei Undo no Kenkyu, vol VI* (Kyoto, *Buraku Mondai Kenkyujo*, 1973), pp 143-203. The Shizuoka group, *Fuzoku Kaizen Domei* (League to Improve Morals), was formed in 1898, see Mahara, *Nihon*, p 114 and Kita p 248. For further details about the groups in Wakayama (1893), Osaka and Nara, see Shiraishi Masaaki, 'Buraku Kaizen Undo to Shoki Yuwa Seisaku' (*Buraku* Improvement and the early *Yuwa* Policy), *Buraku Mondai Gaisetsu* (Osaka, Kaiho Shuppansha, 1977), pp 143-160.
35. Shiraishi Masaaki, 'Tennosei Kokka Kakuritsuki no Buraku Kaizen Undo' (The *Buraku* Improvement movement at the time of the formation of the Emperor system state), *Rekishi Koron*, no 6 (June 1977), pp 96-105.
36. Cornell, p 75.
37. A summary of these three instances of discrimination can be found in DeVos et al, p 38. Ozaki's comments were, 'A combined discussion of the tax problem and naval expansion is as incongruous as a son of a wealthy family walking hand in hand with an *eta* girl.' See also Fujitani, p 98; *Hiroshima-ken; Hisabetsu Buraku no Rekishi*, p 20.
38. Fujitani, p 98; Shiraishi, Tennosei, p 104; DeVos et al, p 39.
39. Yokoyama Gennosuke, *Nihon no Kaso Shakai* (Tokyo, 1898). Reporters and intellectuals in other cities of Japan were 'discovering' pockets of poverty in their urban environment. See Taira, pp 156-7.
40. Nakagawa Yuzo, 'Shin heiminron' (About the 'new commoners'), *Nihonjin* (September 1899). For Yanase's pamphlet see above n 14.
41. This article appears in *Buraku Mondai Seminar* no IV, pp 54-6. See also Fujino, p 49.
42. For example; *Heimin Shimbun*, no 5 (13 December 1903), p 1, carries an article explaining Nakae Chomin's ideas on the assimilation of *shinheimin* into Japanese society which appears to have been written by Maeda Sanyu. In *Heimin Shimbun*, no 15 (21 February 1904), p 7, there is another article by Maeda in which he describes the kind of discrimination experienced by *Burakumin*. – I am grateful to John Crump for directing my attention to these articles.
43. Fujitani makes this suggestion about Nakano, p 99. Shiraishi claims Miyoshi was a member of the *Nihon Shakaito*, '*Buraku Kaizen*', p 150.
44. K B Pyle, 'The technology of Japanese nationalism: the local improvement movement, 1900-1918', *Journal of Asian Studies*, vol XXXII, no 1, pp 51-65.
45. Fujino, p 39.

46. R J Smethurst, *A Social Basis for Pre-War Japanese Militarism* (University of California Press, 1974), p 6. Between 25% and 35% of those who passed the medical went to barracks.

47. R J Smethurst, 'The Creation of the Imperial Military Reserve Association in Japan', *Journal of Asian Studies*, vol XXX, pp 815-828.

48. Quoted in Halliday, p 36, from an article by D Shively, 'Confucian Lecturer to the Meiji Emperor: Motoda Eifu'.

49. W M Fridell, 'Government Ethics Textbooks in late Meiji Japan', *Journal of Asian Studies*, vol XXIX, pp 823-833.

50. Quoted in Fridell, p 830.

51. Quoted in Mitchell, p 25.

52. Quoted in Pyle, p 55.

53. Shiraishi, '*Tennosei*', p 100. Fujino gives the date as 1898.

54. Narisawa, p 144.

55. Shiraishi, '*Buraku Kaizen*', p 152.

56. *Mie-ken: Buraku Shiryo shu II* (Compilation of Documents on *Mie-ken Buraku* history) ed Mieken Koseikai (Tokyo, Sanichi Shobs, 1974), pp 43-58.

57. Oyama Shumpei, *Mie-ken Suiheisha Rono Undoshi* (The *Suiheisha* Worker-Peasant Movement in Mie-*ken*) (Tokyo, Sanichi Shobo, 1977), pp 12-13.

58. *Buraku no Jittai* (Conditions in the *Buraku*). Published by the Fuchu-shi town office (Hiroshima, 1969), p 10.

59. Amano Takuro, 'Buraku Kaiho to Yuwa Undo I' (*Buraku* Liberation and the *Yuwa* movement), *Geibi Chihoshi Kenkyu*, no 60, pp 1-13.

60. Amano Takuro, 'Buraku Kaiho to Yuwa Undo II', *Geibi Chihoshi Kenkyu*, no 61, pp 10-20.

61. Mahara, *Suihei Undoshi*, p 52.

62. It is sometimes suggested that this policy initiative was associated with the fact that one of those involved with Kotoku in the alleged plot to assassinate the Emperor was a *Burakumin*. Arima, later a leading figure in the *Yuwa* movement, certainly seems to have believed this. See his article 'Buraku Kaiho Undo no Yotei' (Main Points of the *Buraku* Liberation Movement) in *Yuwa Undo Ronso* (Tokyo, Sekai Bunko, 1973), pp 149-162 – the article was first published in 1927. As far as one can tell though, none of those allegedly involved in the conspiracy were of *Buraku* origin, but the person to whom Arima referred was probably Takagi Noriaki of Wakayama prefecture who as a Buddhist priest had had some connection with *Buraku* groups. Narisawa, p 145. Fujino, pp 81-3.

63. Narisawa, pp 145-6.

64. Hiranuma Kiichi, 'Chuo Yuwa Kikan to Chuo Yuwa Jigyo Kyokai Shimei' (The role of the Central *Yuwa* Agency and the Central *Yuwa* Project Association), *Yuwa Jiho*, vol 2, no 8 (October 1927), pp 2- 29.

65. For Oe's own account see Kita, pp 236-8.

66. Quoted in DeVos et al, p 40.

67. Akisada Yoshikazu, '1916-22 nen no Yuwa Zaisei ni tsuite' (*Yuwa* Finance, 1916-22), *Ikenobo Tanki Daigaku Kiyo*, no 7 (1976), pp 47-70.

68. *Suihei Undo shi no Kenkyu* I ed *Buraku Mondai Kenkyujo* (Kyoto, 1971), p 18.

CHAPTER THREE

The Emergence of the *Suiheisha* Movement

> Any new idea is the crystallisation of the ideas of thousands of other men.
> Then, one man suddenly hits on the right word and right expression for
> the new idea. And as soon as the word is there hundreds of people realise
> they had this idea long before. When an enterprise takes definite shape in a
> man's mind, one can safely say that numbers of men all around him cherish
> the same or similar plan. That is why movements catch on and spread like
> wildfire.[1]

On 3 March 1922 3,000 *Burakumin* met in Kyoto for the Inaugural Conference
of the *Suiheisha*. At this meeting a movement declaration, general principles and
three resolutions were unanimously approved and at a delegate meeting held in
the evening a set of seven organisational rules was accepted which was to form
the framework within which the movement progressed. Most of the delegates
came from the Kyoto area, but there were representatives from nine other
prefectures, mostly in central Japan. Within a few months five prefectural
groups were formed and by the time of the second conference 60 groups had been
established. Growth in the second year was even more rapid: at the time of the
third conference there were 240 groups scattered over 23 prefectures. But this
was not the first time that an attempt had been made to establish a national
movement of groups based on the *Buraku*. The idea had been proposed by
groups in Kyushu as early as the 1880s, and Miyoshi Iheiji had even managed to
organise a national conference in 1905, though he was unable to forge a
movement from the meeting. Why, then, were they able to succeed in Kyoto, in
1922, when previous attempts had failed?

In this section we will describe the way three young men from a village in Nara
were able to launch a national movement, the situation within the *Buraku*
communities which made this possible and the social environment in which the
ideas that were to inspire the movement's leaders grew and flourished. But
before we can discuss how the *Suiheisha* was created we must map out the general
changes which had taken place in Japan's social and economic structure and had
permitted 'dangerous ideas' from the West to take root in Japan and percolate
down to influence even the *Burakumin*. In other words, we shall try to indicate
that there was a general undermining of belief systems and, more specifically, a
growth of horizontal solidarity which allowed a group of *Burakumin* to establish
for themselves a politically effective identity.

The Rice Riots cast a spectre over all developments in domestic politics in the
1920s and ruling class fears of violent insurrection were compounded by the

impact that both liberal and socialist ideas had on Japan's emerging social movements. Groups and individuals in Japan were already engaged in activity but sought political and social theories to explain what should be done and what could be done. No indigenous system of ideas could do this, but the liberal rhetoric and socialist ideas which received international publicity in 1918 gave apparently coherent explanations of recent history and indicated what kind of action would be taken in the future. Both, in their different ways, encouraged the individual to take action and to form social groups which would ensure social change took place. Although attitudes, particularly those of the more wealthy *Burakumin*, had changed quite markedly in the *Meiji* period, there remained a common conviction that there was something wrong with them and their communities which inevitably led to discrimination. The activities of the *kaizen* activists partially challenged this feeling that discrimination was inevitable by insisting that *Burakumin* could and should improve themselves so that they became socially acceptable, but there was, as yet, no suggestion that what might be at fault was the society's values or the social structure in which the *Buraku* communities were located. After 1918, encouraged by liberal and socialist ideas, groups and individuals within *Buraku* communities throughout Japan were drawing towards the conclusion that direct action was necessary to protest against discrimination, that some kind of change in the social structure was necessary, and that this could be brought about by the combined action of social groups. When the proposal to form the *Suiheisha* was made, there were many in *Buraku* throughout the country who were eager to respond.

Economic and Social Developments – the Rice Riots

The outbreak of war in Europe in 1914 enabled Japan's programme of industrialisation to proceed rapidly. Japan was able to penetrate traditional Western markets in Africa and Asia; there had been large sales of arms to Russia and a boom in the shipbuilding industry. Between 1914 and 1919, the number of factory workers increased from 850,000 in 17,000 plants to just over 1,800,000 in 44,000. Reflecting the growth of investment in modern heavy industry, the proportion of men in these totals rose from one third to one half. In addition to this, there were about 450,000 men employed in the mines.[2] Agriculture, too, so benefited from the growing economy that between the years 1915 and 1919 the real income of an average farm household doubled.[3]

The socialist movement had been driven underground after the trials and executions following the High Treason trial of 1910-1911. However, a liberal-democratic movement was emerging among the urban bourgeoisie. Based essentially on the idea of government for the people (rather than of or by them), they campaigned against the clan-dominated politics and urged the adoption of a more Western approach to constitutional government, even suggesting the adoption of universal suffrage. Apart from matters strictly related to politics, those who supported these liberal ideas in newspapers and magazines voiced their opposition to the old morality of the state and family, opposed militarism, were in favour of education reforms and the spread of a more individualistic morality. The development of the newspaper industry plus the advent of widespread literacy as a consequence of compulsory education meant that these dissenting opinions could be spread rapidly to the remotest village.

Although industrial production almost doubled from 1914 to 1919 and the average rate of profit was around 50% per annum, there was a drop in real wages from a base of 100 in 1914 to 74 in 1916 and to 61 in 1918.[4] Neither did the boom in the agricultural sector benefit the whole farming population. Those who did not possess enough land to produce all the rice they needed, who worked as day labourers in the fields or who produced cash crops other than rice found themselves becoming at least relatively poorer as the increase in the price of rice outstripped the general increase in commodity prices.

In the first six months of 1918 the price of rice more than doubled and continued to increase at a rapid pace during July and August. Peaceful demonstrations of housewives protesting at these high prices soon developed into violent attacks on the shops of rice merchants or government offices. During the late summer the rioting spread across the country; detailed research has identified 636 separate incidents in 33 cities, 104 towns and 97 villages, with perhaps as many as ten million people having participated in these demonstrations of popular discontent.[5]

The overall role of *Burakumin* in these disturbances is hard to assess. About 10% of the 8,200 prosecuted on charges which related to the rioting were *Burakumin*. This at a time when they formed only 2% of the total population. Either this indicates that *Burakumin* took a more active role in the rioting or that police reaction to *Buraku* demonstrations was overly repressive. Certainly in Kyoto the serious, violent rioting originated in the *Buraku* and was only subdued through military intervention. In other towns, too, *Burakumin* played a precipitating role in the outbreaks of violence, a phenomenon which may be explained by the fact that it was the practice in some areas to sell rice in the *Buraku* at prices significantly higher than the current market price.[6] There was also an attempt by some newspapers and members of the government to place the blame for much of the violence on the unruly *Burakumin*.[7] The *Burakumin* seem to have been treated as scapegoats. On the other hand, in many areas the large *Buraku* took no part in the rioting in spite of the fact that many of the poorer *Burakumin* were worst affected by the precipitous price increases. *Buraku* leaders co-operating with the police, in some cases through the mediation of the *kaizen* groups, were quite able to quell unrest.

The Japanese ruling élite, already made nervous by news of the fall of the Romanov dynasty and the, as yet confused, reports of revolution in Russia, were terrified by the implications of these events and took measures to ensure they would not happen again by increasing internal security and developing rice production in Taiwan and Korea. On the other hand, for those who were associated with the emergent working class movements, it was a source of inspiration. The distant and poorly understood Russian Revolution had shown how massive discontent could be channelled to change the nature of the state; the Rice Riots had demonstrated that similar discontent existed in Japan. The problem of channelling it now acquired practical dimensions for the socialist theoreticians. Katayama Sen, later a Comintern executive, wrote in 1931:

> The Rice Riots apparently represented the first encouraging awakening of people in Japan and can be taken to have launched the present revolutionary movement. The revolutionary movement grew a thousand time as much stronger (sic) from the moment of the rice riots.[8]

Knowledge of the Russian Revolution and observation of the Rice Riots brought about profound changes in the thinking of many intellectuals. Perhaps typical of this phenomenon is Kawakami Hajime, a professor of economics at Kyoto University. In a book written in 1914 which sought to highlight the problems of working class poverty created by the prosperity of the capitalist economy, Kawakami took the position of a Confucian moralist appealing to the ruling classes to alleviate the problems of poverty through reforms. From 1918 he began to adopt a class struggle viewpoint and, in the following year, he launched his own magazine *Shakai Mondai Kenkyu* (Studies in Social Problems), which made an important contribution to the spread of Marxism in Japan.[9]

The nature of the contribution of the Rice Riots to the development of the working class and peasants' movements in Japan is harder to assess. Involvement in the violence which occurred in late summer 1918, or, at least, awareness of the nature of the rioting, seems to have made many less reluctant to challenge established authority.[10] Furthermore, demands that the government provide cheaper rice may have led to demands for the reduction of the price of other commodities and to more general demands that the state had an obligation to assist the poor.[11] It is also claimed that the experience of the Rice Riots enabled at least the 'advanced' sections of the rural and urban proletariat better to understand the Russian Revolution.[12] At the very least, the Rice Riots, at the same time, were a product of and contributed to the general atmosphere of uncertainty and loss of confidence in traditional social institutions and value systems. This stimulated both intellectuals and social movement activists to take a fresh interest in alternative systems and organisations.

A general link can be made between the Rice Riots and the emergence of the various social movements, but the evidence of a connection between them and the formation of the *Suiheisha* is contradictory. A general study of this problem concludes that, 'those who took part in the Rice Riots did not usually become central to the *Suiheisha*, rather examples of the opposite are more common.'[13] It is thought that where *Burakumin* did take part in the rioting, they were suppressed with such severity that they were discouraged from taking any further part in protest activity. On the other hand, in Kyoto at least, involvement in Rice Riots seems to have been a precursor to more organised protest activity. Asada Zennosuke, later a leader of the *Suiheisha*, suggests that it was during and after the rioting that it was first proposed that the six *Buraku* youth groups in

Kyoto should form a federation.[14] These youth groups were to be the core around which the Kyoto *Suiheisha* was to develop.

Further research may reveal evidence of some direct connections between the rioting of 1918 and the organisation of the *Suiheisha*, but from what evidence is available at present only two general remarks are justified. The Rice Riots stimulated a general interest in radical ideas and the formation of organised groups which seems to have prompted many *Burakumin* to consider the possibility of forming their own organisation. Secondly, whether justified or not, it was widely believed in government circles that *Burakumin* played a major role in the rioting. For this reason, early in 1919 the central government began to explore ways to pacify *Burakumin* discontent by the formation of a government-led movement and the provision of small amounts of improvement funds. But government policy was no more able to prevent the formation of organised protest in the *Buraku* than it was able to stop the growth of other social movement organisations.

Emergent Social Movements

The Rice Riots gave added force to the arguments of the liberal democrats who were demanding that the government should take measures to expand the franchise to enable the ordinary citizen to play some part in the process of government. The Russian Revolution and Rice Riots demonstrated what could occur when protest was allowed to take the form of direct action instead of being channelled through a system of representative government. Although they were partly inspired by ideas derived from the Western, liberal tradition which had recently been endorsed by President Wilson at the Versailles Peace Conference, much of the support for universal suffrage came from those members of the middle class who regarded it as the best way to insure against violent outbreaks of direct action. Similarly, later in the 1920s, liberal support for programmes of aid to improve the *Buraku* environment was largely inspired by a hope that marginal improvements would discourage radical protest. Nevertheless, the campaigns for universal suffrage commanded much popular support. Mass demonstrations supporting these demands took place in late 1919, early 1920, climaxing with a rally of 75,000 held in Tokyo on 23 February 1920.[15] Popular pressure had little influence. The demonstrations were ignored by Hara Kei, then Prime Minister, and universal manhood suffrage did not come into operation until 1928, by which time the parties in the Diet had lost touch with developments within the social movements.

The labour union movement had changed radically from the Christian-inspired, labour-capital conciliation group that the *Yuaikai* (Friendly Society) had been at its inception in 1912. By 1920 most of the leaders of the labour unions were associated with the socialist or anarchist movements and regarded themselves as the leaders of the class struggle in Japan. However, in the wake of the recession which overtook the Japanese economy in 1920 the unions were forced back on to the defensive and developed mass struggle tactics in order to try to prevent redundancy or wage reductions. The most spectacular display of union power was a strike of 30,000 workers in the Mitsubishi and Kawasaki shipyards of Kobe which lasted fifty days. This strike, which got national publicity, is said to have encouraged many workers' and peasants' groups to engage in organised activity. The same year, the *Yuaikai* adopted a new name, *Nihon Rodo Sodomei* (Japanese Federation of Labour), a title better suited to the more radical organisation it had become.[16] Although there were never more than 8% of the working population organised in labour unions and the national federation was never able to act decisively due to perpetual internal factional rivalry, organised labour did emerge at the start of the 1920s as a potentially powerful social movement.

At the same time, organised tenants' unions were being formed and tenants' disputes were becoming both more frequent and more aggressive. In 1917 there had been 85 major tenants' disputes, in 1921 there were 1,680 in which 146,000 participated.[17] Under the slogan of 'land or freedom', disputes took place across the country, particularly in the central and south western areas, in which tenants demanded the reduction of, or exemption from, rent and sought to establish their 'right of cultivation'. In April 1922 the *Nihon Nomin Kumiai* (Japan Peasant Union) was established to act as a national federation, and by the end of 1924 this had 52,000 members divided between 694 branches.[18] The effectiveness of this organisation, too, was limited by the internal disputes between rival factions but potentially it had great power.

Among the revolutionary left there can be little doubt that at the start of the 1920s the anarchists and syndicalists wielded most influence. Until the time of the Russian Revolution, almost all the revolutionary tradition in Japan had been inspired by such anarchists as Kropotkin and Stirner or such socialists as Morris. Understanding of Marxism was limited.[19] Even as late as 1926, when the syndicalist unions banded together to form the *Jiyu Rengo Rodo Kumiai* (Free Federation of Labour Unions), they claimed a membership of 55,000 distributed between 29 unions. In the same year the syndicalist tenants' union, the *Nomin Jichikai* (the Peasants Self-Governing League, formed in 1925), claimed to have 243 branches and 6,300 members.[20] In the face of the rapid spread of Marxism-Leninism, the anarchist influence so declined by 1931 that the syndicalists could only claim a following of 11,000, the anarchists 2,800. Nevertheless, anarchist ideas propagated by activists in each social movement group were influential throughout the 1920s.

The apparent success of the Russian Revolution gave greater authority to the Bolshevik-inclined factions within the left wing movement. Nevertheless, there was a good deal of co-operation between anarchists and Bolsheviks in organisations like the *Shakaishugi Domei* (Socialist League) and in the production of newspapers such as the *Rodo Undo* (Labour Movement).[21] However, Osugi Sakae's trenchant criticism of the activities of the new Russian régime made any long term co-operation impossible.[22] The final split between the two groups was caused by a disagreement over the practical question of how a

Table 1: *The Size of the Suiheisha, 1926–1941*

		1926	1927	1928	1929	1930	1931	1932	1933	1934	1935	1936	1937	1938	1939[2]	1940	1941[3]
Overall Suiheisha Size (A + B + C)	Groups	367	385	406	398	381	378	346	—	369	276	406	408	414	415	374	347
	Members	44,805	47,925	53,595	53,328	49,162	47,724	35,754	—	44,338	38,889	42,545	45,003	41,085	42,205	40,096	40,538
A National Suiheisha	Groups				319	—	291	259	335	314	349	378	391	391	388	348	310
	Members				48,483	44,246	43,292	27,824	33,133	35,903	35,527	38,449	40,366	38,960	35,527	37,659	36,859
H.Q. Faction	Groups				292	281	275	96	278							346	303
	Members				47,197	43,417	42,465	7,653	28,309							36,159	32,872
Liberation League (Anarchist Faction)	Groups				27		16	4									
	Members				1,286	829	829	226									
Neutral Faction	Groups							107									
	Members							15,549									
Dissolution Faction	Groups							52	57								
	Members							4,396	4,824								
Daiwa Patriotic Movement	Groups															2	7
	Members															1,500	3,987
B Non-affiliated Suiheisha	Groups				24	19	39	48	?	33	20	21	13	20	24	24	35
	Members				1,041	1,832	1,066	5,630	?	3,766	2,197	2,916	2,844	1,992	2,240	2,325	3,569
C Japan Suiheisha	Groups				55	49	48	39	25	22	7	7	4	3	3	2	2
	Members				3,804	3,084	2,464	2,300	2,019	4,669	1,165	1,180	1,993	133	110	112	110

Source: *Suihei Undō Shiryō Shūsei*, Vol III, p1027.

Notes to Table 1:

1. In answer to a question asked in the 50th Diet by Arima on 28 January 1925, the Justice Ministry estimated the size of the *Suiheisha* at 265 groups composed of 33,531 members. This figure presumably relates to the size of the movement in 1924. *Suihei Undo Shiryo Shusei*, vol I, p 370.

2. In the original table compiled by Akisada from documents produced by the *Naimusho*, the total number of *Suiheisha* groups in 1939 is listed as 515 and the number of groups in the National *Suiheisha* is given as 488. In view of what is known to have been happening within Japanese society and the *Suiheisha* at this time such rapid expansion followed by equally rapid contraction the following year seems most unlikely. I therefore concluded that this was a misprint.

3. Similarly, in the column for 1941 the size of the National *Suiheisha* is given as 410 when 310 seems more likely.

A note on the size of the Suiheisha

We have had cause to comment on the increasing or decreasing support given to the *Suiheisha* movement. Evidence of this has largely come from the impressions gained from primary and secondary sources as well as from information about the activities of the groups in Mie and Hiroshima. It is very hard to assess the size of the *Suiheisha* movement. The estimates which exist (see Table 1 opposite) are drawn from reports made to the *Naimusho* (Home Ministry), whose officials compiled a survey every year after 1929 entitled *Shakai Undo no Jokyo x nen* (The condition of the Social Movement in year X). The reports were assembled from the responses of local police to enquiries about how many of the local populace would attend or support *Suiheisha* meetings or *Kyudan* campaigns. Local estimates were added up to provide a total of the amount of support in the prefecture, and reports from the prefectures were used to produce a figure for the country as a whole. It is unlikely that these estimates were very accurate or sensitive to changes which occurred in the movement's size, particularly in the late 1920s. Would the local police have tended to underestimate the number of *Suiheisha* activists in their locality in order to demonstrate their success in containing the movement's development? Or, would they have tended to overestimate the movement's strength at a time when the police were becoming more sensitive to the threat from subversive radical organisations?

After the movement had become a membership organisation in 1925, it should have become possible to draw up membership lists or, at least, to estimate the number of active supporters from the amount of subscriptions paid in by the local branches. However, the membership rules were never strictly enforced. Some groups would contribute very little in spite of having a large, active membership; in other areas a wealthy activist might pay the subscriptions on behalf of a large number of people, even though only a few took part in the group's activities.

Estimates of the extent of the *Suiheisha*'s influence can only be assessed by comparison with the total *Buraku* population but, as has been explained in the introductory section, estimates of the size of the *Buraku* population range between one and three million. Official figures, such as those to be found in Table 1, opposite, are no more than a rough estimate and estimates of the population regarded as *Burakumin* vary greatly, such that all one can say is that probably between one and five per cent of the *Buraku* population regarded themselves or were regarded as *Suiheisha* supporters. This is the group which can be considered to be the 'directed segment' of the movement, the sector of the *Buraku* which will have been influenced to some degree by *Suiheisha* theory and practice. But, as we have seen, there were many outside this group who were inspired by the *Suiheisha* to become involved in some kind of action in the pursuit of their desire for equality of treatment. *Yuwa* policy was directed at restricting the activity of the 'directed segment' of the movement so as to minimise their influence over the 'undirected segment'.

national organisation of revolutionary labour unions could be established. At a conference called to try to resolve this problem in September 1922, the Bolsheviks argued for the creation of a national organisation with strong centralised power; only in this way could the power of the working masses be mustered sufficiently to oppose the power of the capitalist. The anarchists who proposed the formation of a decentralised free federation explained: 'We oppose an organisation which strengthens the chains of authority in order to break the chains of wealth.'[23] The conference ended in chaos; there remained no hope of anarchists and Bolsheviks working together. Reverberations of this anarchist-Bolshevik debate were to be felt in all other social movements including the *Suiheisha*.

On 15 July 1922, the Bolsheviks who had been in the Socialist League met to create the Japanese Communist Party, 'to act positively as a branch of the Comintern and as a leader of the revolutionary movement of the proletariat'.[24] Its existence had to remain a secret, its membership scarcely exceeded fifty, but it achieved some influence both within intellectual circles and within the labour movement. The publications *Marukusushugi* (Marxism) and *Zenei* (Vanguard) served as semi-official organs of the party, being devoted mainly to Marxist analyses of current events and to spreading knowledge about the revolution in Russia. Meanwhile, its members attempted to form party cells within the labour movement in order to increase its prestige and mass support and reduce the influence of the social democrats. Through its diverse activities, the party began to make its presence felt in various sections of the working class movement. However, in June 1923 fifty members of the party were arrested, of whom thirty were brought to trial. Party affairs were placed in the hands of 'caretakers' until the re-establishment of the party in December 1926.

In the early 1920s, then, there was a surge in interest in and activism of groups involved in anti-establishment campaigns, liberal, anarchist and Bolshevik. People throughout the country were encouraged by one or other of these groups to organise to promote change within Japanese society. Liberals and anarchists were most influential at first but, although their numbers remained small, the influence of the Bolsheviks and those associated with them grew rapidly towards the middle of the decade. Their powerful, if inflexible, ideology was to inspire those who became leaders of most social movement organisations. Indeed, it is no exaggeration to maintain that for most of the pre-war period:

> What moulded the spirit of reason and basis of personal responsibility and criticism of authority in Japan was not liberalism but Marxism . . . the only direct opponent of the Emperor system.[25]

The Yuwa Policy – attempts at containment

The government's neglect of the *Buraku* problem ended soon after the Rice Riots. In the autumn of 1918 the *Teikoku Kodokai* carried out a national survey which reported that in none of the *Buraku* where they had a branch established had rioting taken place, but that anger against the government and majority society was mounting.[26] The Home Ministry began to take steps to try to pacify this anger. On 17-19 January 1919 a second conference of the *Saimin Buraku Kyogikai* was held to discuss ways in which basic improvements to *Buraku* could be made and how *Burakumin* could be helped to find work. During the conference some reference was made to concepts of racial equality and national self-determination, but the tone of the conference was set in a speech by Dr Kita Teikichi, who stressed that the problem of the *Burakumin* urgently needed to be solved in order to prevent the spread of socialism among them.

The following month, the *Teikoku Kodokai* held its first *Dojo Yuwakai* (Sympathy/Conciliation Conference). Within this meeting, the liberal tradition was stronger and criticism of government policy more pronounced, but here, too, the main theme was to initiate reform in order to prevent the further radicalisation of the *Buraku* communities. To this end, resolutions were passed demanding that the government provide financial aid for the improvement projects, that the Home Ministry conduct a comprehensive survey of conditions in the *Buraku* and formulate a programme of action based on this, and that the respective ministries see to it that discrimination in the armed forces and in schools was brought to an end. These demands were built into a composite petition which was later presented to the 41st Diet.[27]

In the following year, the Diet gave its approval to the first Central government grant aid to the *Buraku* Improvement Project: 50,000 yen was to be used for this purpose, 43,000 yen of which was distributed to 17 prefectures.[28] A second *Dojo Yuwakai* was held on 13 February 1921 attended by 700, including influential *Buraku* leaders, regional bureaucrats and leading politicians including the Prime Minister, Hara Kei. The mood at this meeting seems to have been more radical. During the debates there were protests about the continuing discrimination that was taking place in the army and the courts and demands that the government provide the sort of cash which would enable real improvements to be made in the living conditions of the *Buraku* communities – about ten million yen per year might be sufficient, it was thought. In the end, though, the resolutions which were passed merely encouraged the prefectural authorities to grant more money for improvement projects and to support *Yuwa* groups.[29] Later the same year, the report of a survey made of conditions within *Buraku* was published and detailed recommendations were made concerning improvements to the environment around the *Buraku*, the provision of better education facilities and the improvement of sanitation and medical facilities. This report was to be the basis for the *Yuwa* policy as it developed in the 1920s.[30]

In 1920 a Social Affairs Bureau (*Shakai Kyoku*) was established within the Home Ministry, one function of which was to administer the funds provided for the *Buraku* Improvement Project. The Home Ministry further decided to encourage local government organisations to develop their own improvement projects and it began to give support to existing *kaizen/Yuwa* groups hoping to establish such a group in each prefecture. To realise this plan, a specialist officer was to be appointed to the prefectural social affairs bureau and by 1921 twelve such officers had been appointed. At the Home Ministry itself, Miyoshi Iheiji, a leading figure in the Okayama *kaizen* movement, was appointed to advise on *Yuwa* policy.[31]

The *kaizen* groups which had been formed in the early years of Taisho seem to have begun to exert some influence over the conduct of local government and to have persuaded them to give some support for *Buraku* improvement projects. In 1916 a total of 30,332 yen was spent throughout Japan on these projects but over 70% of it was expended in the prefectures of central Japan. Most of this money was provided by the *shichoson* (town or village) authorities with lesser amounts coming from prefectural and *gun* (county) bodies, although the proportion of the burden varied greatly according to area.[32] The most tangible aspect of the newly invigorated improvement policy was the provision of monetary aid from central government funds. Although the provision of central government money was a significant policy innovation, it formed only a small proportion of that provided for improvements. As can be seen from the Table, over half of the money was provided by the lowest level local authorities, the remainder coming from the central and prefectural bodies in almost equal proportions. Once again, however, the exact proportions varied greatly according to area.[33] All prefectures where there was a substantial *Buraku* community provided some money for improvement projects, but over 60% of the total expenditure was spent in the Kinki region – an area which, according to the 1935 census, contained 43% of the total *Buraku* population.[34]

Public Aid to the Buraku Improvement Projects 1916-1922

	Central Govt A	Prefecture B	Gun C	Town/Village D	B + C + D
1916		11,027	4,176	15,219	30,332
1917		12,210	5,440	13,520	31,171
1918		14,027	5,621	14,810	34,459
1919		20,761	7,332	24,068	52,162
1920	43,000	50,996	14,818	47,073	112,887
1921	145,760	145,724		361,285	507,009
1922	179,860	181,743		490,704	672,447

Adapted from Akisada, '*1916-22 nen no Yuwazaisei . . . .*', p 54.

There is no direct link between these increases in government funding and the radicalisation of the urban and rural workers before and after the Rice Riots, but it would seem that in the early years more of the money was provided for *Yuwa* groups than for actual improvement projects which perhaps indicates that the priority of policy was one of containment of dissent. The large increases of support for the various projects did not occur until 1920-21 when, for the first time, central government released substantial amounts of money, though by no means as much as had been requested by some of those at the second *Dojo Yuwakai* of early 1921.

Protest against Discrimination

The evolution of the *Yuwa* policy occurred against a background of more vigorous and better organised protest against discrimination. An early example of violent protest against discrimination occurred in the city of Fukuoka in June 1916. An angry crowd of *Burakumin* attacked the offices of the *Hakata Mainichi Shimbun* (Hakata Daily Newspaper) in protest against the fact that it had carried an article which blatantly insulted the *Burakumin* community. The police response was to raid the nearest *Buraku* and arrest 306 people, nearly all the adult males living there, although in the end only 120 of them were brought to trial and only 47 of these were found guilty. This was the first major incident of protest against discrimination and was widely reported in newspapers all over the country. Many commentators suggest that reports of this incident encouraged others elsewhere to engage in vigorous protest.[35]

In the next couple of years, protest against instances of discrimination was channelled through, if not organised by, the groups which in the first place had been established by the local authorities. Most of the members of these groups were young men who frequently came across discrimination in their daily lives and who became resolved to do something to oppose it. To a certain extent, these groups enabled the authorities to keep control over the most restive elements within the *Buraku* communities and they formed the basis of the more closely supervised *Yuwa* movement which was developed in the later 1920s. However, these groups also provided an arena within which *Burakumin* acquired theoretical and practical experience which they were to utilise when establishing *Suiheisha* groups. To develop this point, we will examine the way in which the formation of *Yuwa* groups in Hiroshima and Mie foreshadowed and contributed to the formation of more militant groups.

In the first decade of the twentieth century *kaizen* (improvement) groups had been formed in Hiroshima City and elsewhere in the prefecture. But, nevertheless, there was widespread participation in the rioting of 1918 by members of *Buraku* communities both in Hiroshima City and in towns throughout the prefecture. Rioting in Miyoshi town and Fukushima-cho (part of the city of Hiroshima) was only controlled following the intervention of the army. Still, there was no great haste in introducing a conciliation programme. Not until October 1920 was the *Chiho Kaizen Kyogikai* (Local Improvement Council) formed, presumably following directions sent out by the Home Ministry and, within the next twelve months, groups were set up throughout the prefecture. To back up the efforts of these groups, the amount of prefectural funds provided to assist the improvement projects was increased from 5,000 yen in 1920 to 23,000 yen in 1921. Eighty-three *Burakumin* from groups all over the prefecture were sent to attend the second *Dojo Yuwakai* conference, held in Tokyo in February 1921, and on their return they established the *Hiroshima ken*

Kyomeikai (Hiroshima prefecture Sympathiser Society). At its first meeting, held on 13 March, the group resolved to follow the 'Imperial Way' and faithfully apply the principles set out in the Emancipation Declaration and the Rescript on Education.[36]

Parallel to the development of these officially sponsored groups there emerged a number of more or less independent study groups formed by young *Burakumin*. In spring 1921 Teruyama Masami returned to Fukushima-cho after spending some time at a Buddhist university in Kyoto and Waseda university, Tokyo. On his return, he formed a discussion group, the *Yakushin Seinen Dantai* (Rapid Progress Young men's group), which met regularly to discuss the socialist ideas Teruyama had picked up while at university.[37] They did more than just discuss ideas and became involved in a series of protests against discrimination concerning the use of public baths and discrimination at school. The exclusion of *Burakumin* from a newly-formed youth group in March 1921 led to a prolonged campaign of protest directed against the *gun* authorities which lasted until the following autumn. Elsewhere a league of *Buraku* youth groups was formed to co-ordinate the activities of the groups on the islands of Hiroshima bay (*Tosho Renmei* – Island League). At a meeting held in February 1922 they passed resolutions declaring their opposition to 'sympathetic' actions and all forms of discrimination.[38] The independent groups were moving towards the support of more radical policies.

A slightly different pattern of events emerged in Mie. The first recorded campaigns against discrimination took place in 1917 and may have been inspired by reports of the campaign in Fukuoka which involved the *Hakata Mainichi Shimbun*.[39] A better organised campaign was carried out in 1919 in protest against the use of insulting language by an army officer which resulted in petitions being sent to the prefectural governor and the Army Minister in Tokyo.[40] Following these examples, various groups in Matsuzaka city began to protest about instances of discrimination. These sporadic protests did not lead to any attempts at organised protest until 1921. In that year, Matsuzaka city extended its boundaries to incorporate a *Buraku* community called Amagawa and a movement emerged requesting that the area be renamed because it had started to be used as a term of abuse. This more formal protest seems to have generated the formation of the *Tesshin Doshikai* (Clear Truth Comrade Association), which began to organise the efforts of all *Burakumin* in the prefecture to protest against discrimination.

Following the economic recession of 1920, many of the small factories in Mie closed down and those who had been working in them returned to their families in the rural villages, exacerbating conditions there. Possibly as a result of this, there developed a number of tenants' struggles demanding rent reductions, and tenant unions sprang up throughout the prefecture. One major campaign occurred in the autumn of 1921 and was directed against one of the most important landlords in the Matsuzaka area. It was led by a member of the *Tesshin Doshikai* and many of those involved were *Burakumin*. The campaign reached its climax when four hundred tenants gathered to demonstrate in support of their demands and the following day an agreement was made which promised a 35% reduction in rent.[41] This success seems to have encouraged the leaders of the Mie *Burakumin* groups to develop their own organisation. But, despite the emergence of these groups and although a *kaizen* (improvement) movement had been developed in the late *Meiji* period, there was no attempt made to establish a semi-autonomous *Yuwa* group. Substantial amounts of money were, however, provided to assist with improvement projects.

Throughout the country groups were being formed within the *Buraku* communities to discuss the nature of the prejudice they faced and to organise protest against discrimination. In some, the influence of socialist ideas stimulated criticism of establishment values, but elsewhere, groups developed which were more closely connected with the rise of organisation among the tenants. Whatever their origins, those active in these groups began to demonstrate their frustration with the slow progress of the improvement programmes and the patronising attitudes of those who were involved with their implementation. Isolated criticism was developing into organised protest.

The Proposal to form the Suiheisha

In the spring of 1919 in Kasuyabaru, Wakikamimura, Nara prefecture, the *Tsubamekai* (the Swallow Club) was formed by three young men, Sakamoto Seiichiro, Kiyohara Kazutaka and Komai Keisaku. There had been a strong liberal influence in the area since the nineteenth century and the fathers of both Sakamoto and Kiyohara had been associated with the *Jiyuto*.[42] Sakamoto (b 1892) had led a sheltered childhood made possible by the fact that his father was influential within the *Buraku*, being the owner of a glue factory, so he did not face severe discrimination until he attended Nara commercial school. The experience of discrimination there made a lasting impression on him and, determined to escape from it, he migrated to Manchuria at the age of eighteen, vowing never to return. However, the illness of his elder brother caused him to return home whence he was sent to technical college in Tokyo to study a new process for the production of gelatine.[43] In Tokyo, he lodged with his friend Kiyohara. Kiyohara (b 1895), better known by his pen name of Saiko Bankichi, was the son of a *Jodo Shinshu* priest. He had suffered discrimination from his time at primary school and, though he managed to persevere with his education to middle school level, he found that inequality of treatment there made it impossible for him to complete his full term of study. Artistically inclined, in May 1914 he went to study Western painting in Tokyo, where by concealing his background he was able to acquire a wide circle of friends.[44] At this time, it was becoming possible to acquire translations of novels by such authors as Gorky, Tolstoy as well as the more overtly political works of Kropotkin and religious works on Christianity. Saiko, later accompanied by Sakamoto, like many other of his contemporaries, was eager to study these new ideas. In particular he was seeking to find a means by which he could escape discrimination entirely. For a time he and Sakamoto considered migrating to the Celebes islands (Sulawesi), and even began to learn Malay, but the news of an upsurge of anti-Japanese feeling there forced them to abandon this plan.[45] After their return to Nara, they still maintained contact with their acquaintances in Tokyo and in December 1920 they became members of the Socialist League, being associated mainly with Yamakawa Hitoshi and Sakai Toshihiko. The third of these young men, Komai Keisaku (1897-1945), was the son of a reasonably prosperous wood merchant. After graduating from upper primary school, he went to a private school and then to Tokyo, where he was to study to become a lawyer.[46] He never completed his studies, though while in Tokyo he, too, read much of the socialist and anarchist literature which was being produced and seems to have been particularly influenced by Osugi Sakae.

The *Tsubamekai* – name derived from Saiko and Sakamoto's original plan to 'fly away' from discrimination – at first organised communal bulk purchasing for the *Buraku* and arranged holiday trips for the *Buraku* villagers. Soon, however, they developed a study group and began to build up a library. Between them, they sought to examine the *Yuwa* policy, develop the socialist ideas which they had picked up in Tokyo and apply them in such a way that they would be better able to understand and perhaps solve the problems faced in their everyday lives. The socialist influence in the group was marked, but they were pretty 'easy-going socialists' (*nonki na shakaishugisha*).[47]

In the July 1921 edition of *Kaiho* (Liberation) there appeared an article written by Sano Manabu, a lecturer in law at Waseda University, entitled, 'The liberation of special *Buraku*'. In the first three sections of this article, Sano gives an explanation of the origin of the *Burakumin* problem which seems to draw on the material gathered by Kita Teikichi in his special edition of *Minzoku to Rekishi*.[48] However, Sano suggests that the problem can be treated as if they were a minority group like Jews or blacks in America. In the fourth section he makes his own contribution. Although the prejudice held by many people towards *Burakumin* is nothing but an 'inane social standard', it is one which is supported by a 'solid historical tradition' which 'hinders their economic activity, their social advancement and their acquisition of knowledge'. The efforts of the 'government and philanthropists' to help them have been and will be small. The emancipation of the *Burakumin* must be based on two principles. Firstly, the *Burakumin* must themselves begin to demand the abolition of discrimination against them. 'The destruction of this traditional view of the *Burakumin* can only be achieved by publishing the views of our own groups and making our own demands.' Secondly, since both workers and *Burakumin* are 'economically weak and exploited, in order to build a good society which contains neither exploiters nor oppressors it is necessary for both to form a close union; a joint movement'. In other words, the *Burakumin* should first set up their own autonomous group which, once formed, should co-operate with other groups to overcome all kinds of exploitation and discrimination through the creation of a new society. If this is done Sano foresees 'a better day when, for the first time, all these unfortunate groups will be liberated'.[49]

When Saiko and Sakamoto read this they immediately set out for Tokyo to discuss with Sano how they could set about forming such a movement. On their return they began to sort out the practical details. The name 'Suiheisha' – literally water level (and therefore sometimes horizon) society – was suggested by Sakamoto who only afterwards learnt of the seventeenth century English group, the Levellers.[50] In November they established an office in a small house just outside their village and placed a notice by the window announcing 'Suiheisha Foundation office'. The next major tasks were to organise leaflets and similar publicity for the opening conference which was to be held on 3 March 1922.

For a Better Day

Towards the end of 1921 Saiko moved to live in Kyoto and, supporting himself by working at the gas works, he devoted his evenings to writing leaflets and pamphlets to advertise the forthcoming conference. Most important of these was the pamphlet, 'For a Better Day', written by Saiko following discussions with the others on the need for a pamphlet which would attract a wide spectrum of support for the movement. The pamphlet is a curious mélange of socialist, Buddhist and Christian ideas. It begins with a quotation from William Morris:

> I am Lucifer. I bring out the glimmer of your hopes of happiness and afflict you with suffering . . . .

This is followed by the section of Sano's article on the 'principles of emancipation'. The second section is adapted from an appeal written by Romain Rolland which he wrote to encourage people to attend an International Conference of People's Theatre. The style of the passage is obscure, but the main point is simply to urge people to attend the opening conference. Section three emphasises the point that any activity must be based on self-respect which will not come merely from listening to the improvers; 'change for us' must be 'change by us'. In the next section, entitled 'Destiny', the author criticises the Buddhist ideas of passive acceptance of one's destiny and points out that great religious leaders like Shinran and Jesus of Nazareth both struggled to change their destiny and the life of others. It goes on to criticise the obsession with the past and encourages a positive attitude to the future and the fight 'for a better day'. The pamphlet ends:

> Get up and look. It is dawn. We must dispel the long night of rage, the grief, the enmity, the curses, the hazy bad dream. We must renew ourselves with new blood. Now, let us climb the hill of purification from inferno to paradise. Now, let us rush up this good hill. Those of you who suffer beneath the traditional status system . . . gather together. Receive the baptism of dawn. Worship the rise of the morning star of a better day. Get up and look. It is dawn.[51]

The pamphlet was written in November–December 1921, but they had great difficulty getting it printed. The *Yamato Doshikai* refused to print it because it was too radical. Finally, they were able to get it printed with the help of a reporter from a Buddhist newspaper – *Chugai Nippo* – in Kyoto; then it was distributed to all those on the subscription list of the *Yamato Doshikai*'s magazine *Meiji no Hikari* in January 1922.[52] In the months before the conference over 100,000 assorted leaflets and pamphlets were distributed.[53]

The Movement Develops

The activities of those in the *Tsubamekai* were exceptional only in that they envisaged the formation of a national organisation. In most areas where *Buraku* existed, young *Burakumin* began to participate in groups which discussed how prejudice might be overcome and to protest against specific instances of discrimination. In some areas, Hiroshima for example, these groups were set up by the prefectural authorities and provided with money which came from funds given to *Yuwa* organisations. Elsewhere, as in Mie, the discussion groups were formed independent of bureaucratic control. However, in either case the groups did more than simply discuss the nature of prejudice and began to take part in active protest. Moreover, as radical ideas spread throughout Japan even those groups which had been established by the local government offices to minimise the subversion of Japan's youth began to engage in activities of which their founders will not have approved.

So, as Saiko, Komai and Sakamoto toured the Kansai region to speak at meetings held in *Buraku* communities and to distribute leaflets and pamphlets to publicise the conference which would launch their new organisation, they found a receptive audience. Yoneda Tomi (b 1901) had belonged to a discussion group in his village of Oshima, Nara prefecture, since its formation by the police in 1918. As leader of this group he had even taken part in activities aimed at heightening patriotic feeling among *Burakumin* – in 1920 he joined a party which went to work on the *Meiji Jingu* in Tokyo, a shrine established in memory of the *Meiji* emperor. But he was also a member of a discussion group which was strongly influenced by liberal and Christian socialist ideas. At one meeting of this group Yoneda met Saiko and so, when plans for the foundation of the *Suiheisha* had been formulated, Saiko contacted Yoneda who, with other members of his group, became actively involved in the preparations for the conference.[54]

Minami Umekichi had been one of the most active leaders of the *kaizen* movement in Kyoto for nearly ten years. He had attended meetings of the *Dojo Yuwakai* in Tokyo and had led the local *Yuwa* groups in petitioning the Kyoto authorities to provide more improvement money. Nevertheless, he was becoming critical of the movement's moderate leaders, especially Oe Taku, and was attracted to the more radical ideas which promised more rapid progress.[55] He was a particularly important contact to make at this stage as he introduced them to those involved in the Kyoto federation of six *Buraku* young men's groups which had been developing their own radical ideas and taking part in protest activities. Moreover, because of his experience in the *Yuwa* movement and because he was somewhat older than most of the others so far involved, he was able to command the respect of those both inside and outside the *Buraku* communities.

The propaganda campaign of Saiko and others received the support of the *Chugai Nippo*, a newspaper distributed in the Kyoto area which carried regular reports on the process of the formation of the *Suiheisha*.[56] Then, the *Suiheisha* propagandists' activities received assistance from an unexpected quarter when they were able to use a national conference by *Yuwa* activists to publicise their forthcoming conference.[57]

A group of *Yuwa* activists formed an organisation called the *Dai Nippon Byodokai* early in 1922 and announced that a conference to 'discuss ways of opposing discrimination' would be held on 21 February in Osaka. This gathering, presumably sponsored by the Home Ministry, was intended to launch a new, *Yuwa* style movement which would keep the *Burakumin* under their control. *Suiheisha* activists attended the meeting in order to advertise their conference by distributing leaflets and at one stage they even addressed the conference from the platform. They were so successful that the meeting became in effect a prologue to the formation of the *Suiheisha*. For example, among the 500 delegates in attendance there was a group of three or four from the Mie prefecture *Yuwa* group who met Saiko and took back with them a large number of *Suiheisha* pamphlets. The next month twenty *Burakumin* from Mie attended the *Suiheisha*'s opening conference.[58]

This meeting gave the *Suiheisha* an opportunity to spread their ideas to a wider audience and also gave the *Suiyokai* a chance to contribute to the debate about *Burakumondai*. The *Suiyokai* was a group of socialists based in Tokyo led by the veteran Bolshevik, Sakai Toshihiko, and they produced a pamphlet for this conference which later was distributed throughout the country. The pamphlet, 'The Liberation of the Special *Buraku*', purports to be written by four people, a proletarian, a Special *Burakumin*, an *eta* and a worker. Much more radical than any of the other documents produced, it emphasises the need for an organisation of *Burakumin* that will enable them to regain their self-respect while pointing out that the problem of discrimination can only be solved through the united efforts of organised workers, peasants and *Burakumin* in the creation of a new society. A hierarchy of discrimination is described in which the capitalist despises the worker, the better paid worker despises the poorly paid worker and the lowest paid worker despises the *Burakumin*. To overcome these divisions in society all workers must unite to fight for a change in its basic nature. Finally, *Buraku* workers are warned to beware of the deceptive policies of wealthier *Burakumin*. The Tokyo based socialists sought to influence the nascent *Buraku* movement by introducing notions of class struggle into theories of *Buraku* liberation.[59]

Also from Tokyo, but with a different political orientation, was Hirano Shoken. He travelled from Tokyo to attend the meeting in Osaka only to find that he had been misinformed about the date and had arrived six days early. By chance he heard of the plans of the *Suiheisha* group and went to visit them.

Hirano had been born and brought up in a small *Buraku* in Fukushima prefecture and had come up against discrimination at school, when trying to find work on his arrival in Tokyo and the first time he tried to get married.[60] Eventually he found employment in a print works and became active in the *Shinyukai*, a prominent anarcho-syndicalist union, though it is unclear whether he himself subscribed to their syndicalist ideas.[61] Between 1920 and 1922, he wrote several articles for left wing journals and magazines in Tokyo and from these it is possible to trace the development of his political ideas and his ideas about discrimination.[62] In the earlier articles he relates his own experiences, describing the type of discrimination that existed[63], but in the later articles he begins to suggest that *Burakumin* will have to organise themselves if they are to achieve their own liberation. These later views seem to have developed out of discussions held in a group at Waseda university (the group's name was the *Reimin Soseikai*) which was attended by both Hirano and Sano. Some would even suggest that Sano might have been influenced by Hirano.[64] Hirano was totally opposed to the activities of the *Yuwa* groups and attended the second *Dojo Yuwakai* only in order to heckle the speakers and to distribute a leaflet entitled 'National Self Determination' in which he called on all the *Burakumin* attending the conference to form their own autonomous groups.[65] The following August he had an article published in which he predicted that the *eta minzoku* (race) would lead a violent outburst against the ruling class oppressors using tactics similar to those of the Jewish terrorists in late nineteenth century Russia.[66] After his meeting with Sakamoto and others he returned to Tokyo and hurriedly prepared an article for the 'Labour Weekly' in which he urged all *Burakumin* to attend the forthcoming conference.[67]

Thus in the few months between setting up the office in Kasuyabara and 3 March 1922, the plans of the *Suiheisha*'s founders received widespread publicity and attracted a broad spectrum of support. Left wing journals in both Kanto and Kansai publicised their ideas and left wing groups publicly demonstrated their support for the initiative launched in Nara. Meanwhile, *Suiheisha* ideas were being disseminated through the communication network set up by the improvement movement and the *Suiheisha* activists recruited the support of those who were taking part in the *Yuwa* groups.

The Founding Conference

Official documents reporting on the first *Suiheisha* conference (3 March 1922) indicate that there were 1,000 present, although contemporary 'movement' documents consistently claim 3,000 attended.[68] Most of these were from the Kyoto area; the biggest group of people from elsewhere was of 50 from Nara, although there were representatives from nine other prefectures. The conference opened with a welcoming speech from Sakamoto in which he explained the background to the formation of the movement. Three general principles were then proposed as the basis for the movement's development: 1 We, the *Tokushu Burakumin* shall achieve total liberation by our own efforts. 2 We, the *Tokushu*

Burakumin demand complete liberty to choose our occupations as well as economic freedom and we are determined to obtain them. 3 We shall awaken to the fundamental principles of human nature and march towards the perfection of mankind.[69] These were approved unanimously. Next the movement's declaration was read out and adopted. Written by Saiko (and perhaps Sakamoto), in this statement too we find the rhetoric of the class struggle mingled with the imagery of the poet and student of religion. It urges the rejection of the 'philanthropic' movements which only degrade *Burakumin* and the formation of a movement in which they can regain their self-respect. After many years of oppression, the time has come when 'the oppressor shall be vanquished and the martyr with the crown of thorns be blessed'. The *Suiheisha* is to be formed so that we shall 'never again insult our forefathers or desecrate humanity by cowardice in either word or deed'.[70] The conference then considered three resolutions:

1 If anyone is insulting to us in either word or deed using such names as *Tokushu Buraku* or *eta* we will thoroughly censure the offenders.
2 A monthly periodical called *Suihei* shall be published at the national headquarters in order to strengthen our unity.
3 The East and West Honganji temples of which most *Burakumin* are members are to be approached and asked for their frank opinion on the movement and the reply is to be acted upon.[71]

Following the unanimous approval given to these resolutions, the conference then heard a series of speakers from various prefectures who spoke of the conditions in their regions and of what they hoped the movement would achieve. That evening a smaller group of delegates met to discuss organisational matters. Minami was selected as chairman of the organisation and an office was to be established at his home; to assist him six others were elected to an executive committee.[72] Seven organisational rules were decided upon, but none of these was specific. The central committee (members unspecified) was to meet twice yearly, arrange an annual conference and, where necessary, a special national conference. Regional groups were to be encouraged to affiliate to the national headquarters, but they were free to govern their own affairs as long as they were in accordance with the general principles (although there was no means of expulsion if they did not).[73] The discussion on the rules was followed by a debate over the use of words like *eta, Tokushu, Burakumin* in documents and resolutions adopted by the *Suiheisha*. A representative from Okayama argued that if the words were considered to be insulting then any use of the words should be regarded as objectionable. Yoneda Tomi replied for the executive saying that the words had a historical significance and their use in these circumstances signified the emergence of *Buraku* self-awareness, although he agreed that non-*Burakumin* should not use these words in any circumstances.[74]

Newspaper reports in the days immediately following the conference stressed what were considered to be the radical tendencies within the organisation. The *Chugai Nippo* emphasised the way many of the speakers at the conference had called for the overthrow of capitalism.[75] The Osaka *Asahi Shimbun*, while never actually mentioning the *Suiheisha* by name, carried an article in the 6 March edition in which it equated the problem of the *Buraku* with that of the *Genro*. Both are remnants of the Tokugawa autocracy, both need to be removed. Moreover, in order to prevent especially the young *Burakumin* from becoming 'reds' the government is called on to introduce reforms and give the *Buraku* groups more aid.[76] The formation of the *Suiheisha* received less ambivalent welcome from the left wing press. *Rodo Undo* (The Labour Movement) noted the inconsistency between Japan's insistence on a racial equality clause at the Versailles Peace Conference and the reluctance of the Japanese government to remove the domestic problem of discrimination. The article pledges solidarity with *Burakumin* and urges them to stand and fight with the *Suiheisha*.[77] Meanwhile, the Bolshevik journal *Zenei* (Vanguard), in welcoming the formation of the *Suiheisha*, emphasised that what needed improving was not the *Burakumin* but the society in which they live. The idea that they have special problems which require special treatment was, in itself, discriminatory; the major problem is the existence of capitalist society and the solution to problems such as these will only be resolved by its overthrow.[78]

Despite the fears voiced by the bourgeois press, there does not seem to have been a very strong left wing influence on those who formulated the documents and made the speeches at this time, or if there was, they were careful to disguise it. Indeed, both in the propaganda publicising the first conference and in the documents presented to it, efforts seem to have been made to ensure that there was little to which liberal or Bolshevik, anarchist or nationalist could object. 'Liberation by our own efforts,' 'economic freedom', 'the perfection of mankind' were left undefined. Of the resolutions, the only one that promised to result in any action was that which proposed to censure those who discriminate, although even this was more a case of encouraging something that was already taking place rather than proposing a new tactic. In this early period, then, it was more the style and the rhetoric of the socialists which was borrowed than their ideas or any praxis that might be derived from these ideas. There can be little doubt that this inexactitude was deliberate since the primary aim was to establish a movement with mass support. The success of the founding group is reflected in the fact that not only did their eclectic propaganda attract a wide spectrum of support but also that its leadership managed to include a discontented liberal (Minami), an anarchist (Hirano), a moderate socialist (Yoneda) and two who were identified with Bolsheviks like Sakai (Saiko and Sakamoto). Unity was assured during the initial period of euphoria which accompanied the movement's rapid expansion, but once this ceased and it became necessary to define the movement's aims and means with more precision internal dissension was inevitable.

The Achievement of the Suiheisha

However, if it is the case that there was little that was new in the content of the *Suiheisha*'s ideas, how can we explain the way in which they were found to be so attractive by young *Burakumin* in the few months before the conference and the few years after? The Home Ministry, hoping to strengthen the links between the *Buraku* communities and the Emperor-oriented state network, had encouraged the development of youth groups within the *Buraku*. As this policy developed, it would acquire an extensive bureaucratic framework which would effectively incorporate the *Buraku* communities within the state structure. However, this was something of the future, and the way the *Yuwa* policy developed in the period 1915-22 played a positive role in the *Suiheisha*'s development. By encouraging the formation of *Yuwa/kaizen* groups, the Japanese government had provided *Burakumin* with an arena in which they could acquire the basic skills of leading groups and organising meetings. At the same time, there developed a system of communication and feeling of solidarity between *Buraku* communities both locally and nationally that helped overcome the self-pitying isolation of the impoverished and despised communities. The leaders of the early *Suiheisha* groups at both central and local levels were, almost without exception, former leaders or members of *kaizen* groups. Encouraged by the liberalism of the bourgeois press, and the radicalism of the left wing journals, groups began to appear in the 1920s which questioned the nature of the *Yuwa* policy. This was particularly true in the Kinki area where most improvement money had been spent and where the *Yuwa* groups were most firmly and broadly based. Thus, once the group in Kasuyabaru realised the import of Sano's proposal to form a national autonomous movement of and for *Burakumin*, they were easily able to elicit an enthusiastic response among those *Burakumin* in the surrounding area.

On the surface, there was not yet much difference between the groups and ideas proposed by the *Suiheisha* and those supported by the *Yuwa* movement. There were three small crucial differences of emphasis. Firstly, only *Burakumin* were to be allowed to become members, whereas the *Yuwa* groups had encouraged all to join in the group's activities. Secondly, the previous groups had always sought to appeal to the sympathy of those outside the community and sought their assistance; the *Suiheisha* declared they would achieve their ends 'by their own efforts'. Thirdly, other groups had sought the amelioration of the lot of *Burakumin* within the existing social structure while the *Suiheisha* aimed, albeit in a rather vague way, at the restructuring of society. These views were reflected in the different attitudes towards *Buraku* poverty. The *Yuwa* movement argued that opportunities within Japanese society existed which the *Burakumin* could not or would not take advantage of because of the attitudes they held, whereas those in the *Suiheisha* argued that the will to achieve existed but the opportunities did not and that this was the fault of the social structure. There was a feeling that the *Yuwa* policy did not treat *Burakumin* seriously. Sakamoto felt that the *Yuwa* administrators treated them more like dolls than people.[79] Kimura remembers that the attitude of himself and others in the *Yuwa* groups was one of 'wanting to become human beings' (*ningen ni naritai*) but the *Suiheisha* said '*eta* are human beings too' (*eta mo ningen nanda*).[80] The assertive approach of the *Suiheisha* was what made it so attractive to the young *Burakumin* who were tired of the apologetic attitudes of the *Yuwa* groups.

In attempting to describe how the *Suiheisha* emerged in 1921-22 and to explain why it succeeded in developing so rapidly, the foregoing narrative has tried to elucidate three levels of analysis which together help us to understand the group's birth and growth. In this final section I hope to make clear the theoretical basis on which the narrative has proceeded.

Social movements, at least progressive social movements, are socially creative organisations which make 'self-conscious and successful attempts to introduce innovations into a social system'.[81] Their success will depend on the speed and degree to which their novel ideas can penetrate into the social system. Thus, one can expect that in social systems which value innovativeness, a social movement will be able to grow successfully and one might expect a variety of social movements to thrive. As we have tried to indicate, although industrial and social innovation was encouraged during the *Meiji* period, the government succeeded in limiting the extent of any disruptive repercussions, but, perhaps because of the speed of industrial and social change which occurred in the period 1914-1919, the government lost control over events. During the most liberal phase of the historical period referred to as the '*Taisho* democracy', Japan was open to all kinds of foreign influences, the most important of which can be described as 'liberal' and 'socialist'. The liberals in general seem to have derived inspiration from the ideas avowedly held by the Allies in the War in Europe and the fourteen principles of Woodrow Wilson which led them to take part in the campaigns for universal suffrage and party cabinets and to support the anti-militarist demands of the early 1920s. Socialists, on the other hand, were more impressed by the events in Russia in 1917 and after and the Rice Riots in Japan which persuaded them to support one or other of the peasants', workers' or socialist organisations.

These two patterns were not mutually exclusive and there was a great deal of cross-fertilisation of ideas. It is true that there was no right to form trade unions, that the government had the power to censor newspapers and that the state did use its considerable coercive power to restrict the propagation of left wing thought.[82] Nevertheless, the period 1918 to 1923 was one in which dissent was possible and frequent. It was relatively easy to establish groups whether of liberal, socialist or nationalist orientation and the dissemination of novel ideas to an increasingly literate population could occur with a minimum of state interference.

Within the *Buraku* themselves, there was a subtle change of circumstances which was to make them more receptive to these novel ideas. *Buraku* peasants and workers shared, to a limited degree, the prosperity of the war years and suffered from the recession of the early 1920s. *Burakumin* as proletarians then, shared the experience of the frustration of rising expectations common to the rest of their class. More specifically, however, the spread of the *kaizen* philosophy raised the expectations and aspirations of *Burakumin*. Even though the philosophy was based on a 'reactionary' principle of equality before the Emperor and was conditional on *Burakumin* improving themselves till they matched the standards expected by majority society, it did at least promise equality. Those who managed to meet the necessary criteria and were still not accepted by majority society had good cause to begin to question the policy and indeed the social system that produced it. Moreover, the spread of *kaizen* ideas of equality raised the aspirations of many, even though they would not be able to meet the necessary standards. The *kaizen* groups had not been provided with sufficient funds to make any real difference to living standards within the *Buraku*, but they had busied themselves propagating the idea that if discrimination continued to occur it was against the express wishes of the Emperor. It may not have been very radical or very effective within the majority society, but it did succeed in persuading at least a small section of the *Buraku* communities to begin seriously to consider what an absence of discrimination might be like and how such a state of affairs might be brought about. By provoking a realisation of the 'injustice' of their situation it will have made many begin to feel socially, economically and politically cramped.[83]

The formation of the network of *kaizen* groups in the 1910s (and, as a result of the new policy, in 1920) had a more specific significance for the *Suiheisha*'s development. Theorising about how social movements arise, Freeman emphasises the need for a new movement to utilise an existing network of communication for, if it is to develop rapidly, it cannot rely on one of its own making. Given that such a network exists, it must be 'co-optable to the new ideas of the incipient movement'.

> A co-optable network is one whose members have had common experiences which predispose them to be receptive to the particular new ideas of the incipient movement and who are not faced with structural or ideological barriers to action. If the new movement as an 'innovation' can interpret these experiences in ways that point out channels for social action, then participation in the social movement becomes the logical thing to do.[84]

Once such a situation exists, she argues, all that is required is a crisis to galvanise the network into action in a new direction or a group of persons to begin to disseminate a new idea along this network and/or to begin to weld groups into a movement. The cultural homogeneity of Japan and the uniform nature of the *kaizen* policy had created a network of groups who shared the common experiences of facing discrimination and frustration with the *Yuwa* policy. Experience of the Rice Riots and of the labour union and peasant union struggles, whether direct or not, had broken down the barriers to action. For many *Burakumin*, when the *Suiheisha* was formed, joining in its activities seemed the logical thing to do.

As Barrington Moore Jnr has pointed out, a sense of injustice is an acquired taste, 'a learned response and a historically determined one' which depends on the illusion of the inevitability of (one's own) suffering being shattered.[85] A sector of the *Buraku* population acquired its sense of injustice in the liberal-inspired improvement groups of the late *Meiji* period. The activities of these groups achieved few concrete results, but they did create a climate of opinion among some *Burakumin* which made them receptive to critical ideas – the fathers of both Sakamoto and Saiko were associated with the *Jiyuto*. The sons of the wealthier *Burakumin* also had the time and social space in which to experiment with their ideas. Within the society at large new ideas, mostly from abroad, were challenging all aspects of the traditional value system – its social, political and even religious dimensions. These ideas were introduced alongside the development of capitalism, but up to 1918 the government managed to control their influence. However, the rapid economic expansion which followed was accompanied by social change and the introduction of novel ideas that the government could not control. Objective improvements within the *Buraku* and the increased aspirations they generated made *Burakumin* more open to suggestions that novel solutions were required to deal with old problems. Improvement, minimal reforms and the spread of egalitarian ideas disabused a significant section of the *Burakumin* communities of the idea that discrimination against them was inevitable. Criticism of the idea that suffering was an inevitable part of their destiny can be found in the text of 'Towards a Better Day' and the actions of *Burakumin* from the time of the *Hakata Mainichi Shimbun* incident. It seems safe to say that by 1922 such ideas were widespread. Both liberals and socialists were encouraging them to perceive that the source of their suffering was human society, 'a necessary and first step towards doing something about human misery and unhappiness'.[86] The illusion of inevitability was not yet shattered, but it was becoming transparent.

Notes:

1. B Traven, *Treasure of the Sierra Madre* (Panther Books, (c) 1934), p 34.
2. G M Beckman and G Okubo, *The Japanese Communist Party, 1922-1945* (Stanford University Press, 1969), p 20.
3. Ouchi Tsutomu, Agricultural Depression in Japanese Villages, *The Developing Economies*, vol V (December 1967), pp 597-627.
4. Shiota Shobei, 'The Rice Riots and the Social Problems', *The Developing Economies*, vol II (December 1966), pp 516-534.
5. *Kome Sodo no Kenkyu* (Research on the Rice Riots), ed Inoue Kiyoshi and Watanabe Toru. Vol I-VI (Tokyo, Yuhikaku, 1959-1962). See vol I, p 4, Table 1(b). For a synopsis of the riots see Inoue and Watanabe vol I, Chapter 1.
6. Nakanishi Yoshio 'Kome Sodo Gojunen to Buraku Mondai' (The 50th Anniversary of the Rice Riots and the *Buraku* Problem), *Buraku Mondai Kenkyu*, no 24 (1969), pp 35-47. For example, surveys made in Kagawa, Nara and Kyoto indicated that the price of rice within the *Buraku* was unusually high.
7. Murakoshi Sueo, 'Kome Sodo ni okeru Mikaiho Buraku no Kenkyu' (Research on the Unliberated *Buraku* in the Rice Riots). *Buraku Mondai Kenkyu*, no 3 (1958), pp 72-108. The Minister of Home Affairs, Suzuki, is reported to have singled out *Burakumin* for blame in this respect.
8. Quoted by Shiota, p 517.
9. Shiota, pp 520-521.
10. Ann Waswo, 'Origins of Tenant Unrest', Chapter 13, '*Japan in Crisis*', ed B S Silberman and H D Harootunian (Princeton University Press, 1974), p 380.

11. Inoue and Watanabe, vol V, pp 60-62.
12. Inoue and Watanabe, vol V, pp 252-255.
13. Inoue and Watanabe, vol V, p 291.
14. Personal interview, 30 January 1978.
15. Beckman and Okubo, pp 17-18.
16. S S Large, *Organised Workers and Socialist Politics in Interwar Japan* (Cambridge University Press, 1981), pp 24-5.
17. Shiota, p 523.
18. Dore, *Land Reform*, p 75.
19. A complete translation of *Capital* was not available until 1924 and Lenin's work was hardly known at all until then.
20. The anarchist movement in Japan has attracted little scholarly attention. The material in this paragraph is drawn from an article, 'Anarchy in Japan', *Anarchy* (Second Series) vol I, no 5, pp 5-7.
21. In August 1920, the *Shakaishugi Domei* had been established as a broad based organisation committed to the destruction of the capitalist system and the realisation of a 'society of liberty, a society of equality, a society of peace, a society of justice and a society of friendship throughout the world and mankind'. Despite the growing hostility between Bolsheviks and anarcho-syndicalists, the group attracted a membership of over one thousand and was able to disseminate socialist ideas throughout the nation. Moreover, by bringing together left wing intellectuals and young labour leaders, the League was able to attract the support of the urban and rural working class. It was ordered to disband by the government on 28 May 1921, but even after this time its members continued to be active within local groups. Beckman and Okubo, pp 25-6.
22. In 1922 he wrote: 'the worker-peasant government hindered the advance of the revolution and was a very influential counter-revolutionary element'. And, in the same article, 'the Lenin-Zinoviev group were opposed to the workers themselves controlling production'. Quoted in Tada Michitaro's introduction to *Osugi Sakae; Nihon no Meisha, no 46* (Tokyo, Chuo Koronsha, 1969), p 64.
23. Quoted by Tada, p 66.
24. Quoted by Beckman and Okubo, p 49.
25. Takeuchi Yoshitomo, 'The Role of Marxism in Japan', *The Developing Economies*, vol V, no 4 (December 1967), p 742.
26. Narisawa, p 148; see also an essay by Oe Taku in Kita, pp 236-8.
27. Full text of this petition can be found in Akisada, Yuwa Zaisei, pp 50-51.
28. Narisawa, p 152.
29. Fujitani Yoshio, 'Yuwa Seisaku: Yuwa Undo no Rekishi Tokushitsu' (Historical Characteristics of the *Yuwa* policy and *Yuwa* movement), *Buraku Mondai Kenkyu*, no 37 (May 1973), p 5.
30. Narisawa, p 152.
31. Narisawa, pp 153-4.
32. Approximately 50% came from the *shichoson*, 13% from the *gun* and 36% from the prefectural authorities. The prefectures in which most improvement money was spent were Shiga 32% (of the national total), Nara 19%, Wakayama 7% and Hyogo, Mie, Kagawa 4-5% each. Akisada, *Yuwa Zaisei*, p 61.
33. Between 1920-1922 in Kumamoto, the central government contribution formed 50% of the (small) amount spent on *Yuwa* improvements with nothing being provided by the *shichoson* bodies. On the other hand, in the same period in Nagano the central government contribution came to only 4% of the total *Yuwa* expenditure. Akisada, *Yuwa Zaisei*, p 57.
34. The Kinki region is composed of the seven prefectures Wakayama, Mie, Hyogo, Nara, Shiga, Kyoto and Osaka.

35. *Suihei Undoshi no Kenkyu*, vol II, pp 72-93.
36. *Hiroshima ken: hisabetsu Buraku no Rekishi*, pp 206-9. *Buraku no Jittai*, pp 25-8.
37. *Buraku no Jittai*, p 29. Amano, Buraku Kaiho to Yuwa Undo, part II, p 19.
38. Amano, *Buraku Kaiho to Yuwa Undo*, p 18.
39. *Buraku no Seitai*, vol I, p 99.
40. Oyama, p 23.
41. Oyama, pp 26-7. Buraku Mondai: *Suihei Undo Shiryo Shusei*, vol II, p 645.
42. Kimura Kyotaro, *Suiheisha Undo no Omoide II* (Memories of the *Suiheisha* movement), (Kyoto, Buraku Mondai Shinsho, 1973). p 244.
43. Kimura, *Omoide II*, p 245.
44. Kimura, *Omoide II*, p 140-2; Kitagawa Tetsuo, *Saiko Bankichi to Buraku Mondai* (Saiko Bankichi and the *Buraku* problem), (Tokyo, Toshobo, 1975), p 13.
45. Kimura, *Omoide II*, p 148; Kitagawa, p 42.
46. Kimura, *Omoide II*, p 178.
47. Saiko's description of the group quoted in *Buraku Kaiho to Yoneda Tomi*, p 38.
48. See Chapter 1, note 7.
49. *Kaiho* was a magazine produced in Tokyo between June 1919 and September 1923, edited by Sano Manabu and Aso Hisashi prominent socialists of the time. The article was subsequently reprinted in other magazines, the version quoted here appeared in *Suihei*, no 1 (13 July 1922), (Reprinted by Sekai Bunko, Tokyo, 1971).
50. Kimura, *Omoide II*, p 151.
51. *Suihei Undo Shiryo Shusei*, vol I, pp 21-24.
52. Kimura, *Omoide II*, p 152.
53. *Suihei Undoshi no Kenkyu*, vol II, p 55.
54. *Buraku Kaiho to Yoneda Tomi*, pp 21-2, 27-30, 38-9.
55. Kimura, *Omoide II*, p 251. *Suihei Undo Shiryo Shusei* vol I, pp 215-6. Akisada Yoshikazu, *Suihei Shiso no Seiritsu* (The Formation of *Suihei* ideas), *Rekishi Koron*, no 6 (June 1977), p 111.
56. For example, reports on the progress of the movement appeared in the editions of 7 December 1921; 18 January 1922; 16 February 1922; 22 February 1922. *Suihei Undoshi no Kenkyu*, vol II, p 52 and pp 130-1.
57. For extracts from the articles carried in this edition see *Suihei Undoshi no Kenkyu*, vol II, pp 131-3.
58. Oyama, pp 28-9.
59. The complete text of this pamphlet can be found in *Tokyo Buraku Kenkyukai*, no 8-9 (February 1977), pp 32-8. This is a collection of material about the Tokyo *Suiheisha* edited by Koga Seizo (the pen name of Ogushi Natsumi). Koga suggests that sections of this also appeared in *Rodo Shuppo* (Labour Weekly), no 3 (21 February 1922).
60. These details are taken from an autobiographical article written by Hirano and dated 5 May 1923 entitled Suihei Undo ni hashiru made (Up to the launching of the *Suihei* Movement). Reprinted in *Suiheisha Undo* (Kobe Buraku Kaiho Kenkyukai, 1970), pp 39-47.
61. There is an as yet unresolved minor controversy over whether Hirano ever was an anarchist. The issue is of little importance here but it does have some relevance to trends in the movement after 1923.
62. For an exhaustive list of Hirano's articles written at this time see *Tokyo Suiheisha Kankei Shiryo Shusei*, no 1, edited by Ogushi (Mimeo, Tokyo, 1976).
63. Ore wa Ningen da, *Jiyurodosha*, no 1 (1 March 1920), in Koga, p 28.
64. Reimin Soseikai no Shutai (The shameful conduct of the Poor Peoples' Creation Association) in which he is critical of the condescending attitude of the members of the association. Koga, p 30.

65. This leaflet is reproduced in *Suihei Undoshi no Kenkyu*, vol II, pp 120-121. It also appeared in *Doai*, a *Yuwa* newspaper published in Tokyo in the issue dated May 1921.

66. Eta Minzoku no Hankoshin (The rebellious spirit of the *Eta* people), *Shinyu*, no 15 (August 1921). *Shinyu* was the journal of the syndicalist trade union the *Shinyukai*. Koga, pp 31-2.

67. 'Kyoto e, Kyoto e' (To Kyoto, To Kyoto), *Rodo Shuppo*, no 3 (1 February 1921), Koga, pp 38-40.

68. *Suihei Undo Shiryo Shusei*, vol I, p 20; Ninomiya estimates 2,000, p 128. G Haessler in an article in '*The Nation*' mentions the figure 2,500. Vol 117, no 3035 (5 September 1923).

69. *Suihei Undoshi no Kenkyu*, vol II, p 143. It is believed that the first two of these principles were proposed by Hirano, the third by Sakamoto.

70. *Suihei Undoshi no Kenkyu*, vol II, p 144; see appendix. For a commentary on this declaration see *Saiko Bankichi to Buraku Mondai*, pp 90-97.

71. *Suihei Undoshi no Kenkyu*, p 44.

72. Komai Keisaku, Saiko Bankichi, Sakamoto Seiichiro, Yoneda Tomi from Nara Prefecture, Sakurada Kikuzo from Kyoto and Hirano Shoken from Tokyo.

73. *Suihei Undo Shiryo Shusei*, p 26.

74. *Buraku Kaiho to Yoneda Tomi*, pp 49-50.

75. *Chugai Nippo* (5 March 1922), *Suihei Undoshi no Kenkyu*, vol II, p 147.

76. *Osaka Asahi shimbun* (6 March 1922), *Suihei Undoshi no Kenkyu*, vol II, pp 148-9.

77. *Rodo Undo*, no 3 (13 March 1922), Ogushi, p 8. similar articles also appeared in *Rodo Undo*, no 4 (15 April 1922) and *Rodo Shuppo*, no 9 (6 April 1922), Ogushi, pp 8-9.

78. *Zenei* (April 1922). *Suihei Undoshi no Kenkyu*, vol II, p 151.

79. In an article published in *Suihei*, no 1, p 139.

80. Kimura, *Omoide I*, p 26.

81. J A Banks, *The Sociology of Social Movements* (Macmillan, 1972), pp 16-7.

82. For example, in 1918 some students were arrested for advocating universal suffrage, see E G Griffin, *The Adoption of Universal Suffrage in Japan* (Columbia University PhD, 1965), p 26. In 1920 Morito, a lecturer at Tokyo University, was dismissed for having published an article on Kropotkin, Mitchell, p 47.

83. '. . . the cramped individual is one who not only finds that his basic impulses are interfered with, or that he is . . . deprived of liberty and security but who also feels that this repression is unnecessary and avoidable and therefore unjustifiable.' G S Pettee, The Process of Revolution, quoted in R H Turner and L M Killian, *Collective Behaviour* (Prentice Hall, 1972).

84. Jo Freeman, 'The Origins of the Women's Liberation Movement', *American Journal of Sociology*, vol 78, no 4 (1974), pp 792-811.

85. Barrington Moore Jnr, *Injustice: the social basis of obedience and revolt* (Macmillan, 1978), p 188.

86. Barrington Moore Jnr. p 455.

CHAPTER FOUR

Suiheisha Activity and the *Yuwa* Response

The *Suiheisha* was just one of a number of organisations which were established in the 1920s, most of which derived inspiration from either liberal ideas or socialist ideas or from both. At the time these groups were formed, Marxism-Leninism had won few converts and was rather poorly understood even by those who gave their support to the Bolshevik ideas that were derived from knowledge of the revolution in Russia. The first attempt to form a Japanese Communist Party had not been successful but, nonetheless, the number of Bolshevik supporters grew steadily among those who were actively involved in the various social movements and they began to try to exert influence, if not control, over their groups. They hoped to guide their respective organisations towards adopting joint struggle tactics which would provide the vanguard Leninist groups with a mass following. Resistance to their attempts to dominate the social movements came from both the anarchist and the more moderate of the movements' leaders. However, in many cases internal disputes over policy and tactics, which were provoked by the attempts of the Bolsheviks to guide the movements, resulted in them breaking up into rival organisations competing for membership and unable to act as a spokesman for the social group in whose interests they sought to act. The labour union movement in particular was severely weakened by ideological infighting and fell victim to a series of organisational splits which weakened the movement as a whole.

In its formative years the *Suiheisha* had attracted the support of a wide variety of people of differing political persuasions. It was to be expected that once the early period of expansion came to an end, there would develop a debate over the aims and tactics that the movement should pursue and the type of organisation it should adopt. One of the major themes in the pages that follow will be to assess how the *Suiheisha* handled this internal dissension.

There were two dimensions to the activities which labour unions or peasants' groups initiated. On the one hand, there were local, specific struggles in which groups demanded more pay or reductions in rent and, on the other hand, there were longer-term campaigns for changes in the labour legislation or reform of the system of landholding. These latter campaigns involved varying degrees of commitment to the ideologies of the left. The activity of the *Suiheisha* groups in support of demands for the abolition of formal and informal discrimination can also be divided into two distinct, if overlapping, sectors. In conference motions and committee resolutions they demanded that the Japanese government accept responsibility for the continued existence of discrimination and prejudice which ensured the persistence of impoverished *Buraku* communities. The authorities were requested to prevent overt and covert discrimination in such institutions as the army which were under their direct control and to provide financial assistance to improve living standards within the *Buraku*. Demands for government-sponsored improvements had emerged from 1905 onwards, although little government money was provided for such projects until the late 1910s. However, once the government had overcome its reluctance to take action, which appeared to indicate an admission of responsibility for the plight of the *Burakumin*, many groups and government agencies became involved in the various *Yuwa* (conciliation) projects. By the mid-1920s, a decision appears to have been taken to co-ordinate the activities of these groups and bring them more firmly under government control. The methods adopted by the government to distribute funds to the improvement projects and the way the *Yuwa* groups were placed under the control of an umbrella body presided over by a trusted member of the central bureaucracy will be the subject of the final section of this chapter.

But the *Suiheisha* did more than simply request government assistance to improve their social and economic environment. They backed up their demands for equality of treatment with campaigns directed against those who discriminated against them. All of the local groups became involved in campaigns of protest – *Kyudan toso* – which were aimed at institutions and individuals which displayed any form of discriminatory attitude or behaviour. The ideological arguments consumed much of the time and energy of the movement's leaders, but the local groups' members' time and energy were mainly spent in the organisation of protest against specific instances of discrimination. A consideration of the tactics used and the results achieved by these *Kyudan toso* provides the third major theme of this chapter.

Signs of Radicalisation – the second conference

Although those who were closely involved in the formation of the *Suiheisha* derived inspiration from developments in the working class movement both in Japan and elsewhere in the world, there was little to indicate in the motions and speeches presented at their first conference that the movement would adopt a radical position. For the time being, the movement simply brought together those who were dissatisfied with the *Yuwa* groups and *Yuwa* ideas. Still, a radical caucus grew within the *Suiheisha* movement and made it its self-appointed task to change the orientation of the organisation and its constituent groups and individuals.

Those elected to the central committee at the first conference spent many of the following months attending public meetings held mainly in the Kansai area, to establish prefectural *Suiheisha* groups. Apart from this, they supervised the production of pamphlets explaining the need for a united, autonomous organisation of *Burakumin* and, in accordance with the conference resolution, produced a magazine *Suihei*. This latter was intended to be a monthly magazine, but due to production difficulties only two editions were ever produced, in July and November 1922.[1]

On 17 February 1923 regional delegates met in Osaka to plan the second conference which was to be held the following March. Two important decisions were made. The first was to adopt a *Suihei* flag which had been designed by Saiko, of a red crown of thorns on a black background; an overt manifestation of the breadth of the appeal, the Christian motif, set against the anarchist or socialist background. The second was to draw up an 'Appeal' which could be circulated to *Buraku* groups in order to advertise the forthcoming conference.[2] The appeal begins,

> Proletarians of the whole world . . . all oppressed nationalities under the yoke of capitalist imperialism . . . We the *eta* people appeal to you who are fighting valiantly the final class war against bloodthirsty capitalism.

There follows a description of the suffering endured by the *eta* over the past centuries after which the *Suiheisha* declaration and general principles are reproduced. The *Suiheisha* is described as being involved in 'a fight to take back the human rights of which we have been robbed.' However, the struggle is more than just a fight for civil rights since the *Suiheisha* 'wants to fight side by side with you in our common battlefront of world revolution.'[3] Already the radical influence is more noticeable, due in part to the growing self-confidence of the group's leaders and in part to the encouragement given them by the socialist groups compared to the equivocal response of the liberals.

The conference was opened on 2 March with an address from Minami Umekichi, the chairman, to a gathering of 3,000 (1,800 according to police estimates). After hearing reports on the activities of the central committee and of developments within the movement during the previous twelve months, the conference began to consider the three major resolutions and the 48 motions proposed by the delegate groups. Of the major resolutions one referred to the need to 'thoroughly censure' those who insult *Burakumin*, one demanded basic changes in the government's 'contemptuous improvement policy' and the third resolved to enforce a ban on contributions to the Honganji temple. The other motions considered can be divided into different categories. The largest single group was concerned with types of discrimination against *Burakumin* which had become part of their everyday existence. In particular, motions referred to discrimination in schools, in the army, in temples and derogatory articles which appeared in newspapers. Another group of motions referred to internal affairs; the creation of a Young Men's and a Women's *Suiheisha*, the improvement of *Suiheisha* propaganda, the production of a weekly news bulletin and the need to internationalise the *Suiheisha*. The others were a motley collection of motions which sought to draw attention to the continued existence of old family registers which could be used to ascertain an individual's ancestry, complaints about the government improvement policy, and protest about the presence in the House of Peers of Prince Tokugawa, the direct descendant of the family which had caused the formation of the system of organised discrimination. Attempts were made to avoid 'political issues'. A motion calling for the recognition of Soviet Russia was withdrawn as was one on pacifism; a motion on universal suffrage was rejected as it could promise *Burakumin* nothing and the conference refused to involve itself with the campaign to oppose article 17 of the Peace Preservation Law.[4] The only hint that the movement might become more involved with other groups was approval of a motion urging the formation of tenants' unions in rural areas.[5]

One observer present at the conference wrote later that the ideas of many of the delegates were very close to those of the syndicalists, especially in their stress on direct action and rejection of the suffrage motion.[6] However, the police had given permission for the conference only as long as none of those connected with socialists, labour unions or the Korean independence movement were allowed to attend. In reports from regional delegates we find two themes, the need for solidarity in order to fight discrimination in this society and the need to build an entirely new society in which discrimination would have no place, but in spite of this, the overall tone of the conference was quite moderate. In one of the closing speeches, the speaker denied that the *Suiheisha* movement sought revolution, on the contrary, it aimed at ensuring conditions in the *Buraku* deteriorated no further in order to prevent violent outbursts from the *Burakumin*. Another spoke at length on the importance of Buddhism, Shinran's philosophy and the *Meiji* Charter oath.[7]

Immediately after the conference a delegation of three, Minami, Hirano and Kurisu Shichiro (Osaka), left for Tokyo to present a petition to the ministries of the Army and Navy stating the *Suiheisha*'s opposition to discriminatory practices and demanding that they be stopped. While in Tokyo they met the Minister for Home Affairs Mizuno and later, at the invitation of Arima Yoriyasu, they visited the Diet and discussed the movement and associated problems with members of both houses.[8] Despite the radical rhetoric of some of the movement propagandists, this kind of consultation of the movement's leaders with government officials and party politicians was not unlike that undertaken by delegations from earlier *kaizen* conferences and, as noted in the previous paragraph, there was a significant section of the movement's leadership which advocated a quite moderate approach.

Origins of Division

The growth of the *Suiheisha* was so rapid in the period 1923-4 that groups had to be limited to sending only 2-3 representatives to the third conference. The conference, held once more in Kyoto in March, was attended by over 700 delegates and took place before a large audience of over one thousand; an audience which included both socialists such as Sakai Toshihiko and *Yuwa* supporters such as Kita Teikichi and Arima Yoriyasu. Opening speakers talked enthusiastically about the movement's growth since its foundation, but all were clearly worried about the possibility of division in the movement: a worry caused by the formation of a Bolshevik-oriented youth group the previous November.

For the time being, however, there was no open indication of a split in the organisation although there were signs that the influence of the socialist groups was increasing. At this conference, political issues were discussed openly and, although the motion urging prompt recognition of 'Worker-Peasant Russia' was accepted on the grounds that not to do so would be 'discrimination', the conference declared that it must stand aloof from all political parties and factions. Seven motions deliberated by the conference were connected with the internal workings of the organisation and were chiefly concerned with ensuring the effectiveness of *Suiheisha* propaganda. Opposition to discrimination in temples and shrines, in schools and in the army was reiterated, and protest about the social status of Tokugawa was increased to demands that he resign from his position in the House of Peers. Finally, there were two motions which called for co-operation with movements representing Korean immigrants in Japan and solidarity with the *Koheisha* which had been formed in Korea to fight discrimination against Korea's indigenous minority group, the *Paek Chan*.[9]

Sakai was attending this conference after having been at those held by the *Sodomei* (trade union federation) and the Peasants' Union. Apart from the different colour of the flags, black here, red and blue respectively elsewhere, he noted that there was more open, heated argument here, that there was a greater range of ages among those attending and that there were more women. He is very critical of the anarchist tendency which emerged in the debates over the recognition of Russia and the motions on political activity. He thinks that the movement has outgrown the stage when it can be organised through a loose-knit federation; it now requires a strong, centralised organisation. Moreover, the movement must not remain 'non-political' or separate from the other parts of the proletarian movement, and he remarks that there is a group within the movement who realise that there has to be a three-cornered alliance (*sankaku domei*) of the peasants' and workers' and *Suiheisha* movements.[10]

It is possible to trace the division between the Bolshevik and anarchist groups in the *Suiheisha* right back to the second conference and the debates over the suffrage issue, co-operation with other proletarian groups and the recognition of Russia. However, it would be a mistake to give the impression that the movement was split into two contending factions. At conference, the representatives of these groups were the most vociferous, but a majority of those attending the conferences and in the movement at large allied themselves with neither group. Moreover, even if the debates within the conference hall appear to have been somewhat acrimonious, both in the existing biographies and in interviews former activists remark how, after the conference session was over, anarchists and Bolsheviks would go for a drink together.

Shortly after this conference met, the United States Congress passed a law which was specifically designed to prevent migration from Japan. This measure provoked strong protest from many Japanese, not least from the *Suiheisha*. On 24 April they presented a letter of protest to the American Embassy in Tokyo and on the following Sunday a special conference was held in Osaka. At this meeting the act was condemned as an insult not only to the Japanese people but to all Asian peoples and a resolution was passed calling for a manifesto to be produced and sent to the *Koheisha* in Korea, the *Swadeshi* movement in India and the Asian Co-operative Council in Shanghai.[11] The central committee regarded this as simply a protest against an act of discrimination taken by the United States government, but later the central committee was criticised by the left wing groups for allowing itself to become involved in a campaign which was orchestrated by nationalists within the Japanese government in order to encourage anti-American feelings.

Formation of Local Suiheisha Groups

We have mentioned that the movement spread rapidly and suggested some reasons for this. Let us next describe some of the ways in which *Suiheisha* ideas spread and village and town groups were established.

In Nara prefecture, all those *Burakumin* who were actively involved in *Yuwa* groups were summoned to a meeting in Nara held on 1 April 1922. Addressing the meeting, police and *Yuwa* officials expressed their regret that a radical group like the *Suiheisha* had originated within their prefecture. The speakers hoped that none of those in the *Yuwa* movement would allow themselves to be influenced by this extremist organisation. However, for many of those attending the conference this was the first they had heard of the *Suiheisha* and, far from being warned off joining it, the police descriptions served rather to whet the interest of those at the meeting. That night, Yoneda met a group who had attended this meeting and distributed a number of pamphlets which explained the aims of the *Suiheisha*. They were all very enthusiastic about these new ideas and many of them swore to form a *Suiheisha* group when they returned to their home village. Among them was Kimura Kyotaro who, though he had been active in an improvement group since 1916, was immediately attracted to the *Suiheisha* movement. Soon after his return to his home in Kobayashi he organised the founding meeting of a *Suiheisha* group there which was attended by several members of the National Central Committee.[12] In the rest of 1922 at least 47 major meetings were held, mainly in the Kinki area. Most of these meetings would be attended by at least one member of the central committee and many of them attracted audiences of several hundred. Generally, these meetings were the first step towards organising a local group.

In some areas the existing *Yuwa* groups simply severed their connections with the parent group and adopted the *Suiheisha* name, its ideology and campaign tactics. The six *Suiheisha* groups in Kyoto emerged from six *Yuwa* youth groups.[13] However, in other areas where a network of *Yuwa* groups was firmly established as, for example, in Hiroshima, there seems to have been considerable resistance to the establishment of *Suiheisha* groups. Although there is evidence that young intellectuals from Hiroshima's *Buraku* community were actively participating in left wing groups, they did not attempt to form an independent group.[14] Three of them attended the second National *Suiheisha* conference in 1923 and only after their return home did they begin to make plans for the formation of a *Suiheisha* group. A preliminary meeting was held in June in the offices of the *Yuwa* group and finally, on 30 July, a founding meeting was held in Fukushima-cho at which Minami, Hirano and others from the central committee addressed an audience of 2,000. However, the *Kanto Suihei Shimbun*, reporting on this event, noted that the date chosen for the meeting was the *Meiji Tennosai* (the day commemorating the reign of the *Meiji* Emperor) – an indication that the Hiroshima group was by no means under the control of the left wing groups.[15] Within the next few months, twelve groups are reported to have been established in the prefecture, mainly in the larger *Buraku* located in the towns where handicraft or leatherwork were the main occupations. There were five hundred supporters present at the second Hiroshima *Suiheisha* conference held the following July, which indicates quite a strong support base, but there is some evidence that there would have been more widespread support for the *Suiheisha* had it not been for the strong pressure applied by the police and *Buraku* bosses in *Yuwa* groups to prevent the formation of *Suiheisha* groups. Where groups were formed, they seem to have been composed almost entirely of young men who were not quite so susceptible to pressure from the surrounding society and police.[16]

The situation varied greatly from one prefecture to another. Kitahara Daisaku, a resident of Gifu city, first heard of the *Suiheisha* in articles about the *Koku-Sui* incident (see below), which prompted him to write to the Kyoto office for further information. In reply, he received copies of the *Suihei* magazine, which seem to have encouraged him to form a small group which distributed some leaflets and even began to organise a campaign of protest against discrimination at a nearby school. However, soon after the group was formed Kitahara was summoned by the local police, threatened with arrest and only allowed to go free on condition that the group disband and he cease his correspondence with the *Suiheisha* headquarters.[17] As we shall see later, Kitahara persevered with his radical activity, but it would appear that police activity with or without the support of the *Buraku* bosses (*oyabun*) prevented the formation of the *Suiheisha* in many areas.[18]

On the other hand, in neighbouring Mie the *Suiheisha* was permitted to develop with relatively little police intervention. Shortly after their return from the Inaugural Conference (see above) a group of twenty *Burakumin* began to organise a *Suiheisha* group in the prefecture. A mass meeting was held in Matsuzaka to launch the movement, where an audience of 2,500 (600 according to police reports) heard speeches from Saiko, Sakai and Yoneda on the importance of protesting against discrimination, especially discrimination in the army.[19] Many more meetings were held in the following months, some of them attracting audiences of over 1,000. By the end of 1922 there were ten groups established in Mie prefecture and, just as in Hiroshima, the groups were formed mainly in larger, urban *Buraku* where most of the families relied on handicraft work.[20] In fact, all but two of these *Buraku* had connections with Isehyo, a *zoori* (straw sandal) manufacturer which subcontracted most of its work to families within the *Buraku*.[21] The work was hard and poorly paid, but such home industry perhaps weakened the power of the *Buraku* landlords and established lines of communication between the *Buraku* along which news of the *Suiheisha* could spread.

There seems to have been no common pattern or even sets of patterns to the diffusion of the *Suiheisha* ideas; in some areas the presence of a network of *Yuwa* groups assisted the propagation of *Suiheisha* groups whilst elsewhere *Yuwa* groups were able to contain the spread of radical ideas. In some areas the police seem to have tried to discourage *Suiheisha* activity while police elsewhere paid little attention to it. Similarly, some *Burakumin* responded readily to the new movement while others were less than enthusiastic.

Thorough Denunciation Campaigns

At the first conference it was resolved that:

> If any intent to insult is manifest against us under such names as *eta* or *Tokushu Burakumin* either by word or by deed we shall take resolute steps to denounce the offenders.

Tetteiteki Kyudan toso – thorough censure (or denunciation) campaigns – were the distinguishing feature of *Suiheisha* group activity, especially during the 1920s. It was a form of organised protest which was as specific to the *Suiheisha* as the withdrawal of labour of the industrial union or the refusal to pay rent of the tenants' union. Many of those who had been active in the more radical *Kaizen* groups had already taken part in protest against discrimination by individuals and within institutions like the army. The conference motion gave these actions formal recognition and encouraged others to engage in direct action. In many areas the *Suiheisha* groups only became active when an instance of discrimination provoked their anger and so *Kyudan* was not just the only *Suiheisha* activity that most *Burakumin* took part in but was also the only manifestation of the movement's activity that the majority population encountered. However, as we shall frequently have cause to mention, denunciation of discrimination also took place in areas where there was no formally constituted *Suiheisha* group; throughout its history the *Suiheisha* inspired direct action, it did not control it.

A report on the *kyudan* campaigns of 1922, the first year of *Suiheisha* activity, gives an interesting picture of the kind of protests which were taking place.[22] Most of them were instances where one or more *Burakumin* protested about the use of such words as *eta*, *doetta* or *yotsu* being used either to their face or to a third party.[23] In nearly all these cases the individual or group complained to the person who had uttered the offensive words and demanded an apology. Usually the offender apologised and the matter was closed. Where the *Burakumin* considered the offence to be more serious, they insisted that the offender pay for the insertion of a public apology into a local newspaper or for the production of leaflets. Other cases related to more concrete cases of discrimination. In Osaka a landlord was criticised for saying that he would refuse to let any of his rooms to *Tokushu Burakumin*; when he was challenged about this, he apologised and promised to change his policy. In Hiroshima protests against restrictions on the times *Burakumin* could use the public baths led to the restrictions being relaxed. Several cases concerned acts of discrimination in schools, often just the use of the word '*eta*' in the playground. In such cases the teachers were held responsible for what took place among the children in their charge and were required to make a formal apology to the family of the child insulted.

In very few of these cases can the *Suiheisha* have been directly involved since in these early days the movement was very small. Nevertheless, no doubt those who did become involved in such campaigns were encouraged to do so by hearing news of major campaigns elsewhere in the country. There were several incidents of discrimination which did involve members of the *Suiheisha* in the first few years of its existence which were pursued with particular vigour and which brought the movement substantial publicity. Three of these were regarded by its leaders as having special significance.

A few days after the first *Suiheisha* conference, an incident took place in Beppu, Oita prefecture, which was to become a *cause célèbre* in the movement's early years.[24] For several years a shanty town called Matogahama had been forming on the edge of Beppu populated by former *sanka*, *hinin* and other poor people. At 10 am on 25 March 1922 a group of police arrived at Matogahama and informed those who were not away at work that they could stay no longer and that they had better remove their belongings from the huts as they had orders to burn them down. Pleas were made for more time so that those who were at work could be contacted, but to no avail, and between twenty and thirty houses were destroyed in a fire started by the police. Police spokesmen said at the time that these people had no right to settle there, the district was unsanitary and that criminal types were gathering in the area. However, subsequent investigation revealed that several of the inhabitants of houses which had been destroyed were formally registered as residents, paid local taxes and some were even members of the local reservist association. It is believed that the local police chief had ordered the destruction of this unsightly slum since part of it would be visible from the Crown Prince's train. This incident was widely reported by the daily press and interpreted by *Suiheisha* activists as indicating the way discrimination was institutionalised in the police system and intimately connected with the Emperor system itself. More immediately significant as evidence of the need for the *Suiheisha* was the fact that the local priest, Shinozaki Renjo, tried to get assistance for those who had been dispossessed from both the Honganji temples and from local Christian groups, none of which was very helpful. Finally, while in Kyoto trying to win the support of the main Honganji temple, he came across the *Suiheisha*. Yoneda assisted him in a campaign to demand compensation from the local authority and to seek an assurance that such activities would not recur.[25]

For many *Burakumin* their first experience of insult and blatant discrimination was at school. Only a little over ten years before, separate schools for *Burakumin* had been common in many areas and it was still usual for *Buraku* pupils not to be allowed to sit with non-*Buraku* children, for them to have to use separate lavatories and different eating utensils.[26] Very few *Buraku* students were accepted into upper schools even when their marks warranted it. School, then, was the first stumbling block encountered by *Burakumin* and it is not surprising that many of the early campaigns centred on primary schools. Atypical only in that the action led to arrests and widespread publicity was the campaign which took place in Taisho village, Nara. On 14 May 1922, at the new upper primary school which had been opened only weeks before, one of the pupils called another an *eta*. This incident was reported to the Kobayashi *Suiheisha* and the following day a delegation led by Kimura Kyotaro went to lodge a protest with the headmaster, but he refused to apologise or accept any responsibility. On the sixteenth, a crowd of 300 (200 according to the police) demonstrated in front of the school gates demanding an apology and in the course of the demonstration seven were arrested and charged with incitement to riot. Then police went to houses in Kobayashi village threatening the villagers in an effort to deter them from taking any further part in *Suiheisha* activity.[27] Kimura was singled out as the leader of the campaign and held in prison for seventy days, even though at his trial he was given a suspended sentence. The case received much publicity in *Suihei*, in *Suiheisha* pamphlets and the campaign became a model for similar protests against school discrimination.[28] In the accounts of cases of *Kyudan* which led to police action one finds that throughout the pre-war period a large proportion of the incidents originated in the classroom. Many of the *Suiheisha* leaders have particularly bitter memories of their first realisation of the full enormity of social discrimination which took place at school. Thus when an incident occurred at school the campaign was pursued with more than normal thoroughness.

The cases which attracted police attention and led to protracted disputes occurred when the culprit refused to apologise and the *Suiheisha* overreacted to the stubbornness. In Nara prefecture, a seemingly trifling incident sparked off a major conflict between the left wing supporters of the *Suiheisha* and the right wing followers of the *Kokusuikai*.[29] The right wing *Kokusuikai* had formed branches in many areas in Kinki and found much of its support among the landlords who organised in order to oppose the growth of the peasants unions.[30] In Nara prefecture both of these organisations commanded considerable support and had already come into conflict when the *Kokusuikai* had tried to hinder the *Suiheisha*'s campaigns. The precipitating incident took place in Shitanaga, a community of 82 houses, 424 people.[31] On 17 March a newly married couple were passing through the village and were insulted by a bystander, one Morita, who raised four fingers in derision (a gesture used to indicate a person is of *Buraku* origin). Two youths immediately demanded the old man apologise, but he refused. They contacted the *Suiheisha* and that evening a group of forty *Burakumin* gathered outside his house. Meanwhile Morita had contacted the *Kokusuikai*, who promised to give him their full support. The *Suiheisha* wanted a full apology; the *Kokusuikai* wanted to use the opportunity to oppose the

Suiheisha. By early the next morning 300 *Suiheisha* activists had gathered in a temple yard, most of them armed with bamboo sticks or swords. At 9.30 the *Suiheisha* group moved out, flags and banners waving, with the intention of attacking the *Kokusuikai* supporters who had assembled in a neighbouring temple yard. A small skirmish took place between the two groups in which three *Suiheisha* supporters were injured before the police separated the two sides. Support for both groups continued to arrive throughout the day from within Nara prefecture and from more distant places. Kimura, who by now was the *Suiheisha*'s full time secretary in Kyoto, heard of the incident at 12.00 that day, and after contacting some others he rushed off, to arrive in Shitanaga at 5.00 in the evening. By the morning of the 19th 1,200 *Kokusuikai* members and their supporters from reservist associations and youth groups faced 1,220 *Suiheisha* supporters and fighting once more broke out. While the local police chief was trying to keep the two sides apart and negotiate a settlement, the governor was arranging support from the army and Osaka's police reserve. Finally, on the 20th, three representatives of the *Suiheisha* met with two from the *Kokusuikai* and four mediators from the local government. A solution was proposed by which Morita would apologise as an individual and the dispute between the two organisations would be declared solved. For their part, the police promised there would be no arrests.[32]

This latter agreement was broken and, on the 23rd, 35 of the *Suiheisha* group and twelve of the *Kokusuikai* supporters were arrested. When the cases came before the courts the *Suiheisha* received much heavier penalties than the *Kokusuikai*, thus reinforcing suspicions that discrimination was deeply embedded within the legal system.[33] The greatest burden, however, was borne by those of the Shitanaga *Buraku*, the home of 22 of those arrested. It was estimated that the total cost of legal fees and of supporting those imprisoned was about 5,000 yen , a severe strain on an organisation like the *Suiheisha* which, unlike the *Kokusuikai*, had no wealthy sponsors. These incidents were reported in newspapers throughout the country, giving the *Suiheisha* an unusual amount of publicity. Some *Burakumin* were stimulated by the news to start taking part in their own *Kyudan* campaigns (e.g., Kitahara, see above), but given the predisposition of most of the Japanese public it probably just confirmed their image of the violent, unruly *Burakumin*.

But these are just three examples of incidents from the several thousand which occurred in the first five years of the movement's existence.[34] Of most of the rest we know very little. Only those which involved the police or were reported in the pages of the movement's newspaper, the *Suihei Shimbun*, provide us with some indication as to what kind of issues aroused the anger of the activists. Descriptions of about seventy incidents which took place in the first half of the 1920s can be found in the literature, though we have no way of knowing how representative these are and it seems likely that only the more violent campaigns came to the attention of the courts or were thought worth reporting by the editors of the newspapers.[35]

Nevertheless, more than half of the reported incidents resulted from relatively minor instances of verbal insults directed at *Burakumin* which developed into varying degrees of violence if the offender refused to apologise. As in the earlier period, in particularly serious cases verbal apologies were considered inadequate and written statements were required, either simple letters, the production of leaflets or the insertion of a public apology into a local newspaper. The following is typical of the kind of apology accepted by *Suiheisha* groups at this time:

> I have no words (good enough) to apologise to the Emperor and to all the members of the *Suiheisha* for my having neglected the Imperial edict, issued by the Emperor Meiji on August 28 1871, for having used discriminatory language. I have been impressed by the kind lesson taught me by the honourable members of the *Suiheisha* and I would like to express here my appreciation.[36]

That such letters were accepted by way of apology seems to confirm that the movement, at least at the grass roots level, was scarcely a radical organisation.

When a hot spring owner near Osaka apologised to a *Suiheisha* group they demanded he pay for the production of 500 leaflets and he complied with the request.[37] In order to persuade individuals to issue such statements, *Suiheisha* members would put pressure on the culprit, haranguing him, and sometimes even threatening him with the use of violence. The police took a dim view of this and many were arrested on charges of assault, coercion and blackmail. There were cases which clearly warranted police intervention but, on other occasions, it seems as though the police seized the slightest opportunity to bring charges against *Suiheisha* members in order to hinder the development of the movement.

Even in this early period there were a significant number of campaigns against local public servants, especially priests and police. Such instances were used by the radicals to demonstrate the extent to which discrimination was deeply rooted in the state apparatus. One aspect of the state's response to the formation of the *Suiheisha* had been circulars sent in August 1922 to local government officials at prefecture and town/village levels which ordered them not to permit the formation of separate groups by *Burakumin* and not to allow discrimination to take place in shrines, temples, schools or similar public places.[38] However, this and later instructions on how to handle *Kyudan* campaigns issued after the *Koku-Sui* incident appear to have been less concerned with preventing discrimination or assisting those discriminated against and rather designed to help minimise the disorder which often accompanied the *Kyudan* campaigns.

Campaigns against Buddhist priests had a special significance. A survey carried out in 1921 revealed that over 80% of *Buraku* households were affiliated to the *Jodo Shinshu* (Pure Land) sect, often referred to as the Honganji, which derived its doctrine from the teachings of the Japanese Buddhist prophet Shinran (1173-1262).[39] In the *Tokugawa* period, largely for the sake of administrative convenience, it had been decreed that all *eta:hinin* register with one of the branches of this Buddhist sect and the temples set up in the outcast areas were kept separate from the rest and served by a lowly sector of the priesthood, many of whom might be outcasts themselves. The complex system of branch temples was reorganised in 1876, but institutional discrimination remained.[40] Soon after the formation of the *Suiheisha*, in the summer of 1922, the *Kokui Domei* (Black Vestment League) was formed to co-ordinate the efforts of those who wanted to eradicate this institutionalised discrimination and encourage 'a return to the true spirit of Shinran's teaching'. In particular, they demanded the removal of the rules which segregated *eta* temples, the abolition of separate seating arrangements at other temples and that the black vestment be made standard for all levels of the priesthood. This latter demand was a protest against the practice of having different coloured robes according to the priest's status in the hierarchy.[41] This league seems to have led a series of protests in the Kinki area and gave its support to some of the *Kyudan* campaigns. It is referred to in the conference proceedings as late as 1925, but there is little documented reference to its activities after 1923. Nevertheless, its ideas remained as a strong undercurrent within the movement.[42]

As the *Suiheisha* movement adopted a more radical stance, the demands for reform of the Honganji were dropped and there arose more vociferous criticism of its deceptive ideology and, indeed, of religious ideas in general. It was argued that Buddhist priests and their ideas diverted *Burakumin* energy away from making demands for real improvements. They also pointed out that the donations to the temples, much of which was passed on to the central organisation, were a considerable drain on the communities' resources and they insisted that this money would be better spent on improving the material conditions within their immediate environment. In the later 1920s and during the 1930s successive conferences adopted motions to discourage the donation of money to the Honganji. In fact, these seem to have had little effect, but the central bodies were sufficiently concerned by these protests and criticisms to inaugurate a programme of positive support for the *Yuwa* campaigns. Not, of course, that this improved their image in the eyes of the *Suiheisha* activists who saw this support of the reactionary *Yuwa* programme as confirmation of their suspicions that the Honganji was one of the vestiges of feudal ideas which was sustaining prejudice and discrimination within Japanese society. *Kyudan* campaigns against Honganji priests occur regularly in the later 1920s and throughout the 1930s.

Two overriding impressions remain after considering the large number of *Kyudan* campaigns which took place in the years 1922-26. The first is that often relatively insignificant events triggered off incidents which came to involve large numbers of people and sometimes a great deal of violence. This was as often caused by a stubborn refusal to apologise, on the one hand, as it was by an over enthusiastic desire on the part of the *Suiheisha* to censure every single instance of discrimination in word or deed. It also perhaps illustrates the high degree of tension, of mutual distrust, which had built up between the *Buraku* and non-*Buraku* communities in certain areas. Secondly, the targets for many of these campaigns seem to have been selected indiscriminately. It may well have been that words like *eta* or *chorimbo* aroused deep resentment among *Burakumin* and that angry *Burakumin* were easily organised into *Kyudan* campaigns. However, there was little positive which could be achieved from a campaign which aimed at forcing an apology from someone who was reported to have muttered *eta* while drunk at home, as happened on one occasion. Indeed, the amount of violence which, rightly or wrongly, came to be associated with the *Kyudan* campaigns seems only to have reinforced the stereotype of *Burakumin* as wild, unruly people. There were those in the movement who were beginning to realise the dangers of this tendency and they started to demand the formulation of a more consistent, co-ordinated campaign strategy.

Political Polarisation – the ascendance of the Bolshevik faction

As Sakai had remarked in his article on the third conference which appeared in *Kaizo*, there was a group within the *Suiheisha* which was advocating increased co-operation with other proletarian groups and demanding tighter organisational structure within the movement.[43] On 1 November 1923 thirty young men from *Buraku* in the Kinki area met in Osaka to form the National *Suiheisha* Youth League (*Zenkoku Suiheisha Seinen Domei*). According to the documents produced at this conference, the aim of the group was to establish a 'disciplined organisation of young men' which would combine the strength of the young *Burakumin* throughout the country.[44] At first the group regarded itself as a cultural movement: the opening statement speaks of 'progress from the present society which is symbolised by corruption and gloom to a beautiful pure society'.[45] However, the group adopted a detailed set of organisational rules which specified a hierarchy of committees from village group to national central committee and a monthly subscription was set at 20 *sen* per month, which was to be distributed to different groups of the organisation. As the movement came under the influence of Takahashi Sadaki, it adopted a more overt Marxist-Leninist approach. Born in Oita in 1905, he went to Tokyo in 1921 to study at Tokyo University of Commerce; however, he dropped out in his second year, and from the spring of 1922 he assisted with the production of *Zenei* (Vanguard) and *Shakaishugi Kenkyu* (Socialist Research), both of which became the semi-official organs of the Communist Party. A member of the short-lived first Communist Party, he worked closely with Yamakawa Hitoshi who introduced him to Sakamoto Seiichiro of the *Suiheisha*. In November 1923 Takahashi moved to Osaka and there he established a Marxist-Leninist study group which numbered many of the *Suiheisha* leaders among its members.[46] The early socialist ideologues like Yamakawa considered the *Suiheisha*'s status struggle to be of minor importance, but Takahashi maintained that the *Suiheisha* was an important progressive element within the socialist movement. He argued that the movement should build up a stronger, centralised organisation, rely less exclusively on the *Kyudan* struggle as its main activity and should attempt to raise the political consciousness of the *Burakumin*. If this were done, the class struggle within the *Buraku* would be heightened and gradually the political and economic barriers which separate *Burakumin* from the rest of the working class would break down.[47] His ideas about the *Buraku* problem which he developed in a book and numerous articles were received enthusiastically by the younger activists within the organisation who were becoming dissatisfied with the 'unorganised organisation' (*musoshiki no soshiki*) of the *Suiheisha*.

A monthly newspaper – *Senmin* – was published from February 1924 by the Youth League to publicise its ideas and to create a greater sense of unity among the group's members.[48] Articles in this paper call for a more radical approach to the movement's problems and declare that it is time the movement entered into its second period of growth. In the first period, they argued, priority had been given to growth and propaganda but now a reconsideration of the organisation's internal structure was required. Without strict organisation and discipline, the *Suiheisha* would either be crushed by pressure from the outside or it would crumble from within. Moreover, increased internal strength was an essential prerequisite for the development of the movement from one which simply opposed discrimination to one which took its place in the class struggle.

After the Kato cabinet had promised to introduce a universal manhood suffrage bill in July 1924, the issue of the movement's approach to politics became more urgent. Through *Senmin*, the Youth League argued that the *Suiheisha* must enter the political arena and develop a full programme of political education which would ensure that the *Buraku* masses were not fooled by the bourgeois politicians.[49] By this time, the Youth League regarded itself as the vanguard element within the *Suiheisha* and the influence of Leninist ideas within the group became increasingly strong in both its theory and practice.

The Spy Scandal

The third conference gave its approval to a motion which called on Prince Tokugawa to accept the responsibility that his family bore for having created the system which produced discrimination against *Burakumin*. He was to demonstrate his contrition by resigning his post of Speaker of the House of Peers and by renouncing his peerage. It was hoped that this would be the start of a campaign against the new status system at the top of which were those who held a title of nobility and at the bottom of which remained the *Burakumin*. It was believed that discrimination against the latter would remain as long as there was discrimination in favour of the former. A committee of four – Matsumoto Jiichiro, Matsumoto Gentaro (no relation), Hanayama Kiyoshi (all from Fukuoka) and Minami – was formed to initiate the campaign which was to be directed, not so much at Tokugawa personally, but rather at the status system of modern Japan. However, the campaign did not develop as expected.

In March two members of the committee visited Tokyo to seek an audience with Tokugawa, but their requests were refused. Later, Matsumoto Jiichiro visited Tokyo and even followed Tokugawa home, but he adamantly refused to meet them in spite of continued demands. On 9 July 1924 Matsumoto Gentaro,

Matsumoto Jiichiro and Sato Santaro were arrested and later charged with plotting to assassinate the Prince. They were kept in custody for the most of the summer, during which time Matsumoto Gentaro died either from ill treatment at the hands of the police or from culpable negligence on the part of the prison authorities. When the case was finally brought before a court, Matsumoto Jiichiro and Sato were found guilty of conspiracy to murder and sentenced to four months imprisonment.[50] Apart from providing the movement with its first martyr, the significance of this event is that it indicated the existence of a 'spy' who was privy to the *Suiheisha*'s internal affairs and who passed the information to the police.

Dowa Tsushin was a mimeographed daily broadsheet produced and edited by Tojima Tetsuo from an office in Tokyo. On its front pages it announced its interest in the '*Suihei* movement, International Peace, Korea, Social Problems and Religion'. However, most of the articles concern the *Suiheisha*'s internal problems, the Koreans' campaign for political rights and the progress of 'anti-Japanese ideas' within the social movements.[51] The journal's office was visited frequently by the members of the central committee and it is likely that all of them at some time or other received money or some kind of assistance from Tojima.[52] It would appear that the charges made by the police were not wholly without foundation; Yoneda remembers an occasion when Matsumoto Jiichiro had threatened to kill Tokugawa and produced a knife and a gun but that Hirano had argued against this since it would have given the *Suiheisha* a violent image.[53] It is even suggested that Sato, a young employee (age 20) of Matsumoto, may have actually planned to kill Tokugawa.[54] It seems that these rumours of an assassination attempt were passed by Hirano to Tojima who then gave the information to the police.

From October 1924 the Mie-based *Aikoku Shimbun* had accused Tojima of being a police spy and in November *Senmin* repeated the charge. Their suspicions were confirmed by the reputable *Horitsu Shimbun*, which revealed that Tojima was paid 800 yen a month by the police to produce his broadsheet and provide them with information.[55] The bad feeling created by the 'spy issue' widened the division between the 'gradualist' group on the central committee composed of Yoneda, Hirano and Minami, all of whom had been close to Tojima, and the more radical members of the committee. A special committee meeting was held on the first three days of December at which it was decided that Hirano was to be expelled, Minami would retire from the organisation and Yoneda would apologise and cease to take such an active role. To minimise the discredit to the movement, the headquarters and the *Suiheisha* newspaper's place of publication would be moved to Osaka. The central committee, purged of its moderates, was under the control of Matsumoto Jiichiro, Kimura Kyotaro and Kurisu (Osaka) and the offices were moved to a location where the influence of the Leninist youth group was strongest.[56]

There already existed some tension between the groups in Kansai and those in Kanto and this issue brought the problem to the surface. On 15 December the

Kanto area *Suiheisha* committee met and refused to accept the central committee decision. The following month the decision was published in a magazine which was accompanied by a leaflet produced by Hirano in which he declares his determination to continue the fight against discrimination.[57] A few months later the Kanto *Suiheisha* itself became divided when Hirano was accused of dishonesty in handling money which had been collected to assist those who had suffered in the Serada incident (see below); some of the group remained loyal to him, others refused to associate with him. Although he was to continue to be associated with *Suiheisha* groups in the Kanto area until their dissolution in 1938, he took no further part in the national movement.[58]

The Serada Incident

As those internal disruptions were taking place, a major event occurred in the Kanto region. A *Suiheisha* had been formed in the small *Buraku* of Serada, Gumma prefecture, in July 1922 and it became involved in campaigns against discrimination in schools and in public baths. Perhaps they pursued these campaigns with excessive zeal or maybe their assertive campaigns outraged the surrounding traditional communities, but, whatever the cause, tension built up to the extent that the non-*Burakumin* formed their own vigilante group. Towards the end of December 1923 an old man was overheard by a young *Burakumin* to use the word *chorimbo*, a local term of abuse. The youth demanded an apology, the old man agreed and even promised to give his support to a meeting which was to be held to discourage discrimination. Later, however, he retracted the apology and refused to have anything to do with the public meeting. Despite attempts by both local officials and police to reconcile the two sides, the dispute continued and tension mounted. On 18 January 1,000 villagers led by a group that had been drinking descended on the tiny community of 22 households. In the face of superior numbers most of the inhabitants fled from their houses leaving only seven or eight young men to defend the honour of the *Buraku*. At least four attacks were made on the community, twelve houses destroyed, seven or eight people seriously hurt and many others less seriously injured.[59]

The local police took no steps to restrain the action of this crowd and when a group of them (40-50, depending on the report) was eventually brought to trial they were all given light sentences. Many *Burakumin* felt that this amounted to exoneration of the crime which might open the way for a series of anti-*Buraku* riots of the kind that had taken place in the 1870s. Moreover, when the riot and the subsequent trial were reported in the national press, the report placed the onus of blame on the *Burakumin* who, it was said, had provoked the incident by their aggressive and persistent *Kyudan* campaigns. It seems that there was a growing conviction that it was the *Suiheisha* activists, not the discriminators, who were the cause of all the trouble. Some *Burakumin* were beginning to feel that despite, or rather precisely because of, the *Kyudan* campaigns and other *Suiheisha* activity, discrimination towards *Burakumin* was getting worse.[60] A division was emerging between the radical elements in the new central committee who wanted the organisation to ally itself with the other proletarian groups and increase its own internal discipline, and a group of *Burakumin* who had doubts about the wisdom of associating with such subversive groups and indulging in activities which could provoke a physical and ideological backlash of the sort observed during and after the Serada incident. Such doubts did not result in the emergence of a moderate group, not in the short term anyway, rather they led to the organisation adopting the policies advocated by those in the Marxist group who claimed it would be possible to avoid a backlash by increasing the selectivity in the *Kyudan* campaigns.

The Suiheisha Adopts a Structure – the fourth conference and after

The fourth conference was held at a time of growing popular antipathy towards the organisation and deep ideological and geographical division within the movement. At this conference Matsumoto Jiichiro was elected chairman and under his direction the movement became more organised. Matsumoto was to become the most important single figure in the *Suiheisha* movement and was the leader of the post-war Liberation movement until the time of his death in 1967. He was born in Chikushi-gun, Fukuoka, in 1887 in a fairly prosperous family. Though he experienced discrimination at school, he did well enough to be accepted for entry into a Kyoto middle school. If the move to Kyoto was made in an attempt to escape discrimination it was unsuccessful, and after only a year he left and went to Tokyo, although even there he came across discrimination. He returned to Fukuoka to take his army medical in 1907 after which he left for Manchuria, where he spent three years making a living by peddling medicine. On his return, he formed a construction company which he was to see grow into a large and prosperous organisation. From the beginning of the 1920s he took the lead in local campaigns to oppose discriminatory practices and from 1922 he was involved in preparations to form the Kyushu *Suiheisha*. The founding meeting of this group was held on 1 May 1923, although Matsumoto was unable to attend as he was held in prison between 26 April and 25 June in what is believed to have been an attempt by police to hinder the formation of the group. In 1924 he attended his first national conference and, as we have seen, soon became active in the campaign against Tokugawa. Henceforth he was to be close to the centre of all *Suiheisha* activity.[61]

Because of the dispute between the Kanto and Kansai groups only one of the 400 delegates attending the fourth conference held in Osaka was from Kanto, which allowed the Marxist-Leninist Kansai-based youth group more or less to dominate conference proceedings. Several of the motions repeated the familiar themes of opposition to discrimination in school and in temples, but there were two motions which excited fierce debate and showed that the youth group's policies did not have the unanimous support of the conference delegates. The Osaka group proposed a motion to disseminate political education among *Burakumin* in order to ensure that they would not be led astray by the bourgeois politicians, a motion which followed the line taken by many writers of articles in *Senmin*. Those who opposed this pointed out that the previous conference had resolved to stand aloof from all politics. The motion was eventually passed, but the debate aroused such extreme emotions that at one stage a fracas developed in which two delegates were arrested. However, even more trouble resulted from the other major debate on a motion to establish a committee to organise co-operation with other proletarian groups. Much of the ground covered in the debate was familiar, but in the end the crucial issue which emerged was that of the nature of the *Suiheisha* movement. Those who opposed the Bolshevik tendency argued that the *Suiheisha* was essentially a civil rights movement and, as such, had little to gain from co-operation with the other proletarian groups. The Bolsheviks, on the other hand, argued that discrimination against *Burakumin* was based on the remnants of feudal ideology which was supported by social institutions that the incomplete bourgeois revolution had failed to remove. *Burakumin* must unite with other proletarian groups to ensure the completion of the bourgeois revolution and then maintain the revolutionary impetus to ensure that this was rapidly converted into a socialist revolution which would set up a worker-peasant state as in Russia. Thus the campaigns against discrimination were important, but they must be waged alongside class struggle within the *Buraku* and in co-operation with the other groups engaged in the struggle against capitalism and imperialism both in Japan and throughout the world.[62] At the point when it seemed as though the conference was about to erupt in chaos, the motion was withdrawn and referred to the central committee.[63] Feelings ran particularly high on these issues because many of the Bolsheviks were convinced that the revolution was only a few years away and so it was of vital importance to adopt the correct tactics as soon as possible.

The most important decision taken by the conference was to revise thoroughly the movement's organisational rules. A hierarchical system was introduced in which the size and function of each group, from village group to central committee, was carefully defined. The central committee was to carry out conference decisions and act as the movement's highest organ between conferences. It was to be composed of one representative from each of the eight regions, plus two representatives from the youth group. A fixed subscription was introduced to support the movement's activities and enable it to employ two full-time workers at the Osaka office.[64] Despite strong criticism from anarchists at the conference, the principle of democratic centralism had won a clear victory over the ideas of free federation. Further indication of the Bolshevik control over the new central committee can be found in the Declaration adopted by the conference. It pointed out the need to form a strong organisation which would be able to resist ruling class oppression and shorten the final days of capitalism; iron discipline is required to rescue the *Suiheisha* from its present confusion.

National Conference
Central Committee
                                          Special Committee
Town & village *Suiheisha*   Regional Committee
Peasant Unions
Suiheisha Youth League   Prefectural *Suiheisha*
Women's *Suiheisha*
Young people's *Suiheisha*   Town & village *Suiheisha*

Peasant Unions
Suiheisha Youth League
Women's *Suiheisha*
Young people's *Suiheisha*

Takahashi clearly had a hand in the production of this document and his influence over the Bolshevik group grew as the prominence of the youth group increased. In the autumn of 1925 the Youth League dissolved itself at its second conference and merged with the Communist Youth League. In December the broad based *Zen Nihon Musan Seinen Domei* (All-Japan Proletarian Youth League) was formed from the youth sections of the *Hyogikai* (the left wing of the trade union movement), the Japan Peasants Union, the *Suiheisha* youth league and *Gakuren* (the Communist Party-oriented student group). The principal target of this group was to organise youth groups across the nation to oppose the militarisation of education which had begun in April 1925.[65] Meanwhile, to organise the Bolshevik tendency within the *Suiheisha* movement, the *Zen Nihon Suiheisha Musan Domei* (All-Japan *Suiheisha* Proletarian League) was formed by fifty activists from Kansai and Shikoku. Chairman of this league was Matsuda Kiichi, one of the *Suiheisha*'s full-time workers, but the group was under Takahashi's political guidance.[66]

The division between the *Suiheisha* groups in the Kanto and Kansai areas was not simply the result of regional rivalry or personality clashes. Anarcho-syndicalist ideas remained influential within the labour movement in the Kanto area, especially in Tokyo, for several years after their decline in the Kansai region. But, even in Tokyo, the anarcho-syndicalist movement lost its dynamism after the murder of Osugi Sakae in 1923.[67] However, anarchist ideas continued to play a role within the debates inside the *Suiheisha* in the mid to late 1920s. Those who identified with the anarchist movement placed less emphasis on the importance of the class struggle, advocating instead the adoption of such ideas as 'natural justice' and 'mutual aid', ideas which derived ultimately from translations of the works of Kropotkin.

In 1925 this anarchist tendency held a series of meetings to organise its opposition to the moderate '*Yuwa*-ist' elements on the one hand and the Bolshevik elements on the other. There were never more than thirty at any of these meetings, but among them were Asada Zennosuke and Kitahara Daisaku who were to become leading figures both in the *Suiheisha* and the post-war movement. Their main complaint was that the Bolshevik group was trying to dominate the *Suiheisha* movement and use it for its own ends. They recognised the need for co-operation between their groups and the peasant or proletarian organisations but objected to the *Suiheisha* becoming subordinate to the aims of an outside body. More specifically they objected to the way the movement's newspaper, the *Suihei Shimbun*, had ceased to represent the views of the movement as a whole, nearly all of its articles being written by Bolsheviks. Moreover, they alleged that Takahashi Sadaki, leader of this tendency, was not himself of *Buraku* origin but had insinuated his way into the movement in order that the energy of its activists would benefit the plans of the Bolsheviks.[68] They demanded his expulsion from the movement. Further meetings were held in the spring of 1926 in order to develop a coherent anarchist strategy for the fifth conference.[69]

Regional Reactions

As one might have anticipated, the response to developments which occurred at the conferences and in the central committees varied greatly from one region to another. In Mie, the *Suiheisha* had spread quite rapidly with little police obstruction as did the *Nihon Nomin Kumiai* (Japan Peasants Union). These two groups developed in close association such that by 1925 most of the 22 peasants' groups active in Mie were based in *Buraku* and the local agitational newspaper, the *Aikoku Shimbun*, acted as the mouthpiece of both the peasant and *Suiheisha* movements.[70] A brief perusal of articles carried by this journal indicates that the ideas of the anarchist Osugi Sakae, especially his emphasis on direct action, had a strong influence on the early activists, which might explain the large number of *Kyudan* campaigns and the reputation for violence acquired by the group.[71] But, from the summer of 1924, articles appeared which were highly critical of the anarchist line and called for a new, radical political orientation.[72] The extensive degree of co-operation which existed between the *Suiheisha* and the peasants' movements possibly predisposed the Mie activists towards acceptance of the Bolshevik arguments in favour of greater collaboration between working class movements. The front page of the 1 January 1925 edition of the paper was devoted to an 'Introduction to Marxism' and later that month a Marxist study group was formed; half of its forty members were also members of the *Suiheisha*.[73] An informal youth group was formed to give an enthusiastic welcome to Takahashi Sadaki when he came to the area to address a series of *Suiheisha* meetings and the same group heckled at a meeting addressed by Minami in the following month.[74] This was probably the nucleus of the branch of the *Musansha Seinen Domei* formed in Matsuzaka in November 1925. For the next few years *Suiheisha* activity in Mie was strongly influenced by Bolshevik ideas.

In Hiroshima, the leaders of the *Suiheisha* group were influenced by the ideas of the Socialist League, and soon after the formation of the *Suiheisha* group a number of the *Suiheisha* activists formed a local branch of the Bolshevik *Zenkoku*

Suiheisha Seinen Domei.[75] They took part in campaigns to oppose the Peace Preservation Bill and the Labour Disputes Act, working closely with the other Bolshevik groups, but they could only muster thirteen supporters and it is doubtful whether they had any influence outside Hiroshima city.[76] A strong anarchist tendency also existed within the local working class movement, but an organised faction within the *Suiheisha* group was not formed until July 1927. The workers' and peasants' movements in Hiroshima never produced any outstanding leaders, nor were there any sensational struggles which captured the imagination of those active in the area. For most of the time in Hiroshima, as in most other places, those involved in the social movements spent their time slowly building up groups of workers and peasants in the face of constant police harassment and, in the case of the *Suiheisha* groups, pressure from the *Buraku* bosses and *Yuwa* groups.

In Mie, then, the *Suiheisha* developed into an important social movement and established branches throughout the prefecture. These groups worked closely with the *Nihon Nomin Kumiai* and, perhaps as a consequence of this close cooperation, the *Suiheisha* groups were significantly influenced by the spread of Bolshevik ideas in the mid-1920s which replaced the anarchist influence. In Hiroshima, however, although numerous *Suiheisha* groups had been set up in some of the larger *Buraku*, there was little activity which was co-ordinated with that of the other left wing movements. Only in Hiroshima city was there any cooperation with groups outside the *Suiheisha* movement and even here it involved only a handful of people. So, the heated debates which were taking place within the central committee and at national conference were followed keenly by *Suiheisha* members in Mie but were of little relevance to *Burakumin* activists in Hiroshima. In both areas, though, as important as the developments in the *Suiheisha* were, of equal if not greater importance were the changes which were being made in the *Yuwa* policy and programme.

The Yuwa Policy

(a) *The Formation of the Policy.* The general scope, direction and content of the *Yuwa* policy had been decided by the early 1920s, but there can be little doubt that the intensity with which the policy was pursued increased after the formation of the *Suiheisha* and the rapid spread of its influence. Prodded on by resolutions passed in the Diet and petitions presented to it by *Yuwa* organisations (and the *Suiheisha*), the government formulated a comprehensive *Yuwa* (conciliation) policy and gradually erected a complex bureaucratic structure to administer it.

First mention of the *Suiheisha* in the Diet occurred on 3 February 1923, when questions were asked from the floor of the Lower House concerning the *Suiheisha* movement and the Regional Improvement policy. The questioners noted with alarm the rapid spread of the *Suiheisha* and the danger that this movement might constitute a threat to national stability. On the other hand, other speakers pointed to the incongruity of advocating racial equality at conferences abroad while allowing discrimination to persist at home. In reply, the Home Minister promised to take measures to control the *Suiheisha* if it began to pose a threat to public order and to provide more money to raise education levels, improve the environment and ensure moral improvement in the *Buraku*.[77]

More extensive debate took place in the Diet after the *Kokusuikai-Suiheisha* incident which was widely reported in the newspapers, giving the movement a great deal of publicity. Speakers in the debate mention the existence of discrimination in various aspects of social life and social institutions, notably the army. This was followed by criticism of the way the improvement policy had been applied since it was feared that much of the money had ended up in the hands of the *Buraku* bosses. However, there was little criticism of the policy itself. There was no doubt that the policy was required to keep the peace in the *Buraku*, especially since it was feared that any radical activity that emerged there might spread to the colonies of Taiwan and Korea.[78] In these two debates, although one can detect muted criticism of government policy, there is general agreement that the aim of the policy should be to minimise discontent rather than positively improve conditions in the *Buraku*. Of course, to carry out the former policy involved carrying out some projects that did make real improvements to conditions in the *Buraku*, but in common with the social policy of the period 1900–1920 it was the prevention of radicalism which was the chief target of government policy and liberal criticism of this policy centred on its effectiveness in achieving this end.

The violence of the *Kokusuikai-Suiheisha* incident seems to have prompted the government authorities into taking action. In Nara prefecture, a circular was sent round to mayors, headmasters and police chiefs explaining how discrimination incidents should be handled, and similar circulars were probably issued elsewhere.[79] In May 1923 a meeting was arranged by the Home Ministry at which 23 prefectural governors were informed of the formation of the *Yuwa Sokushin Jigyobu* (Conciliation Promotion Project Section) which marks the start of a formulation of the *Yuwa* programme.[80] At the same time, more money was released for use in the *Yuwa* project and new policies were introduced. The major policy directive which defined the development of the project for the next few years was issued on 28 August 1923 (the anniversary of the promulgation of the Emancipation Declaration). This document reiterated the view that the Emperor had clearly expressed his desire for the emancipation of the *Burakumin*, and thus the main aim of the improvement programmes was to perfect the people's understanding of his wishes in order to remove prejudice completely.[81]

At the time that the Home Ministry was edging towards the formulation of a policy there were four different groups which could claim some degree of influence over *Yuwa* groups and *Yuwa* policies. The oldest of these groups was the *Teikoku Kodokai*, whose earlier phase of development has already been discussed. In 1918–1922 its conferences and meetings had attracted large audiences and much publicity. Oe Taku went on several speaking tours round the country spreading the ideas of his movement.[82] However, on his death in September 1921 the organisation seems to have lost its driving force and its activity declined quite rapidly.

The *Doaikai* (Mutual Love Society), although based in Tokyo, had widespread influence both in the Kanto area and on *Yuwa* movement groups throughout the country. It was founded in April/May and launched as a movement in September 1921 at a meeting of 500 improvement group activists which had been called by Arima Yoriyasu. Arima, the scion of a wealthy noble family whose feudal fief had been Kurume, Fukuoka, had been brought up in the family home in Asakusa, Tokyo. From an early age he had been aware of the great disparity between his lifestyle and expectations and those of the children who lived in the nearby *Buraku*. After graduating from Tokyo University, he entered the Ministry of Agriculture, but he resigned his post there in 1917 in order to be able to spend more time studying social movements and the problems of the poor. He was strongly influenced by the works of Tolstoy with whom he felt some affinity although he never adopted Tolstoy's radical views, remaining a liberal who simply sought to establish greater equality of opportunity throughout Japanese society.[83] He regarded discrimination against *Burakumin* as a stain on the nation's reputation but thought that it could only be removed by *Burakumin* organising themselves. The *Doaikai*'s role was to encourage this self-organisation.[84] In 1924 Arima stood for election to the Lower House in the Kurume constituency and, on taking his seat, joined the *Seiyukai*. For the next few years he was active in keeping the *Yuwa* issue before the attention of the Lower House. Following the death of his father he, somewhat reluctantly, took a seat in the House of Peers in 1929 and throughout the 1930s played an active role on the stage of national politics. Arima had provided 30,000 yen to establish the *Doaikai* and to finance its activities; the government also provided subsidies for some of its projects. The *Doaikai* believed that *Burakumin* must become assimilated into the majority society in order to ensure the well-being of the whole society. Translated into a practical policy, this meant that the group encouraged education projects, land reclamation and work projects. Most of its activities and meetings took place in Tokyo but, through its journal *Doai*, it had a wider influence, especially over *Yuwa* groups in the Kanto area. Arima, through the *Doaikai*, consistently opposed the 'class-oriented' tendency within the *Suiheisha* movement, but in Tokyo the two groups would sometimes organise joint activities (including even *Kyudan* campaigns), and in magazine articles he advocated increased co-operation between the *Yuwa* movement and the *Suiheisha* movement, which he referred to as 'sister movements'.

In December 1924 Arima chaired a meeting of the *Buraku Mondai Kyogikai* (*Buraku* Problem Conference). Sponsored by the *Doaikai*, this group called for the formation of a national league of *Yuwa* groups as a first move in demanding a co-ordinated national policy, a regenerating enthusiasm for *Yuwa* ideas. A committee of eleven was appointed to make further arrangements. The following February, representatives of 16 groups (ten regional groups and six national or religious groups) decided to establish a system to co-ordinate not only the activities of the prefectural groups such as the *Kyomeikai* in Hiroshima but also to form links with religious and education groups to obtain maximum co-ordination of activity.[85] During 1925 representatives of this *Zenkoku Yuwa Renmei* held a series of consultations with Home Ministry officials and leaders of religious groups. The League drew up petitions and presented them to the Diet suggesting, *inter alia*, that at least six times existing levels of funding be provided for the *Yuwa* programmes. In February 1926 and 1927 the League held delegate conferences in Tokyo which deliberated a series of motions all of which, to a greater or lesser extent, demanded the formulation of a comprehensive national *Yuwa* policy.[86] So, at the same time that the left wing groups were extending their influence over those active in the *Suiheisha* movement, we find the liberals associated with the *Yuwa* movement demanding a more effective government policy. It is difficult to prove a direct link between these two phenomena, but those interested in the *Buraku* issue who read the *Suihei Shimbun*, *Senmin* and reports of the conferences cannot have been unaware of the radical forces at work within the *Suiheisha*.

The government did gradually reorganise the administration of its policy. With the reformulation of policy in August 1923, the Home Ministry established the *Chiho Kaizenbu* (Regional Improvement Section) and *Chuo Shakai Jigyobu* (Central Social Project Section) in order to co-ordinate the activities of the various groups associated with the project at central and local levels. In September 1925 the *Chiho Kaizenbu* was abolished and replaced by the *Chuo Yuwa Jigyo Kyokai* (Central *Yuwa* Project Council) which operated within the Home Ministry's Social Affairs division.[87]

In addition to these secular organisations, whether semi-independent groups or government agencies, there were three religious groups which sponsored religious meetings and the publication of material relating to the *Buraku* problem. Both branches of the Honganji set up these groups but that of the western branch, to which about 70% of the *Buraku* communities belonged, was by far the more significant.[88] It formed the *Ichiokai* in 1924 in response to demands that it reform its *Buraku* policy, and in 1925 it spent 16,000 yen on lecture meetings, discussion groups and education projects assisted by government subsidies.[89] The other two groups spent lesser amounts on similar projects to improve the spiritual life of the *Burakumin*. Overall, these groups probably had very little effect, but they may have reduced criticism from those like the Black Vestment League that the Buddhist groups ignored the *Buraku* problem. In some areas, as in Hiroshima, the activities of these groups gave the *Yuwa* campaign a religious dimension, easing the integration of *Burakumin* into a passive acceptance of government policy.[90]

It was becoming clear by this time that the existence of several semi-independent groups was resulting in duplication of effort and was not assisting the development of a co-ordinated national policy. Meanwhile during the 51st session of the Diet a *Yuwa Mondai Kenkyukai* (*Yuwa* Problem Research

Society) was formed of members in both Houses. They recognised the urgency of this problem and discussed ways in which it might be resolved. It was through the mediation of this group that a single united *Yuwa* organisation was formed after many months of discussion. In July 1927 the *Doaikai* and *Teikoku Kodokai* merged with the *Chuo Yuwa Jigyo Kyokai*. The *Zenkoku Yuwa Renmei* was dissolved and its members encouraged to join the *Chuo Yuwa Jigyo Kyokai*. This group met on 16 December 1927 to prepare the basis for its future policies.[91]

Within the newly united *Yuwa* movement, the liberal tendency was represented at the national level by Arima, who became the new Council's deputy chairman. Although it was never a dominant force nationally, this tendency was very important within some of the prefectural associations at least until the mid-thirties. However, the major force within the new movement was that of the nationalists, who sought to bring the whole social movement under state control. The chairman of the new council was Hiranuma Kiichiro, who had been chairman of the *Chuo Yuwa Jigyo Kyokai* since its formation. His approach to the *Buraku* problem was based on a desire to achieve equality and justice within Japan based on the principles laid down by the Emperor. An experienced bureaucrat, he had worked his way up through the Law Ministry to become Attorney General (*Kenji Socho*) between 1912 and 1921 and was appointed a Privy Councillor in 1925. He was also a leading figure within the *Kokuhonsha*, a group which attempted to co-ordinate the activities of ultra-rightists in the army, bureaucracy and political world.[92] As we shall see later, under his chairmanship the *Yuwa* movement was brought under strict central control and became one more part of the national mobilisation policy.

(b) *The application of Yuwa funds.* The reorientation of government policy in late summer 1923 did more than simply reorganise the administrative network. At the same time, more money was made available to assist improvement projects within the *Buraku* and promote the development of *Yuwa* groups. Indicative of the adoption of a more comprehensive programme, the name of the budget was changed from *Chihokaizen Jigyo* (Regional Improvement Project) to *Yuwa Jigyo* (Conciliation Project).

As can be seen from Table 2, the total *Yuwa* budget increased almost 250% in the years 1922-3 following the formation of the *Suiheisha*. Agents from the Home Ministry had tried to prevent the formation of the movement by offering to spend at least two million yen on *Buraku* improvements and give the five *Suiheisha* leaders key positions in the Home Ministry if they cancelled the conference, but the offer was refused.[93] Perhaps most of this additional money was regarded as a way to try to minimise the influence of the *Suiheisha*. It will be noticed that most of this additional expenditure went on new projects; Area improvement, Education aid and aid to *Yuwa* groups. Until 1930, the largest item on the budget was the subsidy given to Regional Improvement projects (see fourth column, Table 2). There were many kinds of projects undertaken by the local authorities all designed to improve the *Buraku* environment; typical

Table 2: *Yuwa Project Funds, 1920–1945*[1]

	Area Improvement Grants	Educational Aid	Aid for Regional Yūwa Organisations	Subsidies to Regional Improvement Projects	Subsidies for Development of Yūwa movement	Funds for 'Emergency' Regional Projects	Emergency Regional Aid	TOTAL
1920				43,000				43,000
1921				145,860				145,860
1922				195,847				195,847
1923	112,000	63,000	106,000	209,745				490,745
1924	112,000	94,500	106,000	198,800				511,300
1925	112,000	126,000	106,000	210,000				554,000
1926	112,000	157,500	106,000	210,000				585,000
1927	112,000	189,000	106,000	210,000				617,000
1928	112,000	189,000	106,000	206,915				613,915
1929	112,000	189,000	150,000	197,600				648,600
1930	95,760	189,000	135,000	168,948				588,948
1931	80,640	180,650	114,750	151,164				527,204
1932	72,576	162,585	103,275	136,048		1,500,000		1,974,484
1933	172,576	162,585	103,275	136,048		1,800,000		2,374,484
1934	172,576	162,585	103,275	136,048		1,000,000		1,794,484
1935	152,576	162,585	103,275	136,048		680,000	220,000	1,234,484
1936	192,576	162,585	164,800	714,523				1,234,484
1937	172,576	182,585	164,800	714,523				1,244,484
1938	172,576	192,585	164,800	700,523		678,800		1,925,930
1939	172,576	192,585	165,800	709,523		158,800		1,438,284
1940	172,576	187,585	164,800	709,523	112,400	46,400	50,000	1,443,284
1941[2]	272,576	187,585	164,800	709,523	112,400	46,400		1,505,460
1942								1,474,310
1943[3]								1,453,216
1944								1,401,176
1945								1,372,995

Notes to Table 2:

1. The main source for this table was found in *Yuwa Jigyo Nenkan*, no 16 (1941), with a few alterations. There are many inconsistencies which occur and recur in these tables which show the yearly *Yuwa* expenses; some misprints have been altered but some unexplained inconsistencies remain.

2. The figures for 1941 and 1942 are the proposed budget for these years, not actual expenditure.

3. The figures for 1943, 1944 and 1945 were found in *Toshi Buraku* (Buraku Mondai Kenkyujo, 1964), p 143. It is not clear whether this is a record of money actually spent or proposed expenditure according to the Ten Year Plan although the former explanation seems unlikely.

projects included improvements to houses and roads, the provision of clinics, improvement of drinking water and sewerage facilities, the building of public baths as well as assistance to those who wanted to emigrate, and projects which aimed at improving the educational and cultural standards within the *Buraku*.[94] These projects were based on plans made following the 1921 survey mentioned earlier, and the fact that the amount of money spent and type of projects funded varied little during the 1920s seems to indicate that the policy followed a model developed before the *Suiheisha* emerged. The pattern of spending on these projects remained the same as before with the central government grant making up only a fraction of the total required for the project's completion, the rest being supplied from prefectural and local government funds. Just as in the pre-*Suiheisha* period, the relative importance of the different grants varied greatly according to prefecture. Why this should be so, is not clear. It may reflect the greater effectiveness of *Suiheisha* or *Yuwa* group campaigns for more improvement money in different areas or may reflect a difference in attitude taken by the local bureaucracies to the *Burakumin* problem or, of course, a combination of the two.

Regional Improvement Project money 1920-1928[95]

Central Government	1,630,000 yen	14%
Prefectural Government	3,260,000 yen	28.4%
Town/village authorities	6,520,000 yen	57%

Regional Improvement Projects in selected Prefectures in 1928[96]

	Total	Central	Govt	Prefectural Govt.		Town/village auth.	
Mie	104,997 yen	9,490	(9%)	22,588	(21%)	72,919	(69%)
Hiroshima	50,123 yen	10,590	(21%)	24,562	(48%)	14,980	(29%)
Kumamoto	4,972 yen	1,660	(33%)	3,972	(79%)	–	

Twenty *Buraku* in twenty different prefectures were designated *Kaizen Chiku* (Improvement areas) and long-term plans of up to ten years were drawn up in order to carry out general improvements to the environment in these communities. In these areas we find the intensive application of improvement projects of the kind described in the previous paragraph.[97] In some prefectures such as Kyoto and Mie these projects were carried out in districts where the *Suiheisha* was growing rapidly and becoming radical, but elsewhere, for example in Hiroshima, the area selected was a relatively isolated village. Even where the policy was not directly designed to pacify an emergent *Suiheisha* group, the use of such a large amount of money on these 'model' projects, which did little to improve overall standards, was regarded as a deceptive policy.

About 30% of the *Yuwa* Project money was spent on providing grants to give worthy *Buraku* children the opportunity to attend middle schools or higher educational establishments. Maximum grants were 330 yen per annum for middle school students and 600 yen to those attending higher specialist schools; there was no obligation to repay this unless the student dropped out in mid-course.[98] At a time when a primary school teacher early in his career was earning no more than 50 yen per month, these grants were quite generous. However, not all students seem to have received a full grant, especially after 1931 when the scheme was extended to assist more pupils without any increase in the programme's budget.[99] Increased equality of educational opportunity may, in some cases, have enabled *Burakumin* to escape the worst aspects of discrimination, but overall it is unlikely to have made much difference to the social structure within the *Buraku*. Most of those who benefited from this scheme were those who in any case belonged to the wealthier sections of the community. To enter middle school it was necessary to have graduated with good marks from upper primary school and there is evidence that few *Burakumin* got that far. Yoneda remembered that of the 60 *Buraku* children who entered primary school with him, only three or four remained until the final year and that he was alone in his years at the upper primary school.[100] Competition to get into the middle school was very tough; only ten children of Kitahara's school year entered middle school the year he graduated from higher primary school (1920) and all of them were from wealthy families.[101] Such anecdotal evidence does admittedly come from the period before the 1920s, but isolated surveys and the overall increase in poverty, especially in rural areas, give us no reason to believe that any improvement took place after 1920. Neither is there any evidence that this policy made any overall improvements to educational standards in the *Buraku*. During the 1920s, education became increasingly oriented towards inculcation of militaristic and patriotic values; by prolonging the exposure of *Buraku* children to such an educational system, the government perhaps hoped to create a dependable bulwark in the *Buraku* communities. Indeed, in the introduction to the education budget which appeared in successive years in the *Yuwa Jigyo Nenkan*, it was clearly stated that the aim of the policy was to create within the communities a reliable, well educated group which would be able to resist the temptation of 'dangerous thought'. Not that the number of children in receipt of such grants was ever very great; in Mie, where the total *Buraku* population was about 42,000 in 1935, only 30-40 *Buraku* children were receiving grants to attend middle school each year.

    More than one fifth of the *Yuwa* budget was spent on subsidising the work of the *Yuwa* group both at the national and local levels. The central organisation, the *Chuo Yuwa Jigyo Kyokai*, absorbed about one-third of this total, in 1930, 58,500 yen of a total of 135,000 yen.[102] Most of this was budgeted for organisational expenses, but there were also research projects, subsidies for public meetings, the production of *Yuwa Jiho* monthly magazine and the *Yuwa Jigyo Kenkyu* every two months (quarterly from June 1932), in addition to the production of thousands of posters and pamphlets. Each regional group was given a yearly subsidy to support its activity. The *Yuwa* project group in Mie for example, budgeted to spend 6,960 yen in 1930, most of which (4,000 yen) was supplied by the central government, the rest coming from the prefecture and other miscellaneous sources. This money was used to subsidise various kinds of meetings and lectures, projects – many of which involved children – and helped to support the production of a monthly newspaper.[103]

As can be seen from Table 2, the early *Yuwa* budget remained relatively stable in the period 1923–1931. It is, however, interesting to note the slight decrease in 1929–1931. The Hamaguchi Cabinet response to the world recession was to adopt a policy of retrenchment and the budget for 1930 was set at 90% that of the previous year, a policy which was continued through the next year, resulting in a further reduction in 1931. That the *Yuwa* budget was cut in accordance with this overall policy seems to indicate that the *Yuwa* policy was accorded no special priority in the government's plans.[104]

Application of the *Yuwa* policy varied greatly from one part of the country to another. In Mie, the first *Yuwa* grants were provided in the Spring of 1919, perhaps in response to the Rice Riots which had been particularly violent in Tsu city. However, throughout the 1920s relatively little money was spent in the Mie *Yuwa* programme.[105] A *Yuwa* policy was not initiated until early 1923, when a *Yuwabu* was set up in the Social Affairs section of the prefectural office. At the same time, a Social Project Council, chaired by the governor, was established to co-ordinate the *Yuwa* projects which were under way and aimed at encouraging economic development in the *Buraku*. By 1926 there were 28 projects being carried out in the prefecture at a total cost of 80,000 yen, one quarter of which came from subsidies provided by either central or prefectural government.[106] Local government bodies were clearly providing improved facilities for the *Buraku* communities, but, despite the radicalism of the *Suiheisha*, no network of *Yuwa* groups was developed.

Meanwhile, in Hiroshima, the network of groups, which was already well established in 1920, was reinforced by the formation of a group of the *Kyomeikai* in March 1921, and soon branches were formed all over the prefecture. Formally it was an independent group sponsored by Maeda Sanyu and wealthy *Burakumin*, but its attempts to promote *Yuwa* ideas were subsidised by central government and prefectural funds. Apart from holding regular lecture meetings, they produced a monthly news-sheet and organised a work introduction service.[107] In addition to this, there was a *Yuwa* project section in the prefecture's Social Affairs office which supervised the improvement projects whose total value in 1926 was just over 30,000 yen, despite the fact that the *Buraku* population was considerably larger in Mie. Supplementary assistance to the *Yuwa* project came from a religious organisation based on the Honganji temples which organised meetings to disseminate religious teachings designed to reduce prejudice, discrimination and militancy.[108]

Despite the rhetoric which accompanied accounts of the progress of the *Yuwa* policy, the whole programme amounted to little more than a series of token efforts at improvement. The core of the scheme – the subsidies provided for regional improvement projects – had been devised in 1921 and did no more than assist with the relatively minor projects planned by local government groups. The projects which were initiated after the formation of the *Suiheisha* seem to have been directly linked to a policy of containment. Grants for the model projects in the twenty selected *Buraku* cost relatively little, affected few people, but did enable the *Yuwa* movement leaders to point to major improvements in the living standards of a few *Buraku* communities which had been carried out under its auspices. Educational aid went mainly to assist the offspring of the *Buraku* bourgeoisie. It was hoped to ensure by this policy the continued existence of a reliable group within the *Buraku* communities and it also provided a means of 'rewarding' the middle class *Buraku* families who co-operated with those who organised the *Yuwa* policies. Many of the *Suiheisha* leaders came from such families and it was considered important to keep this group loyal to the government. Moreover, these families wielded the economic power and political and moral authority within the *Buraku* which could be used to prevent or hinder *Suiheisha* activity.

In many areas the *Yuwa* groups were direct descendants of the *kaizen* (improvement) groups and had a semi-independent status. But after the reorganisation of the *Yuwa* movement in the mid-1920s many of these groups were brought under the control of the central *Yuwa* agency, which was an integral part of the emergent bureaucratic state structure. Liberals and other moderate critics of government policy both inside and outside the *Buraku* communities had for some time demanded that the government should adopt a more active policy to encourage the removal of prejudice and discrimination from Japanese society. After the Rice Riots the government provided a small trickle of funds to assist local projects, but it was only persuaded to take positive measures in order to pacify *Burakumin* who appeared to be turning towards a subversive, foreign ideology.

Summation

One of the reasons for the immediate and widespread appeal of the *Suiheisha* in 1922 and 1923 had been that its propaganda studiously avoided ideological commitment. The founding members were influenced and inspired by diverse and sometimes conflicting ideas – Buddhist and Christian, liberal and socialist. In their early publications, the ideas and images were confused and there was considerable tolerance within the movement for different approaches to the *Buraku* problem. But once the task of establishing the movement had been carried out, the central committee was forced to consider questions of theory and practice which inevitably brought internal dissension. The more moderate of the leaders who were not averse to some degree of co-operation with one or other of the *Yuwa* organisations were removed from positions of influence after the 'Spy Incident', to be replaced by those who favoured more radical theories although not necessarily more extremist activities. Moderates, then, stepped out of the limelight and directed their energies to local issues. However, the anarchist groups which remained influential in the Kanto region, while not capable of challenging the authority of those on the central committee, continued to prevent the Bolshevik group from exercising complete control over the organisation.

Perhaps what is most remarkable about the *Suiheisha* is that, unlike contemporary organisations which were rent apart by internal rivalry, this dissension did not lead to a split and the formation of rival groups. Three factors may explain this. In the first place, there was insufficient internal organisation to ensure that a splinter group would be able to maintain active support for its policies from grass roots supporters. Secondly, the solidarity among *Burakumin* *vis-à-vis* the outside world, though a relatively novel phenomenon, was ultimately stronger than any appeal to political principle. Thirdly, although there was sometimes bitter argument within meetings and at conferences, none of the rival groups constructed a theory to explain the nature of discrimination or a coherent series of suggestions for future movement activity to replace the rather haphazard theory and practice of the *Suiheisha* in the 1920s.

Still, even if, at least by 1925, no split had taken place, there was a clear polarisation of attitudes which was apparent both in the *Suiheisha* groups and *Buraku* communities. This was further complicated by the emergence of the consolidated *Yuwa* policy and the attempt to reform *Yuwa* groups in order to bring more *Burakumin* under government influence. The *Yuwa* movement became better organised and more firmly committed to nationalist principles while the *Suiheisha* was becoming increasingly influenced by the Bolshevik groups. Thus, in those areas where the *Suiheisha* was well established and the *Yuwa* movement organised, the *Burakumin* who was eager to take part in activity to improve his environment was faced with a clear choice.

The *Suiheisha* had acquired a reputation for violence because of the vigour with which it pursued its *Kyudan* campaigns. Yet, as the left wing groups asserted more control, attempts were made to ensure local activists were more selective in their choice of target and efforts were made to link specific incidents with wider issues. Meanwhile, the *Yuwa* groups pursued policies which were designed to make improvements to the *Buraku* environment sufficient to convince at least a section of *Buraku* society of the sincerity of the government's desire to remove discrimination. It was hoped that token improvements backed up by concerted propaganda campaigns carried out by the *Yuwa* groups would lure *Burakumin* away from the *Suiheisha*. It may have been successful to a certain extent. Though no accurate figures exist, various sources give the impression that popular support for the *Suiheisha* movement reached a peak in 1923 and 1924 at the time of the initial burst of enthusiasm. Then, as factional rivalry divided the leadership and *Yuwa* groups were formed as a viable alternative, support for the *Suiheisha* seems to have declined. But, in 1926, the *Suiheisha* became involved in a major campaign which rallied the support of *Burakumin* throughout the country and won the movement the backing of other left wing organisations. It became clear that the *Yuwa* policy alone was not sufficient to contain the growth of the *Suiheisha* movement; more active, repressive policies would be needed to dissuade *Burakumin* from giving their support to leftist groups.

Notes:

1. *Suihei Undoshi no Kenkyu*, vol II, p 156. 3,000 copies of the first edition were produced.
2. *Suihei Undoshi no Kenkyu*, vol II, p 62.
3. Ninomiya, pp 144-5.
4. This law was passed in 1900 in order to control the emergence of social movements, particularly trade unions. Article 17 impartially forbade any agitation which sought to encourage either 'employers to dismiss workers or refuse workers requests for work for the purpose of bringing about a lockout', or 'workers to stop work or refuse offers of employment for the purpose of bringing about a strike'. No case was ever brought against an employer; the act was used, however, in the prosecution of those who organised labour unions or strike activity.
5. Details of the motions put before the conference appear in *Suihei Undoshi no Kenkyu*, vol II, pp 173-6.
6. The observer was Kasuga Masato. *Suihei Undoshi no Kenkyu*, vol II, pp 177-189.
7. For details of these speeches see *Suihei Undoshi no Kenkyu*, vol II, pp 177-189.
8. *Suihei Undo Shiryo Shusei*, vol I, p 41.
9. Further details of the motions debated by the conference can be found, *Suihei Undoshi no Kenkyu*, vol II, pp 203-216.
10. This article by Sakai appeared in *Kaizo*, April 1924, reprinted in *Suihei Undoshi no Kenkyu*, vol II, pp 217-222.
11. For more details see *Suihei Undoshi no Kenkyu*, vol II, pp 225-8.
12. Kimura, *Omoide I*, pp 25-8.
13. According to Asada Zennosuke in an interview, 30 January 1978.
14. Yamagi Shigeru, Taishoki no Hiroshima-ken Shakai Undoshi Gaiyo (An outline of Hiroshima Prefecture Social Movement History in the Taisho period), *Geibi Chihoshi Kenkyu*, vol 74, no 5 (November 1968), pp 10-11.
15. *Suihei Undo Shiryo Shusei*, Supplementary vol I, p 810.
16. *Hiroshima-ken: Hisabetsu Buraku no Rekishi*, p 239.
17. Kitahara, pp 88-90.
18. R P Dore noted an example of this in Omiya *Buraku*, Maizuru city, where the local *Buraku* boss was becoming prosperous and well in with the local authorities and so did not want to see the emergence of a group which might have challenged his position of influence. Private diary shown me by the author.
19. Oyama, p 32.
20. Akisada Yoshikazu, Shoki Suiheisha Undo Shiryo no Danpen (A fragment of material on the early *Suiheisha* movement). *Buraku Kaiho Kenkyu*, no 4 (March 1975), pp 126-9. *Suihei Undo Shiryo Shusei*, vol II, p 275.
21. See *Zenkoku Buraku Chosa*, 1935, pp 104-115.
22. *Suihei Undo Shiryo Shusei*, vol I, pp 256-272. Fifty-four incidents are reported in the account: Osaka 7, Aichi 10, Hiroshima 20, Fukuoka 17.
23. Ninomiya notes the existence of over 30 regional variants of terms like *doetta*, *yotsu*. Appendix I, pp 137-9.
24. This incident is described in some detail in *Suihei Undoshi no Kenkyu*, vol II, pp 250-262.
25. Yoneda Tomi, p 60-63.

26. DeVos and Wagatsuma, p 45-6.

27. Yoneda Tomi, p 71.

28. For Kimura's own account of this incident see *Omoide I*, pp 9-17.

29. The *Dai Nippon Kokusuikai* was founded in 1919, its main sponsor being Tokonami Takejiro, Home Minister in the Hara Kei Cabinet. The main elements in its programme were:

   1   To conduct government so as to make the Throne central and to unify the race.

   2   To preserve the essence of the Japanese people.

   3   To save Asia which, despite the union of Korea and Japan, has been plagued with violence due to human misery. This is the mission of Japan.

   4   To advance faith in the gods and ancestors rectifying pure thought.

   5   To stabilise national livelihood by harmonising labour and capital.
        Kinoshita Hanji, *Nihon Fashisumushi I* (A history of Japanese Fascism) (Tokyo, Iwasaki Shoten, 1950), pp 17-21. D M Brown, *Nationalism in Japan* (University of California, 1955), pp 179-180.

30. Such reports are to be found in Nosei Kenkyu, vol III, no 7 (July 1934). Reproduced in *Suihei Undoshi no Kenkyu*, vol II, p 492.

31. Detailed police reports of the incident can be found in *Suihei Undoshi no Kenkyu*, vol II, pp 262-272.

32. Kimura, *Omoide I*, pp 70-78; Yoneda Tomi, pp 80-84.

33. Of the *Suiheisha* group, 17 were sentenced to between six and twelve months imprisonment, four given suspended sentences and 14 fined between 30 yen and 50 yen. Four *Kokusuikai* supporters were sent to prison for terms ranging from six to eight months, one declared innocent, the rest fined.

34. See Table 4 p 200. Between March 1923 and March 1924 alone there were 1,462 *Kyudan* events, connected with which 162 people were arrested. The top five prefectures in terms of incidence of *Kyudan* events were: Kyoto 206, Yamaguchi 186, Mie 182, Hyogo 179, Osaka 157. Yagi Kosuke, *Sabetsu Kyudan* (Denunciation of Discrimination) (Tokyo, Shakai Hyoronsha, 1976), p 43.

35. *Kyudan* incidents as reported in *Suihei Undoshi no Kenkyu* and *Suihei Undo Shiryo Shusei*: use of *eta* etc. by an ordinary Japanese 31; cases originating in schools 9; cases involving police 4; cases involving other public officials 5; cases involving shrines and temples 3; cases involving reservist groups 3.

36. DeVos and Wagatsuma, p 45.

37. *Suihei Undoshi no Kenkyu*, vol II, p 316.

38. *Suihei Undo Shiryo Shusei*, vol I, p 223.

39. *Suihei Undo Shiryo Shusei*, Supplementary vol I, p 24.

40. DeVos and Wagatsuma, pp 88-90.

41. Articles concerning the demands which emerged from the *Suiheisha* for reform of the Honganji organisation appeared in *Chugai Nippo* between March and June 1923. *Suihei Undoshi no Kenkyu*, vol II, pp 458-467.

42. Hayashi Hisayoshi, 'Suihei Honganji to Kokui Domei', *Buraku Kaihoshi*, no 8 (July 1977), pp 86-111. Contains a critical appraisal of the activities and achievements of the *Kokui Domei*.

43. See above, no 10.

44. Representatives came from groups in Osaka, Nara, Kyoto, Hyogo, Wakayama and Mie. The founding statement produced by this group can be found in *Suihei Undoshi no Kenkyu*, vol II, pp 190-191.

45. Kimura, *Omoide I*, p 91.

46. Further details about Takahashi's early life and the development of his ideas may be found in Okiura Kazuteru, 'Nihon Marukusushugi no hitotsu no Riteihyo –

Takahashi Sadaki no Shisoteki Shiseki' ('A milestone in Japanese Marxism – the tracks of Takahashi's ideas') *Shiso* (December 1976), pp 80-100; Nakamura Fukuji, Takahashi Sadaki to Suihei Undo (Takahashi Sadaki and the *Suihei* Movement), *Buraku Mondai Kenkyu*, no 51, pp 2-39.

47. For a critical appraisal of both Takahashi's ideas and those of the socialist currents present within the early *Suiheisha* see Akisada Yoshikazu, Buraku Kaiho Undo to Kyosanshugi (The *Buraku* Liberation Movement and Communism), in *Nihon Shakaishugi Undoshiron* ed Watanabe Toru and Asukai Masamichi (Tokyo, Sanichi Shobo, 1973), pp 243- 283.

48. The title of the newspaper was inspired by a line taken from the Appeal issued to publicise the second conference which said that *Burakumin* should stop thinking of themselves as *senmin* – lowly people – but as *Senmin* – chosen people. *Suihei Undoshi no Kenkyu*, vol II, p 173.

49. An article arguing this line appeared in *Senmin* (15 October 1924), *Suihei Undoshi no Kenkyu*, vol II, p 402.

50. For a more detailed account of these events see *Matsumoto Jiichiro to Kaiho Undo* (Matsumoto Jiichiro and the Liberation movement) ed *Asahi Shimbun Nishibu Honsha Shakaibu* (Osaka, Buraku Kaiho Kenkyujo, 1973), pp 120-135.

51. I am grateful to Watanabe Etsuji for giving me access to the collection of *Dowa Tsushin* in the collection of documents at the Ohara Shakai Mondai Kenkyujo.

52. Kimura, *Omoide I*, p 117.

53. Yoneda, p 94.

54. Miyazaki Akira, *Sabetsu to Anakizumu* (Discrimination and Anarchism), (Gumma-ken, Isezakishi, Kokushokusensensha, 1975), pp 60-1.

55. The relevant articles from *Horitsu Shimbun* are reproduced *Suihei Undo Shiryo Shusei*, vol I, p 94.

56. For more details about the committee debates see *Suihei Undo Shiryo Shusei*, vol I, pp 94-101.

57. The decisions of the central committee were announced to a meeting in Kanto on 15 December, and a report of the meeting appeared in *Reisen* no 2 (18 January 1925),which also included Hirano's leaflet. Koga, pp 63-4.

58. Hirano is usually considered to have been an anarchist but more recent research suggests that although he certainly was a member of the *Shinyukai* he was never much more than a radical liberal. Miyazaki, pp 29-40. Certainly from 1927, he became involved in an attempt to push part of the Kanto *Suiheisha* movement further to the right when he assisted Minami in forming the *Nippon Suiheisha*, although other documents seem to indicate he was giving his support to the anarchist faction at this time. There is evidence from other sources that at least from 1931 and possibly as early as 1928 he was actively participating in the activities of right wing organisations *Aikoku Undo Nenkan* (Patriotic Movement Yearbook) (Tokyo, 1936), p 44. *Kokkashugi oyobi Kokka Shakaishugi Dantai Shuran* (A compilation of Nationalist and State Socialist Groups) (December 1932) reprinted in 1976 by the Shiso Kenkyu Shiryo Tokushu. For further discussion of Hirano's career see Kinoshita Hiroshi, *Buraku Mondai Kenkyu*, no 31 (November 1971), pp 116-120.

59. For details of the background to this event and the development of the incident see *Suihei Undoshi no Kenkyu*, vol II, pp 272-284 and pp 356-369.

60. See, for example, an article written by Fukugawa Takeshi, *Aikoku Shimbun*, no 32 (15 July 1925), Koga, pp 66-9.

61. For more about Matsumoto's early life see the early chapters of *Matsumoto Jiichiro to Kaiho Undo*.

62. These ideas nearly all seem to have been first developed by Takahashi Sadaki, Okiura, pp 92-6,and Nakamura, pp 31-3.

63. *Suihei Undo Shiryo Shusei*, vol I, pp 104-110,for further details about conference proceedings.
64. Details of the new organisational rules can be found, *Suihei Undo Shiryo Shusei*, vol I, pp 110-111. Though it should be added that in very few areas did the *Suiheisha* groups reorganise themselves exactly as suggested by the new regulations.
65. Beckman and Okubo, p 93.
66. *Suihei Undoshi no Kenkyu*, vol III, pp 163-4.
67. S S Large, *Organised Workers* . . . , pp 44-50.
68. Details of this meeting come from a *Kyochokai* report dated 28 October 1925. *Suihei Undo Shiryo Shusei*, vol I, pp 115-118.
69. *Suihei Undoshi no Kenkyu*, vol I, pp 146, 152.
70. *Aikoku Shimbun* was produced by the Mie prefecture *Suiheisha* and *Nomin Kumiai* between March 1924 and January 1926 during which time 37 editions were produced. The maximum print run produced was 7,000 but the average was nearer 2,000. *Aikoku*, it was explained in the first edition, did not mean patriotism in the 'bourgeois' sense but in its 'real' meaning of caring for the mass of the people.
71. See above note 34.
72. Oyama, pp 61-2.
73. Oyama, pp 74f.
74. Suihei Undo Shiryo Shusei, Supplementary vol I, p 643.
75. Miyazaki, p 106. *Suihei Undo Shiryo Shusei*, vol II, p 400.
76. Yamagi Shigeru, *Hiroshima ken Shakai Undoshi* (A history of social movements in the Hiroshima prefecture) (Tokyo, Rodo Jumposha, 1970), p 387.
77. *Suihei Undo Shiryo Shusei*, vol I, pp 163-5.
78. *Suihei Undo Shiryo Shusei*, vol I, pp 47-67 for a full account of the Diet debate.
79. *Suihei Undo Shiryo Shusei*, vol I, p 223.
80. Fujitani Yoshio, 'Yuwa Seisaku: Yuwa Undo no Rekishiteki Tokushitsu', (Historical Characteristics of the *Yuwa* policy and *Yuwa* movement), *Buraku Mondai Kenkyu*, no 37 (May 1973), p 5.
81. *Suihei Undo Shiryo Shusei*, vol I, p 226.
82. Asada mentions one such meeting, Asada Zennosuke, *Sabetsu to Tatakai Tsuzukete* (Continue the Struggle against Discrimination) (Asahi Shimbunsha, 1969), p 19.
83. For more details about Arima's background see *Tenko-Kyodo Kenkyu*, vol II (Tokyo, Heibonsha, 1960), pp 121-129.
84. Fujitani, *Yuwa Seisaku*, pp 6-7.
85. *Yuwa Jigyo Nenkan*, no 2 (1927), p 181.
86. At the meeting held on 28 February 1926, 32 representatives of regional and national *Yuwa* groups were joined by ten members of the Diet. *Suihei Undoshi no Kenkyu*, vol I, p 149. On 27 February 1927, 60 representatives from 20 prefectures plus 30 members of the Diet-based *Yuwa Mondai Kenkyukai* met to discuss the *Yuwa* movement. *Suihei Undoshi no Kenkyu*, vol I, p 181.
87. *Yuwa Jigyo Nenkan*, no 4 (1929), p 117.
88. DeVos and Wagatsama, p 89.
89. *Yuwa Jigyo Nenkan*, no 1 (1926), p 73.
90. *Yuwa Jigyo Nenkan*, no 2 (1927), p 60.
91. Narisawa, p 183.
92. Hiranuma Kiichiro (1867-1952) was Prime Minister for a few months in 1939 and served as a minister in the second and third Konoe cabinets. After the war, he was designated a 'class A' war criminal and died in prison serving a life sentence. *Encyclopedia Nipponica*, vol 15, p 320.
93. Narisawa, p 166.
94. *Suihei Undo Shiryo Shusei*, vol I, p 228.

95.   *Yuwa Jigyo Nenkan*, no 4 (1929), p 13.
96.   *Yuwa Jigyo Nenkan*, no 5 (1930), p 23.
97.   *Yuwa Jigyo Nenkan*, no 1 (1926), p 4.
98.   *Suihei Undo Shiryo Shusei*, vol I, p 229.
99.   Between 1926 and 1930 the total number of students receiving either of these grants in any one year was 2-300, but in 1931 the number increased to over 800 and by 1937 over 1,000 students were receiving some sort of grant.
100. Yoneda, pp 14-15.
101. Kitahara, p 56.
102. *Yuwa Jigyo Nenkan*, no 5 (1930), p 143.
103. *Yuwa Jigyo Nenkan*, no 5 (1930), pp 195-6.
104. This policy is explained in greater detail by G M Berger, *The Search for a New Political Order* (Yale University PhD, 1972), p 69f.
105. *Yuwa Jigyo Nenkan*, no 1 (1926), p 131, provides an outline of the background to the *Yuwa* programme in Mie.
106. *Yuwa Jigyo Nenkan*, no 2 (1927), p 39.
107. *Yuwa Jigyo Nenkan*, no 1 (1926), pp 176-9.
108. *Yuwa Jigyo Nenkan*, no 2 (1927), p 60.

From left to right: Sakamoto Seiichiro, Kusukawa Yoshihisa, Saiko Bankichi and Hirano Shoken at the time of the founding of the *Suiheisha*

All photographs by Courtesy of the Buraku Liberation League Publishing Division

Medallion commemorating the 14th National *Suiheisha* Conference

Badge made for representatives at the Fourth National *Suiheisha* Conference
(1925)

Suiheisha leaders at the time of the Third National Conference, 1924

Proceedings of the Fourth National *Suiheisha* Conference, May 1925

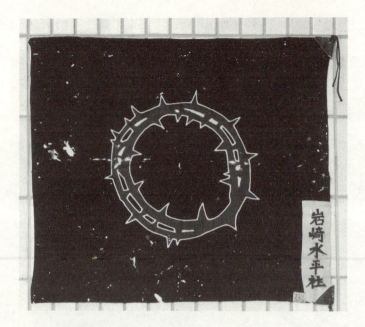

Flag of the Iwasaki *Suiheisha*

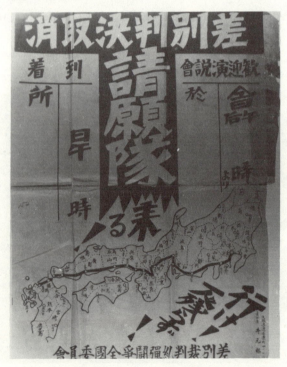

Poster produced for the Campaign in Protest Against the Discrimination Court
Decision, 1933

CHAPTER FIVE

Radical Theory and Practice
and the State's Response

Anti-Militarism and the Fukuoka Regiment Incident

Japanese law required that all males upon reaching the age of twenty present themselves for an army medical examination; of those who passed the medical 25-30% would be ordered to serve a two-year period of military service (four years in the case of the navy).[1] Among the conscripts there were not a few *Burakumin* and many of them experienced severe discrimination during their period of service; indeed, protest about discrimination in the army had been voiced by the *Teikoku Kodokai*, members of the Imperial Diet as well as the *Suiheisha*. There were several ways in which discrimination operated. In some areas, it is said that in the selection of those who were to serve the two-year period there was discrimination in that an unusually high percentage of *Burakumin* was to be found among the conscripts compared to the percentage of the catchment population.[2] In some regiments, there was blatant discrimination manifest in the lists of recruits used by the army bureaucrats; a red mark or the character *toku* (special) was entered by the side of their names.[3] Elsewhere, though no formal marks were made in the registers, army bureaucrats and officers were made aware of the status origin of all the recruits. At the very least, this ensured that the recruit was assigned to the more menial tasks and never received any promotion. Tsurumi Kazuko has shown how the early training of recruits in the Imperial Army was a process of dehumanisation; privacy was destroyed and in frequent inspections violence was used to maximise the distress, fear and humiliation of the recruits. Furthermore, there was a semi-official system of what Tsurumi coyly calls 'hazing' in which the second year conscripts would torment the first year conscripts who were assigned to act as their servants.[4] As can easily be imagined, especially in areas where tension between *Buraku* and non-*Buraku* communities was high, the training process and hazing activities provided arenas in which discrimination could appear in its most overt form. Many *Burakumin* had their worst experiences of discrimination while in the army.

Military discipline made it hard to protest against this kind of discrimination and no incidents of protest were recorded before 1920. A government report shows that thereafter there was a steady increase in the number of protests made against discrimination in the army and they reached a peak in 1927, but there is no indication what connection these incidents had with the activities of the *Suiheisha*.

Protests against discrimination in the army[5]

1921	1	1925	17
1922	3	1926	16
1923	16	1927	21
1924	16	1928	10

In April 1926, two incidents, one in the 19th Tsuruga regiment and one in the 38th Nara regiment, had direct links with *Suiheisha* agitation although these were probably not typical and the connection between the movement and protest in most cases would be indirect. Without doubt, the most important incident involving the army was that which occurred in Fukuoka in which protest about the ill-treatment of *Burakumin* during military service fused with a more general anti-militarist sentiment and threatened to erupt into a major national campaign.

There were two strands of this anti-militarism. The first derived from a 'liberal' dislike of war, a form of pacifism which was common in many parts of the world in the aftermath of the Great War in Europe, exacerbated in Japan by the futility of the Siberian expedition. Such sentiments were even common among members of the Diet who, much to the annoyance of the service ministries, voted to reduce the number of soldiers on active service three times in the period 1922-25. This non-specific pacifism was to continue to be common among the bourgeois intellectuals until the late 1920s. A more radical variety of anti-militarism was held by those associated with the socialist and anarchist movements. In the early 1920s radical pacifism was very popular among young students. One anti-militarist group based in Waseda University attracted 5,000 to a meeting held in May 1923. Anti-militarist study groups were formed in major cities all over the country, often connected to high schools or universities. At the same time, trade unions and the emerging proletarian parties began to include anti-militarist statements in their policies.[6] This dislike of the army was not restricted to intellectuals or left wing groups. It is reported that in the period 1923-27 soldiers would frequently become the object of ridicule on buses and in other public places to the extent that they would not wear their uniforms on their days off.[7]

In many ways 1925 was a watershed year in the pre-war history of the Japanese social movements. The Diet passed a bill to introduce universal manhood suffrage and the government gave its official recognition to Soviet Russia, but in the same year the Peace Preservation Law was passed which was to become the main instrument used to restrict left wing activity. Concurrent with this, the Education minister took first steps to curb the influence of anti-militarism. Early in 1925 regulations were issued which prohibited the formation of pacifist study groups in schools. Then, in July, it was decided that each school above primary level should have a serving army officer attached to it. This measure not only provided employment for those officers made redundant by the reduction in the size of the army but it provided a way of ensuring that military values would become a part of the curriculum in all middle schools and above. The following year, the Cabinet issued instructions to local government authorities ordering them to set up military training centres in each area to ensure that the 80% of the nation's youth which did not attend middle school would receive some military training between leaving school and becoming eligible for conscription or service in one of the reservist associations.[8] Effective from July 1926, all youths between the ages of 16 and 20 were required to attend one of these centres in which, over a period of four years, they would receive over 800 hours of instruction of which 400 would be drill and 100 'ethical' education.[9] Within three months, 12,064 training centres had been established and about 70% of those eligible were attending regularly.[10]

In urban areas there was considerable opposition to this militarisation programme and, as has already been mentioned, the *Musansha Seinen Domei* had been organised to oppose it. On 8 January 1926 a meeting sponsored by the *Suiheisha* was called in Kanehira *Buraku*, Fukuoka, to draw attention to the militarisation programme.[11] One of the speakers at this meeting was Imoto Rinshi, a member of the *Suiheisha* whose activities in the trade union movement had caused him to be blacklisted by companies in the locale.[12] A few days later, he and ten others of the Fukuoka *Suiheisha* Young Men's group joined the 24th Fukuoka regiment to serve their two years conscription and they were accompanied to the gates of the garrison by a crowd of 200, waving red flags and singing revolutionary songs. Within a few days of his joining the regiment, several incidents of discrimination had been reported to Imoto and this information he passed on to the *Suiheisha* group outside. Most of the instances of discrimination involved the use of words like *eta* or *yotsu* to refer to *Burakumin* as well as cases where they were allocated dirty jobs or shoe-repairing. In themselves, these were minor incidents, but they were no doubt deeply distressing for the individual concerned. The main problem arose when protest against discrimination, by either word or deed, was treated by superior officers as impertinence and a breach of army discipline. Army discipline protected the insultor from redress. On 29 January a delegation from the *Suiheisha* visited regimental headquarters to meet the colonel in command and protested to him about the tacit approval the army was giving to discrimination. They demanded that steps be taken to ensure that it cease and asked for permission to hold anti-discrimination meetings within the barracks. He promised to give the matter careful consideration but he made no reply for five months.[13]

Meanwhile the *Musansha Seinen Domei* was developing its campaign to oppose the plans to militarise education and the *Suiheisha* group played a leading role within the Fukuoka area. At the *Suiheisha*'s fifth national conference, held in Fukuoka in May, the movement adopted a 'class-oriented' position and approved a motion to oppose the militarisation of education. Following the conference, the campaign against the youth training centres developed with increased fervour and in Fukuoka they began to demonstrate outside the regimental headquarters.

When negotiations with the regimental commander were resumed, an agreement was reached whereby *Suiheisha* representatives would be allowed to speak about the need to oppose discrimination at two meetings held within the barracks, one for the men, the other for the officers. However, shortly before the meetings were due to be held a letter arrived from the commander saying that the *Suiheisha* had displayed a contemptuous attitude towards the agreement which forced him to cancel the meetings. Later, it was revealed that the cancellation was due to orders from 'higher authorities', probably the Army Ministry.[14] An angry meeting held the next week called for a more intensive programme of protest against discrimination in the army and the military training centres.

Detailed coverage of the incident in the *Suihei Shimbun* had given the issue widespread publicity. In the September edition an attempt was made to co-ordinate the activities of those involved in the Fukuoka campaign with those engaged in campaigns in other parts of the country. Ten thousand special appeals and ten thousand copies of the *Suihei Geppo* (the Kyushu *Suiheisha*'s journal) which gave full details of the incident were distributed to *Suiheisha* and left-wing groups throughout the country. In early October, Matsumoto invited Kimura Kyotaro to come to Fukuoka to assist with the campaign. Despite frequent requests, the army stubbornly refused to attend any meetings with the *Suiheisha* representatives, even refusing offers by the police to act as a third party in an attempt at reconciliation.[15] In mid-October, the Fukuoka regiment while on manoeuvres had deliberately avoided billeting any soldiers in *Buraku* houses. *Suiheisha* activists regarded this as further proof of the prejudice held by the army officers and they began to distribute leaflets encouraging all peasants to refuse to allow soldiers to stay in their homes. Meanwhile, those campaigning against the training centres were encouraging young men to stay away from them and older men to withdraw from reservist associations. Support for the two campaigns was widening; the local peasants' group, the *Hyogikai* and the *Rodo Nominto* (Labour-Peasant Party, formed 1926) were all becoming actively involved.[16]

In the early hours of 12 November police arrested Matsumoto Jiichiro, Kimura Kyotaro and nine others in Fukuoka who had been closely associated with the anti-militarist campaign. Simultaneously, raids were made on the houses of activists in Kumamoto and Osaka and, in the course of the next few days, the houses of *Suiheisha* activists all over the country were searched. Later, at the trial, the prosecution alleged that the campaign was stagnating and that the activists had planned to bomb the regimental headquarters in order to give the campaign renewed momentum. However, the only explosives produced in evidence were two hand grenades which had been brought as souvenirs from the Siberian expedition by the brother of one of the defendants. Prosecution evidence depended on a letter brought to the police by a spy active within the *Suiheisha* in which Matsumoto is said to have ordered some dynamite to make into a bomb. However, the authenticity of this document is in doubt and it may have been 'planted' by the police.[17] Despite confusion among police witnesses as to when the conspiracy is alleged to have taken place, solid alibis being presented by the defendants and the fact that no explosive was ever produced, all the accused were found guilty.[18] Matsumoto was sentenced to 3 years imprisonment, eight others to 3 years and one to 3 months. Of those who went to prison, all of whom were young men, only Matsumoto and Kimura emerged physically unscathed; all the others had their health broken by their period of imprisonment.[19]

The Fukuoka regiment campaign had spread swiftly in the late summer of 1926 by linking the specific demands of the *Suiheisha* with the anti-militarism of left-wing groups. It seems that it was this success which led to the arrest of the campaign's leaders. It is believed that the decision to wreck the campaign was made at high level in or before July which would account for the reversal of the Fukuoka regimental commander's decision.[20] A ban on the reporting of the arrests was imposed and not lifted for three months. This ban, plus the arrests of the campaign's leaders and threats made to other activists, stopped the development of the campaign, although Imoto continued to protest about the incidence of discrimination in his regiment. He had never intended his activities to become the start of an anti-army struggle but began his protests because it seemed the natural thing to do. By ensuring that the rest of his behaviour was beyond reproach he was able to continue to protest to the commanding officer each time an incident was brought to his attention. This did not endear him to the colonel, but by his careful tactics he was able to alleviate conditions for *Burakumin* in the Fukuoka regiment during his period of army service.[21]

The army was regarded by the *Meiji* oligarchs, particularly Yamagata, as that which safeguarded the essence of the nation, a view which was shared by Yamagata's successors, Generals Tanaka and Ugaki. The strong criticism of Ugaki's militarisation programme and the demands for the right to protest against discrimination within the army threatened to undermine the whole system of military values and were an indirect attack on the Emperor system itself. As Steinhoff points out, the

> Emperor system was carefully built up during the late nineteenth and early twentieth centuries into a powerful integrative force, bolstering political authority, facilitating communal activity and reducing internal conflict.[22]

An attack on this system did not have to be effective to elicit a powerful response, any movement appearing to subvert its values had to be stopped before its influence grew. The harsh sentences meted out to those who had been involved in the Fukuoka campaign were a consequence of the anti-military aspects of the campaign and were not directly related to the protests against discrimination in the army.

Although it was not possible to revive the campaign, it inspired others to take part in protests which ultimately forced the army to adopt a formal policy of non-discrimination. The most spectacular of these was Kitahara's Direct Appeal to the Emperor. Kitahara had joined the Gifu *Suiheisha* at the age of 19 and had been active in the anarchist tendency.[23] He was ordered to serve his period of conscription in the 68th Gifu regiment starting in January 1927, and shortly before joining he announced in an article that, although he felt guilty about leaving the movement at a time when the Fukuoka regiment issue was still unresolved, it was important to learn how to use a gun.[24] After joining the army, in spite of being troubled by illness, he made a nuisance of himself protesting about incidents of discrimination and also kept in contact with the *Suiheisha* groups outside. During his first year in the army he was imprisoned for short periods twice and spent five months in hospital.[25] He recovered in time to take part in a series of army manoeuvres held near Nagoya in November in which 40,000 troops participated. These were the first army manoeuvres to take place in the presence of the new Emperor and they were to end with a grand parade before him on 19 November. As Kitahara's platoon marched towards the Emperor, he left his platoon, took 15-16 paces towards the dais and, taking a written appeal from his pocket, announced his name and rank and calmly spoke the words 'Direct Appeal'.[26] When Kitahara refused to withdraw quietly he was dragged off and locked in the garrison prison. A reporting ban was immediately imposed. Within a week he was tried before a special military court and sentenced to a year's imprisonment. He claimed in his defence that he had suffered from severe discrimination while in the army and had been unable to obtain any satisfactory replies to his complaints, thus the Direct Appeal was his only alternative.[27]

The tradition of 'Direct Appeal' (*Jikiso*) goes back at least to the *Tokugawa* period. Faced with an instance of blatant injustice the subject, usually a peasant, would, as a last resort, appeal direct to the *daimyo* or *shogun* demanding that the wrong be righted. Direct Appeal in the *Tokugawa* period was a final recourse since, whether successful or not, the petitioner would invariably be executed for his insolence. Kitahara was not, however, putting his life in danger for, before deciding to make his appeal, he had consulted the military regulations and discovered that the maximum penalty he would suffer was two years, imprisonment and that, as long as he was careful not to display too much disrespect, he could be reasonably certain to receive only a one-year sentence. The petition which he attempted to give the Emperor was accordingly couched in reverent tones, pointing out the existence of discrimination within each regiment and the perversion of justice which was taking place in Fukuoka where the police had framed the *Suiheisha* leaders.

Four days later, the newspaper ban was lifted and the incident was front page news in all the major newspapers, some of them even bringing out special editions. Most of the reports carried Kitahara's appeal in full and the event seems to have prompted the publication of many articles in a variety of magazines which discussed the nature of discrimination in Japanese society in the 1920s and how it could be removed.[28] Kitahara was well aware of the paradox of an anarchist appealing to the Emperor to assist *Burakumin* in their struggle against discrimination but, by his actions, he gave the *Suiheisha* movement publicity both in Japan and the world (an article appeared in *The Times*, 14 December 1927). For a short while at least it was possible to discuss the problem of discrimination openly in the press. Further, it is no coincidence that a few weeks after the incident the Army Ministry sent instructions to all regiments on how to deal with the *Yuwa* problem.[29]

There were no more campaigns as spectacular as this, but over the next few years incidents of discrimination in the army provoked occasional protest campaigns. Notable examples took place in the 22nd Ehime regiment (1928), the 18th Aichi regiment (April 1930) and the Fukuoka regiment (1933).[30] These campaigns centred on demands for the right to protest against discrimination within the army which persisted despite the new regulations.

Bolshevik Attempts to Control the Suiheisha

One might have expected that the enthusiasm generated in the wake of the Fukuoka Regiment Campaign and the publicity provided by Kitahara's Direct Appeal would have launched the *Suiheisha* into a period of fresh activity. This, however, did not occur. Indeed, the *Suiheisha* movement was not to re-establish itself as a mass movement until the mid-1930s. The reasons for this are numerous but can be placed into three broad categories. Firstly, the leaders of the movement expended their energies on internal factional rivalries with the result that the day-to-day tasks of co-ordinating the various regional group activities were ignored. Secondly, the increasingly repressive measures enacted by the state, especially after the passage of the Peace Preservation Law, deliberately sought to disrupt the activities of all the social movement organisations. Thirdly, in its early years the aims of the *Suiheisha*'s leaders were clear: to build an organisation of and for *Burakumin* and through this organisation encourage *Burakumin* protest against discrimination. By 1925, these tasks had been accomplished; but, now the organisation had been created, in which direction should it proceed? What should its priorities be? Perhaps these questions were never simply put, but the debate within the *Suiheisha* over the next few years which was to absorb so much of its members' energy amounted to a series of attempts to formulate clear answers to them.

In March 1926 the *Rodo Nominto* (Worker Farmer Party) was formed with three of its central committee also leading figures in the *Suiheisha* movement – Matsuda Kiichi, Ueda Onshi and Saiko Bankichi.[31] Originally a social democratic party, this soon became the most radical of the legal parties and closely allied to, if not the front organisation for, the Japan Communist Party. Much of the debate which was to occur in the movement over the next few years would be centred on how far the *Suiheisha* should be in the control of those who were at least Marxists, if not party members.

At the fourth *Suiheisha* conference held the previous year, those allied to the Bolsheviks had successfully insisted on changes being made to the movement's internal organisation which gave the central organs greater authority over its constituent bodies. At the fifth conference, held in Fukuoka in May 1926, they succeeded in changing the movement's political orientation.[32] The theme of the conference seems to have been to replace the 'bourgeois liberalism' which had guided the movement hitherto with more radical, socialist ideas. First indications of this appeared in the opening description of the movement's aims and principles which contained some fairly obvious paraphrases of Marx.[33] But the most significant event was the change made in the *Suiheisha*'s general principles. Following a confused debate, conference finally accepted that the first two of the principles should be kept almost unchanged but that the third should be deleted and replaced with,

> Because we recognise the *raison d'être* of discriminatory attitudes, we will develop our movement following the guidelines of a clear class consciousness.[34]

It was argued that such a clause was essential in order to clarify the difference between the *Yuwa* groups and the *Suiheisha* movement, but it also cleared the way for increased co-operation between the *Suiheisha* and other working class movements.

However, the Bolshevik group did not exert complete control over the conference proceedings. Pressure from the anarchist group had forced the central committee to investigate Takahashi Sadaki's background. They found no evidence to support his claim to *Buraku* origin and therefore recommended his expulsion from the movement, a motion which was supported by a large majority of those at the conference.[35] The anarchist group also prevented the approval of a motion which would have pledged the *Suiheisha* to give its support to the proletarian party; code for the *Rodo Nominto*. While the Bolsheviks argued that the *Suiheisha* was involved in a struggle against feudal ideas which could only be overcome in the process of class struggle in co-operation with the proletarian groups, the anarchists insisted that the *Suiheisha* was more like a national movement and therefore had little to gain from taking part in class struggle politics. Since the movement had adopted the 'class consciousness clause' it was perhaps natural that it should give its electoral support to the class party, but there were many in the *Suiheisha* who favoured adherence to the movement's policy of keeping aloof from party politics, any variety of which supported the ruling class. Debate on this issue generated such strong feelings that it was decided to defer the discussion to a later date.[36]

Although not unopposed, the Bolshevik faction was clearly dominant and its success stimulated the organisation of its critics within the *Suiheisha*. Following his expulsion from the movement's leadership after the spy incident, Minami Umekichi had continued to involve himself in the activities of *Suiheisha* groups in the Kanto area. In the latter part of 1926 he developed the idea of establishing a pure *Suiheisha* which would oppose the faction that currently controlled the movement. A meeting was held at his house in January 1927 at which representatives from 18 areas agreed to form the *Nippon Suiheisha*. Its declaration and general principles were the same as those adopted by the

Suiheisha at its first conference. They argued that, in the course of its swing leftward towards proletarian politics, the *Suiheisha* had lost its original spirit. They resolved to make the *Suiheisha* as it had been.[37] But it never developed into a movement of any significance. Its influence was restricted mainly to the Kanto area and even after the arrest of the Bolsheviks and their supporters in the late 1920s the police estimated its size to be, at most, 3,000 at a time when they thought the membership of the movement as a whole was 53,000.[38] Thereafter its support dwindled rapidly.

Minami even attempted to form a political party based on this group, but this was even less successful. It never received the support of more than a handful of the wealthier *Buraku* households.[39] Between them the *Suiheisha* and the *Yuwa* groups provided sufficient choice for *Burakumin* activists; there was no middle ground for the nationalist *Nippon Suiheisha* to occupy.

At the other end of the political spectrum, the anarchists were attempting to devise a consistent policy and a coherent organisation which would enable them to resist the rise of the Bolshevik faction. In November 1926 they organised themselves into the National *Suiheisha* Liberation League (*Zenkoku Suiheisha Kaiho Domei*) declaring at their first meeting that 'our movement is based on a clear class consciousness, and is a self-liberating movement of *Burakumin*'. But they were very critical of the way the Bolshevik tactics in the peasant and labour movement had led to factional splits which had weakened the movement as a whole. They pointed to the way Bolsheviks within the *Suiheisha* were making the movement subordinate to the requirements of an outside body.[40] The intellectual leader of this group was the Tokyo based Fukugawa Takeshi, who elaborated his ideas in a series of articles published between 1926 and 1929.[41]

To summarise his arguments; he maintained that discrimination against *Burakumin* is not based simply on either 'race' prejudice or 'class' prejudice but that it contains elements of both. Under Marxist leadership, Fukugawa predicted, the *Suiheisha* would disappear into the class movement, but he was not convinced that discrimination would be eliminated in the course of the class struggle. The *Suiheisha* must remain aloof from political parties and ensure that only *Burakumin* are allowed to become members in order to maintain its integrity. Although the movement needs the understanding and co-operation of those active in other sectors of the working class movement, such co-operation must be undertaken with clear aims in view and must not mean that the interests of the *Suiheisha* are subordinated to those of other groups. The ultimate target must be the end of all forms of discrimination and exploitation and the *Suiheisha* should advance as one wing of the *Jinrui Kaiho Undo* (Liberation Movement of the Human Race).

These ideas were articulated best by Fukugawa, but they are to be found in all the leaflets, conference speeches and journals produced by the group. Opposing Marxist ideas with ones based on concepts of 'humanism' and 'mutual aid' the anarchists reached their widest audience in 1927 when the Anarchist-Bolshevik controversy within the *Suiheisha* was at its height. Behind the arguments now was the concern of members that the movement was beginning to stagnate and the problem was to find a strategy which would revitalise it.

Meanwhile the Bolshevik group within the *Suiheisha* was growing in size and influence. Although the conference in Fukuoka had not approved the motion to become involved with 'proletarian parties', in October 1926 a 'National *Suiheisha* League to Support the *Ronoto*' was formed. Groups were established in more than ten prefectures which sought to educate the *Buraku* masses to ensure they give their support to the proletarian parties in the forthcoming election.[42]

In December 1926, the Japanese Communist Party was formally, but secretly, re-established as a branch of the Comintern. Since early 1926 there had been a Marxist-Leninist study group based in Osaka which had acted to co-ordinate the activities of the various Bolshevik groups and individuals and from early 1927 this group became the base for Communist Party recruitment.

From the time of its reformation the party embarked on a policy of 'forming factions in labour unions, peasant unions, labour farmer parties, youth organisations'.[43] Kasuga Shojiro, who had spent eighteen months at the Eastern Workers Communist University in Moscow, was sent by the Central Committee to establish the party in the Kansai area. His job was to encourage the formation of party 'cells' in factories and 'factions' within groups such as the *Suiheisha*. One of the *Suiheisha* faction, Kishino Shigehara, had been associated with the first JCP in Tokyo but had escaped arrest. He had returned to Osaka where he ran a successful business as a pharmacist at the same time as being closely involved with the left wing of the *Suiheisha*. He had worked closely with Kimura Kyotaro in publishing *Senmin* and its successor *Seinen Taishu* (Youth Masses). Moreover, he was the regional organiser of the *Zen Nihon Musan Seinen Domei*, which soon became the legal front organisation of the Communist Party's youth league.[44] Another member of the faction was Matsuda Kiichi. Born into a poor *Burakumin* family in Osaka, he was a member of the left-wing study group which formed around Takahashi, was a full time worker for the *Suiheisha* after the fourth conference and became chairman of the *Zen Nihon Musan Seinen Domei* when it was formed in September 1925. From around this time, he began reading the works of Lenin and left-wing periodicals and joined the party in January 1927. Kimura Kyotaro, the other full time worker, was also closely associated with the party but it is not clear whether he was ever a party member.[45] As we have seen, he was always actively involved in the movement's affairs particularly in the production of the newspapers *Senmin* and the *Suihei Shimbun*. He later admitted to having been strongly influenced by Marxist magazines and left-wing newspapers especially the works of Lenin and Fukumoto, leading theoretician of the Communist Party at this time.[46] As Kimura saw it at the time, the liberation of the *Burakumin* would only be achieved when the class system based on exploitation was overthrown and replaced by an egalitarian society under the dictatorship of the proletariat.

Saiko Bankichi had progressed in his political thinking from Tolstoyan humanism and Owenism to a study of Marxism and, apart from his commitment to the *Suiheisha*, he was also actively involved in the peasants movement as well as the *Ronoto*. During the summer of 1927 this group, under Saiko's leadership, co-ordinated the campaigns of the *Ronoto* candidates who stood for election to the prefectural councils in the Kansai area. None of them was elected, but each candidate gained considerable support.[47] Following the election, the group formed itself into the *Suihei* faction bureau with Kimura as its chairman. Saiko was finally persuaded to join the Party, although he was later to maintain that he did this not from any commitment to Marxist ideology but to demonstrate his opposition to government oppression.[48] This group of four made up the Communist Party faction within the *Suiheisha* although they were later joined by two others, Kamemoto Genjuro and Honda Ihachi, in February/March 1928. The aim of the faction was to ensure that *Suiheisha* policy reflected the overall party strategy and that activities were organised in co-ordination with those other groups within the orbit of Bolshevik influence.

However, there was abundant evidence that the *Suiheisha* movement was rapidly losing strength. The sixth conference, scheduled for May 1927, was not held until December of that year and only 100 delegates attended the meeting which was held in Hiroshima. For much of the time the discussions followed a familiar pattern: the ways in which discrimination continued to manifest itself in the army, schools, marriage, etc., the deceptive nature of the *Yuwa* policy which was attempting to place *Burakumin* under the control of the state.[49] About such matters there was broad agreement. But, once more, the controversial issue was over political participation and, in particular, whether the *Suiheisha* should support the *Ronoto* in the forthcoming election. So great was the disruption caused during this debate that the police ordered the meeting to disperse and the conference business was concluded the following day at a different location.[50]

There are scraps of evidence which suggest that perhaps by 1927 the influence of radical socialist ideas was already past its peak and that the moderate grouping was growing in strength. Early the following year Imoto Rinshi, having completed his two-year term of military service, was appointed as a third full time worker in the Osaka office alongside Kimura and Matsuda. His expenses were provided by Matsumoto Jiichiro and this seems to have been an attempt to exercise a moderating influence on the *Suiheisha*'s central organisation.[51] But, at the time, this was far from obvious to either *Suiheisha* activists or to the government officials who were charged with the duty of keeping the social movements under control.

For the moment the Communist Party faction had a secure foothold within the *Suiheisha* movement's headquarters and, despite the fact that active support for the movement was declining, many groups were coming under the influence of those associated with the Party. Leaders of the *Yuwa* movement were taking steps to improve their image and organisation in order to win over those who were finding they could not support the radicalised *Suiheisha*. But these cosmetic changes brought few immediate results and more vigorous measures had to be devised to dislodge the Bolsheviks from their dominant position within the *Suiheisha*.

The Machinery of Integration and Repression

In 1925 the Kato Cabinet had formally recognised the Soviet Union (February) and passed the Peace Preservation Act (April) and the Universal Manhood Suffrage Law (May). It was feared that the restoration of diplomatic links with Communist Russia would encourage the growth of left-wing groups which would work to undermine the basis of the Japanese state. It was important, therefore, that universal suffrage worked in such a way as to increase the loyalty and co-operation of the citizen with the state – as its liberal advocates like Ozaki had said it would – without opening the door to disintegration of the social structure that might take place if socialist ideas became widespread. There was probably no formal deal between the Privy Council and the Cabinet to pass the Peace Preservation Law in exchange for the Suffrage Law, but some sort of agreement certainly existed.[52] When the Suffrage Act was being deliberated in the Diet, 'Home Minister Wakatsuki felt obliged to assure the Diet that the Suffrage Bill was not designed to promote democracy'.[53] Nevertheless, the act abolished the tax qualification and gave voting rights to nearly all the male population over the age of 25; slightly less than 20% of the total population was now eligible to vote.

In the deliberations on the Peace Preservation Bill there was widespread anxiety expressed that links would be formed between the Soviet Union and the Japanese Communist Party.

> These agitators are people to be greatly feared since we cannot give them the proper punishment for this kind of terrible crime.[54]

When the Peace Preservation Bill became law these 'terrible crimes' became punishable. The Act, as amended in 1928, made it possible to arrest and prosecute anyone who was a member of a group which planned making basic changes in the national polity (*kokutai*) or 'anyone who commits acts in order to further the aims of such a group'.[55] In effect, the Act decreed as outside the range of subjects acceptable for political debate: discussion of the political system, the economic system, traditional social relationships and 'symbols of the nation'. Throughout the late 1920s and 1930s this Act was used to harass groups and individuals who were critical of government policy, and as Japanese involvement on the Asian continent deepened and the possibility of war with the USSR increased so the definition of what was within the acceptable area for political debate became more and more narrow.[56] Moreover, the amendment to the Act ensured that the active political groups almost immediately set up self-policed limits to their activities.

We have already seen how, in 1925, the Education Ministry took measures to increase the militarist element in school education and the life of young men and the reaction to attempts to oppose this. In December 1924 the Tenants Dispute Law had been passed to try to damp down radical activity in rural areas and in 1926 a Labour Disputes Mediation Act was introduced in an attempt to limit trade union activity. On nearly all fronts, then, the government was attempting to control the development of oppositional activity among its subjects.

The first general election held under the provisions of the Universal Manhood Suffrage Act took place on 20 February 1928 and the Communist Party decided to give positive support to the 40 *Ronoto* candidates, eleven of whom were actually Communist Party members. Its overall strategy was to use the election to raise the political consciousness of the Japanese working masses, but they also hoped that if the *Seiyukai* (the ruling party) could be prevented from achieving an absolute majority in the Lower House the Diet would have to be dissolved once more, resulting in political confusion and the possibility of armed insurrection.[57] The Communist Party faction within the *Suiheisha* campaigned on behalf of Saiko, who stood for election in the Nara constituency, and he received 300 yen from the party to help his campaign.[58] Matsumoto Jiichiro and Miki Seijiro of the *Suiheisha* stood as *Ronoto* candidates in Fukuoka and Okayama. None of them was elected, but they all received a substantial section of the vote: Saiko 8,779, Matsumoto 5,992, Miki 5,154.[59]

In the election campaigns Communist Party activity came more into the open. Then, orders came from Moscow to recruit more labourers into the Party through mass organisations like the *Ronoto*. This made the Party even more vulnerable.[60] A large collection of documents had already been amassed by the police which enabled them to build up a comprehensive picture of party activities. In the early morning of 15 March a series of raids was made on 50 left-wing organisations and many private houses; 1,600 people were arrested. Communist Party membership had been estimated at about 100, but it was discovered that there were 409 members and 500 candidate members, a great shock for the investigating police and the politicians.[61] The story of these raids was not released to the press until 10 April when a formal ban was placed on the *Ronoto*, *Hyogikai* (the left wing trade union organisation) and the *Musansha Seinen Domei*, all of which had been Communist Party front organisations. Justifying the police raids, Prime Minister Tanaka said they, the Communists,

> would fundamentally change the national polity unbroken through the ages ... and have as basic policies the protection of the Soviet Union and granting of complete independence to the colonies. They have printed and distributed unspeakable assertions regarding the government – diabolical acts beyond description which neither heaven nor man can permit.[62]

Not all party activists or sympathisers were caught in these arrests and those who had not been captured began to recreate the *Ronoto*, rebuild the *Hyogikai* and re-establish the Party. To do this many students were sent back from the Eastern Workers Communist University in Moscow, among them Takahashi Sadaki. This group managed to restart some publications and distribute some leaflets, but on 16 April 1929, 700 arrests were made in raids carried out nationwide and all the key party members were caught.

Over 20 leading *Suiheisha* activists were held in the 1928 arrests including all of the 'faction bureau' and the leaders of the Youth Organisation. The movement was paralysed. The only national activity was organising the conference; few groups bothered to continue to pay money to central funds. The anarchist *Kaiho Renmei*, curiously unsympathetic to the fate of their arrested comrades, issued a statement in May in which they maintained that the enemies of the *Buraku* masses were, on the one hand, the government *Yuwa* league and, on the other, the Communist Party/Youth League. There was nothing to choose between the bourgeois politicians and the new rulers of the working class who sought to control the masses in the name of liberating them.[63] The *Suiheisha* had lost its most energetic activists and remained divided within itself.

From Disarray to Reunification

Less than six months after the previous conference, the seventh *Suiheisha* conference was held in May 1928 in Kyoto. The atmosphere of repression was maintained by the presence of 500 police surrounding a meeting attended by only 502 *Suiheisha* supporters.[64] Moreover, despite the fact that a major theme of the conference was to reunite the movement, this meeting was boycotted by the members of the twelve groups associated with the anarchist Liberation League (*Kaiho Renmei*). They objected to the way the decision had been taken to change the location of the conference from Nagoya, where their strength lay, to Kyoto, where the *Ronoto* faction remained influential.[65] It may have been true that the movement's remaining leaders feared the rise to prominence of the *Kaiho Renmei* group, though not for the reasons the anarchists suggested. Perhaps they were concerned that if this radical group were to gain control of the movement, it would be ordered to disband as had the *Hyogikai* and other left-wing organisations. On the second day of the conference, a *Kaiho Renmei* supporter burst in to the conference hall scattering leaflets which explained the reasons for their boycott. This incident provided the police with an excuse to disperse the meeting and the conference was not permitted to reconvene.[66]

This left the *Suiheisha* movement in complete disarray. Activity in the country at large was, in any case, dwindling – *Suiheisha* groups are reported to have held 391 meetings in 1928 and only 117 in 1929.[67] In Hiroshima, the nine groups listed in police reports existed, if at all, on paper.[68] In Mie, the *Ronoto* had put up candidates for the local elections of 1927 and a candidate in the general election of 1928. Communist Party influence grew through contacts made in these campaigns, but in the series of arrests following 15 March all leaders of the *Ronoto* and the Peasants Unions were detained by the police and this included ten *Burakumin*. Those who remained at liberty tried to regroup and form organisations committed to the use of 'legal tactics'. Police reports on these attempts commented on how the *Suiheisha* acted as the nucleus (*botai* – literally mother group) around which the new organisations were created.[69] However, in the first few months of 1929 police attending meetings and demonstrations began to arrest all those they considered to be the leaders. Few were held in gaol for very long, but sustained group activity became difficult, if not impossible.[70]

Nevertheless, in the summer of 1928 Matsumoto and Sakamoto made a final attempt to re-unite the movement. They sent circulars to all the prefectural organisations proposing to hold a meeting of representatives of prefectural groups which would prepare the way for the development of a united movement. Twenty-five representatives from 18 prefectures attended the meeting held on 15 July. Apologies were made for the lack of preparation for the previous conference, the organisational rules were amended and financial arrangements were revised.[71] Thus a degree of formal unity was achieved, but they appear to have been unable to revive mass activity.

The movement lost more of its activists in the arrests of April 1929, and in the same month Matsumoto went to prison to serve a three-and-a-half year sentence for his part in the Fukuoka Regiment incident. This left Sakamoto and a handful of others to ensure the *Suiheisha*'s continued existence. They went ahead with arrangements for the eighth conference to be held in Nagoya in November.

The night before the conference, there was no money to pay for the hall and only 15 delegates were expected to turn up. On the day 58 representatives arrived, but it was clear that the movement faced severe difficulties. It had little money; a campaign launched the previous year to raise 1,000 yen to support the publication of a newspaper had succeeded in generating a meagre 74.52 yen.[72] Once more the theme was national unity and, despite rather heated debates, agreement was finally reached that the two main issues were to oppose the *Yuwa* policy and to establish a campaign to improve living conditions in the *Buraku*.[73] Soon after this conference, the anarchists decided to dissolve their organisation.[74] Though weak, the *Suiheisha* was united once more.

Kyudan Campaign Continues

Despite the organisation's internal problems and the disruption caused by the arrests in 1928 and 1929, *Kyudan* campaigns continued to be carried out across the country in the latter half of the 1920s (see Table 3). Although there was a clear drop in the total number of discrimination incidents from the peak in the years 1924-5, during this later period there were still over 500 major incidents each year. Further detail about a small number of these cases, most of which involved the police at some stage, enables us to make some general remarks about the kind of campaigns which were being undertaken, though it should be remembered that not all of these directly involved the *Suiheisha*.[75]

In the first place, the number of campaigns directed against ordinary citizens undertaken in response to a verbal insult, though still the most numerous, seem to have become less important. There were still those who used *eta* and *chorimbo*, but it would seem that the general population was becoming, if not more tolerant of *Burakumin*, then more wary of referring to them in ways they considered insulting or, if neither of these, then were more willing to apologise when

Table 3: *The Incidence of Reported Discrimination in each Prefecture, 1927–1938*

	1927[1]	1928	1929	1930	1931	1932[2]	1933	1934	1935	1936	1937	1938[3]
Tokyo	5	6	6	13	6	1		9	1		7	6
Saitama	76	28	18	19	22	22		58	25	21	21	15
Gumma	14	15	26	38	57	54		67	51	34	23	19
Shinagawa		1	1			1		1	1			
Tochigi		2	1	6	2	8		2	5	3	6	3
Ibaragi	7	7	2	3		3		4	3	4	1	2
Chiba				1		1		7	8		1	2
Fukushima		1			1			2				
Nagano	18	21	17	16	18	19		12	8	14	10	24
Yamanashi									2		1	
Shizuoka	5	9	5	6	12	8		11	3	3	5	7
Aichi	12	14	3	6	20	9		9	5	8	4	
Gifu	4	14	3	7	12	3		4	5	1	4	2
Yamagata											1	
Fukui	7	2	5	4	5	3		2	4	3	2	3
Toyama	1	2	2	1	3	3		7	11	9	7	8
Niigata			1			2			2	1		1
Shiga	2	3	3	12	11	1		12	7	5	3	6
Wakayama	13	19	13	21	6	15		28	19	16	16	20
Kyoto	20	36	17	18	17	16		33	33	30		27
Osaka	44	32	21	21	40	24		47	25	35	19	30
Hyogo	49	45	34	34	41	40		23	35	22	39	33
Nara	9	38	28	37	99	69		58	39	30	21	24
Mie	40	43	20	35	46	33		36	28	27	18	23
Tottori			5	5	3	5		13	6	5	8	5
Shimane	10	12	1	5	10	9		10	9	7	4	8
Okayama	36	52	47	49	67	95		73	53	81	48	46
Hiroshima	35	64	58	33	33	51		50	57	55	29	36
Yamaguchi	11	12	10	17	14	17		23	29	19	11	18
Tokushima	5	7		9	10	20		31	25	25	24	17
Ehime	13	11	30	27	37	25		38	45	49	31	39
Kochi	11	12	19	19	35	31		35	25	16	13	14
Kagawa	27	28	21	25	30	18		38	26	24	20	9
Fukuoka	79	47	47	40	34	28		52	67	57	44	28
Oita		6	3	6	8	10			8	5	11	6
Saga	7	7	3	14	17	3		8	9	6	3	6
Kumamoto	6	22	8	5	5	3		14	32	34	18	7
Miyazaki			2	2				1		1		1
Nagasaki	1	2	4	2	5	2		5	4		1	2
Kagoshima				1				1				2
	567	620	484	557	736	652		824	715	650	474	499

Source: *Suihei Undō Shiryō Shūsei*, Vol III, p1029.

Notes to Table 3:
1. The year between 1927 and 1931 begins in November the previous year and ends in October, thus '1927' refers to the period from 1 November 1926 to 31 October 1927.
2. From 1932 the 'year' is defined as beginning on 1 January and ends on 31 December.
3. No breakdown by prefecture is available after 1938.

challenged so that such incidents never developed into campaigns. On the other hand, it is probable that the greater experience of *Buraku* leaders, whether or not they were members of the *Suiheisha*, made them more selective in the kind of incident they chose as the focal point for a campaign. Police reports for 1930 and 1931 remark on a tendency to protract those campaigns which involved schools, public officials or other local notables in order to maximise publicity. The same reports note a reduction in the amount of violence associated with the campaigns.[76]

As in the earlier period, the number of campaigns which centred on discrimination in primary schools occupy a prominent position. Usually they were generated by the use of a word like *eta* by the teacher or between the pupils, but in either case the headmaster was held responsible for what had taken place in his school and it was he who was requested to apologise and sometimes even to resign. In most cases about which we have further evidence the impression is that the incidents occurred within the context of inter-group tension within the village, of which these incidents are a clear manifestation. A major campaign developed in Okayama in 1930 when it was discovered that one teacher was segregating his classes into *Buraku* and non-*Buraku* groups. At first he said this had been to stop the spread of trachoma, then that the class was divided according to ability, and finally that it happened by accident. The *Burakumin* did not believe him, and two days after the discrimination had been noticed they organised a 'school strike' and no *Buraku* children attended classes for a month until the headmaster and teacher had been transferred. Even then, the struggle continued for another six weeks as the *Burakumin* demanded that the local authorities running the school accept their responsibility and apologise. From being an isolated incident, the campaign had developed into a political struggle against the village authorities and it is probably significant that the father of the offending teacher owned a lot of land in the village.[77] In this campaign, we see the adoption of two new elements to the *Kyudan* strategy. First, criticism did not stop with the headmaster but included reference to the local education board and in some cases to even higher authorities. Secondly, there was the adoption of the 'school strike' in which *Burakumin* kept their offspring away from school in order to put pressure on the headmaster and authorities to issue apologies or in some cases to make changes in the curriculum. Outrage provoked by a specific event was used to mobilise *Burakumin* to mount a wider campaign against the local authorities.

Another large group of incidents involved public officials like village mayors, police, prison officers and doctors who were criticised for making insulting remarks about *Burakumin*. The *Suiheisha* regarded such remarks as demonstrating the degree to which discrimination was deeply ingrained within the thinking of the Japanese people, especially the minions of the capitalist/landlord ruling class. One blatant instance occurred in a pamphlet produced by the Home Ministry in 1927 which gave instructions to the local police forces on the new election law. In it, '*tokushu Burakumin*' are referred to as being equivalent to 'inferior' (*teikyu*) or 'untrustworthy' people (*shinyo jubun narazarumono*). The *Suiheisha* lodged a protest and the pamphlet was revised and an apology issued.[78]

One of the most important campaigns of the early 1930s took place in Nara and took the form of criticism of one Dr Funagi. At a meeting of local doctors he had used four fingers to refer to *Burakumin* patients and the incident was brought to the attention of the local *Suiheisha*. As Funagi was an important figure within the local community, serving on many committees as well as being a police surgeon, the *Suiheisha* decided to widen the campaign against him and many villages in the area began to take part. Quite soon, he agreed to make a public apology and distribute 7,000 leaflets, but seeing there was an opportunity to develop the campaign its leaders, Sakamoto, Yoneda *et al*, decided to extend their criticisms to include the local health authorities. Unfortunately, during one demonstration outside a hospital a policeman had a heart attack and died. The demonstrators were held responsible for this, several of them were arrested and the campaign lost its momentum.[79]

A more important trend was the increase in incidents which emerged from demands for equal access to communal facilities like common woodlands which many *Buraku* communities had been deprived of in the local government reforms of the late nineteenth and early twentieth centuries. Several campaigns of this nature had been initiated by the *Suiheisha* group in Mie during the late 1920s.[80] In 1931, for example, a large meeting was held in Ise-mura to protest about the fact that, although the local temple owned over 100 *cho* of land (over 245 acres) in the vicinity, only non-*Burakumin* were allowed to use it. As the campaign for equal access developed over the next few years it acquired an anti-religious dimension although it is not clear what results were achieved.[81] The growth of demands for equal access to communal property reflected an increase in *Burakumin* self-confidence derived from the development of group strength from within the *Buraku* communities as well as encouragement from groups outside, whether associated with the *Yuwa* or *Suiheisha* movements. These campaigns may also have been indirectly encouraged by the way that universal suffrage made it possible for *Burakumin* groups to discover how much land was communal. Their participation in local affairs gave them confidence to demand what they saw as rightly theirs.

Another prominent feature of the campaigns is the censure of those who published material containing derogatory remarks about *Burakumin*. In general, these campaigns involved local newspapers and were successful in producing public apologies. The *Beppu* evening newspaper in 1928 carried an article which a local group considered to be insulting. They demanded an explanation and urged people not to buy the paper until an apology was made. The campaign was a success, the newspaper printed an apology and distributed 10,000 leaflets condemning discrimination.[82] In May 1930 the Tokyo *Suiheisha* complained about an article in the prestigious *Chuo Koron* and the magazine produced an apology.[83]

After Kitahara's 'Direct Appeal', the Army Ministry had issued instructions to each regiment detailing ways in which the 'Yuwa problem' was to be handled so as to avoid discrimination. Nevertheless, there is evidence that Burakumin were rarely, if ever, promoted, tended to be given dirty jobs or jobs which involved leather work, and were still the butt of insulting remarks. Although it was no longer easy to communicate with any outside groups, such incidents did lead to a few protest campaigns. Despite the fact that more Burakumin were having to seek work outside the Buraku community, there were remarkably few incidents involving discrimination in employment. The only major incident occurred in Kyoto, where the Suiheisha protested to the owners of the Guge silk mill that although they employed over 13,000 people none of them were Burakumin.[84] However, the campaign was not brought to a satisfactory conclusion.

Only two-thirds of those campaigns about which we have more information involved Suiheisha groups and we may suppose that fewer than half of the incidents in any one year were directly connected with a branch of the national movement, especially likely at a time when we know there was a reduction in Suiheisha activity. Police comments on the campaigns note how most incidents were settled amicably with a verbal apology. The Suiheisha campaigns of the 1920s do seem to have encouraged Burakumin, even those not in the movement, to protest against insult and to object to discrimination when faced with it in their daily lives. Where the Suiheisha was directly involved they seem to have made sure that the incidents were placed in their social context so that the protest was not simply about the scornful attitude of an individual but about the existence of a system in which an individual can be influential despite the fact that he holds blatantly discriminatory views about Burakumin. In the campaigns concerning access to common land we also note that they aimed at longer-term targets than simple apologies and were edging towards making demands the fulfilment of which would result in the general improvement of living standards within the Buraku communities.

So, in contrast to the evidence of weaker support for the Suiheisha groups at grass roots level, there are indications that active opposition to instances of discrimination continued into the late 1920s and early 1930s. Possibly the continuation of activity in this the 'undirected' sector of the Buraku movement provided the basis upon which the Suiheisha was able to rebuild its organisation in the 1930s

The Suiheisha in the 1920s

At the time of the launching of the Suiheisha movement there was a great deal of overlap of Suiheisha and Yuwa attitudes, a considerable area of agreement about their liberal policies. But during the 1920s the liberal position came under attack from both sides as the Yuwa movement adopted a more reactionary, nationalist ideology at the same time as the Suiheisha adopted a more radical, left-wing position. Traditional social pressures backed up by the state machinery in the form of the Special Police and organisations established in the period

1905–10 had until 1918 been sufficient to prevent the emergence of autonomous social movements like the *Suiheisha*. But it was inadequate to prevent the influx of foreign ideas after 1918 which inspired the formation of the various social movements. In the 1900s, when autonomous groups of *Burakumin* had started to organise themselves, the only readily accessible ideology which could be used to support their demands was that of the liberal critics of the clan dominated government. By the mid-1920s this had been superseded by the anarchist and Marxist critiques of Japanese society. Neither of these systems of ideas seems to have been fully appreciated by its adherents, but they did provide a base from which it was possible to challenge the Emperor system around which the new status hierarchy had been constructed. The anarchists, sometimes with the support of the liberal or rightist groups, put up some resistance to the attempts of the Bolshevik groups to dominate the *Suiheisha*, but by 1925 the Marxists more or less controlled the *Suiheisha*. Even those such as Imoto Rinshi and Asada Zennosuke, who never became party members, were regular readers of *Sekki* (The Red Flag) and other Communist Party journals.

Of course, the Communist Party exerted a considerable influence over all the left-wing organisations of the time, but there are quite specific factors which explain the success of socialist ideas among the *Suiheisha* leaders. The subversive foreign ideas of liberalism, socialism and anarchism had encouraged some Japanese to regard society as a structure made for and by human beings, a structure which could be changed by human action and thus the hardship and suffering caused by a particular social system or belief were not inevitable. Having rejected this notion of inevitability though, many socialists and anarchists adopted a naive belief that Japanese society could and would be revolutionised within the space of a few years and a new society would emerge in which there would be none of the evil aspects of the old society. The imminence of The Revolution made it vitally important to adopt the correct theory and tactics immediately and this, in part, explains the intensity of the debate between Bolshevik and anarchist. The scientific socialism of the Bolsheviks, which appeared to demonstrate how the process would occur, eventually attracted more adherents than its less well organised opponents. *Suiheisha* activists had perhaps more reason than most to want to create a new society in which there was no room for the prejudice and discrimination of the past and they enthusiastically supported the Bolshevik ideas.

There were two other, more specific reasons for the *Suiheisha* activists' attraction to Bolshevism. Many of the early *Suiheisha* leaders had been inspired to become involved in left wing groups by the news of the Russian revolution and the way it had led to the liberation of the Jews in Russia. Many believed that, just like the Jews in Russia, the *Burakumin* had a special role to play in the revolutionary process.[85] A second reason which may have predisposed many of the *Suiheisha* leaders towards accepting the vision of a new society presented by the socialists was the similarity with the view presented by Buddhism. In conversation, Kimura Kyotaro and others refer to the similarity between Buddhism and Marxism which made transition between the two systems of ideas relatively easy. In the early 1920s newspapers carried articles explaining that when the Buddhist saints of old talked of equality, they were expressing the same sentiments as modern man in his demands for democracy.[86] Even Sano Manabu indicated in an article written in the early 1920s that he considered the aim of creating a *Suihei* society as being a modernisation of Shinran's notion of an ideal society and that this differed very little from what Marx and Engels foresaw would be created after the decay of capitalism.[87] The use of oriental imagery to convey occidental theories was more than just a propagandist's device. The way many Japanese absorbed Marxist ideas within a Japanese matrix of thought helps to explain how many of them were able to adopt socialist ideas with such ease and relinquish them a few years later with so little difficulty. Buddhism, especially Shinran sects, had been a particularly important influence on most *Burakumin* and it may well be that the similarities between Shinran's Buddhism and Sano's Marxism facilitated the acceptance of Bolshevik ideas among the *Suiheisha*'s leaders.

It is usually predicted that a social movement will adopt a more bureaucratic framework as time progresses and that increased bureaucratisation plus the appointment of full-time workers will tend to make the movement more conservative. This did not happen in the *Suiheisha* in the 1920s. Those who were most insistent that the movement become better organised were the Communist Party sympathisers whose recommendations were opposed by the less radical groups. Furthermore, the appointment of full-time workers who were associated with the Bolshevik grouplets ensured there was considerable pressure from the centre of the movement encouraging left wing policies. After the arrest of the communist sympathisers, a more moderate, social democratic faction emerged which looked to Matsumoto Jiichiro for leadership. But the emergence of a more moderate group had less to do with changes which were taking place within the organisation and is better characterised as the adoption of 'legal tactics' at a time when the definition of what was legal was rapidly becoming narrower. Matsumoto was later to establish himself as the movement's leader, but during the 1920s no leader or leadership group emerged. In the early years, the loose, federalist structure of the organisation made this difficult, although despite the structurelessness an unofficial group composed of Saiko, Sakamoto, Minami, Kimura and Hirano seems to have directed the movement. Only at the fourth conference was an organisational structure established, but even then no structured organisation was established which could firmly link the local group to the central *Suiheisha* institutions.

The *Suiheisha* movement inherited many of its values from the *kaizen* groups which preceded it and adopted others from contemporary social movements. The conference debates and the discussions in the movement's journals can be seen as a process in which the movement deliberated to what extent values inherited from previous groups were relevant to its present and future and how far the tactics and experiences of other social groups could help to devise strategies for the movement's progress or for specific struggles. All activists involved in the campaigns aimed at the creation of a state of affairs in which all

Burakumin would be able to play a full and equal part in social affairs to the extent that their former feudal status became irrelevant. Government policy, that of the *Yuwa* groups and that of the right wing of the *Suiheisha*, was to insist that such equality was the sincere desire of the Emperor which could only be realised when his subjects changed their attitudes to agree with him. Totally opposed to this view of the problem and the policies which were derived from it, was that of the anarchists and Bolsheviks who argued that such equality could not be achieved without the complete destruction of feudal ideas, Japanese society and capitalism. Between these extremes was a third tendency which argued that what was required was the reform of a wide range of social institutions to a greater or lesser degree which might ultimately lead to or necessitate the 'overthrow of capitalism'. But because of the need to adopt 'legal tactics' they argued it was not opportune to be openly committed to this latter, long term target. This more 'realistic', moderate policy, which was supported by Matsumoto and his followers, was adopted by the movement during the 1930s. It is the development of this policy and the parallel formulation of a more inclusive *Yuwa* policy that we shall examine in the next section.

Notes:

1. Smethurst, *Pre-war Japanese Militarism*, p 6.
2. Imoto Rinshi recollects that about 10% of the conscripts in his regiment were *Burakumin* although *Burakumin* made up only 3% of the population of Fukuoka prefecture. Interview, 14 November 1977.
3. DeVos and Wagatsuma, p 51.
4. This is described in detail in Chapter Three, Socialisation for Death, Tsurumi Kazuko, *Social Change and the Individual* (Princeton University Press, 1970).
5. *Suihei Undoshi no Kenkyu*, vol III, p 34. The figures are taken from a report published by the *Rikigunsho* in 1934.
6. Shindo Toyo, *Fukuoka Rentai Jiken* (The Fukuoka Regiment Incident) (Tokyo, Gendaishi Shuppankai, 1974), pp 50-8.
7. Watanabe Toru, 'Taisho Demokurashii to Guntai' (Taisho democracy and the army), *Buraku Kaihoshi, Fukuoka*, no 10 (February 1978), p 38.
8. Smethurst, *Pre-war Japanese Militarism*, pp 37-8.
9. Smethurst, *Pre-war Japanese Militarism*, p 40.
10. Shindo, pp 46-7.
11. *Suihei Undoshi no Kenkyu*, vol VI, p 57.
12. Interview, 14 November 1977.
13. Shindo, p 100.
14. Shindo, pp 105-6.
15. Shindo, p 111.
16. *Suihei Undoshi no Kenkyu*, vol VI, pp 67-8.
17. Shindo, pp 144-5.
18. Kimura Kyotaro, *Omoide I*, p 195. See also Matsumoto Jiichiro, *Buraku Kaiho e no Sanjunen* (Thirty years towards *Buraku* Liberation), (Tokyo, Kiudai Shisosha, 1948), p 98.
19. Kimura, *Omoide I*, p 197.
20. Kimura, *Omoide I*, p 192. Kimura notes the transfer of a Public Prosecutor from Yamaguchi to Fukuoka which took place at about this time. It is said that he had

destroyed the *Suiheisha* movement in Yamaguchi prefecture and was expected to have similar success in Fukuoka. Interview with Kimura, 31 January 1978.

21. Interview, 14 November 1977.
22. P G Steinhoff, *Tenko: Ideology and Societal Integration in Pre-war Japan* (Harvard University PhD, 1969), pp 14-15.
23. *Suihei Undo Shiryo Shusei*, vol III, p 207.
24. The article was later published in the *Zenkoku Suihei Shimbun* (15 July 1927), *Suihei Undoshi no Kenkyu*, vol III, p 271.
25. Kitahara, pp 110-115.
26. The text of the Direct Appeal was as follows:
    'A reverent complaint:
    1   Within the army, discrimination against we *Tokushu Burakumin* occurs as frequently as under the feudal system; protest against it occurs often but the attitude of the authorities towards solving the problem is not at all sincere towards those who are discriminated against, but rather is oppressive.
    2   The attitude of the authorities towards this problem is the same within every regiment in the country and remains unchanged as can be seen in the internal military regulations.
    3   Because of the struggle against discrimination which took place in the 24th Regiment, several victims of discrimination are being sent to prison because of a crime fabricated by the police.
    I humbly beg you to give the situation reported above your careful consideration.
    Showa 2 (1927) November 19
    68th Regiment, Platoon 5,
    2nd class private Kitahara Daisaku.'
    The Japanese text appears in *Suihei Undoshi no Kenkyu*, vol III, p 272.
27. *Suihei Undoshi no Kenkyu*, vol III, p 274.
28. Articles about the incident appeared in most publications, a selection of these articles can be found Kitahara, pp 145-150.
29. Kitahara, p 144. *Hiroshima-ken: Hisabetsu . . .* p 240.
30. Further details of these campaigns can be found in *Suihei Undoshi no Kenkyu*, vol III, pp 325f; 362-4. *Suihei Undo Shiryo Shusei*, vol II, pp 524-5, vol III, p 63.
31. Kimura, *Omoide I*, p 202.
32. According to one report 158 of the 261 delegates came from Fukuoka prefecture. Miyazaki, p 163.
33. *Suihei Undoshi no Kenkyu*, vol III, p 120.
34. *Suihei Undo Shiryo Shusei*, vol I, pp 127-8. The proposed platform had been:
    '1   Complete censure of all discriminatory speech and action directed at us.
    2   Total rejection of the *Yuwa* policy and patronising policies of the government which are aimed at deceiving *Burakumin* .
    3   Remove the *Buraku* Liberation movement from the list of violent groups.
    4   Oppose all religious teaching which stupefies the spirit of *Buraku* Liberation.
    5   Defend *Buraku* workers politically and economically.'
35. The problem of Takahashi's background is a complex matter. Beckman and Okubo say quite simply 'eldest son of an ex-samurai family' (p 383). Watanabe Toru thinks that if he really had been a *Burakumin* it would have been fairly easy to prove and he would not have left for Moscow before the fifth conference. However, it is suggested by others that his real mother was of *Buraku* origin but that his father divorced her when he learnt of her true status only after she had borne him a son, Sadaki. His father soon remarried, Sadaki was brought up by his stepmother and only later discovered the circumstances of his birth. Nakamura, p 4. Okiura, p 92.
36. *Suihei Undo Shiryo Shusei*, vol I, pp 138-140.
37. *Suihei Undo Shiryo Shusei*, vol I, pp 157-8.

38. *Suihei Undo Shiryo Shusei*, vol III, p 511.
39. *Suihei Undo Shiryo Shusei*, vol II, pp 441-3, 511-2.
40. *Suihei Undoshi no Kenkyu*, vol III, pp 170-1.
41. Fukagawa's articles on which the following is based are: Kaiho Undo Dantai no Gensei (The present state of the Liberation Movement Groups), *Kaiho*, vol 5, no 16 (December 1926), in Koga, pp 184-190. Kodo ni Riron ni Sozo no Suihei Undo (The recent *Suihei* movement) *Kaizo* (June 1929). Koga Seizaburo, *Tokyo Suiheisha to Hikaku Sangyo Rodosha* (The Tokyo *Suiheisha* and workers in the leather industry) (Tokyo Buraku Kenkyukai, 1977), pp 24-28.
42. On 5 June 1926, a meeting to support the *Ronoto* was held in the small town of Takada, Nara prefecture. About 600 people attended, of whom about half were *Burakumin*. Yoneda, p 148.
43. *Suihei Undo Shiryo Shusei*, vol I, pp 145-7. See also *Suihei Undo Shiryo Shusei*, vol II, pp 31, 49-56. Much of the information about the Communist Party activity in what follows comes from the answers given to questions asked by police investigators during the period of interrogation following the arrest of the left wing leaders in March 1928 and April 1929. A selection of documents taken from police records appears pp 30-164.
44. *Suihei Undo Shiryo Shusei*, vol II, pp 32, 56-61.
45. He maintains that although he knew of the existence of the party from January 1927 and worked closely with those who were members he never actually joined the party.
46. *Suihei Undo Shiryo Shusei*, vol II, pp 63-76. Fukumoto Kazuo (1894-19) was the theoretical leader of the reconstituted Communist Party. In his writings he stresses two themes; firstly the party must be composed only of genuine Marxists, no 'reformists' were to be admitted to party membership, neither was the party to seek united left wing alliances. What was required was a vanguard party which would capture the leadership of the proletarian movement when the decisive moment came. This moment was not far off since the struggle against the autocratic system of government was essentially a process of completing the task of the bourgeois revolution which 'will be transformed into a proletarian revolution through an inevitable and inherent dialectical process'. Beckman and Okubo, pp 108-116.
47. *Suihei Undo Shiryo Shusei*, vol I, p 147. In the Kansai area the *Ronoto* candidates received the following support in prefectural elections:

	Votes received	Votes needed for election
Kyoto	1,002	1,671
Osaka	984	1,646
Nara	902	2,083

48. *Suihei Undo Shiryo Shusei*, vol II, pp 78-9. Kitagawa, p 132.
49. For details of the conference debates see *Suihei Undoshi no Kenkyu*, vol III, pp 96-105.
50. Yamagi, *Shakai Undoshi*, p 384.
51. Interview with Imoto, 14 November 1977.
52. Griffin, pp 183-9.
53. Halliday, p 119.
54. Quoted in Mitchell, p 65.
55. Further details about the Peace Preservation Law may be found in Steinhoff, pp 36-40.
56. Between 1928 and 1934 there were 48,545 arrests made under this Act, but in only 8% of these cases (4,066) were formal charges made. This may indicate that it was a 'difficult law to prosecute' or it may simply demonstrate how it was used to harass left wing groups and make sustained activity difficult. Steinhoff, p 6of.
57. Beckman and Okubo, pp 148-9.
58. *Suihei Undo Shiryo Shusei*, vol II, p 81. Saiko was to say later that he did not realise

that this money came from the Party. He thought it was from *Ronoto* funds.

59. *Suihei Undo Shiryo Shusei*, vol II, p 22.
60. Steinhoff, p 92.
61. Mitchell, p 86.
62. Beckman and Okubo, p 156.
63. *Suihei Undo Shiryo Shusei*, vol II, p 440.
64. *Suihei Undoshi no Kenkyu*, vol III, pp 105-7.
65. Miyazaki, p 168.
66. The full text of this leaflet can be found *Suihei Undo Shiryo Shusei*, vol II, pp 24-5.
67. *Suihei Undo Shiryo Shusei*, vol II, p 443.
68. *Suihei Undo Shiryo Shusei*, vol II, p 462.
69. Oyama, p 149.
70. Oyama, pp 154-8.
71. For details of this meeting see *Suihei Undo Shiryo Shusei*, vol II, pp 24-5.
72. *Suihei Undoshi no Kenkyu*, vol III, p 126.
73. *Suihei Undoshi no Kenkyu*, vol III, p 132.
74. *Suihei Undoshi no Kenkyu*, vol III, pp 202-3.
75. To indicate the types of campaigns being pursued in the period 1927-33 I have classified them according to the following types:

Cases of simple verbal insult	16
Cases involving public officials	11
Cases involving use of communal facilities (usually land)	9
Cases involving schools	6
Cases involving the army	6
Cases involving the media	5
Cases associated with factories	4
Cases involving the police	3.

This is a classification of the incidents which are reported in the collections of documents *Suihei Undoshi no Kenkyu* and *Suihei Undo Shiryo Shusei*. Presumably they are the major campaigns undertaken in this six year period.
76. *Suihei Undo Shiryo Shusei*, vol II, pp 523, 596.
77. *Suihei Undoshi no Kenkyu*, vol III, pp 285-297.
78. *Suihei Undoshi no Kenkyu*, vol III, p 339.
79. *Suihei Undoshi no Kenkyu*, vol III, p 298 and *Suihei Undo Shiryo Shusei*, vol II, pp 597-8. It is suggested that one reason for trying to prolong the campaign was that Yoneda and Sakamoto wanted to use it to build support for their anti-headquarters faction.
80. Oyama, pp 169-179.
81. *Suihei Undoshi no Kenkyu*, vol III, p 370.
82. *Suihei Undoshi no Kenkyu*, vol III, p 346.
83. Koga. *Shiryoshu*, pp 122-3.
84. The incident took place in 1928. *Suihei Undoshi no Kenkyu*, vol III, p 344.
85. Hirano certainly seems to have believed this and it seems to have been quite a common notion among the *Suiheisha* leaders and activists within other left wing movements. Koga, *Shiryoshu*, p 31, Akisada Yoshikazu, Buraku Kaiho Undo to Kyosanshugi (*Buraku* Liberation Movement and Communism), *Nihon Shakaishugi Undoshiron* ed Watanabe Toru (Tokyo, Sanichi Shobo, 1973), p 258.
86. *Chugai Nippo*, 22 April 1922, *Suihei*, p 79.
87. The article appeared in *Kaiho*, May 1923, reproduced in *Suihei Undoshi no Kenkyu*, vol II, p 450.

CHAPTER SIX

Yuwa Organisation and *Suiheisha* Theory

At the start of the 1930s the *Suiheisha* was very weak and seemed unlikely to be able to survive as a national organisation; many of its leaders were in prison and reports from both urban and rural areas indicate there was little grass roots activity apart from the occasional *Kyudan* campaign. On the other hand, the *Yuwa* policy had been revised in the later 1920s and the *Yuwa* movement placed under the leadership of one of the prominent right wing politicians. It seemed poised to fill the vacuum left by the rapid decline of the *Suiheisha*.

More money was allocated by the government for the improvement of the *Buraku* environment and living standards and for subsidising the activities of the *Yuwa* groups at all levels. Nevertheless, the *Suiheisha* re-emerged as an important social movement in the period 1933-1937. In the chapters which follow we will seek, firstly, to describe the economic and political background against which this takes place; secondly, to explain the revival of the *Suiheisha* movement and the strengthening of the *Yuwa* policy and, thirdly, to chronicle the series of events which led to the virtual unification of the two movements in the wartime conditions of 1937-1940.

This chapter will begin with an outline of the general political and economic conditions in Japan and a brief look at the living conditions in urban and rural *Buraku*. Then, we will examine the changes which were taking place in the formulation of the *Yuwa* policy at the national level before looking at a few examples of the organisation of the *Yuwa* groups at the local level and assessing their effectiveness. The final and longest section of this chapter will analyse the attempts made by the remaining *Suiheisha* leaders to regenerate their movement by devising a coherent theory which could inform group activity.

Political and Economic Trends – The Political Atmosphere

Many liberal intellectuals and members of the political parties had optimistically interpreted the constitutional developments of the early 1920s as presaging the emergence of a 'Western style' party cabinet system, but by the mid-1930s such optimism had disappeared. Even Minobe Tatsukichi, a prominent liberal constitutional theorist, began to question the desirability of allocating to the parties a central role in government and he started to express doubts as to whether even the Diet had a role as a legislative organ. Hamaguchi Osachi was attacked by a 'patriotic youth' on 14 November 1930 and died the following year; Inukai Tsuyoshi fell victim to a military assassin's bullet on 15 May 1932, bringing the era of party government to an end. Both of these Prime Ministers had sought to maintain the control of the Cabinet over the armed forces – the navy and army respectively – but neither had been successful. When Inukai had sought to implement a policy which would have brought the Manchurian crisis to a speedy conclusion, his Army Minister informed him that the Cabinet's decisions were not necessarily binding on the armed forces and, in spite of Cabinet opposition, the plans to seize southern Manchuria were implemented. For the next four years the government would be led by Admirals – Saito Makoto and Okada Keisuke – for 'an interim period', but by the end of this time neither of the two main political parties had sufficient strength within the political framework nor sufficient support from the public outside to enable them to re-assert their control over events. Once the parties lost their position of power, their prestige dwindled rapidly and it became difficult for them to recruit those with technical expertise, such as bureaucrats and financiers, as they had no tangible rewards which could be distributed among potential recruits and this resulted in further criticism of the low level of expertise of party members. While the prestige of the political parties moved inexorably down this spiral, that of the military and civil bureaucracy increased as they used their position to persuade the masses that only they could deal with the 'Emergency'.

The party leaders themselves lost their enthusiasm for party-centred politics, having neither a theoretical basis from which they could criticise the growth of military and bureaucratic influence, nor a popular base. The parties in the Diet had, at the best of times, operated within a closed world of factional rivalry with only tenuous links with local party organisations. From 1932 the centralisation of the local administrative system undermined what remaining influence these local groups had. At the grass roots level, people regarded the Diet system with disinterest, if not distrust. During the 1920s the parties had claimed that they had a rightful place at the centre of the political system as representatives of the people. They were now rejecting the theoretical implications of such a claim at a time when it was, in any case, ceasing to be true. Now it was the armed forces which were claiming to represent the people. By 1935 the four organisations connected with the reservists' association could claim membership of between eleven and twelve million.[1] On the one hand, these groups were a 'bulwark of national cohesiveness' acting as the local representatives of martial and national values, able to damp down social unrest, and, on the other hand, able to act collectively as a mass patriotic pressure group. On such occasions as the controversy over the London Naval Treaty and during the Manchurian crisis they demonstrated, demanding that the government take a stronger stand, with a fervour that often exceeded that of the army itself. Because of their connections with these bodies the army officers could claim, with some justification, that they were more closely in touch with the people than were the party politicians.

During the time when the parties had been relatively significant within the political framework, they had shown little interest in the problems of the *Burakumin*; now that their influence and prestige were in decline, there was no reason to suppose that the *Suiheisha* should turn to them when there was pressure on them to dissociate themselves from the left wing groups. The Communist Party continued to exert powerful influence over the leaders of the *Suiheisha*. In spite of the arrests of 1928 and 1929, which had resulted in the capture of the Party's leading theoreticians, by 1932 it was re-established with a total membership of 400. However, mass arrests in the autumn of that year destroyed the party organisation completely and no subsequent attempt to re-form the party succeeded. In the years 1931-3 the mass base of the party's potential support was systematically harassed; over 10,000 arrests were made each year on charges relating to alleged contraventions of the Peace Preservation Act. On the university campuses, the threat of arrest created an atmosphere in which,

> fear of prosecution was so great that it established in the students a sharp sense of limits beyond which they must not think rationally.[2]

As the party organisation was destroyed and its potential supporters harassed, its policies were losing credibility. The 're-conversion' (*tenko*) of Sano Manabu and Nabeyama Sadachika was followed by the *tenko* of 35% of those Party members in jail in the first month following and 65% of those awaiting trial in the next six months.[3] The party did not analyse these defections seriously, its only response being to call them traitors and petty-bourgeois elements, but debate over the issues raised by the 're-conversions' divided the remaining sympathisers. Party popularity during the early 1930s was not helped by their insistence on referring to their potential allies in the social democratic movement as 'social fascists'. By the time they did come round to accepting the idea that a united front policy was necessary, they were too few in number and not trusted by any on the left wing to be able to make the policy effective.

The social democratic parties joined forces to form a united Social Masses Party and in the election of 1936 they managed to establish themselves in the Diet having won a sizeable proportion of the popular vote. The presence of a group of 'proletarians' seems to have enlivened the Diet's debates, but they were too few in number and their arrival too late to reverse the process in which the civil bureaucracy and military were increasing their power. In any case, the content of their programmes was changing significantly. Europe had always been the source of inspiration for the social democratic groups. However, in Britain and France the activity of the social democratic movement had declined in the face of economic confusion and in Italy and Germany the left-wing movements had been, or were being, destroyed. Moreover, in a general sense, the mobilisation of the League of Nations to oppose Japan's manoeuvres in Manchuria was presented by the media in a way which discredited the West and Western ideas. From the mid-30s those active in the social democratic movements were turning away from their early ideological sources and were looking towards 'Japanistic' (*nipponshugi*) theories of renovation and Nazi theories of the state and political movements to inform their political activity. As the formerly social democratic groups adopted more rightist policies, by mid-

1938 'leftists and rightists (were) so alike in organisation and tactics it was hard to tell them apart'.[4] With the disappearance of the Communist Party and with little to be gained from association with the established political parties, the *Suiheisha* allied itself with the social democratic groups and ultimately found that it too was forced to adopt a right wing political position supporting the war in Asia and mobilisation at home.

The Economic Environment

These political developments were taking place in the context of profound changes in the Japanese economy. The urbanisation of the country continued; the proportion of the population living in rural areas fell from 82% in 1920 to 67.2% in 1935 while the number of people living in cities with a population of one million and over rose from 6.2% to 16.1%.[5] This process was accompanied by the cartelisation of all major industries. The financial crisis of the late 1920s had wiped out thousands of small businesses while the larger conglomerates like Mitsui and Mitsubishi were able to extend their direct and indirect control over an increasing number of commercial and manufacturing industries. Moreover, from 1932 this process was assisted by the Japanese government which gave financial aid to subsidise further mergers.[6] Whereas previously the bulk of Japan's industrial production had come from light industry, notably textiles, there was more investment in heavy industry. In the period 1930-35, the share of total production which came from heavy industry or chemical production increased from 38.2% to 52.3%.[7] This increase in industrial production resulted from investment in heavy plant which was financed partly by the large corporations and partly by the increase in military expenditure which rose from 406 million yen in 1931 to 1,021 million yen in 1935.[8]

In the wake of this industrial expansion, one might have expected urban living standards especially to rise and the trade union movement which had been growing steadily during the 1920s to expand still further. In fact this does not appear to have been the case. Figures on the cost of living and wages indicate that between 1928 and 1938 there was a slight decline in real wages in manufacturing industries. Further, although the absolute number of unionised workers continued to increase until 1936, the percentage unionisation of the workforce reached a peak of only 8% in 1931. There was little effective co-operation between the unions; three-quarters of them belonged to a nationalistic federation, the remainder divided their support between the centrist (social democratic) and leftist groups. Trade unionists were under the close scrutiny of the special police and were liable to be arrested for any real or suspected 'thought' crime. The number of these special policemen was increased in the Tokyo area from 70 in 1928 to 380 in 1932 with similar expansion taking place elsewhere in the country.[9] Overt suppression of union activity plus the change in political climate which placed increased emphasis on the nation working together to overcome the problems of the national crisis led to a marked reduction in strike activity during the 1930s.

In rural areas in the 1920s the standard of living of most of the peasant farmers had, at best, been frugal, but towards the end of the decade their living conditions declined still further. In the first place, bumper harvests in the years 1927-31 drove prices down to ruinously low levels. Secondly, an important cash element in the income of many peasants came from the sale of silk cocoons. However, due to the world recession, the price of raw silk dropped from a post-war high of 222 in 1925 (1914 = 100) to 151 in 1929 and 67 in 1931,[10] thus further reducing peasant income. So low were the living standards in many rural areas that the health of the young conscript soldiers seems to have been adversely affected and army officers and the reserve associations urged the government to take some measures to assist the peasants. Measures to stabilise the price of rice were introduced in 1932-3 and a reformed rice control system was instituted in 1936; government assistance was also given to ease the burden of debt on the peasant farmer.[11] These measures made real improvements, but were unable to restore living standards to their 1920s level.

Peasant unions had been particularly active in the south-west of Japan where the drift of young men to the cities had reduced the amount of competition for land which enabled peasants to demand lower rents with less fear of reprisals. However, during the 1930s the movement was forced to drop these aggressive demands and adopt more defensive tactics. The recession in industry had cut off the means of escape from rural life and, since the government paid the laid off workers their fare home in an attempt to reduce the number of urban unemployed, many peasant families found their already depleted earnings had to support more dependants. Despite this, there were twice as many tenancy disputes from 1932 to 1941 as there had been from 1917 to 1931. However, there were three important differences in the nature of these campaigns. In the first place, the number of people involved in each dispute dropped significantly and the total land area concerned was much smaller. Secondly, the type of dispute had changed considerably; in the 1920s most of the disputes centred round demands for a reduction in rent, in the latter period a large number of the disputes were in opposition to attempts by the landlords to evict existing tenants in order to lease the land to new tenants or farm it themselves. Thirdly, and perhaps most significantly for our study, whereas until the late 1920s most of the disputes had taken place in the west or south-west of Japan – areas where there was a relatively high concentration of *Burakumin* – during the 1930s the disputes tended to occur more in the east and north-east, there being a marked decline in peasant activity in the Kinki area.[12]

Living conditions in the Buraku

Having produced a general sketch of the political and economic context within which the *Suiheisha* operated in the 1930s, let us now consider the conditions which existed in the *Buraku* communities. A 1933 survey estimated the average income of farming households at 727 yen p.a.; but according to the same survey, it was less than half this in the *Buraku*: 304 yen.[13] However, surveys in some rural prefectures indicate incomes much lower than this. It is reported that in Okayama, for instance, the average income of the *Buraku* communities was 137 yen p.a. compared to an average of 283 yen p.a. in the neighbouring communities (and in one village the difference was 52 yen: 239 yen).[14] Fewer peasants owned their own land and the average size of landholdings was smaller. The Okayama report indicates 7.0 *tan* in the non-*Buraku* and 3.6 *tan* in the *Buraku* compared to the national average of 10.5 *tan* and 4.2. These rural *Buraku* were very badly affected by the recession of the late 1920s, their small landholdings making them particularly vulnerable to market fluctuations. Conditions in many rural *Buraku* were described as the worst in living memory.[15]

Poverty in the rural *Buraku* communities encouraged migration to the towns and cities, especially after 1930, and yet conditions in the urban *Buraku*, where migrant *Burakumin* would usually find themselves, were bad and getting worse. A survey of conditions in Kyoto in 1938 found that only 57% of those living within the *Buraku* areas had been born there and over 60% who had moved into the *Buraku* had migrated since 1932.[16] Further, we are told that the rate of migration into Kyoto was not as high as in other cities.[17] Another survey, taken in 1932, found that 42.5% of *Buraku* were 'poor', earning less than 45 yen a month, compared to 2.7% in the rest of the city excluding the six *Buraku*.[18] Many small *Buraku* enterprises were forced out of business in the period 1927-33, notably small scale tanning and leather industries. Moreover, those in 'new' *Buraku* occupations, like rickshaw men, were facing unemployment, forced out of business by motorised transport such as the train and bus. For these reasons, *Burakumin* became more reliant on finding day labour outside the *Buraku*, but this increased their vulnerability to economic recession and to instances of discrimination. In 1932, one third of *Burakumin* labourers were employed for fewer than 15 days a month.[19] Wages paid to *Buraku* labourers were much lower than the national average: about 66 *sen* compared to a normal day wage of 1.42 yen.[20] Between 1927/8 and 1938/9, when two surveys were carried out in Kyoto, the number of families earning less than 20 yen a month increased from 4% to almost 40%.[21]

Housing conditions reflected this increasing poverty. In 1927/8 the population density of the six Kyoto *Buraku* was already six times that of the surrounding areas, but despite this the population increased by 15% in the next ten years. Although some money was provided to improve housing, in all but one of the six communities the proportion of housing officially described as inadequate increased and reached 96-99% of the total.[22] Competition for scarce housing caused rents to rise despite deteriorating conditions so that a growing number of families began to pay rent daily rather than monthly. Water supply and drainage were inadequate and most families shared toilet facilities with the result that contagious diseases spread rapidly. The incidence of tubercular and similar diseases was high and more than 40% of children suffered from trachoma compared to 3% in the rest of the population.[23]

In other words, despite ten years of *Suiheisha* agitation and *Yuwa* policy, not only did the conditions in the *Buraku* lag a long way behind those in the majority communities in both urban and rural areas but, especially in the cities, the gap between the two was actually widening. Despite the general revival of the economy by the mid-1930s high unemployment and abject poverty in the *Buraku* continued until at least 1937-38.[24] The developments in the *Suiheisha* movement, then, take place in a general context of reduced activity of those in the worker and peasant movements and against a background of falling living standards for most *Burakumin*. One of the major themes of the theoretical and practical struggles that took place within the movement was to find some way in which they could explain the reasons for this downward spiral process and find a way to reverse the trend. However, before we can discuss how the movement set about doing this we must consider the developments in and the effects of the *Yuwa* programme.

Yuwa Policy in the early 1930s

Although it is difficult to demonstrate a clear link, it is surely no coincidence that at the same time the Japanese state was clamping down on the activities of *Suiheisha* leaders steps were also being taken to persuade *Burakumin* that the state was also interested in improving their lot within the bounds of existing social structures. The first steps towards the development of a coherent policy had been taken in the mid-1920s when the various *Yuwa* groups active at the national level were merged into one under the control of the Home Ministry (*Naimusho*). Then, in early 1928, the Central *Yuwa* Project Council (*Chuo Yuwa Jigyo Kyokai*) was established and a policy document was produced which urged more people to become involved in the projects which were designed to remove prejudice and realise equality of opportunity. In its first year the Central *Yuwa* Project Council planned two events. A national *Yuwa* day was to be held on November 3, the anniversary of the birthday of the *Meiji* emperor who had emancipated the *eta:hinin* from their status restrictions. An enormous effort was expended in publicising the *Yuwa* message on this day; an estimated eleven and a half million leaflets and pamphlets were produced and meetings held in over 500 towns and villages.[25]

Secondly, in order to co-ordinate and encourage the activities of those involved in *Yuwa* projects or *Yuwa* groups, a national *Yuwa* conference was held in mid-December 1928. In some respects the discussions of the 431 delegates were similar to those of the early *Suiheisha* conferences. They discussed how instances of discrimination should be dealt with; how discrimination could be removed from within the education system; and it was even proposed that the family registration law be revised to make it more difficult to ascertain an individual's past social status.[26] There was some criticism of government policy and it was proposed that more money should be released for use on *Yuwa* projects; it was pointed out that the government had spent huge sums rescuing some of the larger banks from collapse though it spent very little assisting the poor. However, as well as those critical, liberal voices there were others, probably a majority who emphasised the need to enact policies which would prevent the spread of 'dangerous thought' which was weakening the *kokutai*.

This latter sentiment was more pronounced at the second national *Yuwa* conference held just over two years later in February 1931. Though as many as 31 motions were discussed in the course of the proceedings, the underlying theme was what form the *Yuwa* policy should adopt in the light of the political and economic crises which were overtaking Japan. Once more there was some criticism of government policy. It was pointed out that much of the *Yuwa* money was spent by *Yuwa* groups and organisations while very little went to provide *Burakumin* with the assistance they so clearly needed. There were specific suggestions that central government and local authorities should do more to improve facilities in the *Buraku* and create, for example, apprentice training schemes.[27] Many delegates were concerned that measures continued to be taken to minimise the influence of the *Suiheisha* and leftist thought; specifically it was suggested that more energy be directed towards the political education of *Burakumin* to prevent them from being used by the proletarian parties.[28] Some in the *Yuwa* movement were beginning to realise that without a change in the attitudes of the wider society, no matter how much money was spent, the position of *Burakumin* would change very little. At the same time, there were others who argued it was equally important to acquire a better understanding of the roots of prejudice and its role within twentieth century Japan. No conclusions emerged from these discussions, but several delegates called for more 'scientific' research into the *Buraku* problem.[29]

However, if there is some evidence that at the national level there was genuine concern for the plight of *Burakumin* and a desire to resolve some of their problems, the dominant trend was for the *Yuwa* project administration and *Yuwa* groups to be consolidated into one administrative network under central government control. Indeed, there is abundant evidence which supports the criticisms of both *Yuwa* and *Suiheisha* activists that very little of the money spent on *Yuwa* projects benefited *Burakumin*, and that often *Yuwa* projects were little more than an extension of the state security apparatus.

In Hiroshima, for example, following the reorganisation of *Yuwa* groups in the prefecture in 1928 a *Yuwa* Project Committee was established in Takasaka village, Toyoda *gun*. The mayor and his deputy occupied the top two positions with the rest of the committee being composed of headteachers, police, priests and local government officials. It received funds from both the prefecture and the village – 75 yen from each – but in 1928 most of this money was used for official expenses, 26 yen was used to finance a series of lectures and only 10 yen was spent on improving facilities in the *Buraku* community.[30] Only in 1932 when central government began to provide funds for the relief of poverty did this committee begin to organise improvement programmes.

Large amounts of money had been provided by prefectural and local government in Mie for the various improvement projects during the 1920s, but no attempt had been made to establish a network of *Yuwa* groups in the region. In 1934 steps were taken to remedy the situation. In that year an organisation calling itself the *Kyoaikai* (Mutual Love Association) was established with the support of the prefectural Social Affairs Bureau and the local branch of the 'special police'. The society promised to take a lead in improving educational facilities and living standards in the *Buraku*. At early meetings talks were given by police officers on the need for a *Yuwa* programme and, perhaps because these lectures did not attract large audiences, in September the police visited factories in the area in order to persuade *Burakumin* to take a more active part in *Yuwa* group activities.. In an attempt to demonstrate their sincerity they even persuaded a spinning mill to employ seven *Buraku* girls. But the society was not just interested in supporting the *Yuwa* programme, it was also used by the police to supervise the activities of former *Suiheisha* activists. This became clear in November 1934 when 13 *Suiheisha* members who had been arrested the previous March were released from prison, the charges against them suspended. The police seem to have regarded their decision to join the *Kyoaikai* as proof of their '*tenko*'. Their release may even have been conditional on their joining this group. One concludes that the 'special police' participation in the *Kyoaikai* was to enable them to keep an eye on potential subversives.[31]

This pattern seems to have been repeated across the country wherever there were *Buraku* communities. Where *Yuwa* groups had been formed without official support in the early 1920s, by 1930 they nearly all had been brought under the control of government officials. In part this was no doubt the product of a desire to take the initiative away from the *Suiheisha* at a time when the movement had been weakened by the arrests of its leaders and internal disagreement. But it was also one more manifestation of the general expansion of the power of the bureaucracy which was occurring in all sectors of Japanese society at this time. Still, it did seem that for the first time the state had accepted that it had some responsibility to improve conditions in the *Buraku*. No doubt the officials actually involved in implementing improvement projects, some of whom may have been *Burakumin* themselves, were genuinely concerned to do all that was possible to minimise prejudice and discrimination. Nevertheless, despite these attempts to demonstrate the government's genuine concern, there was no response to the demands made at the *Yuwa* conferences to introduce measures to make discrimination illegal and to change the family registration laws to make it more difficult to investigate an individual's status origin. Even such moves would not, of course, have removed discrimination at a stroke, but they would have demonstrated that the government was prepared to take a lead and it might have contributed somewhat to reversing the downward spiral of prejudice → discrimination → poverty → prejudice.

No such imaginative moves were made. The dominant trend in all aspects of Japanese economic and social life was towards strengthening its corporate character. The *zaibatsu* were increasing their hold over the economy; militaristic control over the lives and minds, especially of the rural villagers, was increasing through the extension of the activities of the reservist associations; the liberal ideas of intellectuals and party leaders were eclipsed with the rise in prestige of the military and civil bureaucracy. *Burakumin* had been little affected by the attempts to develop a strong national consciousness; the *Yuwa* policy can be seen as an attempt to remedy this and bring them into a system of state control. Hence, despite all the rhetoric, the increased emphasis placed on building an administrative framework occurred at the expense of making real improvements and in the absence of legislative measures which would positively reduce discrimination. Throughout the rest of the decade, the *Yuwa* movement was to be developed as a means of social control.

The Suiheisha in Search of a Theory

Following the eighth national *Suiheisha* conference held in Nagoya (1929), one reliable observer remarked of the *Suiheisha* movement,

> two general tendencies are observable
> 1 the internal division which marked the preceding period has materially lessened so that unity in policy at least in form is apparent and that, as a result,
> 2 there are indications of a tendency for the *Suiheisha* to enter the political arena with a united front.[32]

However, the movement was facing several major problems. In the first place, most of the movement's branches had ceased to be active and had stopped holding meetings locally or making any financial or other contributions to the prefectural or national committees. This led to major financial problems and the movement was unable to pay even its immediate bills such as rent for the office or payment for the telephone. A general awareness of these problems provoked many of the movement's activists to seek a way to reverse the decline. It was clear to many that this could only come about from the framing of a theory which would indicate new developments in the movement's practice. But where was the movement to look for guidance? By now, most of the leaders realised that the movement for *Buraku* liberation had several unique aspects which meant that it was unable to borrow and adopt tactics used by other left wing groups in the world in the same way as the peasants and working class movements could. Nor could they expect much guidance from those active in other social movements within Japan. Though they might find useful hints on what sort of theory and tactics might be appropriate, ultimately the only way they could discover if ideas were suitable was to try them out. The corollary of this argument was (and still is) that no one outside the movement may criticise its tactics. This latter point was not immediately apparent, but throughout the changes made in the movement's theories in the following few years the constant theme is the search for a theoretical framework whose practical implementation would lead to the revival of the movement.[33]

Dissolution Proposed

So, at the same time as the *Yuwa* movement was reorganising itself and its members were starting to enquire why discrimination continued to exist in Japanese society, a similar process and similar debates were occurring within the *Suiheisha*. The theoretical perspectives were, however, quite distinct. Critics of the *Yuwa* leaders were liberals, while those who were critical of the *Suiheisha* leadership derived their ideas from Marxism-Leninism.

Despite the arrests of 1928 and 1929, Marxist ideas still circulated quite freely in Japan as the Communist Party slowly began to rebuild its organisation. There do not seem to have been any party members in the *Suiheisha* at the start of the 1930s, but Asada Zennosuke, formerly of the anarchist tendency, was reading such Marxist journals as *International, Marxism* and *The Worker* as well as participating in the activities of the local branch of *Sohyo*.[34] And the influence of Asada and others of his persuasion was growing within the *Suiheisha* movement. At the ninth conference, held in Osaka in December 1930, the discussion on the reasons for the movement's weakness was conducted almost entirely in terms which derived from Marxist sources. One major obstacle to establishing the *Suiheisha* as a mass movement was, it was argued, that working conditions inside the *Buraku* were still 'semi-feudal' in that the workers relied both socially and economically on the factory owner. Moreover, those who found work outside the *Buraku* were day labourers rather than regular employees and thus were a 'lumpen proletarian element'. Neither the bourgeoisie nor the lumpen proletariat could be relied on in the class struggle. In order to develop into a reliable mass movement, the *Suiheisha* must demonstrate to its membership the 'material basis of discrimination'. Thus far none of its campaigns had affected the material and social roots of discrimination which lay in the feudal and semi-feudal present in Japanese society. The concrete manifestation of this discrimination was the extreme poverty in which most *Burakumin* lived. But *Burakumin* were not alone in this since both workers and peasants were being impoverished by the development of capitalism. A strong mass organisation would be able to co-operate with the workers' and peasants' organisations to effect the overthrow of the already weakening monopoly capitalist system.[35]

Reflecting this new, radical analysis, several proposals were made for changes in the Basic Principles. After discussion within the central committee, it was decided to remove the section which referred to demands for 'total economic freedom and freedom of occupation' and replace it with,

> We, *Tokushu Burakumin*, desire to recover the right to live and to acquire political freedom.[36]

Clearly, the influence of the Marxists such as Asada and later Kitahara was on the increase, though the movement continued to be supported by such moderates as Sakamoto and Yoneda.

During the next twelve months Asada continued his attempts to develop a rigorous analysis of the *Buraku* problem, being strongly influenced by publications which originated in the Soviet Union. Early in 1931 he came across a ten-page article entitled, 'The role of the revolutionary trade union movement in Japan', which was based on resolutions passed at the Fifth Profintern conference held the previous August. Its central argument is that the trade unions should aim to build a united proletarian front from below in order to encourage class struggle and defend themselves against 'white terror, fascism and social fascism'. In particular, there were two sentences which caught Asada's eye,

> ... left-wing trade unions must take the initiative in the struggle against relationships which split the working masses into antagonistic groups, against exclusionism, against insolent attitudes towards Chinese, Korean or Taiwanese workers, and against all forms of social prejudice. Revolutionary trade unions, unlike the reactionary or moderate unions, must unite with workers of all races.[37]

Then, in April 1931, the Communist Party issued a draft set of 'Political Theses' which were intended to act as a guide for the activity of its members over the subsequent years. Comintern strategy towards Japan was somewhat ambiguous due to the confusion which surrounded the fall of Bukharin and the rise of Stalin and because of the paradoxical way Japan was regarded as a potentially fascist state despite the fact that its bourgeois revolution was incomplete. Nevertheless, it was argued that the only way to resolve the various class contradictions was by establishing a 'united front from below based on the idea of class struggle'.[38]

Asada tried to apply these general guidelines in his analysis of the problems of the *Burakumin*. Quite simply, his conclusion was that the *Suiheisha* only served to perpetuate divisions within the working class movement and thus was fulfilling a reactionary role. Therefore, the *Suiheisha* should disband and its members give their individual support to the peasant or proletarian movement as appropriate.

It should not be thought that this was an eccentric interpretation of Comintern policy. At the same time, trade unions set up by and for Koreans working in Japan were under pressure to disband and join the relevant Japanese union. The Korean Workers League agreed to disband in October 1930, and twelve months later the Tokyo branch of the Korean Communist Party was dissolved and Koreans resident in Japan were encouraged to join the Japanese Communist Party.[39] Moreover there were others in Japan who were developing similar ideas. Kitahara Daisaku, after his release from the army, moved to live in Tokyo where he joined the local *Suiheisha* and for a short time studied at *Nihon Daigaku* (Japan University). At this time he came across members of the Communist Party and, though he did not become a member until April 1933, he was strongly influenced by Comintern policy. In March 1931 he became one of the five full time workers in the *Suiheisha* office and thus exerted considerable influence on the movement's policy.[40]

A few days before the tenth conference convened in Nara in December 1931, Asada, Kitahara and a couple of others met in Kyoto to discuss their ideas and write a leaflet to be distributed at the conference. During the first part of the actual conference proceedings it became clear that this group which was sympathetic to the Communist Party line was exerting strong sway over the course of the debates. For example, it was proposed that the *Suiheisha* should co-operate with other working class organisations to oppose the 'evil laws' such as the Peace Preservation Law, though it was made clear that such joint activity should not include co-operation with 'social fascist' groups. There was even a motion introduced which condemned the imperialist war in Manchuria, although the police who were supervising the meeting would not permit it to be discussed. On the other hand, there was substantial discussion of more mundane issues such as the publication of a newspaper and ways to generate more income for the movement. Debate on the movement's policy document was heated. In the version which was finally accepted, conference committed the movement to raising the class consciousness in the *Buraku*, clarifying the basis of discrimination, exposing the deceptive nature of the *Yuwa* policy and demonstrating the real significance of the imperialist war.[41]

In a sense, the debate which followed only developed these ideas to their logical conclusion. Imoto Rinshi, of the Kyushu federation, proposed that the *Suiheisha* should disband and its members join the appropriate worker or peasant union. Already a leaflet, written by Asada and Kitahara but bearing Imoto's name, had been circulated to all at the conference. It began by noting that the *Suiheisha* was inactive on all fronts and that there was an obvious need to reorganise the struggle. But, the leaflet argues, the only possible way forward is in co-operation with the workers and peasant movements for there can be no *Buraku* liberation without the liberation of the proletariat as a whole. The *Suiheisha* had developed as a mass organisation on the basic premise that *all Burakumin* are brothers and *all* non-*Burakumin*, whether workers or capitalists, peasants or landlords, are real or potential enemies. This led to 'exclusivist' theories and indiscriminate tactics of total censure which cut the *Suiheisha* off from contact with the other proletarian groups. Most workers and peasants within the *Suiheisha* divide their energy between status struggles and class struggles, but, since the roots of discrimination lie deep within the 'semi-feudal' capitalist system, status prejudice can only be removed by the total overthrow of this system which will be achieved following the heightening of the class struggle. Status struggles which direct energy away from the class battlefront are thus an obstacle to progress toward the proletarian revolution. Moreover, the *Suiheisha* contention that *Burakumin* can be liberated within the capitalist system supports the ruling class position and is not much different from the attitude of the *Yuwa* movement. The pamphlet points out the tendencies which existed in the movement to support the 'fascists' and gives as an example the formation of the Kanto *Yuwa* Promotion League composed of former *Suiheisha* activists, and it warns equally of the dangers of the parliamentarianism of the 'social fascist' groups. It ends calling for members to reject the social democrats and fight for a revolutionary class consciousness and a movement led by the proletariat.[42]

In his speech in support of the dissolution resolution Imoto repeated many of the arguments outlined in the leaflet. The only reason that the *Suiheisha* movement had not played an even more reactionary role was that it was closely connected to the workers' and peasants' movements. To prevent the *Suiheisha* movement being used by the ruling class against other sections of the proletarian movement, it should dissolve itself.

Not surprisingly, the *Suiheisha* headquarters faction strongly opposed these suggestions. One of the central committee argued that the *Suiheisha* had a positive role to play as a mass organisation and that these young theorists were simply indulging in 'left-wing infantilism'. Nevertheless, they won the support of a large group at the conference and the debate became so heated that the police threatened to disperse the meeting.[43] The matter was referred to the central committee for further consideration.

Dissolution Considered

From the time of the arrests in the late 1920s, the *Suiheisha* movement had been divided into two groupings, one, based on the Osaka-Kyoto activists, remained close to the Marxist grouplets and favoured the adoption of what, by this time, were 'illegal' tactics, the other, more moderate, group got its main support from the Kyushu federation and favoured 'legal' tactics. Throughout the 1920s the *Suiheisha* groups had been closely connected with the peasants' movement and when, in 1931, it split between those who supported the social democrats – the *Zenno* – and those whose allegiance lay with the illegal Communist Party this division was reflected within the *Suiheisha* movement. Furthermore, many of those who in the 1920s had actively supported the anarchist tendency, in the 1930s were giving their support to the social democrats. Typical of these was Fukugawa Takeshi, leader of the Tokyo *Suiheisha* group, and member of the national central committee. It will be remembered that, from as early as 1927, Fukugawa had been critical of the Bolshevik tendency and had predicted that, if their ideas were developed to their logical conclusion, they would recommend the dissolution of the movement. Now that the movement's Marxist sympathisers were proposing precisely this, Fukugawa lined up with the social democratic group. Most influential of this group was Matsumoto Jiichiro, who had been in prison since April 1929 and was not released until two weeks after the tenth conference. On his return to the *Suiheisha* office, he was not at all pleased to discover that the dissolution proposal had been issued in the name of the Kyushu federation. This division immanent within the movement came out into the open in the course of the first few months of 1932.

There were important questions of theory which emerged in the dissolution controversy which exacerbated the *Suiheisha*'s internal dissension, but it could scarcely have happened at a more inopportune time. *Kyudan* – protest against discrimination – continued to take place, but police estimates indicated that within the previous twelve months there had been a large drop in the size of the

movement's active supporters. The dissolution issue, deferred by the conference, was discussed at the central committee meeting held in March 1932.
However, Matsumoto proposed that a decision of such importance should not be
taken lightly or hastily and that they had better further defer the decision for
consideration at the next committee meeting. Matsumoto refused to attend this
meeting held in July and the dissolution issue was again deferred for discussion
at the next conference.[44] It was quite possible that the movement might have
collapsed before the conference took place; only the regular monthly contributions of 50 yen from Matsumoto kept it solvent. It had been proposed at the July
meeting that the next conference should be held in Osaka the following
December. However, in September two of the three standing committee
members left the office in Osaka for home, leaving just Nishida from the
Fukuoka group to keep the movement's affairs ticking over. It was clear there
was no chance of holding a conference that year: so, on 30 November it was
decided that the conference would be held early the following year in Fukuoka
where Matsumoto would pay most of the expenses. There were only four
attending this meeting and two of them were prevented from resigning only by
Matsumoto's persuasion.[45]

At a time when the central group was scarcely able to keep the movement in
existence at a minimal level, the dissolutionist group launched a campaign
throughout central Japan to attract support for their ideas. The supporters of the
anti-headquarters faction met in Kyoto in March and May 1932 to discuss how
they would organise themselves and at the second meeting they announced they
were to be known as the *Zensui Kaisho Toso Iinkai* (National *Suiheisha*
Dissolution Struggle Committee); they published a pamphlet critical of the
headquarters faction and planned the production of a monthly news sheet which
would publicise the progress of their cause. Police reports indicate that by the
end of the year they had support from as many as 4,300 individuals in 51 different
groups.[46] As their influence developed they formed strong links with the *Zenkyo*
and *Zenno* National Congress groups – the Communist Party oriented workers'
and peasants' organisations. Joint meetings were organised to discuss both the
problems of discrimination and the wider issues which confronted the working
class movement as a whole. In some areas the dissolutionist groups even
distributed *Sekki*, the Communist Party newspaper, but such close connections
made the movement vulnerable to police harassment, and in the course of the
year 115 were arrested of whom 43 were later charged.[47]

However, while these groups were trying to establish a strong faction within
the *Suiheisha* in order to ensure the movement's formal dissolution at the next
conference, the Comintern issued a new set of 'Theses on the Situation in Japan
and the tasks of the Communist Party' which corrected some of the 'mistakes' in
the Profintern's advice and the draft theses of 1931. It was now asserted that the
'forthcoming revolution . . . (would be) . . . a bourgeois-democratic revolution
with a tendency to grow rapidly into a socialist revolution'.[48] Within this new
framework, the struggle against 'feudal' elements was considered to be playing a

positive role in clearing the way for this bourgeois-democratic revolution and thus the *Suiheisha*, rather than dividing the proletarian movement, was in fact playing an important part in the struggle which would lead to a full socialist revolution. These new theses made the activities of the dissolution group redundant but, Asada maintains, it was not simply the change in theoretical leadership which led them to abandon their ideas. They had hoped that by linking up with an 'objective' movement like the peasant movement, the progressive elements in both organisations would be encouraged to assert their influence, but when they tried to put their ideas into practice they began to realise that the workers' and peasants' movements were so divided into different factions that close co-operation of the kind they had envisaged was not a practical possibility.[49] Thus, it was because the new ideas had proved impractical as well as because they had been countermanded by revised party policy that the group abandoned their dissolution plan.

On 20 February 1933, shortly before the eleventh conference, the members of the dissolutionist group met to reconsider their position. They admitted that they had underestimated the role of the *Suiheisha* in the revolutionary struggle and overestimated the imminence of the revolution which had made dissolution such an urgent issue. Nevertheless, they produced a pamphlet which urged total opposition to the 'feudal' elements within capitalism which supported the continued existence of prejudice and discrimination against *Burakumin*. At the subsequent conference and over the next few years members of this group agitated to encourage the development of a consolidated theory which would generate tactics to make the movement relevant to the struggles of the *Buraku* masses in their everyday life and which would encourage them to take their place in the wider class struggle. Although there had been debates before in which issues of principle were important, until the dissolution proposal there had been no attempt to formulate a theoretical framework in which the *Burakumin* struggles were explained and encouraged. An understanding of how the new theory developed and its major premises is important if we are to explain the revival of the movement and, though it is outside the scope of this work, the theoretical issues debated in the 1930s have considerable significance in the post-war liberation movement. In the next few pages we will attempt to describe the development of this theory and explain its content.

Buraku Iinkai Katsudo

Although the overwhelming majority of the 158 delegates at the eleventh conference were from Fukuoka or Kyushu, which might have enabled Matsumoto and the moderate group to dominate the conference, the debates and documents seem rather to reflect the ideas of the more radical tendency. Four major motions were debated and passed; 'fascism' in Japan which supported the imperialist war in China was to be opposed, as was the 'social fascism' of the social democrat groups who gave their tacit approval to imperialism; consumer unions were to be organised as a practical means of alleviating the poverty caused by the economic recession and inflation; they agreed to support the Japan Proletarian Cultural Movement which would raise the level of consciousness of the culturally and politically backward *Buraku* masses;[50] they also agreed to take a positive role in the Japan Workers' Relief Society, a non-party organisation which assisted workers' and peasants' groups with their legal and medical problems. As was to be expected, the main debate was over the new struggle policy and the conference declaration. The former issue was referred to the central committee and the declaration was eventually passed as proposed by the central committee.[51] The following day (4 March) a mass meeting was held to commemorate the movement's ten years of activity. All the speakers mentioned the need for co-operation with the workers' and peasants' movements and in the major speech Matsumoto declared that it was the aim of the *Suiheisha* to create a society in which there was neither discrimination nor exploitation and that the *Suiheisha* would continue as long as either existed.[52] The committee met the same day. After selecting new delegates, it was decided that the headquarters office which had temporarily been transferred to Fukuoka would be re-established in Osaka and a new policy document was accepted.[53] In May, the committee met again to formulate policies on how the anti-fascist struggle and the unification of the movement were to be carried out. It was resolved to restart the newspaper, though this was not carried out and Matsumoto agreed to donate 300 yen required to maintain the office in Osaka. In general, public meetings would be held and leaflets produced in order to promote the policies of the *Buraku Iinkai Katsudo* and oppose the government's *Yuwa* policy.[54]

The *Buraku Iinkai Katsudo* (*Buraku* Committee Activity) was a strategy devised by the leftist tendency within the *Suiheisha* in the aftermath of the abandonment of their dissolution proposals. Though the content of the proposals derived directly from the experiences of the activists in the *Buraku* struggles in the previous ten years, the main inspiration for the framework of the proposals came from the *Nomin Iinkai Katsudo* which had been developed by the Communist Party oriented *Zenno* National Congress group.[55] The basic format of the ideas emerged at the eleventh conference; then, in the following year, they were developed until they were set out in a statement in July 1934.[56]

The main author of the statement was Kitahara Daisaku, who though he had been one of the protagonists in the dissolution debate had retained his position as a full-time worker in the Osaka office. He became a Communist Party member in April 1933 at a time when the Party was trying to recover from the devastating series of arrests of the previous autumn and he was set the task of establishing a faction group which would place the *Suiheisha* under Party control. As a first step towards this, he began to distribute *Sekki* (Red Flag) among *Suiheisha* members. As we shall see, all activity in the summer and autumn of 1933 revolved around the Takamatsu campaign and Kitahara was at the centre of this, but he went underground after hearing of the arrests of Imoto and Matsuda in October. Then he moved to Tokyo, where he hid in the house of Yamamoto Masao, one of the more liberal of the *Yuwa* programme administrators.

In his spare time here, he prepared a series of theses on the status struggle in which he attempted to formulate a theoretical foundation for the *Suiheisha*'s activities based on the ideas outlined in the '1932 theses'. But a more influential document which was written at the same time and based on the same principles was the pamphlet '*Buraku Iinkai Katsudo ni tsuite*' (About the *Buraku* Committee Activities). While in Tokyo, he had managed to maintain contact with the Party leaders and on 30 December he left the metropolis for Kyushu, where he intended to expound his ideas on how the movement should develop and establish *Sekki* readers' discussion groups which would form the basis for the revival of the Party. Unfortunately these plans were never fulfilled as he was arrested in Fukuoka on 28 January.

The pamphlet he had written was finally published in July 1934 in the name of Imoto Rinshi. It seems to follow the original statement very closely although Kitahara now claims that it was altered without his knowledge by Imoto and/or Asada. In fact, the pamphlet itself was banned by the government and was never allowed to be circulated, but it still is worthy of attention as it was the crystallisation of the ideas held by those active in the campaigns in the period 1933 to 1936 and helps to explain both how and why the movement was able to develop so rapidly in these years.

The first of the pamphlet's sections discusses the world economic crisis, noting that only Soviet Russia had been unaffected by it, and that while Japan's economy had been revived by the increased military spending following the outbreak of war in China the workers in both factories and fields suffer beneath 'colonial-like exploitation'. Although all sections of the working population suffer beneath this exploitation, in rural areas the *Burakumin* farm smaller areas of poorer land, while in the towns, despite the rapid development of capitalism as a whole, the tiny factories in the *Buraku* tend to use antiquated methods and be run on feudal *oyabun-kobun* lines. Thus, *Buraku* are said to suffer beneath both feudal status oppression and capitalist colonial-like exploitation. After a description of the emergence of the *Suiheisha* and a review of the development of the *Yuwa* policy, comes the key section entitled, 'The significance and function of the *Buraku Iin Katsudo*'. Here it is explained that a basic requirement is to revise the tactics of the *Kyudan* struggle so that, on the one hand, it becomes part of the wider struggle undermining the base of the Bourgeois-Landlord-Emperor system, which is the core of the feudal status network that fetters *Burakumin* in all aspects of their social life. On the other hand, each protest against a specific instance of discrimination must contain concrete demands for the provision of facilities which will raise the cultural and economic levels of the *Buraku* communities. The *Meiji* bourgeois revolution did not destroy all the feudal structure but used some of that which remained to build up a new power structure – for example, the upper segments of the old ruling class were awarded the equivalent of several million yen in compensation for their loss of feudal privileges and around them a new status system was erected. At the other end of the status hierarchy, another feudal remnant were the 'special' *Buraku* who, though formally liberated, were given no cash grants which might have enabled them to overcome the results of centuries of formal discrimination. Thus, they were not able to take part in the process of modernisation with the result that they are now subject to the same obligations as the rest of the citizenry but have none of the benefits. The reason for the existence of the 'special' *Buraku* is the '*special*', feudal nature of Japanese capitalism – the relationship between the two is likened to that of the light bulb and the generator – and thus it is the whole system which is to be opposed. When protesting about incidents of discrimination the *Suiheisha* must be careful to distinguish between those members of oppressed and exploited groups who, deceived by the divisive ruling class policy, discriminate against *Burakumin* and those incidents which involve intellectuals, bureaucrats and other minions of the ruling class. Each *Kyudan* campaign must encourage the unity of all oppressed people while, at the same time, indicating the severely impoverished state of the *Burakumin* and making clear the connection between this state of affairs and the feudal nature of Japanese capitalism.

Perhaps the most important innovation is the insistence that *Suiheisha* activity should not simply revolve around protest against discrimination. Groups must form committees (*iinkai*) whose activity (*katsudo*) must centre on the needs of the *Burakumin* themselves. At the lowest level this means helping to sort out domestic problems, medical problems and tax payment, giving advice on contraception, loans and legal problems and writing letters for people. From this basis, groups could form consumer unions to purchase such essential foodstuffs as rice, *miso* and *shoyu* in bulk. Then, with a thorough knowledge of the real needs of the *Buraku* communities, the *Buraku Iinkai* can effectively oppose the deceptive *Yuwa* policy while demanding the state finance real improvements which will materially benefit the lives of ordinary *Burakumin*. In particular, the *Iinkai* are to prevent the misuse of *Yuwa* money on schemes designed to bolster the authority of the local *Buraku* bosses. Furthermore, *Burakumin* are encouraged to play an active role in local politics, to participate in elections and, once having achieved positions of influence, must take care to act on behalf of not only those active in the *Suiheisha* but of all the *Buraku* masses. By winning the confidence of the *Buraku* masses in the fight to improve the quality of their everyday lives, the movement will be able to mobilise them in the wider class struggle which has the long term political aims of overthrowing the capitalist system in Japan.[57]

Until the tenth conference, held in December 1931, there had been little attempt to define the '*Buraku* Problem' or analyse the nature of discrimination within the context of Japanese capitalism. Most *Burakumin* had had a poor education (if any) and the level of political consciousness was generally so low that in the early years the *Suiheisha* groups had been little more than 'left wing gangs'.[58] From the time of the fifth conference, the movement's activities had begun to approach some of the political problems although the anarchist/Bolshevik debate never developed much theoretical depth. The first attempt to confront the basic theoretical problems came when Asada and Kitahara tried to apply the principles laid down by the Profintern and in the 1931 draft theses to the practical situation of the *Suiheisha* at a time when it was becoming at best stagnant and at worst reactionary. In the end, this proved to be a false start though, nonetheless, a start had been made. When the 1932 theses were produced putting more stress on the democratic phase of the forthcoming revolution, more gradualist tactics could be contemplated. Yet, as has been mentioned above, it would be a mistake to imagine that *Suiheisha* leaders changed their strategy simply in order to harmonise with Comintern policy. The proposed tactics of unification with the splintered workers' and peasants' movement proved impractical and the *Iinkai Katsudo* married the new theory to the practices in *Kyudan* struggles which were already being developed by groups throughout the country, albeit in a piecemeal way. The authors of the *Iinkai* policy thus analysed and projected existing trends in *Suiheisha* group activity while trying to orient these campaigns towards involvement in the wider class struggle. The immediate tasks of improving the *Buraku* standard of living were linked to the middle- to long-term project of overthrowing the Emperor–centred capitalist system.

It was essential that this political perspective remained closely linked to the immediate reformist issues, for without it the *Buraku Iinkai* could easily be incorporated into the scheme for improvements which was being advocated by the *Yuwa* movement. *Burakumin* were encouraged to demand the state bear the full burden for the complete improvement of the *Buraku* communities, *Buraku* committees were urged to involve themselves in the allocation of *Yuwa* funds; without the political perspective the movement could easily find itself becoming an adjunct to the *Yuwa* programme. As we shall see later on in our discussion of the *Yuwa* programme, the immediate aims and organisational methods of the new *Suiheisha* plans and the *Yuwa* programme were similar in many ways. For the time being, however, the movement was able to maintain its leftist political perspective in the formulation of policy and tactics. For the first time, in 1933, a more or less coherent theoretical framework had been developed which could be used to inform the movement's practice. It is unlikely, however, that the renovation of theory alone would have been sufficient to revive the movement's activities: what was required was an opportunity to put theory into practice on a wide scale. The Takamatsu campaign provided the *Suiheisha* with an ideal opportunity to test the effectiveness of the new theory.

Notes:

1.   Smethurst, *A Social Basis for Pre-war Japanese Militarism*, p 151.
2.   Mitchell, p 151.
3.   Beckman and Okubo, p 250.
4.   Mitchell, p 178.
5.   Cho Yukio, 'Showa economy to military economy', *The Developing Economies*, vol V, no 4 (December 1967), pp 568-596.

6. Halliday, p 127.
7. Cho, p 570.
8. A H Gleason, 'Economic Growth and Consumption in Japan' in *The State and Economic Enterprise in Japan* ed W W Lockwood (Princeton University Press, 1965), p 443.
9. Mitchell, p 119.
10. W W Lockwood, *The Economic Development of Japan* (Princeton University Press, 1968), p 57.
11. Dore, p 100. The legislation easing the debt burden was the Debt Clearance Unions Law of 1933.
12. For a detailed analysis of tenancy disputes in the 1930s, see B A Waswo, *Landlords and Social Changes in Pre-War Japan* (PhD Stanford University, 1969), Chapter Six.
13. Haraguchi Eiyu, *Buraku Mondai ni Tsuite* (On the *Buraku* Problem) (Fukuoka, 1969), p 26.
14. *Suihei Undo Shiryo Shusei*, vol II, pp 601-603.
15. *Suihei Undo Shiryo Shusei*, vol III, p 78.
16. Okayama Tetsuo, Daikyoka Zengo no Toshi Buraku to Suihei Undo (Conditions in the City *Buraku* at the time of the Great Depression and the *Suihei* Movement), *Buraku Mondai Kenkyu*, no 41 (March 1974), pp 64-78.
17. Akisada Yoshikazu, '1930 nendai Zengo ni okeru Toshi Buraku no Jotai to Dowa Jigyo ni tsuite' (Conditions in the Kyoto *Buraku* in the 1930s and the Dowa project), *Buraku Kaiho Kenkyu*, no 1 (October 1972), pp 52-75.
18. Akisada, '*1930 nendai Zengo . . .*', p 57.
19. Okayama, p 68.
20. Mahara Tetsuo, *Suihei Undo no Rekishi* (A history of the *Suihei* Movement) (Kyoto, Buraku Mondai Kenkyujo, 1973), p 185.
21. Okayama, p 64.
22. Akisada, '*1930 nendai Zengo . . .*', p 59.
23. Akisada, '*1930 nendai Zengo . . .*', p 66.
24. It was estimated that in 1937 27% of the *Buraku* working population was unemployed; moreover, the number of *Burakumin* classified as 'destitute' by the Kyoto authorities increased from 331 in 1927-8 to 1,547 in 1937-8. Akisada, '*1930 nendai Zengo . . .*', p 73.
25. *Suihei Undo Shiryo Shusei*, vol II, pp 167-9.
26. *Suihei Undo Shiryo Shusei*, vol II, pp 169-223 is a complete report of the proceedings of this conference.
27. *Suihei Undo Shiryo Shusei*, vol II, p 453.
28. *Suihei Undo Shiryo Shusei*, vol II, p 543.
29. *Suihei Undo Shiryo Shusei*, vol II, p 556.
30. *Hiroshima ken: Hisabetsu Buraku no Rekishi*, pp 252-3.
31. Oyama, pp 228-230.
32. Ninomiya, p 133.
33. This explanation of the frame of mind of the *Suiheisha* leaders in the early 1930s was suggested to me by Asada Zennosuke in an interview, 30 January 1978.
34. Asada, pp 94-5, 112-3.
35. *Suihei Undoshi no Kenkyu*, vol III, pp 137-143.
36. *Suihei Undoshi no Kenkyu*, vol III, p 209.
37. Kitahara Daisaku, p 23. The full article appeared in '*Intanashionaru*' (International), vol 4, no 14 (November 1930), pp 109-119.
38. Beckman and Okubo, p 204.
39. For further details about how the Korean activists implemented Comintern instructions see Iwamura Toshio, *Zainichi Chosenjin to Nihon Rodosha Kaikyu*

(Koreans Resident in Japan and the Japanese Working Class) (Tokyo, Azekura Shobo, 1972), pp 178-197.

40. The other four were Izumino Tokizo, Yoneda Tomi, Hishino Teiji and Itoma Choichi, although none of them spent all their time in the office. Kitahara, p 221.
41. *Suihei Undoshi no Kenkyu*, vol IV, pp 69-76.
42. *Suihei Undo Shiryo Shusei*, vol II, pp 592-5.
43. *Suihei Undoshi no Kenkyu*, vol IV, pp 192-195.
44. *Suihei Undo Shiryo Shusei*, vol II, pp 614-5.
45. *Suihei Undo Shiryo Shusei*, vol II, p 616. This meeting was attended by Matsumoto, Sakamoto, Izumino and Kitahara. Kitahara now claims that he and Izumino threatened to resign in an attempt to put pressure on Matsumoto to ensure he continue to supply the monthly donation which kept the movement solvent. He had stopped providing this money because Kitahara and Izumino were supporting the dissolutionist group. Kitahara, p 236.
46. *Suihei Undo Shiryo Shusei*, vol II, pp 610-612. See also Appendix 3.
47. *Suihei Undo Shiryo Shusei*, vol III, p 15.
48. For full text see Beckman and Okubo, pp 332-351.
49. Asada interview, 30 January 1978.
50. This was a JCP front organisation. Beckman and Okubo, p 214.
51. Details of the conference debates can be found in *Suihei Undoshi no Kenkyu*, vol IV, pp 83-5.
52. *Suihei Undoshi no Kenkyu*, vol IV, pp 207-210.
53. *Suihei Undo Shiryo Shusei*, vol III, pp 20-1.
54. *Suihei Undo Shiryo Shusei*, vol III, pp 24-5.
55. Kitahara, p 238.
56. Kitahara, p 273-4.
57. The full text of this document can be found in *Zenkoku Suiheisha: Gojunenshi* (The National *Suiheisha*: Fifty years history) 3rd edition (Osaka, Buraku Kaiho Shuppansha, 1975), pp 158-176.
58. This is Asada's phrase. Interview 30 January 1978.

CHAPTER SEVEN

Suiheisha Revival and *Yuwa* Renewal

For a time it had seemed as though the reduction in popular support for the *Suiheisha* was an irreversible trend. The movement seemed likely to disappear entirely in the face of competition from the better organised *Yuwa* movement and the inability of the *Suiheisha* leaders to agree on a basic policy. But quite suddenly, after years of internal division and weak leadership, in the early part of 1933 the *Suiheisha* became united and was determined to revive the movement. Despite the lack of centrally co-ordinated activity in the late 1920s and early 1930s, there is plenty of evidence that groups and individuals, many of whom had never been associated with the *Suiheisha*, became engaged in protest against discrimination. In other areas, local *Suiheisha* groups continued to organise and protest irrespective of the absence of guidance from a national organisation. So, in both the 'directed' and 'undirected' sectors of the *Buraku* communities activity continued; what was required was an issue and the reformation of a dynamic national leadership to galvanise the dormant *Suiheisha* movement into a new era of activity.

Separate but parallel to the changes that had taken place within the *Suiheisha*, the *Yuwa* movement in the early 1930s emerged as a unified organisation, half government, half popular (*hankan-hanmin*). Which half dominated varied according to the level in the hierarchy, across time and from place to place. While the central organisation was firmly in the control of Home Ministry bureaucrats, at the local level many *Yuwa* groups were responsive to the demands and requests of the local population. However, as the central government control of Japan became more pervasive even the local *Yuwa* groups were placed under central control. At the same time as the *Suiheisha* movement began to re-establish itself as a nationally important social and political force, the *Yuwa* movement was provided with more funds and accorded a clearer role in the central government's plan to revise and strengthen Japan's economic structure. Then, resources which had originally been provided to assist recovery from economic recession were rechannelled into a more ambitious programme which had wider, social aims. This ten-year plan aimed at the complete elimination of prejudice and discrimination against *Burakumin* within a decade. In the second part of this chapter we will examine how this policy emerged, but first we will describe the campaign which led to the revival of the *Suiheisha* as a mass movement.

The Takamatsu Discriminatory Court Campaign

On 3 June 1933, Hisamoto Yukitaro (aged 33) and Yamamoto Yoneichi (38) were sentenced by the Takamatsu Regional Court to 12 and 10 months imprisonment respectively having been found guilty of abducting a girl with intent to marry her. The two were stepbrothers who, in mid-December the previous year, had returned to Shikoku on the ferry after completing some business in Okayama. During the voyage they met and fell into conversation with Ishihara Masae, aged 19, a waitress at the Café Royal. After the ferry had docked, the three went to eat together and, when it became too late for the girl to return home, she stopped with them at a local inn. Already the possibility of marriage between Ishihara and Hisamoto had been mentioned in conversation. She had agreed to the proposal on condition that her father give his approval and that the 37 yen loaned to her father by the café which was to be paid off by her future earnings was repaid. For the next few days, the girl stayed with Hisamoto at the house of one of his friends. However, they were neither able to win her father's approval for the marriage nor raise the necessary 37 yen. Moreover, when her father heard of his daughter's plans, he filed a complaint of abduction with the police and preliminary investigations began on 20 January.[1] At the trial, it was explained that Hisamoto had been married before but that in May or June 1932 he had got a divorce and was due to take custody of his four-year-old son from January 1933. Hence, one supposes, his desire to remarry. The prosecution alleged that when the two defendants had first talked with the girl they had claimed to be connected with the motor car trade – an occupation with considerably more prestige than their scrap metal business; they had made no mention of Hisamoto's previous marriage and they had not told her of their 'special status'. Thus, in three different ways they had deceived her. Following this initial deception, the prosecution charged the defendants with having contrived to keep her from her parents by allowing her no opportunity to escape. Hisamoto was accused of the crime with Yamamoto as an accomplice; both pleaded guilty to the charges.[2]

On 20 June the Takamatsu *Suiheisha* contacted the headquarters office in Osaka and on the 27th Imoto Rinshi arrived in the city to investigate the case, followed the next day by Kitahara. In an attempt to forestall any trouble the police arrested them and expelled them from the prefecture, although they were soon permitted to return. On the basis of reports from these two, the Central Committee decided to organise a national campaign and on 19 July a special campaign committee was formed to publicise the issue and to produce regular news sheets to keep all the prefectural groups informed of developments in the campaign. The *Suiheisha* argued that during the trial both prosecution and judge had placed great emphasis on the fact that the stepbrothers had concealed their 'special status' from the girl and that this was the key point in the prosecution's case. They argued that what the pair were really charged with was having concealed their special status in order to marry an ordinary girl. Although they were prepared to admit that the girl did not know of their status, they argued it was not relevant to the case.[3] It was feared that if this court decision established a precedent it would place a legal onus on *Burakumin* to disclose their former status when applying for a job or getting married or be liable to be accused of deception. This would, in effect, have nullified the Emancipation Declaration. Nevertheless, the campaign was initiated with some trepidation on the part of the *Suiheisha* leaders since it was feared that too much stress on the fact that it contravened the declared wishes of the Emperor might give the campaign a reactionary character that could get out of control.[4] It would seem that even the leaders were not entirely confident about the efficacy of the *Buraku Iinkai* strategy.

The campaign was a huge success. Its main demands were for the release of the two defendants, the nullification of the court's decision and the removal from office of the public officials who had taken part in the proceedings. However, there was plenty of scope in the course of the campaign to bring out more general issues. At the highest level, they connected this specific incident with the general trend of repression of progressive ideas and were somewhat fearful that it marked the first move in a campaign of organised discrimination against *Burakumin*. It was compared to the overtly discriminatory laws which were being passed at that time in Germany against Jews, reports of which appeared in newspapers at the time the Takamatsu campaign was being launched.[5] At another level, the campaign stressed its opposition to the *Yuwa* policy. It had been discovered that as early as 25 May the local *Suiheisha* group had first taken up the issue and had tried to develop a campaign in co-operation with the neighbouring Kagawa group but that the *Yuwa* group had obstructed the development of the campaign.[6] This fitted in well with the *Suiheisha* criticism of the deceptiveness of the *Yuwa* policy. In addition, discrimination in marriage, the poverty which prevented them from being able to raise 37 yen and the fact that they had low status occupations were major problems which faced most *Burakumin* at some stage in their lives and thus it was relatively easy to mobilise support for the campaign. Furthermore, in accordance with the *Iinkai Katsudo* principles, the local campaign committees which were established across the country were encouraged to link the campaign with specific demands to their local government bodies for the provision of facilities to improve the economic and cultural conditions within their communities. If the local authorities refused to accede to these demands, the committees were to encourage *Burakumin* not to fulfil the 'three great obligations' of military service, tax payment and school attendance, since it was argued that, if the state provided the individual with no rights, the citizens were not obliged to fulfil their duties.

During July, meetings were arranged in most of the prefectures of central and western Japan and the campaign broadened, getting support from groups like the *Shakai Minshuto* (Social Democratic Party), Osaka branch, and the *Ronobengoshi dan* (an association of left wing lawyers).[7] On 28 August, the anniversary of the Emancipation Declaration, a meeting was held in Osaka, attended by delegates from 25 prefectures, to organise their demands and to

spread the campaign to each area of Japan. Great care was taken to emphasise the
political dimension of the campaign; Kitahara explained that the campaign was
being undertaken to oppose the reactionary, fascist trends in Japanese society
and indeed that it was one part of the worldwide anti-fascist movement. In the
same speech, he demanded the government provide more facilities to improve
the *Buraku* and began to criticise the large amount of military expenditure, but at
this point the attending police ordered him to stop.[8] The following day the
committee met to decide on future tactics and planned a march from Fukuoka to
Tokyo, a distance of 1,200 km, holding meetings along the way to give their
campaign more publicity. The police forbade them to do this, so instead, they
left Fukuoka on 1 October by train and, having held meetings at various points
en route, they arrived in Tokyo on 19 October. There the delegation presented a
petition signed by 50,000 people to the Justice Ministry and, with the assistance
of some sympathetic lawyers, entered into negotiations with Justice Ministry
officials. These latter, while expressing regret over what had happened,
maintained that they were unable to do anything about it. When it appeared that
the negotiations were getting nowhere, the campaign committee began to
consider more radical tactics such as encouraging a mass refusal to pay taxes and
there were even some suggestions that another Direct Appeal was being planned.
The police at least seem to have believed this rumour and all the Osaka
based campaign committee were arrested on 21 October and held in prison for
ten days.[9] Towards the end of November, the Justice Ministry issued a
statement recognising and regretting the fact that the court had displayed a
discriminatory attitude. A few days later, the chief judge at the trial announced
his retirement, the police chief resigned and the prosecutor was transferred
to Kyoto. On 7 December both the accused were released from prison on
parole.[10]

The campaign against the public prosecutor was taken up by the Kyoto
Suiheisha in the spring of 1934 and as a result of the protests he was finally
transferred to Hokkaido.[11] The immediate demands of the campaign had been
met, but it had not been without its casualties as police supervision of the
campaign had been strict. In some towns where those travelling from Fukuoka to
Tokyo had stopped, the police had forbidden meetings and the campaign's
leaders were imprisoned many times. In the aftermath of the campaign, the
police in some areas tried to reassert their control. In the largest *Buraku* in
Takamatsu, 61 were arrested of whom 50 were later charged, a move which
destroyed the local organisation. Imoto and five others were arrested once more
and detained for a week.[12] However, these arrests were unable to prevent the
general revival of the movement. In the course of the campaign, it is estimated
that about two-thirds of the total number of *Buraku* communities had taken part
in some kind of activity; the multi-faceted nature of the campaign had made it
easy to mobilise support and the insistence that groups link the campaign to local
issues helped to keep the momentum going.

The Reappearance of Regional Groups

At the start of the 1930s the Hiroshima *Suiheisha* was virtually inactive, any *Burakumin* interested in improving their lot had no alternative but to join one of the numerous *Yuwa* groups. However, the Osaka based campaign committee contacted one of the former leaders, Takahashi Sadao, and from 10 August 1933 he began to organise local activities to collect money for and publicise the importance of the Takamatsu Discriminatory Court Campaign. Later that month, Matsumoto Jiichiro went to Hiroshima to address two large meetings in the city. These were attended by former activists from all over the prefecture, from Miyoshi in the north to the islands in the south, and they mark the revival of *Suiheisha* activity in the prefecture.[13] The Takamatsu protest committee stopped in Hiroshima on their journey to Tokyo and spoke at nine meetings in the course of five days.[14] Yamagi estimates that, during the early autumn, over two-thirds of the prefecture's 500 *Buraku* played some part in the campaign.

Just as the Takamatsu campaign was reaching its peak, the attention of the campaign committee was directed towards an instance of discrimination which had taken place on Edajima, in Hiroshima bay. A group of 30 men had set upon seven or eight *Burakumin* in what was the culmination of a series of disagreements which had originated in the participation of a *Buraku* community in a local religious festival held on 5 October. The committee investigated the background to the incident and prepared a report which was critical of the way the police had dealt with it. A pamphlet based on this report was produced and distributed widely in a campaign demanding some kind of retribution for the injuries suffered by the *Burakumin*. Somewhat reluctantly the *Yuwa* group gave its support to the campaign and largely due to its intervention a settlement was reached which provided 800 yen paid in compensation to those who had been injured, the local mayor apologised on behalf of his villagers and twelve of those who had taken part in the assault were arrested, tried in Kure and, ultimately, fined.[15]

The first meeting of the re-invigorated Hiroshima *Suiheisha* was held on 1 April 1934 and was attended by 40 delegates from across the prefecture. The discussion covered four major topics; the need for more genuine improvements, opposition to the *Yuwa* plan, opposition to fascism and demands for the freedom to oppose discrimination in the army.[16] This latter issue was specifically connected with a campaign concerning discrimination in the Fukuyama regiment. The statement adopted by this meeting seems to have been based on the *Buraku Iinkai Katsudo* principles, the application of which enabled the movement to maintain the momentum built up during the Takamatsu campaign. During the next few years, *Suiheisha* groups re-emerged and even *Buraku* communities where there was no formally constituted group began to initiate *Kyudan* campaigns; between 1934 and 1936 the number of *Kyudan* campaigns in Hiroshima was among the highest in the country.[17]

In Mie, probably because neither a strong *Yuwa* movement nor overt police obstruction had hindered the movement's development in its early years, the

Suiheisha and particularly the left wing elements managed to establish broad based support among the *Buraku* masses which facilitated the continuation of organised activity even in the face of police harassment in the late 1920s and early 1930s. Periodic arrests of the movement's leaders as suspected Communist Party sympathisers do not seem to have affected the size of the support for the *Suiheisha*; in 1932, for example, it was reported that in Mie prefecture there were 25 *Suiheisha* groups with influence over about 1,600 supporters[18] The communist oriented trade union group *Zenkyo* and the left wing of the peasants group *Zenno* were active in Matsuzaka and, until March 1933, there was a *Sekki* reading group which may have been intended as a precursor to the formation of a party cell. At this time, however, the police arrested 152 under the Peace Preservation Law of whom 75 were members of the *Suiheisha*, successfully smashing the left wing organisation. After this, the only organisations with a broad base of support were the *Suiheisha* and the Peasant Union, both of which began to adopt legal tactics.[19]

Leaders of the Mie *Suiheisha* took part in the dissolution debate, but the acrimonious argument that took place at national level does not seem to have caused much division within the group. Perhaps co-operation between the *Buraku* and the organised peasant movement had developed to such a degree that the dissolution arguments seemed irrelevant. Although there remained a strong *Suiheisha* presence in the prefecture, purely *Suiheisha* activity in the area declined between 1930 and 1933; there were fewer *Kyudan* campaigns as activists devoted their time to more specific issues.[20] The Takamatsu campaign did not have the effect of dramatically reviving a moribund organisation as in Hiroshima for the simple reason that the movement in Mie was in a much healthier state. Still, Asada and Matsuda of the Osaka campaign committee visited the prefecture in mid-July 1933 to encourage popular support for the campaign. Following this, a campaign committee was set up in Matsuzaka and a newsletter was circulated to local groups but, just as the campaign was getting under way, its leaders were arrested, stopping it in its tracks.[21]

Nevertheless, the revival of the National *Suiheisha* and the production of new tactics do seem to have stimulated the Mie movement. The frequent arrests of its militant leaders persuaded the groups to avoid 'illegal' tactics which involved co-operation with the underground Communist Party or one of its front organisations. The groups now found guidance in the principles outlined in the *Buraku Iinkai Katsudo* documents. Between July and September 1934, a series of meetings was held to discuss these ideas and ways in which they might be put into practice. During the following autumn, the town and village groups organised campaigns which concentrated on the economic and political problems which were encountered in the course of protest against status discrimination.

Thus, the *Suiheisha* movement at all levels, from local branch to national committee, was revived in the wake of the Takamatsu campaign and the debate over the movement's tactics. In the course of the campaign, the organisation had won the support of the wider left wing movement; the Social Democrats and the Peasants' Unions gave active support and there were even two articles in the Communist organ, *Sekki*, urging workers and peasants to stand beside their *Suiheisha* comrades in their struggle against the Emperor system.[22] However, though it might not have been apparent at the time, these left wing groups were becoming weaker; their activities were being circumscribed by police supervision which made independent activity increasingly difficult and many were on the point of being overtaken by the tide of nationalism. In the summer of 1934 the *Suiheisha* movement was revitalised with a united organisation, a coherent theory and a host of active groups with a strong mass following, however it stood alone.

Consolidation of the Rapid Expansion

One hundred and twenty five delegates met in Kyoto on 13 and 14 May 1934 to attend the twelfth national conference. They heard of the progress of the previous year, the developments in the ideas of the *Buraku Iinkai Katsudo* and the extent to which the Takamatsu campaign had revived previously dormant groups and even caused some groups to be formed where previously none had existed. It was, however, carefully pointed out that the revival was mainly due to the correct application of the principles devised and propagated since the last conference.[23] Several of the motions considered by the conference were concerned with the revision of bye-laws, the movement's finances, the selection of officers as well as the usual debate on the struggle programme and the conference declaration. Two substantial motions were considered. It was decided to carry out a thorough survey of *Buraku* all over the country, since without detailed information it was not possible to formulate an effective policy. The other motion notes a trend towards unity in the two tendencies of the peasants' movement and resolved that the *Suiheisha* should encourage the trend.[24]

The enlarged central committee elected at the conference met to consider future activities on 24 May at which meeting bye-laws were revised and a standing committee elected. Asada and Imoto, who were the leading advocates of the *Buraku Iinkai Katsudo* approach, proposed that, in future, members of the *Suiheisha* refer to themselves not as *tokushu Buraku* but as *hiappaku* (oppressed) *Buraku*. They explained that they were not 'special' but merely one section of the oppressed masses and by making this alteration in their self-appellation their political position *vis-à-vis* the class struggle would be clarified. In a more practical vein, it was decided to revive the newspaper, the 1,000 yen guarantee money would be provided by Matsumoto and publication was to begin in the middle of June.[25] Previous meetings had made similar resolutions without any success, but this time, after some delay, the first edition of the new series of the *Suihei Shimbun* appeared on 15 November 1934. For the next 20 months it was to appear at monthly intervals.[26]

Late in 1934 an article appeared in the newspaper *Yorozu Choho* written by a reservist officer about the current corruption scandal which had involved the

Minister of Railways. The article was entitled *Kijin and Eta* (Nobles and *Eta*) and it contained several overtly insulting references to *Burakumin* including the assertion that *eta* are not capable of understanding the morality of human ethics. Imoto, Matsuda and others on the central committee decided that they could not let this go unchallenged and they started a campaign which they hoped would not only expose the continuing discrimination in the army but also develop into an anti-fascist struggle, for they had discovered that the article's author, Lt Gen Sato Kiyokatsu, was a member of the *Meirinkai*, a right wing group. Early in 1935 they arranged a meeting with the general and the editor of the magazine and, contrary to expectation, the affair was settled amicably. The general apologised and agreed to put a written apology in the *Yorozu Choho* and arrange to have an article explaining the *Buraku* problem published in the reservists' magazine, *Senyu*. The editor also apologised and promised to publish an article on the *Yuwa* project.[27]

With the immediate goals successfully achieved, the committee attempted to prolong the campaign by pointing to examples of discrimination in the army. The *Suihei Shimbun* in 1935 and 1936 carried several reports of *Kyudan* struggles against discrimination in the army. One result of this was that, in January 1937, 1,500 copies of a magazine entitled *Jinmin Yuwa e no Michi* (The Path towards Human Conciliation) were circulated to regional army headquarters throughout the country having been partially financed by a donation from Lt Gen Sato.[28] This was followed by a series of detailed instructions on how officers should deal with the *Buraku* problem. They were warned not to use discriminatory language, care was to be taken in billeting so that none was offended and they were to permit no 'loose language' among soldiers in the ranks. When incidents did occur, they were to be treated as isolated events, the soldiers involved were not to be allowed to protest and any attempt to relay information about such events to outside groups was to be strongly punished.[29] After this time, no further incidents were reported which involved the army; however this seems to be less the result of a genuine reduction of discrimination than the imposition of tighter discipline after the outbreak of hostilities in China in 1937. Certainly there is anecdotal evidence that during the war some regiments kept registers which included lists of *eta* who were often, unknown to themselves, grouped together in one platoon and given the most dangerous tasks, such as being the first sent to wade ashore on assault missions.[30]

The campaign against Sato was one of the major topics discussed by the thirteenth conference (4-5 May 1935). During the following year criticism of the persistence of discrimination in the army was to be a major theme as was the demand for more control over the use of the *Yuwa* development funds. Linked to these demands were ones which had grown out of the campaigns for a fair share in the use of common land; now they demanded a right to play an active part in village affairs. One new issue arose from the realisation of the influence that the media exerted on public opinion through films, plays and novels; where discriminatory attitudes were located they should be strongly criticised.

As a whole, the *Suiheisha* movement was becoming more moderate. The report to the conference urged the movement's supporters to be aware that the masses judge the whole movement by one wrong act and that a rash action might separate them even further from the masses. Under the influence of the state-controlled mass media and the pervasive influence of the army through the reservist associations, public opinion was moving further to the right to the extent that demands that the *Suiheisha* keep in tune with the masses were in fact a call for moderation. The notions discussed by the conference provoked little controversy; there were plans for a Youth group, for more regional conferences and reorganisation of the movement's finances. A programme on how to fight discrimination was presented to the conference and a proposal was introduced to launch a petition demanding more *Yuwa* money. Both were passed. The conference declaration remarks that after the Takamatsu campaign there were more demands for increased freedom but now it was more important to concentrate on the improvement of living conditions.[31]

The movement seemed to be in a healthy state. Over the previous year the *Buraku Iinkai Katsudo* principles were further elaborated to form a policy which encouraged activity among a wide number of groups and which gave the whole movement stability. The newspaper, edited by Asada, appeared each month during 1935 and spread news of the concrete application of these principles. Not that there were no problems. There was still a division between the Kyushu and Kinki federations which dated from at least the time of the dissolution issue and the theoretical and emotional differences manifested themselves in the form of a minor squabble over the use – or misuse – of funds which broke out between Asada and Imoto in the summer of 1935.[32] For the moment, at least, these problems were soon solved. More ominous were the reports from Nara prefecture that several of the *Suiheisha* movement's founding leaders had renounced their left wing ideas and had formed a group based on ideas of 'state socialism'. In the Kanto area, too, a trend towards supporting a more overtly nationalist Emperor-centred policy was emerging. Hirano Shoken had been active in the Kanto region since 1932 trying to organise a movement which would unite the local *Suiheisha* and *Yuwa* movements and initiate a policy which would completely solve the economic and spiritual problems of the *Buraku* by restoring the Emperor to the centre of the political and economic system.[33] The next year a group led by Hirano representing the Kanto *Suiheisha* league visited the Meiji and Yasukuni shrines bearing a banner which read 'A Prayer for the Solution of the Emperor's Crisis'.[34] There were, then, a few potential problems, but for the moment the *Suiheisha* was stronger than ever with a committed active leadership, a strong mass following and a clear, coherent theory. Let us turn next to consider how the *Yuwa* movement and policy developed during the early 1930s.

The Yuwa Programme:
From Emergency Improvements to the Ten Year Plan

The *Yuwa* policy was becoming more closely integrated into overall government policy and, as Japan became more involved in war on the Asian continent, it became subordinate to the requirements of the war economy. In the course of this process, the liberal current of ideas fades away and nationalist themes and slogans dominate to the exclusion of all else. This should not be surprising since although the funds allocated to the *Yuwa* project in (say) 1935 amounted to less than 0.055% of the national budget, the *Yuwa* administration was by no means a peripheral government agency. It was closely linked to the Home Ministry's Social Affairs Bureau and the *Yuwa* chairman, Hiranuma Kiichiro, was a prominent politician throughout the 1930s who served as Prime Minister between 5 January and 30 August 1939. In the early 1930s the *Yuwa* policy played a role in the government's attempts to slough off the effects of the worldwide depression and then, from the mid-1930s, the *Yuwa* programme became one part of the policy to mobilise the entire nation behind the war effort.

The Emperor, whose grandfather had emancipated the *eta:hinin*, had always occupied an important role in the propaganda of the *Yuwa* movement and its antecedents. From 1931 onwards, the first chapter of the *Yuwa Jigyo Nenkan* (*Yuwa* Project Yearbook) was entitled 'The Imperial Household and the *Yuwa* problem'. Each year this began with a brief overview of the role of the Imperial Family in the emancipation of the *Burakumin* and then demonstrated how the present Emperor continued to take an interest in the problem. For example, in 1931 three of the *Yuwa* project officials were invited to join the Imperial Cherry Blossom viewing party and in the autumn two more (from Kyoto and Shizuoka) joined the Chrysanthemum viewing party.[35] This custom had commenced in 1928 and continued until 1937 when presumably the emergency conditions made these private parties inappropriate.[36] The reason for inviting them may have been to demonstrate that even he had no qualms about mixing with those involved in the *Yuwa* programmes, although it is not known whether any of these *Yuwa* officials were themselves *Burakumin*. On the other hand, the Emperor's patronage of the *Yuwa* movement may simply symbolise the way central government was taking control of the *Yuwa* organisations.

The Emergency Facilities for Regional Improvement

Abroad the army's obsession with the threat to Japan posed by an unstable China was to lead to the situation where army officers fabricated an incident on the Manchurian railway providing them with an excuse to become directly involved in Chinese affairs. At home, a new economic policy was launched which would both revitalise the economy and provide relief for the rural areas which had been harshly affected by the recession. Increased military spending directly and indirectly encouraged investment in modern heavy industrial plant. Meanwhile on 22 August 1931 a rice support policy, a loans assistance policy and a series of public works projects were announced. This latter policy committed the government to spending 860 million yen over a period of three years on improvements to roads, ports, riverbanks and hillsides. Such public spending was designed to ensure smooth economic expansion and to overcome the worst effects of the depression and dislocation caused by the rapid economic changes. At first it had seemed that there would be no alterations to the *Yuwa* policy, indeed the budget planned for 1932 was less than the previous year. Then, on 28 August, apparently without any consultation with the *Yuwa* leaders, it was announced that additional Emergency Improvement money would be made available to assist alleviate the particularly severe poverty which was to be found in the *Buraku*.[37] This extra money, which over the next four years would amount to nearly 5 million yen, rather than being used to expand existing projects was to be spent on new projects.

Most of this improvement money was simply spent on the improvement of roads; in 1932, such projects absorbed 90% of the 1 million yen extra money provided for the *Yuwa* project.[38] These projects not only assisted the improvement of the environment, but also provided work for *Burakumin* in the locality. In Hiroshima, for example, in 1932 there were 146 projects to build and improve roads at a total cost of 93,803 yen of which 85,000 yen was provided by central government under the emergency fund scheme. Around 60% of the money was paid out in wages to *Burakumin* labourers at a rate of 80 sen per day, a low wage even for day labourers. Throughout the four years in which the emergency funds were provided, most of the money seems to have been spent on road improvement schemes.[39]

In northern prefectures, the project work seems to have been carried out mainly during the winter when people were not so busy in the fields. In the south-west, slightly more money would appear to have been spent on improving communal facilities other than roads. Most places reported an improvement to economic conditions in the *Buraku* as a result of these projects and that they had side effects like encouraging tax payment and savings.[40] Other reports commented on the uplifting 'moral' effects of the projects. Saitama prefecture reported a decrease in support for the *Suiheisha* and increased support for traditional Japanese customs and for the government. Ibaragi noted that road improvements made it easier for *Buraku* children to get to school. In Yamanashi it was reported that road improvements made it possible for cars and carts to get to the *Buraku* which had increased trade with the surrounding area and thus assisted the economic regeneration of the region's *Buraku* communities.

While these projects were being implemented the central *Yuwa* agencies were planning a more comprehensive analysis of the contemporary *Buraku* problem. In September and October of 1932, the *Chuo Yuwa Jigyo Kyokai* issued two reports, the first outlining the major economic problems being faced by the *Buraku* communities and the second suggesting strategies which could be adopted to assist the regeneration of the *Buraku* economies. The former report noted that *Burakumin* had much smaller landholdings than the average peasant and that previously they had relied on remittances from their daughters working in the cotton mills and similar factories or on day labour in the off-season to make ends meet. Now that this work was not available many were unable to pay rent or bills and in some places were being evicted from their land. In urban areas, there was very little modern industry, little access to finance except at high rates of interest and a level of discrimination which prevented *Burakumin* from moving freely to find work. If these economic problems could be solved, it was argued, then the other problems would be overcome. It was estimated that the emergency money would provide work for *Burakumin* in about one third of the nation's *Buraku* communities, but although this would give them immediate aid it was no solution to the problem. This could only be achieved when the *Burakumin* themselves took the lead in the regeneration of their own economic environment. Property owners and *Buraku* intellectuals were to be encouraged to conduct surveys of their own community's economic facilities and to formulate five or ten year plans to restructure the whole community. It was suggested that these plans could be based on co-operative unions which would be able to co-ordinate the activities of all the *Buraku* residents and make efficient use of the available resources. Low interest loans were to be provided to assist these co-operatives. The second report covered much of the same ground as the second part of the first except that the principles were described in much broader terms and examples provided of how a rural co-operative might be organised.[41]

However, these plans were not adopted very extensively for the time being. One aspect of the new programme was to train *Yuwa* group leaders. Men aged between 25 and 40 were chosen from among the leaders of the *Buraku* communities to attend four-day courses at which they would hear lectures from professors from the Imperial universities and central *Yuwa* group leaders who explained the aims of the *Yuwa* policy and how it was to be put into operation. When they returned home, they were expected to form groups which acted on these principles. Between September and December of 1932, 43 groups were established in 33 prefectures.

Some of the newly trained *Yuwa* leaders tried to put into practice the principles they had been taught in their training courses, even though there was not much money provided to assist them. In Nagano prefecture, one very poor *Buraku* of 26 households made plans to form a co-operative organisation within the village to organise vegetable plots, the production of rope and straw bags and to improve silk cultivation. The drinking of *sake* was discouraged and, the report claimed, there had been a 40% reduction in its consumption.[42] In Okayama, a more ambitious plan was devised for a slightly larger community of 46 households. Although landholdings were very small – 3 *tan* compared to an average 10.9 per household in the surrounding district – they proposed to make maximum use of the land available by increasing productivity by about 45% using new techniques which would, for example, eliminate the rice borer. Vegetable gardens were to be enlarged, unused land was to be used to grow cabbages, melons and fruits. It was planned to make the community self-sufficient in *shoyu* and *miso* and to introduce animal husbandry and rabbit breeding over a five-year period. School attendance would be encouraged and adult education was to be used to develop an attitude of service to the state and to teach young girls to be good and graceful housewives.[43]

Summarising the effect of the emergency programme, it was claimed that *Buraku* attitudes had softened, there was now a more positive evaluation of the *Yuwa* policy, and tax payment had increased. However, since most of these reports came from groups who were implementing these projects, one suspects that they were a little more enthusiastic than the results may have merited. *Suiheisha* comments on these programmes are almost all scathing attacks on their deceptive nature, although the provision of some work and the improvement of roads may have helped some *Buraku* families through the worst of the depression and provided an infrastructure which would benefit the area as a whole. The fact that the *Suiheisha* at its twelfth and thirteenth conferences had demanded that more money be provided and the scope of the project be extended suggests that those already in operation were having some beneficial effects on *Buraku* life. The *Buraku Iinkai Katsudo* proposals dismiss the emergency funds as a pacification exercise and the practical application of the project seems to have taken on such qualities, but there were strong similarities between the *Iinkai Katsudo* proposals and the plans for the regeneration of the *Buraku* economies. Both began with a review of *Buraku* poverty, both stress the necessity of raising the economic and cultural standards of the *Buraku* communities and both emphasise that this can best be done by *Burakumin* themselves forming their own groups within which a new co-operative spirit would be born. To be sure they were founded on very different political principles, one seeking to build a movement which could contribute towards the collapse of capitalism and the other aiming at finding a 'solution to the national crisis and national unity in accordance with the task of building the nation'. Still, in the short to middle term the aims were in theory similar and in practice almost identical.

There was, however, good cause for complaint that the *Yuwa* project was deceptive and, in itself, discriminatory against *Burakumin*. The average daily rate paid to *Burakumin* labourers was around 80 sen which is indeed what a *Burakumin* might expect, but at that time the usual rate for such work was around 1.40 yen. Thus the *Yuwa* authorities seem to have been perpetuating the low level of *Buraku* wages. There have been several suggestions that much of the money budgeted for road improvements was never spent on *Buraku* roads. In one area of Hiroshima prefecture, the reports suggest that only 30% of the money was used in the *Buraku* communities, the other money being spent on projects in non–*Buraku* areas.[44] In another district, also in Hiroshima, it was alleged that only 30% of the money was spent on *Buraku* improvements, the rest being used to build a house for the leader of the *Yuwa* group.[45]

From Mie comes evidence that, in 1934, a group of *Burakumin* opposed a *Yuwa* plan to spend 5,000 yen on the reclamation of a plot of waste land since this would be of most benefit to the landlord and do little to improve the lives of the

Burakumin. Instead, they wanted the money spent improving the community's drainage system which would benefit everyone.[46] These examples of misuse of *Yuwa* funds lead one to suspect both that a substantial proportion of improvement money was never spent in the *Buraku* and that at least some of that which was benefited the *Buraku* élite rather that the *Buraku* masses.

It might also be argued that the amount spent on the emergency *Yuwa* projects was less than might have been expected. Large sums of money were spent on assisting the poor among the 70 million majority population, whereas less than 1% of the total was spent on the emergency *Yuwa* project. By its own reckoning, the *Yuwa* administration could point to a *Buraku* population of one million and Arima considered this to be an underestimate, the true total being closer to two million. Moreover, there were numerous reports which indicated that poverty within the *Buraku* was a much more serious problem than in the majority community. If the programme had been concerned with equitably distributing funds to assist all the nation's poor, one might have expected a greater amount of money to be spent on the emergency *Yuwa* funds. That it was not would seem to indicate that the *Suiheisha* was correct to regard it as a programme primarily aimed at pacifying disgruntled *Burakumin* and deceiving them into believing that the *Yuwa* programme was genuinely concerned with improving conditions in the *Buraku* communities.

Government expenditure 1931–36, compared to the
Emergency Yuwa Project [47]

	Total	Military	(Manchuria)	Temp Relief Project	Emergency *Yuwa* Project
1931	1477	455	76	–	–
1932	1950	686	278	163	1.5
1933	2255	673	196	214	1.8
1934	2163	943	159	145	1.0
1935	2206	1033	184	–	0.68
1936	2282	1078	207	–	–
				million yen	

The reports issued in 1932 provided an analysis of the problems of *Burakumin* and some strategies which might be used to solve some of them. They seem to form the first step towards the development of a consolidated *Yuwa* policy. The next step in this direction was the formation of a *Yuwa* education policy. Since 1923 funds had been available to provide grants for deserving *Buraku* children to attend middle schools and institutes of higher education. However, this did little to raise the general standard of education of those in the *Buraku* or to reduce prejudice among the non-*Buraku* population. Some prefectures had allocated time for *Yuwa* education in their schools, but it was not until 1928 that the *Chuo Yuwa Jigyo Kyokai* adopted the idea of spreading *Yuwa* principles through the classroom and even then no guidelines were suggested, individual prefectural committees being left to formulate their own curricula. For most of the 1920s *Yuwa* education, in the sense of spreading *Yuwa* ideas among the majority population in order to reduce their prejudices, meant little more than the production and distribution of large quantities of pamphlets and leaflets. The production of these leaflets and the holding of *Yuwa* group meetings were generally co-ordinated around special events like the *Yuwa* day. The first of these was held on 3 November 1928, but the next not until 14 March 1930. Thereafter, the date remained the same until 1938 when it was decided to extend the programme to last for one week, renamed the *Kokumin Seishin Sodo Yuwa Shukan* (National Spiritual Mobilisation *Yuwa* Week). These days became the focal point for a huge amount of *Yuwa* activity; for example, in 1933 the 29 prefectural groups produced nearly two million pamphlets and over half a million posters, handbills and other publications and held 139 meetings which were attended by over 15,000 people.[48] Yet, despite these annual flurries of activity, little co-ordinated educational policy was enacted until 1933–34.

The two national *Yuwa* conferences in 1928 and 1931 had spent considerable time debating the issue of *Yuwa* education and after both of them petitions were presented to the Ministry of Education recommending the propagation of *Yuwa* ideas in schools, particularly primary schools. The first move towards implementing such a policy occurred in 1932 when a circular was sent to all public and private universities demanding that they disseminate *Yuwa* ideas in their institutions. Later that same year, the Education Ministry social affairs section produced a statement on the problem of discrimination. In it they argued that progress towards the solution of the *Yuwa* problem was hindered by the general lack of understanding of the nature of the *kokutai*, there was an urgent need to develop the idea that the whole nation is one big family united before the Emperor, and, if only this were properly understood, discrimination would disappear.[49] This statement provides a clear outline of the sort of ideas which lay behind the development of the *Yuwa* education policy and demonstrates that in its basic approach the *Yuwa* policy had progressed very little since the time of the early *kaizen* groups.

In the years 1933 and 1934, prefectural and municipal bodies began to develop their own *Yuwa* education programmes to be used in schools and youth groups. Finally, in December 1934, the *Chuo Yuwa Jigyo Kyokai* issued a policy statement which outlined the basic aims of *Yuwa* education. In its preamble it recognises three major targets:

1 To foster the spirit of respect for human character and universal brotherhood (*shikai doho*).

2 To make clear the process of the formation of the Japanese race and to foster the spirit of national unity.

3 To recognise the roots of the concepts of customary discrimination and foster a spirit of progress based on self confidence.

The substance of the document explains in detail how *Yuwa* ideas are to be introduced into the curricula of primary schools, middle schools and teacher training colleges as well as indicating ways in which these ideas could be propagated in youth groups, mothers' groups and other adult organisations.[50]

These principles were shortly incorporated into the Ten Year Plan which established a programme organised on three levels:

1 The training of *Yuwa* education leaders

2 The development of the organs of *Yuwa* education

3 Research projects on the results and methods of *Yuwa* education policy.

Every year a group of 40 to 50 school inspectors was invited to attend a five day conference organised jointly by the Education and Home Ministries at which they heard lectures and took part in discussions on various aspects of the *Yuwa* education project.[51] At the prefectural level, courses and lecture meetings were held for school teachers, organised presumably by the school inspectors, and groups of teachers who were interested in the issue of *Yuwa* eduction were formed at prefectural and town/village levels to discuss methods and problems of teaching *Yuwa* principles. In addition, 14 prefectures established research groups to monitor the progress of the *Yuwa* education policy.

By 1940 *Yuwa* education programmes were operating in 35 prefectures, although how widely and effectively the ideas were disseminated within the schools is hard to ascertain.[52] It is also hard to discover how much money was spent on the education project since no separate figures appear in the material. Clearly, the effectiveness of such a project would not depend simply on how much money was allocated to it, but it would indicate what priority the plans were given. From what material is available it does not seem that the project was given high priority. At best, it unequivocally established the principle that *Burakumin* children were entitled to equality of opportunity and this would at least tend to dissuade schools from continuing overt segregation in the classroom. The number of officials and teachers involved in the campaign was very small and the content of the education programmes was little more than an extension of, or an additional buttress to, the Imperial family/nation *Kokutai* ideas which were being given increased prominence within schools from the mid-1930s. In other words, the *Yuwa* education policy derived less from a decision to use education as a means of reducing prejudice for its own sake and more from the perceived need to increase feelings of national solidarity at a time of international crisis.

The Ten Year Plan

The funds for the 'Emergency Facilities for Regional Improvement' more than tripled the amount of money that was being spent on the *Yuwa* project, but it was made clear that this was to be a temporary measure designed to deal with the urgent problems caused by the economic recession. However, demands were made both by those active in the *Yuwa* movement and by *Suiheisha* supporters that the government should initiate a more comprehensive policy of state assistance. Requests for more money for the *Yuwa* projects, clearer leadership from the central body and more encouragement for the education programmes had been expressed at the meetings of the representatives of the prefectural *Yuwa* groups held annually in February between 1928 and 1935. In the later years, there was much discussion on how the *Yuwa* policy should be developed when the emergency programme came to an end. At the meeting held in 1935, it was resolved to formulate a programme for the consolidated progress of the *Yuwa* project and a committee of 13 was formed to sort out the details of a ten-year plan. This plan should aim, it was decided, at raising 'consciousness' inside and outside the *Buraku* community so as to improve relations between the minority and majority communities, attention was to be directed towards regenerating the *Buraku* economy and raising the cultural level within the *Buraku*, and, finally, the possibility of co-operation with the *Suiheisha* was to be considered. By June, the committee had worked out a detailed report which was explained to a meeting of representatives of the prefectural groups; 50 million yen was to be spent over the next decade in ways which would raise the economic and cultural level of the *Buraku* to that of communities elsewhere, prejudice and discrimination would be eliminated and the *Yuwa* problem completely solved. On 22 and 23 August, the Third *Zenkoku Yuwa Dantai Rengo Daikai* (National Conference of the League of *Yuwa* groups) was held in Tokyo and attended by 469 representatives from 38 regional groups. Other issues were discussed, but it was clear that the main purpose of the conference was to launch the Ten Year Plan and, in doing so, ensure that the largest possible number of activists became aware of its content and purpose.[53]

Much is made of the Ten Year Plan both by its critics and supporters. There are detailed notes on the theory and practice of each aspect of the problem and series of tables showing in detail the proposed expenditure. However, there was nothing new in the principles of the plan, they had already been developed in the two reports produced in 1932; all it represented was a detailed application of these principles. Moreover, as a glance at Table 2 (page 104) will reveal, the introduction of the plan in 1936 did not lead to an increase in government expenditure on the *Yuwa* project. What appears to have happened is that money previously provided for the 'emergency' projects and spent on the improvement of roads was redistributed to subsidise the regional improvement projects and grants to assist the *Yuwa* groups' activities. The target budgets, described in considerable detail in the plan, were never fulfilled. In the first year, 5,968,647 yen was to have been spent and the total was to drop to 4,078,532 yen in the final year, yet, as is clear from Table 2, actual expenditure was never more than about 35% of the projected figure and for most of the time it was considerably less than this.

According to the plans, around 80% of the total expenditure was to be directed towards *Jikaku Kosei* (regeneration of consciousness); these were plans to improve the physical environment, 'revival of industry' projects and education/cultural projects in approximately equal amounts, but it is hard to tell from the way the material is presented where most of the cash was actually spent. One gets the impression that, despite the elaborate plans discussed in the document, the way in which the *Yuwa* project funds were used and the type of project undertaken remained much the same as before. Area improvement grants continued as before; the previous plans to make improvements to 20 *Buraku* came to an end in 1932 and, in the following year, a new series of projects was launched, this time in 23 prefectures. Some of the projects were to last for ten years, but most were scheduled to be completed in three, four or five years with the cost ranging from 430,000 yen (Kyoto, Shichijo) to 10,000 yen (Shizuoka).[54] As before, these projects were mainly concerned with improvements to roads, drainage systems, water supply and housing.

In 1936 an increased amount of money was given to assist the activities of the *Yuwa* groups. The same document which outlines the Ten Year Plan also puts great emphasis on the importance of establishing a hierarchy of *Yuwa* administration which would permit the efficient organisation of *Yuwa* policy from national to village level. The country was divided into six regions – Kanto, Chubu, Kinki, Chukoku, Shikoku, Kyushu – to form a four-tier administrative structure, national, regional, prefectural and town/village, with each level being accorded a specific place in the decision-making structure.[55] Women's and young people's groups were to be organised to develop those aspects of the *Yuwa* programme that were relevant to them. At the lowest level in the hierarchy, corporate unions were to be formed of peasants and workers to operate as consumers' and producers' organisations. Under the guidance of the benevolent *Yuwa* officials, these groups would prevent the spread of 'class consciousness' and 'anti-capitalist' ideas as well as ensuring the efficient utilisation of resources within the *Buraku* communities.

The distinction between the *Yuwa* project administration and the formally independent *Yuwa* groups, already vague, was disappearing entirely. In 1935 all the prefectural *Yuwa* groups had their offices located within the local government office building[56] and a report on the state of the *Yuwa* movement in Hiroshima shows that all but one of the local *Yuwa* group's thirty branches had their offices located in the local police station.[57] In Mie prefecture the activities of the *Yuwa* groups in some places had to come under the control of the Special Police and become part of the system which administered the 'protection and supervision' of those who had undergone a *tenko* and aimed at ensuring that this thought reform continued. So, at the same time that more funds were made available for the improvement of conditions in the *Buraku* and a large amount of publicity was aimed at convincing *Buraku* and non-*Buraku* alike that more money was being spent than was in fact the case, government control over the *Yuwa* administration and groups became stronger.

This was not an isolated phenomenon; there were parallel developments in other social spheres. The reservist association which had between eleven and twelve million people under its direct or indirect influence was placed under the direct control of the Army Minister in 1936. At the same time, the youth training centres were merged with the supplementary technical schools such that the military indoctrination network involved more than half of the nation's young males plus a large number of young women.[58] In 1934 the Osaka based *Naisen Kyowakai* (Korean Harmony Committee) recommended the adoption of a uniform national policy towards Koreans resident in Japan. A national organisation was to be formed to supervise this policy which would develop close links with the police and place special emphasis on the education project which would deepen consciousness of the *kokutai* among Koreans. The following year *Chuo Kyowakai* was established as a semi-official government body under the guidance of the Home Ministry. Within the next twelve months, district and branch offices were set up throughout the country in order to promote harmony between Japanese and Koreans while at the same time placing the suspect Korean population resident in Japan more firmly under the supervision of the central government.[59]

The bureaucratisation of the *Yuwa* programme, therefore, fits into an overall pattern of strengthening government control over all aspects of the nation's life. As the bureaucrats, in co-operation with the military, consolidated their control over the higher echelons of political power, they incorporated into their spheres of control all those elements which had escaped their influence. It might be argued that this process represents the recognition by the state of its responsibility towards its impoverished citizens, that finally representatives of the *Burakumin* were being allowed access to the decision-making process. However, since it took place alongside the repression of leftist elements at a time of 'national emergency', it seems more realistic to characterise this process 'as the suborning of dissident elements and their conversion into agents of control for a powerful state'.[60]

Suiheisha and the new Yuwa policy

The *Suiheisha* had consistently criticised the *Yuwa* programme as being deceptive and in the early 1930s these criticisms became more detailed. A prominent criticism was that little of the money ever reached the *Buraku* communities; a pamphlet in 1933 notes that 22% of the *Yuwa* budget was used to assist *Yuwa* groups whose major role was to obstruct *Suiheisha* activities; 35% was spent on the education of *Buraku* children, the major aim being the dissemination of reactionary ideas; 29% of the total was spent on special area projects which had little general effect such that only 10-20% of the total amount was devoted to improving conditions in the *Buraku*.[61] Similarly the Ten Year Plan was attacked because of the large amount that was spent on administration and the small proportion of the total which was used to improve living conditions. The plan as a whole was compared unfavourably to giving toffees to crying children and it was pointed out that the apparently large sums of money that were being promised amounted to only 1% of the total given in compensation to the dispossessed feudal rulers after the *Meiji* restoration.[62] Hiranuma's dual role as chairman of the *Yuwa* committees and leading activist in the *Kokuhonsha* continued to attract criticism, the latter group being called a fascist organisation and likened to the Italian blackshirts or the German Nazis.[63]

Nevertheless, with the adoption of the *Buraku Iinkai Katsudo* strategy, the emphasis changed from one of outright opposition to one of ensuring that the money was used in ways which would most effectively improve living standards. At first, the local groups attempted to point out the reactionary nature of the overall programme and specific projects, but as they became involved in the allocation of *Yuwa* funds the *Suiheisha* groups began to lose their independent identity. In some areas, specific improvement projects did make a very real difference to the quality of life in the community; they would have to do so to make the *Yuwa* programme at all credible, but this was not the major effect of the plan. The plan reorganised the *Yuwa* groups and placed them, and thus the *Buraku* they represented, under closer government control. Secondly, using the improvement funds almost as a lure they were able to co-opt *Burakumin*, often the most active *Burakumin*, on to their improvement committees, thus placing the *Buraku* communities more effectively under government control. This meant that in many areas between 1935 and 1937 many village and town level *Suiheisha* groups became part of the *Yuwa* network.

Mobilisation of the Japanese population to serve the needs of the nation at war is not usually considered to have started until the summer of 1937.[64] But it seems difficult to regard the implementation of the Ten Year Plan as anything other than an attempt to prepare *Burakumin* for full participation in the national effort. At the same time of course, it was necessary to try to reduce some of the hostility of the majority population so that *Burakumin* could move more freely within majority society. And yet we must be careful not to view the plan as being simply part of an inevitable drift towards war and defeat. Certainly there appear to have been strong tendencies towards increased centralised control of society by the bureaucracy, and the *Yuwa* administration was not exempt from this, but the new plan can be regarded as deriving from three related though quite distinct preoccupations of the *Yuwa* administrators.

In the first place, there was genuine desire among at least some of those involved in the *Yuwa* programme to remove prejudice and discrimination both for the sake of *Burakumin* and the whole society. No doubt this motivation was often obscured by more pragmatic considerations discussed below, but it should not be forgotten that many of the *Yuwa* programme administrators, if not *Burakumin* themselves, were in daily contact with *Buraku* communities and will no doubt have argued within the Home Ministry for the provision of more resources to extend their schemes. In retrospect it seems strange that the government should have committed itself to the provision of large sums of money for the *Yuwa* programme immediately prior to embarking on an aggressive policy abroad which was to lead to an escalation of the war in China. However, in 1935 when the Plan was being devised there was no fear of a drift towards war, nor any realisation that war would have disastrous consequences. On the contrary, it is reported that there was at this time a feeling of prosperity and optimism generated by the partial economic recovery and supported by a sense of international security.[65] In this context it is understandable that the *Yuwa* officials were able to persuade the Finance Ministry that more should be provided to assist those who had benefited least from the economic recovery.

Benevolence, then, was one motivation behind the Ten Year Plan, but it was not the only one. Unemployment in the majority society had been reduced by the rapid expansion of heavy industry which was mainly the result of increased military expenditure. However, there remained pockets of high unemployment in the *Buraku*. For the nation to make maximum use of its human resources, the *Yuwa* movement had to improve educational standards within the *Buraku* and break down the barriers of discrimination in the society outside. The need to employ all Japanese in the task of building the nation was recognised by all sectors of the political élite and this probably explains why funds continued to be provided for *Yuwa* projects long after the outbreak of open hostilities. Indeed, the prompt apologetic reaction of people such as Lt Col Sato to *Suiheisha* criticism suggests that there was a desire even among those on the right wing to encourage the integration of *Burakumin* so they could serve in all social institutions from the army to the factory.

High unemployment and impoverished living conditions in the *Buraku*, obvious manifestations of inequality, encouraged *Burakumin* to support their left wing movement. By the mid-1930s most of the left wing movements and political parties were small in size and were abandoning their more radical policies. Indeed, in 1935 the *Suiheisha* was probably the only organisation with a mass following which persisted in criticising the drift towards 'fascism' at home and the tendency to become more heavily involved on the Asian continent. Police repression had not, by itself, been sufficient to prevent strident criticism of domestic and foreign policy and the *Suiheisha* posed an ideological challenge to the claims of the Japanese state. The repressive policy continued, but through the application of a renewed *Yuwa* policy which promised to reduce unemployment, raise living standards and remove discrimination, the Japanese government sought to give support to those within the *Suiheisha* movement who were urging its leaders to abandon leftist ideas and adopt a nationalist ideology to guide its activities.

Notes:

1.   The original incident and subsequent campaign are documented in *Suihei Undo Shiryo Shusei*, vol III, pp 29-59 and *Suihei Undoshi no Kenkyu*, pp 260-298. Detailed documentary evidence of all aspects of the campaign can be found in *Suihei Undo*

Shiryo Shusei, supp vol II, pp 1139-1500, though my account is based mainly on the former two sources.

2. *Suihei Undo Shiryo Shusei*, vol III, p 34.
3. *Suihei Undoshi no Kenkyu*, vol IV, p 261.
4. Interview with Imoto, 14 November 1977.
5. *Suihei Undo Shiryo Shusei*, vol III, p 40. For example, a report about the so-called Nuremberg Race Laws had appeared in the *Osaka Mainichi Shimbun*, 27 July. These were the laws forbidding miscegenation and cohabitation of different races.
6. S Moroka, Suiheisha: Takamatsu Chino Sabetsu Saiban Kyudan Toso : (The Takamatsu Court Discrimination Censure Struggle) *Gendai no Me*, vol 14, no 2 (1974), p 119.
7. *Suihei Undo Shiryo Shusei*, vol III, pp 35-6.
8. *Suihei Undo Shiryo Shusei*, vol III, pp 41-2.
9. *Suihei Undo Shiryo Shusei*, vol III, pp 52-3.
10. Moroka, p 128.
11. Moroka, p 129.
12. *Suihei Undo Shiryo Shusei*, vol III, pp 55-6. Moroka, p 128.
13. Yamagi, *Hiroshimaken Shakai Undoshi* (1970), pp 671-2.
14. Yamagi, (1970), p 673.
15. Yamagi, (1970), pp 674-6. *Buraku no Jittai*: Hiroshima-ken Fuchu shi p 43. *Suihei Undo Shiryo Shusei*, vol III, pp 61-2. Perhaps one reason that this campaign had attracted the attention of the campaign committee is that in 1927 there had been a major campaign on the island against a local mayor which itself was related to earlier anti-discrimination campaigns. Nakano Shigeru, *Hiroshima ken: Suihei Undo Shi* (A History of the *Suihei* Movement in Hiroshima Prefecture). First published 1930. Republished 1971.
16. *Suihei Undo Shiryo Shusei*, vol III, pp 247-8, Yamagi, p 681.
17. 1934: 50 incidents reported, no 5 in the country; 1935: 57 incidents reported, no 2 in the country; 1936: 55 incidents reported, no 3 in the country. Figures from *Suihei Undo Shiryo Shusei*, vol III, pp 199, 254, 305.
18. Oyama, pp 205-6. A Special Police report gives a list of 25 groups active in Mie in June 1932 with a total of 1,164 members. *Suihei Undo Shiryo Shusei*, vol II, p 646.
19. Oyama, p 218. *Suihei Undo Shiryo Shusei*, vol III, p 16.
20. Oyama, p 212.
21. *Suihei Undo Shiryo Shusei*, vol III, p 35.
22. Moroka, p 126.
23. *Suihei Undoshi no Kenkyu*, vol IV, p 98.
24. *Suihei Undo Shiryo Shusei*, vol III, pp 221-4. Despite the firm resolve to carry out the survey demonstrated by this resolution, it does not seem to have been translated into any practical activity.
25. *Suihei Undo Shiryo Shusei*, vol III, pp 224-5.
26. *Suihei Undo Shiryo Shusei*, vol III, p 204.
27. *Suihei Undo Shiryo Shusei*, vol III, pp 282-5. See also, *Suihei Undoshi no Kenkyu*, vol IV, p 392 and Yagi, pp 105-7. Associated with the *Kokuhonsha* (in which Hiranuma was a leading figure) the *Meirinkai* was composed of officers from the upper echelons of the military with a small but homogeneous membership. Tanin and Yohan categorise it as a reactionary group for it advocated the abolition of the party system though it favoured the retention of the Diet. Tanin and Yohan, pp 267, 273.
28. Yagi, p 106.
29. *Suihei Undo Shiryo Shusei*, vol III, pp 511-2.
30. One example of this is recorded in *Hiroshima Ken: Hisabetsu Buraku no Rekishi*, pp 246f. It seems unlikely to have been an isolated case.

31. *Suihei Undo Shiryo Shusei*, vol III, pp 264-276.

32. *Suihei Undo Shiryo Shusei*, vol III, pp 277-8.

33. *Suihei Undo Shiryo Shusei*, vol II, p 613.

34. Kitahara, p 241.

35. *Yuwa Jigyo Nenkan*, no 6 (1931), pp 2-3.

36. *Yuwa Jigyo Nenkan*, no 16 (1941), pp 7-8.

37. *Yuwa Jigyo Nenkan*, no 8 (1933), p 8.

38. 1,347,813 yen of 1,500,000 yen. *Yuwa Jigyo Nenkan*, no 8 (1933), p 136.

39. For example, the emergency fund money in Hiroshima was spent in the following way:

	No of projects	Cent Govt Grant	Amount for Labour	Total
1932	146	85,000 yen	57,851	88,868
1933	272	101,000 yen	60,622	106,236
1934	187	55,000 yen	33,188	58,898
1935	196	34,000 yen	22,342	37,289

Suihei Undo Shiryo Shusei, vol III, p 123.

40. This and the summary of reports noted below is derived from a detailed account of the implementation of the emergency fund plan in most parts of the country. The report is dated June 1934 and is reprinted *Suihei Undo Shiryo Shusei*, vol III, pp 99-117.

41. Edited highlights of these reports can be found in *Suihei Undo Shiryo Shusei*, vol III. The first entitled Keizai Kosei e no Michi (The Path to Economic Regeneration) appears pp 77-86, the second with the title Keizai Kosei Undo ni Kansuru Yoko (A general plan for the Economic Regeneration Movement), pp 87-92.

42. *Suihei Undo Shiryo Shusei*, vol III, pp 134-5.

43. *Suihei Undo Shiryo Shusei*, vol III, pp 175-185.

44. *Hiroshima ken: Hisabetsu Buraku no Rekishi*, p 268.

45. *Buraku no Jittai: Hiroshima ken Fuchushi*, p 45.

46. *Suihei Undoshi no Kenkyu*, vol IV, p 357. It is not clear how this campaign was resolved.

47. The main part of this table is taken from M Takahashi, 'The Development of Wartime Economic Controls', *Developing Economies*, vol V, no 4 (December 1967), p 654, who gives his source as *Showa Zaiseishi*, vol III, 1950. I have added the figures referring to the Emergency *Yuwa* project.

48. *Yuwa Jigyo Nenkan*, no 8 (1933). pp 358-360.

49. *Yuwa Jigyo Nenkan*, no 8 (1933), pp 14-15.

50. *Suihei Undo Shiryo Shusei*, vol III, pp 437-8.

51. See, for example, *Yuwa Jigyo Nenkan*, no 12 (1937), pp 185-9, for a detailed description of one such conference.

52. *Suihei Undo Shiryo Shusei*, vol III, p 443.

53. For more details of the plan's formation and an account of events at the third conference see, *Suihei Undo Shiryo Shusei*, vol III, pp 345-357.

54. *Yuwa Jigyo Nenkan*, no 8 (1933), pp 25-6.

55. *Suihei Undo Shiryo Shusei*, vol III, pp 375-6.

56. *Yuwa Jigyo Nenkan*, no 10 (1935), pp 23-30.

57. *Suihei Undo Shiryo Shusei*, vol III, p 902. The exception, the Kure group, was based in the town hall.

58. Smethurst (1974), p 43.

59. Iwamura Toshio, pp 268-271. The Koreans resident in Japan, like the *Burakumin*, were regarded as being likely targets for the left wing groups and, indeed, a large proportion of the support for the Japanese Communist Party in the 1930s came

from the Korean communities.

60. J T Winkler, Corporatism, *Archive Europeene Sociologie* (1976), p 101, quoting P Selznick, TVA and the Grass Roots.
61. *Suihei Undoshi no Kenkyu*, vol IV, pp 294-5.
62. *Suihei Undoshi no Kenkyu*, vol IV, p 401.
63. *Suihei Undoshi no Kenkyu*, vol IV, p 391.
64. This follows the periodisation suggested by T R H Havens, *Valley of Darkness* (New York, W W Norton, 1978), p 7.
65. Havens, pp 2-3.

CHAPTER EIGHT

Suiheisha, *Yuwa* and the War

The greatest change in the theory and practice of the *Suiheisha* during the first half of the 1930s was the increased prominence of pragmatic politics. This was, in part, necessitated by the fact that the decline in living standards in the *Buraku* was so serious that first priority had to be given to the advocacy of policies which would produce immediate effects. When the Communist Party endorsed a more realistic assessment of the prospects for the revolutionary movement in Japan which gave the *Suiheisha* an important role to play in the removal of 'feudal' remnants from society the way lay open for them to adopt a range of policies which would be popular with the masses. The third constraint on the progress of *Suiheisha* theory and practice was, of course, the tolerance of the police. It became increasingly difficult to criticise any aspect of government policy without risking arrest or the confiscation of offending documents. If the *Suiheisha* were to be effective in doing anything to reduce prejudice and discrimination and relieve poverty in the *Buraku* it had to gain access to government funds and ensure that they were utilised to best effect. As this process continued, so the *Suiheisha*'s ideas and activities began to resemble those of the *Yuwa* movement, and there arose suggestions that the two movements should co-operate and, later, merge identities. Thus, by the end of the 1930s, we find leaders of the *Suiheisha* movement advocating policies that less than five years before they would have denounced as 'fascist' and 'imperialist'. This change of ideas was, for the movement as a whole, a slow process and took place in a social and political environment in which all those who remained active were adapting their theories to take into account the need to support the Japanese state at a time of crisis. Before we explain the changes that took place in the *Suiheisha*, we must try to outline the political changes which were taking place in the surrounding society.

The Political Background

As indicated earlier, once the established political parties lost their grip on political power in 1931 they lost most of their prestige and this ensured that they would never regain a prominent political role. The political changes which took place at Cabinet level in the late 1930s were complex, but apart from the efforts made by Prince Konoe to moderate the influence of the army on government policy, the government remained firmly under the control of the military and civil bureaucracy and was virtually impervious to any criticism that might originate from the established parties. For our purposes this is important in that it meant that if and when those active in the *Suiheisha* turned away from leftist politics and groups there was no central or even moderate right wing political party to which they could turn. By this time, the parties' grass roots organisations had atrophied, never having been strong, and it was apparent to all that they were politically impotent.

At the other end of the political spectrum the Japanese Communist Party had been removed as an effective actor on the political stage by the arrests of 1931 and 1932. As Beckman and Okubo write,

> The history of the Japanese Communist Party as a political organisation terminates with the 1932 arrests.[1]

Isolated groups were to emerge from time to time, but they were always arrested before they had the opportunity to develop the large organisations they planned. These arrests were a formidable deterrent to many, but for others the Party was discredited in the eyes of activists in search of an organisation after the well publicised *tenko* of many of its former leaders and the abrupt change in policy in 1932 made for the convenience of the Comintern. For the time being at least, the social democratic groups appeared to be a more viable alternative.

The non-communist leftist groups emerged from the 1920s in a state of disarray, but by 1931 the two major parties were the National Farmer-Labour Masses Party (*Zenkoku Rono Taishuto*), which claimed a membership of 60,000, and the Social Democratic Party (*Shakai Minshuto*), which had a membership of 63,000. They differed mainly on the issue of the Manchurian venture. The Social Democrats took a guarded position in their response to the outbreak of hostilities combining a determination to advance the cause of democratic socialism with a desire not to alienate the military and a hope that the *zaibatsu* and capitalism itself would be kept out of Manchuria. On the other hand, the NFLMP openly opposed Japanese policy in Manchuria, demanded the withdrawal of troops and was very critical of the SDP for pandering to this trend towards 'fascism'. However, in the general election of 1932 the total poll received by the parties of the left dropped to one half that of the previous election and both parties were weakened by the depression which had greatly reduced available funds. In May of that year Akamatsu Katsumaro, secretary-general of the SDP, who had been trying to lead the party in the direction of national socialism, finally left the party, taking with him a substantial group of followers, and subsequently formed the *Nihon Kokka Shakaito* (Japan State Socialist Party). Meanwhile, the NFLMP also split when a section of its membership tried to force the adoption of a motion favouring 'a practical strategy suitable to our state and society'.[2] The defection of these nationalist elements stimulated the unification of the remaining majority factions in the formation of the *Shakai Taishuto* (Social Masses Party). The new party adopted policies which included absolute opposition to imperialist and capitalist wars, support for the principle of equality of all the races of the world, the reduction of the financial and tax burden on the masses, measures which would stabilise their livelihood through the state control of staple industries and the introduction of proper labour legislation and comprehensive housing and medical care services.[3] However, they saw little hope that the masses would turn towards the Diet to change matters and the party leaders, Aso Hisahi in particular, were less anti-military than anti-bourgeoisie and anti-capitalist. By the mid-1930s the SMP leaders did not regard the party's anti-fascist and anti-capitalist principles as precluding the possibility of an alignment with some of the young nationalist army officers. Aso was encouraged by 'the union of class-oriented thought with renovationist Japanism' and he envisaged a new Japanism emerging in which those ideas,

> which had previously emphasised the historical qualities of Japan and ignored the nature of the world, would gradually merge with a more 'leftist' spirit of reform which had hitherto emphasised only the nature of the world while ignoring the historical qualities of Japan.[4]

These social democrats were staunchly anti-communist and decidedly anti-capitalist, but they were unclear what they supported. During the 1930s they adjusted their position for tactical reasons to the extent that all that remained unchanged was their opposition to the established Diet parties.

In its early years the *Suiheisha* movement had been opposed to participation in Parliamentary politics, but from 1927 members stood for election to positions in the Diet as well as prefectural and town or village councils. Positive participation in the governmental process at all levels was one of the strategies recommended in the *Buraku Iinkai Katsudo* programme as a way in which *Burakumin* could ensure that *Yuwa* money was efficiently allocated to improve conditions in the *Buraku*. In 1932 there were only 38 *Suiheisha* representatives on town councils in central and western Japan, but two years later over 270 *Suiheisha* members sat on councils from prefectural to village levels.[5] Members were instructed that in both central and local elections they should not vote for the candidates put forward by the established parties – the 'running dogs' of the capitalist/landlord class – but should support those who could be trusted to work in the interests of the oppressed classes; in most areas this meant they would give their support to the SMP.[6] This increase in active participation in the local elections occurred as the movement's leaders and mass support were changing their primary allegiance from the 'illegal' strategies of the communist groups to identification with the legal tactics of the social democrats.

However, the most important breakthrough for both the SMP and the *Suiheisha* came in the elections held on 20 February 1936. Thirty candidates were put forward including Matsumoto Jiichiro, who stood in the Fukuoka constituency, and he was one of the 18 who were elected. His participation in the peasant unions as well as his experience in the *Suiheisha* had enabled him to attract a wide spectrum of support; it is thought that only 6,000 of the 15,000 votes he received came from *Burakumin*. Once in the Diet, Matsumoto worked within the left wing of the SMP trying to organise a united front of proletarian groups.

After their success in the 1936 general elections, there seemed to be at least a possibility that the leftist forces might be able to exert some influence over government policy through the Diet and reverse the trend towards militarisation. Already, in January 1936, proletarian groups both inside and outside the Diet had met to discuss the idea of a popular front, but the series of discussions was interrupted by the imposition of martial law following the abortive military coup of 26 February. Nevertheless, a group continued to keep these ideas in circulation and, shortly after martial law restrictions were raised, in early July, the Labour-Farmer Proletarian Council was formed with three basic aims:

> to form a united anti-fascist political front of the proletarian class, to expand and extend the labour unions and peasant unions, to protect and expand the economic and political gains of the proletariat.[7]

Matsumoto Jiichiro and Kuroda Hisao of the *Zenno* tried hard to persuade the SMP to merge with this new organisation, but their efforts were unsuccessful. At its December conference a statement was issued which labelled the popular front movement as 'an unrealistic struggle which ignores the social forces of our country'.[8] Kuroda and Matsumoto even held meetings with the leaders of the established parties hoping to form a broad, anti-fascist front which would protect Parliamentary government and political freedom, but their proposals were ignored. Thus, by early 1937, the advocates of a popular front policy were isolated from the other political groups and it was decided to establish a separate political party, the *Nihon Musanto* (Japan Proletarian Party), in February 1937. Its first platform was banned for being too radical and a more moderate statement had to be produced.

In the subsequent elections in April, the proletarian parties increased their representation in the Diet from 23 to 36 and the popular vote for the left wing groups increased from about 500,000 in 1936 to over one million in 1937. However, only one candidate representing the *Nihon Musanto* was elected. Throughout its development the popular front movement had been subject to the close surveillance of the Special Police as it was suspected of being a Communist Party front organisation carrying out the Seventh Comintern Congress policy which called for the creation of broad, anti-fascist popular movements.[9] On 5 December 1936, 1,300 suspected party members were arrested and some of these had been active in the popular front movement. Fearing arrest and the suppression of the movement, they could not overtly oppose the war after the outbreak of hostilities in the summer of 1937; instead, they issued a statement demanding the peaceful resolution of the conflict, government assistance to those families who had sent their men to the front, full wages for soldiers and a reduction in rent for those families supporting active soldiers.[10] However, in the long run, this evasive attitude made no difference for the authorities became persuaded that they had to suppress the non-communist left wing groups as well. In December, the *Nihon Musanto* and associated groups were ordered to disband and 400 of those belonging to these organisations were arrested. At the same time, the SMP expelled all those who had advocated the popular front policy and denied that it had any connection with any of the dissolved organisations.

In October 1937, Kamei Kanichiro, now leader of the SMP, announced that the Party was no longer to be regarded as 'socialist' or 'democratic' and he began to do research on Nazi theories of the state and devise strategies to convert the Party into a mass organisation which would supplant the established parties.[11] The following month the Party made significant changes in its platform; the clause about the 'liberation of the proletarian classes' was replaced by one referring to the 'stabilisation of the people's livelihood', the overthrow of capitalism was changed to the reform thereof and a clause was introduced vowing support for the *kokutai*.[12] The Party gave its full backing to the war effort and its leaders sought unification with the nationalist reform groups in order to build up a mass movement outside the Diet. Kamei foresaw the formation of a new mass party led by Konoe although Konoe himself refused to have anything to do with such plans. During the next few years the SMP entered into negotiations with other parties and groups in an attempt to form a new movement, but with no success. Following its failure to create a 'unitary, national, totalitarian party' through merger with the *Tohokai*, in February 1940, the Party broke down into its factional elements and Aso Hisashi led it into dissolution on 6 July in what were preliminary moves to the formation of the Imperial Rule Assistance Association (*Taisei Yokusankai*).[13]

The Development of Right Wing Elements within the Suiheisha

The *Nippon Suiheisha*, founded by Minami Umekichi at the height of the anarchist-Bolshevik struggle, continued to exist in name, but it had ceased to be active and none of his attempts to launch new right wing groups had been successful. In the Kanto area, Hirano was encouraging the *Suiheisha* groups to develop a more overtly nationalist orientation and was advocating co-operation between the *Suiheisha* and *Yuwa* groups. Generally however, those who felt unable to work in the leftist *Suiheisha* would join one of the *Yuwa* groups if they wanted to involve themselves in projects to improve the lot of their fellow *Burakumin*.

Right wing criticism of the *Suiheisha* which sought to influence its policy from within, as opposed to *Yuwa* criticism of the movement which was aimed at reducing its influence and ultimately replacing it, appeared in the mid-1930s from a group which was centred on those who had been the movement's radical leaders in the mid-1920s. Passing reference has already been made to the phenomenon of *tenko*, the process by which communists, socialists, and later liberals disavowed their left wing principles and publicly announced their commitment to Japanese nationalist values. The process began in June 1933 when Sano Manabu and Nabeyama Sadachika made the surprise announcement of their disillusionment with Comintern policy and their reconversion to a belief in the importance of the Emperor-centred state.[14] In the following years, many of the former members of the Communist Party issued similar statements either spontaneously or at the prompting of prison officials. In nearly every case, the statement began by acknowledging a reawakening of national pride and belief in the importance of the Imperial family, they criticised the Comintern's advice as misleading and affirmed their support for the war in China on the grounds that it was a war of liberation of the Asian races.

One of the first of the former *Suiheisha* leaders to announce his conversion to a form of Emperor-centred, state socialism was Saiko Bankichi. As he was released in February 1933, his cannot be said to have been a typical *tenko* statement since it was made before the process of encouraging conversions in exchange for reduction in sentences was institutionalised. Nevertheless, his statement, produced shortly before being permitted to leave prison on parole ten months before his sentence was complete, bears all the hallmarks of a *tenko* statement.[15] On his release from prison, he got married and settled in Nara, where he contacted Sakamoto and Yoneda and began to discuss with them how he might disseminate his nationalist ideas. Akamatsu Katsumaro had left the SDP early in 1933 after disagreements over the issue of supporting the war in China and in April 1934 he was instrumental in establishing the *Nihon Kokka Shakaito* (Japan State Socialist Party) which sought 'to construct a new Japan without exploitation on the basis of the national spirit of millions of people under one ruler'.[16] Saiko, Sakamoto and Yoneda decided to join this party but remain within the *Suiheisha* movement in order to criticise the activities of the left wing group hoping to convert the whole organisation to the ideas of state socialism. By 1934 they seem to have attracted support from over 800 former *Suiheisha* members although their influence outside Nara prefecture seems to have been minimal. Nevertheless, they published a newspaper – *Gaito Shimbun* – in which they developed their ideas on how a *Showa* restoration would overthrow capitalism and create a new Japan in which there would be no exploitation. The selfish, egoistic, private production system which had developed under capitalism would be replaced by a communal system based on the Imperial family system and, in this way, economic and spiritual poverty would be overcome.[17] Later articles explained how these ideas could be applied both to solve the national crisis and the problems faced by the *Buraku* and peasant movements; the creation of this new society would usher in an era in which there would be no exploitation of the peasant nor prejudice or discrimination against *Burakumin*. The paper was produced until December 1938. In 1936, however, they parted company with the Japan State Socialist Party to form the *Kokoku Nomin Domei* (Loyal Peasants League). This group regarded peasant poverty as the basis of the nation's problems and they maintained that if only the peasantry united in solid support of the principles of the *Kokutai* all the problems could be solved. Saiko stood in the 1937 election as the *Kokoku Nomin Domei* candidate but was not elected, nor did the league's ideas attract much mass support.[18]

Kimura Kyotaro had been in prison for seven and a half years by the time he was released in September 1935. He, too, had been persuaded to produce a *tenko* statement in exchange for his release and he remembers being shown a copy of the statement produced by Sano and Nabeyama.[19] After his release, he remained under close supervision and had to report to the police once a month. This made it hard for him to establish any open links with those still active in the *Suiheisha* movement though he was aware that there was much that needed to be done to remove discrimination. He became active within his community's peasants' co-operative and attempted to organise a group to discuss how they could make improvements to their environment. Kimura and his colleagues from his time in the Communist Party, Kamemoto Genjuro and Nakamura Tadayoshi seem to have been influenced by Saiko's group and they started to produce a newspaper called the *Shinsei Undo* (Regeneration Movement) in which they tried to explain how the principles of *Nipponshugi* (Japanism) would liberate the *Buraku* economically, politically and socially.[20] The newspaper folded in December 1938, but the group seems to have maintained its connections with those who were demanding the *Suiheisha* movement adopt renovationist policies.

Kitahara Daisaku was arrested in January 1934 and, in the course of his interviews with the police, he began to have doubts about the correctness of the '1932 Theses' and was particularly worried by rumours of the 'lynching' of a suspected police spy by the Party's leaders.[21] In his *tenko* statement, he is critical of the Comintern's lack of concern with Japanese tradition and its total lack of understanding of the *Buraku* problem. He recognises the need for democratic economic change, but it must be one which preserves the *kokutai* and respects the national spirit. In the final section, he suggests the adoption of various policies all of which involve co-operation with the *Yuwa* movement which would contribute to a complete solution of the *Buraku* problem.[22] He was released in June 1935 and spent the next six months recuperating at Matsumoto's expense. Although he, too, continued to be subject to visits from the Special Police once or twice a month, this did not prevent him from working for Matsumoto. At first he assisted him with the election campaign and later he worked as his secretary in Tokyo, where he became actively involved in the attempts to form a popular front of proletarian groups. However, he claims that there was an atmosphere of factional rivalry which built up around Matsumoto and because of this he resigned from his position in the summer of 1938.[23]

Although the *Suiheisha* movement had managed to rebuild its central organisation and rejuvenate its local branches with co-ordinated campaigns and a coherent theory, it was revived at a time when the social democratic movement was divided and abandoning both socialist and democratic policies. Many of the most active members in the social movements were re-orienting their activism from a situation where they derived their ideological support not from socialism or Marxism but from Emperor-centred Japan. That Kitahara was permitted by the police to become active in the *Suiheisha* once more and was accepted by fellow activists after making what was presumably a genuine *tenko* statement, indicates the extent to which the *Suiheisha* was officially regarded as being at or near the centre of the acceptable political spectrum.

Suiheisha Activities on the Eve of War

There was still some commitment to radical ideas though. The major themes of the national conference planned for April 1936 in Saitama were opposition to fascism at home and war abroad. However, the conference was never held as the Saitama authorities refused to permit it on the grounds that not only was it adjacent to an area which was still under martial law (after the February 26 incident) but also because the themes were held to be subversive.[24] The 14th conference was not finally convened until March of the following year by which time the *Suiheisha* movement had adopted an ambivalent, not to say confused policy. On the one hand, they continued their criticisms of the *Yuwa* policy. The *Yuwa* projects were described as attempts by the ruling class to disguise the fact that discrimination emerges from the very system which supports the ruling class and the increasing concentration of Japanese capitalism was described as providing the economic basis for the growth of fascism. Moreover, the Ten Year Plan was said to be mainly concerned with strengthening the reactionary rule of bureaucratic fascism. Nevertheless, members were urged to take part in *Yuwa* activities in order to reduce their reactionary character and in order to co-ordinate the demands of the *Buraku* masses for a more thorough policy of improvements.

Thus far the policy was in line with the principles adopted a few years earlier. However, it was also decided to change the movement's Basic Principles. The 'class consciousness' clause was regarded as inappropriate as the *Suiheisha* was now considered to be not a class organisation but a movement founded on the basis of a common status consciousness; the concept of the 'right to live' was rejected as an abstract concept which had no practical meaning; and the 'by our own efforts' clause was described as having been originally introduced as a reaction to the activities of the *kaizen* (improvement) groups of the 1910s but which had led to 'exclusivism'.[25] These three planks of the old platform were replaced by one which read:

> We will protect and extend our human rights and freedom in all political, economic and cultural aspects by group struggle and achieve the absolute liberation of the oppressed *Buraku*.[26]

Two emergency motions were discussed, one demanding limitations on the privileges of the aristocracy (one of Matsumoto's major concerns) and another asking for state assistance for the families of soldiers serving at the front. There was also some concern expressed about the state of the movement's finances, which were not sufficient to keep the central organs afloat. Not much seems to have resulted from these complaints for when in the following July, 200 yen was urgently required, the problem was only resolved when Matsumoto agreed to provide half of it.[27]

After the conference Imoto Rinshi and six others were arrested and detained in prison, being suspected of planning to create a Communist Party cell within the *Suiheisha*.[28] The reaction of some of the movement's leaders to this was curious. At the next meeting of the central committee, which was held to cope with the disruption caused by these arrests, one member announced that while he regretted that Imoto had been arrested, it was important for the progress of the *Suiheisha* that all left wing elements be removed from the organisation. He even opposed the movement's continued support for the Social Masses Party on the grounds that it gave the impression that the *Suiheisha* was under Comintern directives.[29] Such views were perhaps not prevalent but they were becoming increasingly common.

So, while there continued to be some continued allegiance to left wing ideas (or at least left wing rhetoric), by revising the movement's basic principles the distinction between the *Suiheisha* and the *Yuwa* movements was eliminated. The *Suiheisha* was responding to demands from within and without that it adopt a more 'realistic' approach and this inevitably meant that it became hard to distinguish from its government sponsored rival.

Suiheisha activity in Hiroshima had recommenced in the wake of the Takamatsu campaigns and at least between 1934 and 1936 an annual prefectural conference was convened to discuss past campaigns and plan the future activities of the town and village groups. There had been an abortive attempt to revive the Communist Party cell in April 1934, but the group was destroyed when all its members were arrested.[30] After this there is no evidence of any attempt being made to create a left wing movement in the area, even the Social Masses Party was unable to establish a base in the prefecture.

This did not inhibit the development of the *Suiheisha*'s campaigns. The groups responded enthusiastically to the campaign against Lt Col Sato and it was developed in conjunction with demands for a comprehensive *Yuwa* policy in the armed forces. At the prefectural conference held in Fukuyama (5 April 1935) it was decided to send a delegation to the naval base in nearby Kure to demand the incorporation of *Yuwa* principles into their code of practice.[31] Some demands which emerged at these conferences calling for the formation of a united, anti-fascist front indicate that some of those who were active in Hiroshima were sympathetic to the attempts to form a popular front, but most of the campaigns which were waged against instances of discrimination or concerning the application of *Yuwa* funds had little overt political dimension. In general, the *Suiheisha* groups in Hiroshima concentrated on campaigning for more money to improve housing standards or to assist the development of projects such as oyster farming in some of the poor *Buraku* fishing villages. Conferences and co-ordinated campaigns continued until early 1937, but after this time there was a drop in organised activity.

As one might have expected, the supporters of the Mie *Suiheisha* were much more active politically than their counterparts in Hiroshima. In the spring of 1935, the reformist and radical wings of the peasants' movement were reunited and support developed for the Social Democratic Party. No left wing candidate stood in the elections of 1936, but in 1937 Ueda Onshi, a founder member of the *Suiheisha* and former member of the Communist Party, stood for election to the

Lower House.[32] Despite a donation of 1,000 yen from Matsumoto to assist his campaign and the support of *Suiheisha* and Peasant Union members, Ueda was not elected. Nevertheless, the campaign generated sufficient interest in the Social Masses Party to warrant the formation of a Mie branch of the party on 9 June. It was hoped to establish a network of groups across the prefecture starting from the *Suiheisha* and Peasant Union members who had taken part in the election campaign, which would unite working class strength in the area.[33] The group sponsored candidates in local council elections, and by the end of 1937 there were four of its members sitting on town councils and it had 16 representatives on village councils, 14 of whom were *Burakumin*.[34] Although there were now no Communist Party members in Mie, there were a few who, like Ueda, had been active members and several of these became interested in the activities of the Popular Front groups in Tokyo. However, simultaneous with the mass arrests in Tokyo, on 30 December a total of 86 people were arrested in Mie because of their links with the Popular Front movement. Only six of them were ultimately charged, but these arrests mark the end of concerted left wing activity in the prefecture.[35]

Suiheisha groups continued to exist, on paper at least, in both Mie and Hiroshima for the next three years and there were *Kyudan* campaigns carried out in their name. There was, however, a marked decline in activity co-ordinated either between groups within the prefecture or between national and local levels of the *Suiheisha* organisation. Although the central organs of the *Suiheisha* movement were to continue to exist until the early 1940s, from 1937 their activities were of increasingly little consequence to the mass of *Burakumin*, even those who had once been active supporters.

Kyudan Struggles – 1933–1940

After the movement's revival in 1933 and the adoption of the principles of the *Buraku Iinkai Katsudo*, the number of censure campaigns increased once again. As can be seen from Table 4 (see over), the number of incidents reported to the Home Ministry remained higher than that of the late 1920s until 1936, and even after 1938 there was not the sudden disappearance of overt discrimination and organised opposition to it that one might have expected. What is remarkable is the increase between 1933 and 1934 in the number of incidents which were resolved by an unconditional apology; the proportion increased from 14% to 54%. This trend continued until 1938 when over three-quarters of the cases were settled in this manner. This change can be explained, in part at least, by reference to the advice given in the principles of the *Buraku Iinkai Katsudo* that groups should try to resolve incidents in such a way as to 'encourage the unity of all oppressed people'. From around this time, too, the *Yuwa* groups began to play a role in some of the disputes, mediating between the antagonistic parties, thus contributing to peaceful settlements.

From 1932 the Home Ministry categorised *Kyudan* incidents according to the reason for the original complaint (see Table 3, p 134), although since we do not

Table 4: *Reported Incidents of Discrimination and their Resolution, 1922–1942*

	Number of Incidents	Type of Discrimination					Mode of Solution				Unresolved	Dealt with by Justice Ministry
		Spoken	Action	Written	Treatment	Other	Unconditional Apology	Conditional Apology	Spontaneous Disappearance	Other Solution		
1922¹	69											
1923	854											
1924	1052											
1925	1025											
1926	825											
1927	567											
1928	620											
1929	484						31	384	17	20	36	6
1930	557						60	392	46	21	29	9
1931	736						69	525	67	36	27	12
1932	652	506	75	9	52	10	101	386	65	74	16	10
1933²	752											
1934	824	632	93	31	46	22	123	507	76	79	20	19
1935	715	555	81	19	50	10	390	125	64	114	22	–
1936	650	498	81	18	39	14	386	147	46	57	13	27
1937	474	387	45	6	29	19	324	73	25	33	19	12
1938	499	416	43	5	24	11	379	41	27	43	9	17
1939	417	358		17	18	24	352		51	–	14	9
1940	373	330		14	18	11	338		26	–	9	3
1941	348	322		8	10	7	322		25	–	1	10
1942	294	263		8	12	11	260		29	–	5	4

Source: *Suihei Undo Shiryo Shusei*, Vol III, p 1028

1. The source table had no entry for 1922; this figure was found *Suihei Undo Shiryo Shusei*, vol I, p 256.
2. The original table contained no figures for 1933; this figure was found *Suihei Undo Shiryo Shusei*, vol III, p 14.

know what definitions were used to classify these incidents, the information is
not as useful as it might be. It does confirm what has been said previously that a
majority of the incidents (over 75%), resulted from spoken insults while only
around 5% actually involved discriminatory treatment. If we turn to examine
those incidents which resulted in police intervention and/or publicity in the
Suihei Shimbun the pattern appears to be similar to that described before. Many
cases involved schools and in the campaigns which developed it was usually
insisted that the headmaster accept responsibility for the incident, though
occasionally criticism was also extended to include the local government
authorities. A large group of incidents involved the police, usually when they had
made a wrongful arrest. Such events, the protesters claimed, provided evidence
that the police still held the idea that *Burakumin* constituted a criminal class. The
other incidents involving the army, public officials, shrines and temples also
centred on the use of insulting words or, more rarely, discriminatory actions
which in some, usually small way were considered to reinforce prejudice against
Burakumin.[36]

One major change in emphasis that occurred was the emergence of campaigns
complaining about prejudice in the mass media, especially in films and radio.
Two films in particular were strongly criticised for containing scenes which the
Suiheisha argued would perpetuate existing stereotypes. The second campaign
was particularly interesting in that the film '*Fujin Sendara*' was set in Edo in the
Tokugawa period and examined the problem of marriage and society at the time
of Danzaemon and Kuruma Zenhichi. When first informed of the *Suiheisha*'s
objections the writer of the script is said to have retorted that he had written
about the lives of the *hinin* and the story had nothing to do with the *Buraku*
problem. Still, the *Suiheisha* persevered and was able to persuade those involved
of the connection between the portrayal of prejudice on the screen even in
histories and the recreation of discrimination in contemporary everyday life.
Finally, the producer of the film admitted that the film probably could
encourage negative stereotypes and even expressed himself grateful to the
Suiheisha for making him examine the problem in depth. No longer was the aim
of the movement simply to wring an apology out of the alleged discriminator but
rather the *Kyudan* campaign was seen as an almost educational process which
sought to make him or her realise the harm that they were causing, whether
intentional or not.[37]

Radio, too, was subject to *Suiheisha* protests. On 25 December 1935, in a
programme about the *Meiji* radical Nakae Chomin, there was material broadcast
which was clearly insulting to *Burakumin*.[38] Imoto and others immediately sent
protests to the offices of the radio company in Tokyo and Osaka. The company,
NHK, was controlled by the Ministry of the Post Office and, after a meeting with
the *Suiheisha* representative in March, they agreed to take care to ensure that no
more derogatory remarks would be made and that time would be set aside for
serious discussion of the *Yuwa* problem. Furthermore, a committee was
established of programme controllers and representatives from the *Suiheisha* to

discuss ways in which this time could be used. One result was that on 28 August 1937 Matsumoto made a broadcast to the whole nation on the significance of the Emancipation Declaration and how the discrimination which continued to exist should be overcome.[39]

After the decision taken in 1937 to give, at first qualified, support to the drive for national unity, the *Suiheisha* central committee and later the conferences urged the local groups to conduct their *Kyudan* campaigns in co-operation with the *Yuwa* groups and other government bodies. If the incidents were handled in an enlightened manner they would serve to foster the development of national unity which was essential for the success of the new order in East Asia.[40] There was no immediate reduction in the total number of discrimination incidents, although by 1940 there were about half as many as there had been at the peak in the 1930s and about 90% of the campaigns were being settled with a simple apology. It seems that by this time the *Suiheisha* was having very little direct influence on the protests. The Home Ministry reports give detailed information on the 417 incidents of 1939 and only 38 (9%) involved groups associated with the national *Suiheisha*, 14 involved other groups, 44 were associated with the *Yuwa* groups and the other 321 incidents involved no intermediary group.[41] In 1941, the only other year for which similar figures are available, only 14 incidents involved a group belonging to the national *Suiheisha*, a mere 4% of the total.[42] It seems reasonable to conclude that the *Kyudan* incidents were not manifestations of *Suiheisha* activity and that there was no direct relationship between the number of *Kyudan* struggles and the level of *Suiheisha* activity. One suspects that the number of incidents that involved *Suiheisha* groups declined quite sharply towards the end of the 1930s, but these figures demonstrate that the movement inspired many to continue to protest against instances of discrimination even after the formally constituted *Suiheisha* groups disappeared (see Table 3, p 134).

Despite 20 years of *Suiheisha* campaigns and the much publicised appeals for national unity, there were still public officials who displayed overt prejudice in public pronouncements even during the war. In 1939, in Kyoto, a village mayor was gratuitously insulting towards *Burakumin* at a ceremony to send off a group of newly-recruited soldiers.[43] In Wakayama in 1942 at a memorial service for soldiers killed in battle there is reported to have been an instance of blatant discrimination which provoked protest from leaders of the *Buraku* communities.[44] During the late 1930s the press was brought firmly under state control. Under the pretext of the need to save paper the number of daily newspapers shrank from several hundred to 54, virtually one for each prefecture, and the content of these papers was carefully screened.[45] One assumes that it would no longer be possible to report an instance of discrimination or protest against it so that if such events did take place no record of them would remain. There is some suggestion that *Burakumin* were somewhat less cowed by the authoritarian powers acquired by the state in the war years than their fellow citizens. There are reports of *Burakumin* in Nara prefecture organising to demand increased rations in 1943 and later that year in Gumma prefecture some *Burakumin* began to demand rent reductions, but the movements were easily controlled. It is impossible to say how extensive this *Burakumin* resistance to wartime controls was, though it is unlikely it was widespread. Nevertheless, there appear to have been rumours spread which suggested that bands of *eta* were seeking to hasten Japan's defeat by derailing trains and burning factories in the hope that discrimination would disappear in a defeated Japan.[46] Apparently the efforts of both the *Yuwa* and *Suiheisha* movements had not been sufficient to dispel popular beliefs about the un-Japaneseness of the *Burakumin*.

The Suiheisha and Yuwa Movements and the Outbreak of War

During the summer of 1937 Japan's commitment to war in China deepened after the Marco Polo Bridge and Shanghai incidents. On 11 September, an enlarged central committee meeting was held to discuss how the *Suiheisha* should react to the emergency; a statement was produced, mimeographed and circulated to all the local branches. While they looked forward to a rapid return to peace and a situation of mutual co-existence between the Japanese and Chinese people, they felt obliged to participate in the plans to foster national unity on the basis of which the *Yuwa* problem would be solved. They urged the government to continue to improve living standards despite its wartime obligations, special assistance was to be given to the families of active servicemen while at the same time they instructed their members to seek solutions to the *Kyudan* campaigns which would positively contribute to the strengthening of national unity.[47] It will be noticed that despite the slightly increased stress on national unity this policy statement reflects quite closely that which the *Nihon Musanto* (Japan Proletarian Party) produced at the same time and it seems safe to assume the committee was strongly influenced by them.

As the war in China became the major issue in Japanese politics, so the military influence over government policy increased. In March 1938 a National Mobilisation Bill passed through the Diet giving the government wide powers of control over the nation's resources and personnel whether directly or indirectly connected to the war effort. It allowed for the control of prices and goods, the regulation of wages and working conditions and there was to be stricter censorship of the press and other media.[48] The aim was to 'utilise human and material resources to the full extent of the total power of the nation for the attainment of defence purposes' and to establish a legal framework which would strengthen the powers of intervention of the state into the economy.[49] Furthermore, the importance of securing access to Manchuria and Northern China increased as Japan was excluded from access to raw materials elsewhere in Asia by action taken by the United States and Britain. Plans were made to co-ordinate the Japanese economy with that on the continent through development corporations and these plans were popularised at home in propaganda about the forthcoming 'New Order in East Asia'.

The size of the *Suiheisha* during the late 1930s, at least according to Home Ministry reports, seems to have remained fairly stable although our knowledge of the state of local groups makes us doubt whether there was much grass roots activity. Even the police reports note a reduction in activity, the abandoning of struggle tactics and the adoption of co-operative tactics based on the principles of *kokutai*. Successive central committee meetings held in February, April and June 1938 adopted policies which encourage collaboration with government policy and indicate a total rejection of the movement's political principles. At the June meeting, it was decided to replace the basic principle introduced the previous year with one that read:

> Conforming to the essence of the *kokutai* we will contribute to national prosperity by the perfection of conciliation among the people.

At the same meeting, a draft movement plan was presented which recommended positive co-operation with national mobilisation, co-operation with the developments on the Chinese continent including support for the emigration policies, and demands for the reform and extension of the *Yuwa* programme.[50]

These trends towards support of the government policy were confirmed at the Fifteenth conference held the following November in Osaka. The 77 delegates at this conference supported motions and statements endorsing the war in China since, after all, it was Japan's historical duty to free the subject Asian races from the fetters of British and American imperialism and build a new co-prosperity sphere in East Asia. The basic revision of the Japanese urban and rural economy which would occur within this new order would create the circumstances in which a solution to the *Yuwa* problem would take place. There was some criticism of the continuation of discrimination in the army and of the activities and statements of one of the *Yuwa* movement leaders, but this took place within very rigid restrictions which were enforced by the attendant police; even a motion suggesting the reform of the nobility system was ordered to be erased from the minutes. Further advice was given on how the *Kyudan* struggles were to be carried out. *Suiheisha* and *Yuwa* groups were to co-operate with each other to mediate in such disputes where the overall aim should be to encourage the general mobilisation of the national spirit. The motion passed at the previous conference which described the *Yuwa* policy as deceptive was called a 'mistake' and the conference decided that it was important to co-operate with the *Yuwa* groups at all levels even though the Ten Year Plan needed to be revised to take into consideration the changes in national circumstances. The day after the conference, the *Suiheisha* delegates met with 39 representatives of *Yuwa* groups, the Honganji and other organisations to discuss ways in which the gap between the two organisations could be bridged and to work out common approaches to the problems caused by discrimination.[51]

The *Yuwa* project gained a new significance in the context of the national emergency and the plans for the co-prosperity sphere. At an extraordinary meeting of *Yuwa* group leaders held in October, it was decided that the movement should participate in the drive for national mobilisation, individual groups were to make *Burakumin* aware of the significance of the emergency and show how it gave them a chance to prove themselves.[52] The next month, more detailed proposals were made itemising the kind of work the groups should become involved in. Four main areas were indicated: encouragement of enlistment, promotion of the development of productive power, strengthening *Yuwa* groups, and taking a lead in assisting *Burakumin* to find new jobs. To assist the movement fulfil these aims a supplementary budget of 678,000 yen was provided, of which 200,000 yen was to assist *Burakumin* to change their occupation and 360,000 yen was to aid the unemployed.[53] Government surveys indicated that about 35% of the population in the *Buraku* was either unemployed or under-employed and that the number of unemployed was increasing at a rate of 15,000 a year. *Yuwa* programmes were devised to employ this surplus population and, in particular, they were to be directed towards the war supply industries.[54] Those who could not be employed were encouraged to migrate. Over 15% of the money allocated in the Ten Year Plan was to have been used to encourage migration and, though it is not clear what kind of priority was given to these plans, there appears to have been a large amount spent on holding meetings to encourage migration to Manchuria and Mongolia and in some cases migrants were given monetary assistance from *Yuwa* funds.[55]

The *Yuwa* movement fitted in well with the plans for National Mobilisation. As already mentioned, in 1938 the *Yuwa* day was extended to last a week and was renamed the National Spiritual Mobilisation *Yuwa* week. Within the *Buraku* communities, the *Yuwa* groups took on the tasks of encouraging the mobilisation of soldiers and workers and assisting the families that were left behind.[56] It was expected that soldiers would fight better (and workers work harder) if they were assured that their families were being looked after at home. There was special concern about the state of the leather industry which had been adversely affected by the sudden drop in imported hides and import of tannin. The government organised co-operatives of leather producers through which the scarce raw materials were distributed.[57] Where there was an insufficient supply of hides to keep the leather factories open, *Burakumin* were recruited into the munitions industry. Thus the *Yuwa* movement mobilised the *Buraku* workforce to ensure it best served the national interest. As the state of emergency became more serious, so the problem of solving the *Yuwa* problem was seen to be more urgent, or at least it was more important to convince people that something was being done. However, within the movement the nationalist ideas predominated and the liberals who had formed an important tendency in it were forced to resign.[58]

The Movement's Final Years – divided once more

The influence of the *Suiheisha* group was declining because of the restrictions placed on it by the police and because, even in these final years, internal divisions once more absorbed much of its leaders' time and energy. We have already indicated that from 1934 there was a group in Nara centred around Saiko Bankichi which was advocating uncritical support for the aggressive foreign policy and calling for a *Showa* restoration to solve all domestic problems. Both the *Gaito Shimbun* and *Shinsei Undo* had argued that the *Suiheisha* should abandon its exclusiveness and join in the wider struggle for renovation of the country in the process of which problems like *Buraku* discrimination would disappear. From early 1939, there was no disagreement over whether these ideas should be implemented, but there were differences over how they could be applied.

The activities of the national *Suiheisha* centred on Matsumoto and those close to him. In July 1939 a meeting of the movement's six leading activists was held to decide on their attitudes to the current political situation and how the movement should develop in the future. It was resolved to spend more energy putting into effect the motions passed at the previous conference and to encourage *Burakumin* to become positively involved in the creation of the new order in Asia.[59] Three thousand copies of a special edition of *Zensui News* were printed and circulated in order to spread these ideas. The general message contained in the circular is that discrimination is an obstacle to national unity and is something which cannot be overcome by seeking assistance from capitalist or liberal institutions but can only be removed by the creation of a new national order within which the miserable economic and cultural conditions in which *Burakumin* now exist will disappear. Although they seek to encourage the renovation of Japan they are not uncritical of the *Yuwa* policy; they point to the results of *Yuwa* surveys which indicate the extent of *Buraku* poverty, they urge that more money be spent on the *Yuwa* project, and object to the way *Yuwa* activists try to give the impression that the problem will soon be solved.[60]

The central caucus of the movement moved closer to a total acceptance of government policy but it was criticised for its 'liberal' policies by a group composed of former *Suiheisha* and former *Yuwa* group leaders. After Kitahara resigned from his job as Matsumoto's secretary, he found a job with the *Dai Nippon Rengo Seinendan* (Greater Japan Alliance of Youth Groups), a nationalist organisation. He now lived in Tokyo and he and Yamamoto Masao were members of the *Tokyo Kokutai Kenkyukai*, and under the influence of this group they began to develop their criticisms of the contemporary *Suiheisha* policy. With these two as the leading elements, in February of 1939 the *Yamatokai* was formed from the nationalist elements from the *Suiheisha* and the 'progressive' elements of the *Yuwa* movement.[61] The following October, Nozaki Seiji, formerly a leading member of the *Suiheisha*, wrote a statement on behalf of the group in which he is strongly critical of the *Suiheisha* for clinging to individualist ideas. The capitalist *zaibatsu* power must be destroyed and be replaced by a new corporate state based on co-operative groups within which systematic discrimination would disappear. The *Suiheisha*, he argued, had no reason to exist at the same time as the *Yuwa* movement and therefore should dissolve itself.[62] These ideas were supported by Asada, Matsuda and several others who had previously been members or sympathisers of the Communist Party. They held a preliminary meeting at a hot spring resort in Tottori late in 1939 and resolved to form a new movement. On 3 April a meeting of 40 delegates met in Osaka and agreed to publish a regular paper, to establish an office in Tokyo and hold meetings throughout the country to launch the *Buraku Kosei Komin Undo* (*Buraku* Welfare Citizens Movement).[63] They criticised both the 'class' and the 'liberal' aspects of the *Suiheisha* and wanted it to develop into a new kind of people's movement based on co-operative units which would oppose both capitalism and communism; in its present state it was a hindrance to the solution of the *Buraku* problem. They were equally hostile towards the *Yuwa* movement and attacked it for being based on liberal ideas, for being remote from the lives of *Burakumin* and for encouraging begging attitudes. Contacts were made with groups and activists in various parts of the country and they planned to hold a national conference on 28 August, a move that was deliberately provocative since the *Suiheisha* was planning to hold a conference on the same day.

While this group was establishing their organisation and elaborating their political position, Matsumoto and others were preoccupied with the fruitless task of trying to organise a new political movement based on the Diet. In fact, the differences between the two groups amounted to very little and, personal antipathies aside, it came down to the fact that Kitahara *et al.* argued that during the 'emergency' there was virtually no discrimination and thus no need for the *Suiheisha* or *Yuwa* movements, whereas Imoto and Matsumoto argued that even during the 'emergency' the movement was needed to oppose incidents of discrimination and demand more improvements.[64] An example of discrimination took place in the Diet, as if to prove Matsumoto's point, when one of the members made an insulting reference to *Burakumin* during a debate on education (February 1940). The issue was taken up by Matsumoto and an apology received.[65] By mid-summer 1940, there was little to distinguish the two groups. Imoto produced a pamphlet entitled 'The new party of the whole nation and our attitude' in which he discussed the plans to set up the new national organisation under Konoe's leadership. At a central committee meeting held on 4 August it was decided that the *Suiheisha* could not afford to be left out of the new political order.

Following this, 6,000 leaflets were produced to publicise the forthcoming conference which was to be held in the Honganji temple in Tokyo on 28 August. Nearly 200 delegates attended this conference, but there was little discussion or controversy. The first two motions passed were ones of praise to the Imperial Army and thanksgiving to the injured soldiers. The only document of interest which was produced at the conference was the declaration which explained how the *Suiheisha* and *Yuwa* movements had started from different positions but now had the same aims and so should work together within the new order. Japan was, it was said, in the process of constructing a new world order and a new Japan in which the feudal remnants of the old order would be removed as would capitalism, liberalism and individualism. Preparations were made to establish the *Daiwa Kokumin Undo* to co-ordinate the activities of the *Yuwa* and *Suiheisha* groups.[66]

The *Komin Undo* had always contained latent tension between the former *Yuwa* members who regarded the movement as a study group or vanguardist organisation and the former *Suiheisha* leaders like Nozaki and Asada who wanted to develop the organisation as a mass movement. The former group controlled the finances which came from Arima via Yamamoto, while the latter group had the energy, gave the movement its dynamism and, for the time being, was predominant.[67] Their conference, held in Osaka, was attended by over 100 delegates, but there was very little productive which came out of it. A long declaration was produced discussing the movement's political background and its attitude to the current crisis, but the conclusion, that both the *Yuwa* and *Suihei* movements had fulfilled their historic role and should form a new movement, was very similar to that passed the same day at the *Suiheisha* conference. The whole movement then was agreed, in principle, that they should take active part in the new political order which was to be led by Konoe.

Throughout the summer of 1940 many political groups, social movement organisations and labour unions had dissolved their organisations in anticipation of the formation of a new organisation to be led by Konoe. Utilising a new leadership principle, this organisation would unite civilian and military interests and provide political leadership for the masses. All Japanese would be recruited into vocational and cultural groups which would be linked together through a 'nucleal' group which would act as a link between the central government and the individual, to formulate policies and organise support for them. On 17 September, it was announced that the nucleal group was to be known as the *Taisei Yokusankai* (Imperial Rule Assistance Association – IRAA). Less than a month later the movement's organisational network and social programme was announced and the general objective was specified as 'fulfilling the way of the subject in assisting the Imperial rule'. At least in its early stages, the movement promised different things for different people. Konoe hoped to organise a political base from which he could oppose the militarists and obtain a peaceful settlement to the war in China and also regarded it as a bulwark against social revolution.[68] Meanwhile, Aso Hisashi considered it a means by which the mass energies of socialism could be preserved and Ozaki Hotsumi thought that it contained the 'germs of a Leninist party which could replace the decimated and tactically bankrupt Japanese Communist Party'.[69] Its liberal supporters – Arima Yoriyasu was its first secretary general – hoped that the new movement would be able to impose its will on the army and army-dominated bureaucracy. However, the movement was never allowed to develop a political role. From January 1941 it was not permitted to formulate its own policies, the leadership of the movement was, in effect, ceded to the Home Ministry and the Army subverted the association as a convenient organisational device for placing the economy on a wartime basis.

Throughout 1939 and 1940 Matsumoto and Imoto had been engaged in negotiations with *Yuwa* officials considering how far they could co-operate with each other and what form this co-operation could take. In September the

Suiheisha and *Yuwa* representatives were joined by two delegates from the *Kosei Komin Undo* group to discuss the movement's future. The following month, further meetings were held, culminating in an enlarged meeting of 64 delegates held on 2 November. Here Matsumoto and Imoto explained the developments of the past months and recommended to the delegates that they agree to the dissolution of the *Suiheisha* movement and give their full support to the *Daiwa Hokoku* movement whose founding meeting was to be held the following day. Representatives of all the interested groups attended this meeting which was chaired by retired General Shimamoto. Its aims – to build and serve the new order and work with the IRAA – were unanimously approved and a central committee of 18 was elected of whom five had been leaders of the *Suiheisha*. Though the nature of this group is by no means clear it would seem to be an example of the 'vocational and cultural' groups which were to be established within the IRAA's umbrella structure.[70]

The *Kosei Komin Undo* central committee met in Osaka to discuss the new situation and, although there was general disagreement with the new movement's aims, they were persuaded by Kitahara to abandon their oppositional attitudes and work for the achievement of their aims from within the *Hokoku* movement. Moreover, now that the *Buraku* movement was committed to working within the IRAA, the *Kosei Komin Undo* had fulfilled its original aims and they formally dissolved the movement leaving just a research group to maintain contacts between the members.[71] *Yuwa* groups were instructed by the central organisation to co-operate with the new movement. A special conference was scheduled for early December at which the formal dissolution of the *Suiheisha* would be announced. Instead, a special committee meeting was held at which it was agreed to participate actively in the new movement and Matsumoto, Yamamoto Masao and General Shimamoto planned a speaking tour of central and western Japan during which they could urge local *Suiheisha* and *Yuwa* groups to join the *Hokoku Undo* and co-operate with local branches of the IRAA.[72]

Although the respective leaders of the two factions had claimed to be acting on behalf of the national movement there was little activity outside the central offices. In Mie, most *Suiheisha* activity had ceased with the mass arrests of 1937, but there are reports that *Kyudan* campaigns continued during 1938 and 1939.[73] Ueda Onshi, who had been a member of the JCP and later the SMP, assisted Kitahara, Asada and the others to build up the *Kosei Komin Undo* although he does not seem to have had much success in establishing the movement in the Mie area. On 30 September, Ueda held a meeting in Matsuzaka to form a local branch and 36 people attended the meeting.[74] But on 9 December, the group announced its dissolution and resolved henceforth to co-operate with the IRAA.[75] After this Ueda seems to have assisted with the administration of *Yuwa* funds in his home prefecture.

The *Kosei Komin* movement does not seem to have had any influence in Hiroshima, but three of the Hiroshima *Suiheisha*'s leading members did attend the founding meeting of the *Daiwa Hokoku Undo* in November 1940. They invited members of the new movement's committee to visit the prefecture and, in the following March, two meetings were held in Hiroshima and Fuchu which were addressed by General Shimamoto and Yamamoto Masao. Both meetings were attended by over 100 people and following them two branches were set up.[76] In April, the local *Yuwa* group, the *Kyomeikai*, merged with the prefectural branch of the IRAA, and its town and village committees dissolved into their local IRAA groups at the same time. Meetings were held in late May 1941 to announce the formal dissolution of the remaining *Suiheisha* groups.[77] Presumably the two branches of the *Hokoku Undo* continued to exist a little longer although there is no indication what activities, if any, they took part in or when and how they ceased to exist.

The negotiations and mergers which took place in autumn 1940 were intended to culminate in a meeting held on 10 and 11 December to celebrate the 2,600th anniversary of the founding of the Japanese state at which it was hoped all the groups would be united in one patriotic movement. The meeting was held in the presence of 1,000 delegates from all kinds of groups and addressed by the Minister of Health and the Minister of Education. Its message was that the *Yuwa* movement had an important role to play in the building of the National Defence Structure.[78] However, the *Suiheisha* did not announce its dissolution. The reasons for the impasse reached in the negotiations between Matsumoto and the former *Yuwa* movement group are unclear, but they seem to have something to do with a personal reluctance on Matsumoto's part to allow the *Suiheisha* to disappear after he had spent so much time and money developing it in the previous ten years. He did, nevertheless, embark on a speaking tour of Western Japan in the spring of 1941 which it was hoped would result in the formation of regional groups. A conference called by the *Hokoku* movement was held in May in Osaka and was attended by over 700 delegates; a majority came from the Kinki area but there were representatives from all six of the *Yuwa* regions. These activists discussed the practical problems of co-operating with the IRAA as well as the aims of the movement which were defined as practising a morality based on the *kokutai* spirit, to strengthen national defence and to encourage international co-operation based on the morality of the Japanese people.[79] At a central committee meeting held in August 1941 it was claimed that former *Suiheisha* groups were holding meetings expressing support for the new movement; already they had the support of six prefectural groups, 20 town groups and 6,000 activists and they aimed at a mass following of 50,000.[80] It is hard to decide what those active in this movement hoped to achieve, all one can say from examining the documents that remain is that the function of the meetings held by the movement was to try to stimulate patriotism among the *Burakumin* communities.

The *Chuo Yuwa Jigyo Kyokai* began to co-operate with the activities of the IRAA soon after it was established in October 1940 and changes were made in the Ten Year Plan to facilitate this co-operation. As has already been indicated, from this time the local *Yuwa* groups were urged to work with the branches of the IRAA. The activities of the *Yuwa* movement were made subordinate to government control in June 1941 when its name was changed to the *Dowa Hokokai* (*Dowa* Public Service Group).[81] Previous leaders of the movement with the exception of Hiranuma were set aside and control passed into the hands of the senior civil servants from the main ministries and the IRAA. By the end of the year the group was completely absorbed into the IRAA.[82]

For a time at least the *Yuwa* projects continued as before but with a stronger emphasis placed on the encouragement of migration to Manchuria and Mongolia. One might have expected that, as the hostilities on the Asian continent increased, and especially after the outbreak of the Pacific war, the *Yuwa* projects would have been abruptly brought to a halt, yet there is evidence that money continued to be provided for projects in such areas as Kyoto until as late as 1945.[83] As was pointed out earlier, there remained pockets of resistance to government policy in the *Buraku* and perhaps the government felt obliged to continue to finance the policy which ensured close control of the *Buraku* community with one element of tangible improvements as proof of the genuine desire of the government to treat them as equals. Secondly, as many of the surveys had indicated, there was a high level of unemployment inside the *Buraku* and the main aim of this wartime *Yuwa* policy may have been to direct surplus labour to places at home or abroad where it could be utilised to build up the national defence state.

Despite Matsumoto's frequent protestations of his desire to dissolve the *Suiheisha* movement and form a new organisation, it still existed at the end of 1941. In December, the *Suiheisha* was designated as a 'shiso kessha' (thought group) and ordered to disband. This it did formally on 20 January 1942 although Matsumoto issued a statement at the same time declaring that he did not regard the *Buraku* problem as solved and he reserved the right to revive the group at a later date.[84] The *Dowa Hokokai* continued its activities throughout the war years supervising projects to co-ordinate the leather industry and to monitor living conditions within the *Buraku* communities. Many former *Suiheisha* activists found employment within its constituent groups.[85]

The Final Years

The main theme of our discussion of the changes which took place in the *Suiheisha* and *Yuwa* movements in the 1930s is the convergence and merger of the two organisations and their ideologies. However, 'convergence' perhaps gives a misleading impression since it implies that fundamental changes took place in both movements which led them to meet at some mid-point, whereas, as we have seen, the changes took place within the *Suiheisha* as it abandoned its leftist and liberal positions to adopt the nationalist orientation of the *Yuwa* movement. From as early as 1933, there were many similarities in the policies of the two groups towards *Buraku* improvement; what separated them was their ideological orientation. The *Suiheisha* clung to its radical ideology as long as and perhaps longer than any other social movement organisation in Japan but, in the end, the movement's leaders gave their full support to the government's domestic and foreign policy. There were clearly very specific reasons explaining why individuals changed their political views which are related to the nature of Japanese society and of the socialist movement within Japan, but the phenomenon is one that can be observed in other states, especially at times of international crisis or war. Discussing the support given by the German social democrats to the 1914-18 war, Barrington Moore Jnr points out how there were heavy sanctions imposed on those who refused to co-operate with the war effort but substantial rewards offered to those who did. All that was required was 'sensible' co-operation with the government. The choice was to go along with the nationalist tide or risk the destruction of the organisation to which they owed their status and had, for a long time, devoted their energy and intelligence.

> . . . to resist the patriotic upsurge meant disgrace and insult . . . , the opposite meant acceptance in a euphoric if ephemeral brotherhood.[86]

The Japanese social democrats of the mid-1930s, like their German counterparts in 1914, chose co-operation when the only alternative was personal and organisational destruction. The *Suiheisha* was one of the last organisations to capitulate to the patriotic upsurge, but by late summer 1937 it had formally renounced its left wing views. Because their status depended on the continued existence of the *Suiheisha* and partly because the leaders seem to have retained some scepticism about the ability of the government to eliminate prejudice and discrimination, the negotiations concerning the merger of the *Suiheisha* and *Yuwa* movement were long and tortuous. Kitahara and Asada, who seem to have taken the radical, right wing ideas seriously, wanted the merger to lead to the formation of a mass movement which would take its place alongside other movements within the framework of the IRAA. Matsumoto's motives, as ever, were not so clear, but one suspects he was stalling for time hoping for a peaceful solution to the war in China which would enable him to relaunch his *Suiheisha*.

Although the organisation continued to exist until 1942, the *Suiheisha* ceased to be effective as a mass movement from around 1937. Publicity surrounding the Takamatsu campaign and the new organisational principles developed by Asada and Kitahara created renewed interest in the movement and encouraged *Burakumin* to engage in protest against discrimination. However, police harassment and the government-orchestrated patriotic propaganda persuaded most *Burakumin* that their activity had better be channelled through the *Yuwa* groups which would ensure that it contributed to national unity. Autonomous organisations of *Burakumin* disappeared after 1937, though protest by individuals continued. As our study of the *Suiheisha* in Mie showed, even where the movement had had a broad, well-established radical base both groups and activists abandoned their militancy after 1937. Negotiations between the *Suiheisha* and *Yuwa* group leaders took place on a high level which, despite their claims, was remote from the lives of most *Burakumin*. Once the *Suiheisha* announced its support for national mobilisation in 1938 the practical distinction between the *Suiheisha* and *Yuwa* movements disappeared; henceforth they co-operated to organise *Burakumin* behind the drive for national unity. *Suiheisha* leaders may have had some reservations, but most *Burakumin* seem to have believed that the result of the war in Asia would be the creation of a new form of society in which their former feudal status would be irrelevant. When the euphoria of the early war years had worn off, the social and economic controls imposed by the war Cabinet prevented any organised protest.

Before moving on to more general observations in our concluding remarks, a comment on the nature of the *Suiheisha* movement and *Yuwa* programme in the 1930s: in an earlier chapter, we traced the development of the two organisations as they emerged in the 1920s but at each stage it was difficult fully to comprehend either since their ideas were diverse, their activities poorly co-ordinated. Only in the late 1920s can one perceive a sense of unity within the two movements and only from the early 1930s is it possible to indicate a broad direction in which the two are heading. Of course, there never was the degree of formal unity and ideological coherence within the *Suiheisha* that its leaders tried to suggest, as is perhaps indicated by their inability to establish the organisation on a firm financial basis. However, a national structure was formed and a body of literature produced which attempted to give the movement a clear theoretical orientation. For the first time there was a sustained theoretical debate about the nature of discrimination in Japanese society. Similarly, the *Yuwa* movement elaborated its policy and the improvement programme. Both movements seemed to mature in the 1930s and develop a sense of purpose neither had in the 1920s. Though further discussion of this point is outside the brief of this work, we would suggest that the post-war *Buraku* Liberation Movement and *Dowa* policy derived a great deal from the experiences of their forebears in the 1930s. Developments within both groups, particularly the acrimonious theoretical debate which has raged within the liberation movement for the past 15 years, cannot be fully comprehended without reference to the *Suiheisha* of the 1930s when the theoretical issues were first confronted and the outlines of the major arguments first described.

Notes:

1. Beckman and Okubo, p 238.
2. Beckman and Okubo, p 222.
3. Beckman and Okubo, p 222, n 66 quoting Evelyn Colbert. *The Left Wing in Japanese Politics* (New York, 1952), pp 35-6.
4. W D Wray, Aso Hisashi and the search for reform in the 1930s, *Papers on Japan*, vol 5 (Harvard University, 1970), p 65.
5. *Suihei Undo Shiryo Shusei*, vol III, p 231. There were 274 councillors who were supported by the National *Suiheisha*, 28 who had the support of other *Suiheisha* groups as well as 184 who had *Yuwa* group support.
6. See for example an article in *Suihei Shimbun*, no 10, 5 August 1935. *Suihei Undoshi no Kenkyu*, vol IV, p 312.

7.   W D Wray, The Japanese Popular Front Movement, July 1936 – February 1938, *Papers on Japan*, vol 6 (Harvard University, 1972), p 113.

8.   W D Wray (1972), p 113.

9.   Beckman and Okubo, p 255. Also, in February 1936 Nosaka and Yamamoto, the senior surviving members of the JCP now based in Moscow, issued a 'Letter to the Japanese Communists' which was to supersede the 1932 Theses. In this they call for the creation of a popular front to oppose fascism. For complete text see Beckman and Okubo, pp 352-361.

10. W D Wray (1972), p 125.

11. G M Berger, pp 230-231.

12. W D Wray (1970), p 73.

13. That the SMP should have negotiated with the *Tohokai* demonstrates how far to the right it had moved. The *Tohokai*, led by Nakano Seigo, boasted a million members who 'affected black shirts in imitation of the European fascists'. G M Berger, *Parties out of Power in Japan 1931-1941* (Princeton University Press, 1977), p 144.

14. Beckman and Okubo, pp 246-8, provide a detailed analysis of the statements issued by Sano and Nabeyama which became models for other *tenko* statements.

15. The declaration he made which appears to have resulted in his early release from prison was entitled '*Matsurigoto*' and appears in *Saiko Bankichi Sakushu* (Selected works of Saiko Bankichi), vol I, pp 15-25.

16. Quoted by Beckman and Okubo, p 222.

17. This is a summary of an article in the first edition of *Gaito Shimbun* dated 10 September 1934. *Suihei Undoshi no Kenkyu*, vol IV, pp 466-7. Subsequent editions of the newspaper elaborated on these ideas. According to Kimura, Saiko wrote or provided the inspiration for most of the articles, Sakamoto supplied the money to subsidise the paper's production and Yoneda organised its sales. Interview, 30 January 1978.

18. *Suihei Undo Shiryo Shusei*, vol III, p 506. Neither this group nor the newspaper they produced had much influence outside Nara prefecture.

19. Interview, 30 January 1978.

20. A selection of articles which appeared in this journal appear in *Suihei Undoshi no Kenkyu*, vol IV, pp 469-474.

21. Kitahara, p 276.

22. Kitahara, pp 278-281 for the text of his *tenko* statement.

23. Kitahara, pp 308-9.

24. *Suihei Undo Shiryo Shusei*, vol III, pp 309, 485.

25. *Suihei Undo Shiryo Shusei*, vol III, pp 490-1.

26. *Suihei Undoshi no Kenkyu*, vol IV, p 154.

27. *Suihei Undo Shiryo Shusei*, vol III, p 495.

28. *Suihei Undo Shiryo Shusei*, vol III, p 496. Proof that Imoto had direct links with the Comintern was that a copy of the Dmitrov report, which advocated the united front tactic to oppose fascism, was found in his possession. It now seems that this document was 'planted' in his office shortly before his arrest, following which he was kept in solitary confinement for eighteen months before being released on bail. At his trial he was given a five-year suspended sentence. Interview 14 November 1977.

29. *Suihei Undo Shiryo Shusei*, vol III, p 495.

30. Yamagi, (1970), p 681. *Suihei Undo Shiryo Shusei*, vol III, p 247-8.

31. Yamagi, (1970), pp 765-6.

32. According to Beckman and Okubo (pp 191, 237), Ueda had been a member of the Communist Party since the late 1920s and shortly before his arrest in April 1933 was a member of the Party's central committee.

33. Oyama, pp 260-2.

34. Oyama, p 271.

35. Oyama, pp 272–5.
36. A breakdown of discrimination incidents 1933–1940.

Simple verbal insults by an ordinary citizen	9
Incidents involving a school	7
Incidents involving the police	8
Incidents involving the media	6
Incidents involving the army	5
Incidents connected with shrines or temples	4
Incidents involving other public officials	4
Incidents concerning the use of communal facilities	2

37. Yagi, pp 113–7.
38. 'Nakae who was elected by a *tokushu Buraku* in Osaka called Watanabe *mura* became a Dietman without spending a penny and even when he attended the Diet he said nothing, just sat there picking his nose . . .' quoted by Yagi, p 118.
39. The full text of the broadcast can be found in *Suihei Undo Shiryo Shusei*, vol III, pp 502–5.
40. *Suihei Undo Shiryo Shusei*, vol III, p 602.
41. *Suihei Undo Shiryo Shusei*, vol III, p 603.
42. *Suihei Undo Shiryo Shusei*, vol III, p 737.
43. *Suihei Undo Shiryo Shusei*, vol III, p 604.
44. *Suihei Undo Shiryo Shusei*, vol III, p 1017.
45. Havens, pp 62–3.
46. *Suihei Undo Shiryo Shusei*, vol III, p 1018. Similar rumours were spreading at the same time about Koreans who were believed to be involved in sabotage and other fifth column activities.
47. *Suihei Undo Shiryo Shusei*, vol III, pp 498–9.
48. G M Berger, (1972), p 202f.
49. Takahashi, p 659.
50. *Suihei Undo Shiryo Shusei*, vol III, pp 546–7.
51. *Suihei Undoshi no Kenkyu*, vol IV, pp 167–9. *Suihei Undo Shiryo Shusei*, vol III, pp 551–4.
52. *Yuwa Jigyo Nenkan*, no 13 (1938), p 68.
53. *Yuwa Jigyo Nenkan*, no 13 (1938), p 99. Of this 66,000 yen was provided to assist communal projects and 32,000 yen to encourage the growth of a dependable *Burakumin* leadership.
54. These figures are taken from the introduction to *Yuwa Jigyo Nenkan*, no 14 (1939).
55. *Suihei Undo Shiryo Shusei*, vol III, p 385.
56. *Yuwa Jigyo Nenkan*, no 13 (1938), p 203.
57. Koga, *Tokyo Suiheisha to Hikaku Sangyo* . . ., pp 220–1.
58. At least Yamamoto Masao was forced to resign in the summer of 1938 and he implies that others resigned at the same time. *Yuwa Undo no Kaiso* (Reminiscences of the *Yuwa* movement) in *Yuwa Jigyo Kenkyu*, vol 4.
59. *Suihei Undo Shiryo Shusei*, vol III, p 594.
60. *Zensui News*, 1 August 1939. *Suihei Undoshi no Kenkyu*, vol IV, pp 421–5.
61. *Suihei Undo Shiryo Shusei*, vol III, p 678.
62. *Suihei Undo Shiryo Shusei*, vol III, pp 595–6.
63. For more details concerning this conference see *Suihei Undo Shiryo Shusei*, vol III, pp 664–9.
64. *Suihei Undo Shiryo Shusei*, vol III, p 597.
65. *Suihei Undo Shiryo Shusei*, vol III, pp 648–9.
66. *Suihei Undo Shiryo Shusei*, vol III, pp 657–663.
67. *Suihei Undo Shiryo Shusei*, vol III, p 692.

68. Konoe's attitude towards the IRAA is discussed in detail in Berger (1972), pp 451-5.
69. Aso's attitude is discussed in W D Wray (1970), p 77. Chalmers Johnson outlines Ozaki's hopes for the organisation in *An Instance of Treason* (Tokyo, Tuttle, 1977), p 120.
70. *Suihei Undo Shiryo Shusei*, vol III, pp 685-7.
71. *Suihei Undo Shiryo Shusei*, vol III, pp 682-3.
72. *Suihei Undo Shiryo Shusei*, vol III, p 708.
73. Oyama, p 281.
74. *Suihei Undo Shiryo Shusei*, vol III, p 682.
75. Oyama, p 288.
76. *Suihei Undo Shiryo Shusei*, vol III, p 751.
77. *Suihei Undo Shiryo Shusei*, vol III, pp 905-6.
78. *Yuwa Jigyo Nenkan*, no 16 (1941), p 28. *Suihei Undo Shiryo Shusei*, vol III, pp 708-711.
79. *Suihei Undo Shiryo Shusei*, vol III, p 743. The number of delegates attending the conference were: Chubu 20, Kanto 43, Chukoku 26, Kinki 500, Shikoku 39, Kyushu 23.
80. *Suihei Undo Shiryo Shusei*, vol III, p 747.
81. Fujitani Toshio, *Yuwa Jigyo Kenkyu Somokuji* (Introduction to the general index of the collection of the copies of *Yuwa Jigyo Kenkyu*), (Republished Sekai Bunko, 1974) p 74.
82. *Suihei Undo Shiryo Shusei*, vol III, p 919.
83. Fujino, p 317-9.
84. *Suihei Undo Shiryo Shusei*, vol III, p 921.
85. Fujino, p 302-3.
86. Barrington Moore Jnr, p 488.

Conclusion

Active protest against discrimination first emerged at the start of the 20th century when a small group of *Burakumin* made the initial, tentative suggestions that they should be treated as equals. In order to ensure that this took place, fellow *Burakumin* were urged to improve their living standards and life styles so that they were more acceptable to their majority neighbours. This scarcely seems to be a radical prescription for action, but the very fact that they were organising themselves without the state structure forced the *Meiji* bureaucrats to take an interest in the issue for the first time since the promulgation of the Emancipation Declaration in 1871. It is no coincidence that at precisely the same time other branches of the government were starting to take an active interest in other groups which were developing critiques of Japanese society and politics. The state was successful both in its attempts to control the first autonomous *Burakumin* organisations and to crush the infant socialist movement. However, it was not possible to cope with their challenge so easily when they were to re-emerge in the late 1910s, but then too the response to the emergence of political protest was a programme of social control.

In the previous chapters we have been concerned with discussing the details of the development of the *Suiheisha* movement and the attempts to prevent its influence through the *Yuwa* organisation. Here, in this final section, I want to return to some of the broader questions mentioned in the introduction. Firstly, I will outline what seem to me to be the main themes in the history of the development of the *Buraku* liberation movement in the first half of this century. An understanding of the circumstances which led to the successful proposal to establish the *Suiheisha* helps to explain a great deal of the changes which took place after its launch. Secondly, I will turn to a discussion of the relationship between the *Suiheisha* and its social and political contemporaries, particularly the other left wing social movements. The relationship between the rival *Suiheisha* and *Yuwa* groups and organisations and the nature of the *Yuwa* policies is another theme which has run through all the account of developments of the 1920s and 1930s and I will suggest how this might be characterised. Then, having briefly summarised the argument on each of these topics I want to outline what might be considered to have been the achievements of the *Suiheisha*.

From the time of the Restoration, the Japanese ruling class was keenly aware that Japan is a particularly vulnerable member of the community of nations such that both domestic and foreign policy decisions have had to be tailored to take into account the international environment. However, *Meiji* policy towards *Burakumin* was one area least affected by such considerations. Advisers to the new government cannot have been completely unaware that within the recent past the United States had abolished slavery, the Tsar had liberated the serfs and that educated opinion in the civilised west was opposed, in principle at least, to racial or status discrimination. But it seems unlikely that such knowledge had much influence on the decision to remove formal status restrictions which impeded *Burakumin* mobility and it is more probable that it was simply part of the process of dismantling the feudal social structure. Indeed, the lack of positive aid after formal emancipation reinforces this impression.

Despite the prophylactic measures initiated by the *Meiji* oligarchs, liberal ideas spread slowly, if unsurely, throughout the country in the final decades of the nineteenth century. The permeation of western ideas of liberty and democracy provided *Burakumin*, amongst others, with a set of values with which to judge the actions of central and local government and encouraged them to devise strategies to improve the way they were treated by contemporary society. Yet it was not just the subversive element within the liberal ideas nor the presence of sympathetic radicals outside the *Buraku* which generated the early *kaizen* groups. Structural changes in rural society which increased inter-communal contact; aspirations for equality of treatment inspired by a modicum of primary education; the fact that material success achieved by a certain sector within *Buraku* society was not rewarded by commensurate social esteem; all these internal changes produced a segment within *Buraku* society which was receptive to liberal ideas. The liberal tradition was absorbed into the value system of these communities and, though it remained dormant for a generation, it prepared *Burakumin* for the more radical ideologies which were put before them in the 20th century.

At the turn of the century, the *Meiji* oligarchs concluded from their observations of events in other industrialising countries that precautionary measures were required to prevent the spread of socialism and similar 'individualist doctrines'. Details of the social policy adopted at this time have already been examined and the significance of the policy will be discussed later. At this point, it is sufficient to note that the policy was successful for a while in isolating the Japanese people from liberal and socialist ideas which were spreading rapidly elsewhere in the world. In order to restrict the development of autonomous *Burakumin* organisations which, it was thought, would be easy prey for the socialist movement, the government adopted a policy to integrate these groups into the structure of local government. Improvement groups would, it was hoped, prevent the spread of radical ideas to the *Buraku* by publicising the egalitarian nature of the Emperor-family ideology and subsidising the implementation of a few minor improvements. But, contrary to expectations, the early *Yuwa* policy proved to be of major importance in enabling the *Suiheisha* to spread so rapidly when it was set up ten years later.

In the first place, the administrators of the *Yuwa* policy tended to treat all *Burakumin* as a group and thus encouraged *Burakumin* to regard themselves as members of a minority group. Especially among the better-off, middle class

Burakumin, a sense of solidarity emerged in the period 1910-1918. Secondly, those who became actively involved in the government supervised groups soon became dissatisfied with the token efforts taken to implement the promises of equal treatment. Criticism of the policies of the oligarchic government was mounting in other sectors of society and this encouraged *Burakumin* criticism of the inadequacy of the *Yuwa* policies. Within these groups *Burakumin* acquired a sense of the injustice of discrimination against them and learnt the skills needed to hold meetings and run groups. Thus, when the suggestion to form the *Suiheisha* was made there was already established a communication network which could be used to disseminate the idea and a large number of *Burakumin* who were receptive to these new ideas.

Once established though, from where did the *Suiheisha* movement's leaders receive their inspiration? In the early groups, one can find representatives of organisations which extend across the political and religious spectra, but after the first couple of years it became apparent that those most active within the movement allied themselves with either its Bolshevik or anarchist sectors. Indeed, it appeared for a while as if the *Suiheisha* would split into rival factions as had happened to other left wing groups. This internal factional fighting produced fierce debates at the almost-annual national conferences although at first the debates contained little discussion of the nature of prejudice in Japan or specific tactics to be used to overcome discrimination. In part this was due to the over-optimism of both anarchists and Bolsheviks concerning the imminence of The Revolution which would, it was confidently predicted, with one cathartic sweep solve all the problems of the oppressed masses. During at least the early 1920s both anarchists and Bolsheviks were most impressed by what they perceived to be happening in Russia. There the Jews had played a key role in the growth of the revolutionary movement and the Bolshevik victory had removed all forms of discrimination from Russian society. Many imagined that *Burakumin* had a similar role to play within the revolutionary movement in Japan and that status prejudice which divided the oppressed masses would break down in the course of the revolutionary struggle against Capitalism such that neither prejudice nor discrimination would exist in the post-revolutionary society. As the anarchist influence within the left wing movement declined, so within the *Suiheisha* too Marxists, whether members of the Japan Communist Party or not, established themselves in the key positions within the movement's hierarchy. In other groups this had been the prelude to organisational division. This did not occur in the *Suiheisha*, partly because of the disorganised state of the movement, partly because solidarity between *Burakumin* proved stronger than loyalty to ideology and partly because the Communist Party faction was not formed until comparatively late and its activities cut short by the arrests of March 1928.

The arrests of the late 1920s removed Communist Party members from the *Suiheisha* leadership, but the Marxist influence was not eliminated. Indeed, of the foreign ideologies influential in Japan in the 1920s the Marxist tradition proved to be the most resistant to the growing nationalist current and it was particularly important within the *Suiheisha* until the outbreak of open hostilities in China. In the early 1930s, a time when most sectors of Japanese society were becoming introspective, the leaders of the *Suiheisha* such as Asada and Kitahara were still looking abroad for suggestions as to how the movement be reorganised. The 'Dissolution campaign' was inspired by an interpretation of Profintern advice and Comintern decisions and took the movement to the brink of collapse, but it did stimulate real consideration and discussion of the nature of discrimination against *Burakumin*. In the end, these discussions were resolved less by reference to ideas from abroad and more by an examination of the requirements of the *Burakumin* themselves. After more than ten years of encouraging active opposition to discrimination and long debates on the movement's theory, the *Suiheisha* finally began to consider the real needs of those on whose behalf they were campaigning. Despite the negative aspects of the dissolution debate it marked a watershed in the movement's development.

Nevertheless, despite the more moderate, inward-looking policies pursued during and after 1933, the movement maintained a strong adherence to a radical political perspective longer than any contemporary organisation. This calls for an explanation which must include several related sets of factors.

In a very general sense, there is considerable evidence that the isolation of the *Buraku* from the majority community made their inhabitants less vulnerable to outside pressure to conform whether this pressure be applied by the local society or the police as agents of the state. After two centuries of systematic exclusion from the majority community and over 50 years of discrimination in modernising Japan, the *Burakumin* were not as susceptible as others to the nationalist myth that all social problems would be resolved in a renovated Japan. This may explain the reluctance of many *Burakumin* to abandon their left wing views although of course most were forced to modify their ideas in order to remain at liberty.

The *Yuwa* policy tacitly recognised that *Burakumin* felt apart from Japanese society and much of its propaganda and many of its policies were directed towards overcoming these feelings of alienation. Their exclusion from Japanese society was clearly a hangover from *Tokugawa* society and most interested observers could agree that it was a 'feudal remnant'. The *Yuwa* activists were perplexed by this. To the extent that they had a theoretical framework, it was one which regarded Japan as a modern, capitalist nation in which status discrimination had no reason to survive. Hence, perhaps, the production of policies aiming to eliminate it from society in the near future and their confusion when prejudice and discrimination persisted despite *Yuwa* measures.

For the Marxists of course the survival of feudal attitudes and social groups presented no theoretical problem. Many of them would argue that the *Meiji* Restoration had been an incomplete bourgeois revolution which had failed to root out all the feudal social structures from Japanese society. The survival of the Emperor and the nobility was one example of this and, at the other end of the social hierarchy, the persistence of *Buraku* communities and discrimination against them provided further evidence of the inadequacy of the 19th century capitalist revolution. There was, on occasion, division within the movement about the practical implications of this theoretical explanation of *Buraku* persistence, and the tactics recommended to the movement varied according to the requirements of Comintern policy. But no alternative framework of analysis was ever presented; for *Suiheisha* activists it was the only theoretical framework which could both explain the persistence of the *Buraku* problem and suggest a way forward. The power of the Marxist explanation is demonstrated by the way that even after such radicals as Kitahara and Asada gave their support to the nationalist organisations the language they use in their propaganda betrays their adherence to a theoretical structure which was similar to that suggested by the Marxist model.

The internationalist dimension to Marxism was also particularly attractive to *Suiheisha* leaders. In a general sense there was the obvious attraction of a system of ideas which promised liberation of all oppressed members of society and urged the solidarity of all groups beneath the Red Flag. More specifically, some of the older members of the *Suiheisha* leadership, Matsumoto and Sakamoto for example, had lived and worked in China and Manchuria and had witnessed the high-handed manner with which the Japanese government officials and merchants treated the native Chinese. These attitudes closely resembled those of the domestic authorities towards *Burakumin* and there seems to have developed from these observations strong feelings of sympathy and solidarity with the victims of Japanese imperialism abroad. For some *Burakumin*, the Marxist analysis of the Japanese state – oppressing those abroad while operating a semi-colonial system in certain sectors of the domestic economy – was more than a theoretical structure and seemed to be confirmed by the experience of the *Suiheisha* leaders. These feelings of solidarity with the Chinese, deeply rooted in a common experience of hardship, go a long way towards accounting for the fact that the *Suiheisha*, as late as 1937, was still criticising the 'fascist' government's domestic and foreign policy. Indeed, it seems that most of the movement's leaders only became supporters of government policy once they had been persuaded that Japan's China policy was fundamentally anti-imperialist aiming to free the peoples of Asia from the yoke of Western imperialism.

Tenants' groups and trade union organisations had, in the 1920s, professed their support for radical change within Japan and international solidarity with oppressed peoples. However, by the early 1930s most of these groups had been deprived of their most radical leaders and their mass membership pacified by the improvement of economic circumstances following the changes in the agricultural support system and increased wages and lower unemployment which followed the change in government policy in 1932. Although the *Burakumin* groups too suffered police harassment, they enjoyed few of the benefits of the new policies; there was little to entice them away from their radical ideas. Poverty, poor housing and inadequate education persisted in spite of repeated government promises to make improvements. Neither the overall economic policy nor the various *Yuwa* projects caused marked improvements within the *Buraku*. So, while most of Japanese society was benefiting from material improvement from 1932 onwards, *Burakumin* poverty continued, and under these conditions it is not surprising that they continued to support their organisation which was demanding radical reform. The leaders of the *Suiheisha* were able to rely on mass support for their radical demands well into the 1930s.

The early *Yuwa* policy was formulated, albeit in a vague form, in the final years of the *Meiji* period and was implemented by the police and local authorities so as to bring recalcitrant *Burakumin* under the influence of the state. This relatively benign policy was continued until, following the Rice Riots and the formation of the *Suiheisha*, *Burakumin* were perceived as being not merely a source of disunity but as posing a threat to order and potentially subversive of the national well-being. It became clear that a more sophisticated and comprehensive policy was required. Various organisations with differing degrees of association with formal government agencies responded to the new situation in different ways until it was decided that this pluralist approach was resulting in the dissipation of effort and waste. So, in 1927/1928, just as plans were being implemented to increase the militarist content of education and restrict the activities of left wing groups, a consolidated *Yuwa* policy was launched and a co-ordinated network of *Yuwa* groups was established. Despite this, the *Suiheisha* continued to exist, and from 1933 displayed an alarming degree of vitality and influence over *Burakumin*. Then, once more in conjunction with other changes in government policy, the Ten Year Plan was introduced with the unstated aim of reducing and removing the influence of the *Suiheisha*. At first the *Yuwa* groups were not able to take the initiative away from the *Suiheisha*, not at least until the consolidation of the rest of the corporate state structure after 1937, after which time the *Suiheisha* groups were absorbed fairly rapidly into the *Yuwa* movement.

Status discrimination in Japan was considered to be undesirable because it was a source of disorder and disunity, not because it represented a transgression of any abstract or legal principle of equality. Accordingly, the *Yuwa* policy aimed at pacifying *Burakumin* rather than attempting to introduce reforms which might have reduced prejudice and demonstrated the government's firm commitment to ending discrimination. For example, *Suiheisha* and *Yuwa* conferences urged the government to remove from public view the records of the *Jinshin Koseki*, the national census made in 1873 which often included reference to former *eta:hinin* status. This would have made it more difficult to discover an individual's status background. It would not have dramatically reduced social prejudices but it might have prevented some instances of discrimination and would have demonstrated the government's firm resolve to oppose feudal prejudice. That no steps were taken leads one to conclude that the *Yuwa* policy was at best a half-hearted improvement policy. The principal aim of the *Yuwa* programme was to subordinate dissident elements within the *Buraku* and to convert (or reconvert) the autonomous groups which had been formed into agents of social control. The

Yuwa policy was little more than a consolidated effort to incorporate *Burakumin* into the national structure.

Finally, we must assess the *Suiheisha*'s achievements. Unlike many of the organisations which were formed in the early 1920s whose existence was somewhat ephemeral, the *Suiheisha* survived for nearly 20 years even though there were times when it came perilously close to collapse. Simply to continue for so long was an achievement in itself, demonstrating, perhaps, that it was fulfilling a need and contributing in some way to the improvement of the life of *Burakumin*.

In the short term, it seems clear that the presence of the *Suiheisha* organisation and its local groups provoked the central and local authorities to provide more money for the improvement of the *Buraku* environment than would have been the case if *Burakumin* had remained in isolated groups. Much of the *Yuwa* money was used on projects directly linked to pacification programmes tied to the overall corporatist policy; some of it was misappropriated by the projects' administrators but some of it was used to improve living conditions within some *Buraku* communities. We have been critical of the way the money was distributed and the kind of projects which were implemented, but there can be little doubt that *Burakumin* would have received even less than they did had it not been for the existence of the *Suiheisha*.

There were some groups and individuals who became involved in active protest against discrimination even before the *Suiheisha* was formed, but they were relatively few in number. However, in the few years following the creation of the *Suiheisha*, several thousand instances of protest were recorded. Probably very few of these protests involved formally constituted *Suiheisha* groups and most of those who took part in them will not have regarded themselves as members of the *Suiheisha*. On the other hand, most of them will have been inspired to become involved in direct action by hearing or reading of the *Suiheisha*'s activities or even by reading material produced by one of the *Suiheisha* groups. To a certain extent it may be that the early *Kyudan* campaigns did little to improve the image of *Burakumin* in the eyes of the majority population. Such campaigns were perhaps a necessary first step towards the acquisition of self-confidence among the hitherto socially oppressed groups, the degree of violence was probably exaggerated by the press reports and in any case the movement soon learnt to develop more cautious tactics and to be more selective in the campaigns which were pursued. The early campaigns seem to have led to a marked reduction in overt insults and in some rural areas the systematic exclusion of *Burakumin* from communal facilities was ended. In the short term, then, they led to a considerable improvement in the life of *Burakumin*. Moreover, these campaigns seem to have established the principle that discrimination should not be tolerated. The continuation of a relatively large amount of *Kyudan* activity even after the *Suiheisha* had ceased to be able to provide a positive lead indicates that there was now a substantial sector of the *Buraku* community which was no longer prepared to endure insulting behaviour which they previously had accepted as normal. The tactics used in both major and minor campaigns had developed to quite a sophisticated level by the mid-1930s and they provided the post-war liberation movement leaders with a fund of experience on which to draw when they were launching the new organisations.

However, in asserting that *Burakumin* should be accorded equal civil rights and even be given government assistance, the *Suiheisha* was forced into a position of criticising government policy. Further, their insistence that *Burakumin* should organise their own liberation 'by their own efforts' placed the movement to the left of the liberals whose notion of democracy was government for the people rather than of or by them. From a political position which was well to the left of centre at its inception, the *Suiheisha* soon adopted a Marxist perspective and this was to be dominant within the movement throughout the 1930s for reasons already discussed. This was of significance for groups outside the *Buraku* too, for as our study of the Mie group demonstrated, particularly in the 1930s, the *Suiheisha* was often the largest, most persistent left-wing organisation in an area and this provided continuity and co-ordination for the activities of the left wing peasants' and workers' movements. In a more general sense, *Suiheisha* demands for equality of treatment and the activities undertaken in pursuit of these demands contributed to the development of democratic thought and practice in Japan. So, even if the *Suiheisha* had little short term success in eliminating status consciousness, it had a significant impact on pre-war Japanese society.

Opposition to prejudice and campaigns against discrimination, neither of which have much to do with the ballot box, are not generally regarded as evidence of democratic political activity. But the acquisition of a sense of injustice which makes one determined to ensure that one's society lives up to its egalitarian principles and even to try to create different social conditions in which the notion of equality is interpreted more broadly, provides at least one basis for the development of democratic ideas. Moreover, the experience of putting these ideas into practice, whether within one's village or at the national level, was one which had political lessons for all those who took part. However misguided some of its policies and activities might have been, there can be little doubt that the *Suiheisha* contributed to the democratic current within pre-war Japanese society both by spreading liberal and socialist ideas among the *Buraku* communities and by forcing the members of the liberal and socialist movements to consider more carefully the problems of the rights of the individual citizen within Japanese society.

Possibly because they proved unable to resist the rise of nationalism, the left wing political groups are not usually given much credit for their contribution towards the evolution of democratic thought within Japan. Nevertheless, the activities particularly of the grass roots organisations encouraged individuals and small groups to act to defend their right to earn a living or improve their working conditions to ensure respect for themselves and their families, presumably three of the basic preconditions for any kind of democratic activity. In some cases these

movements may even have stimulated some to consider the possibility that
existing social arrangements could and should be changed to permit a more
equitable distribution of the social product. The left wing organisations never
influenced very many, they were helpless in the face of the ideological and
repressive might of the corporate state. Nevertheless, they were one of the few
sections of pre-war Japanese society which put up any opposition to the
regimentation of the 1920s and 1930s or offered any resistance to the process of
incorporation into the state structure. Their contribution to the development of
progressive thought in Japan was perhaps not apparent until the late 1940s, but it
was important to the growth of the various post-war left wing movements. Of the
pre-war left wing organisations the *Suiheisha* was the mass movement which
clung most tenaciously to its Marxist perspective and held out longest against
emasculation by the nationalist ideologies.

An assessment of the final achievement of the *Suiheisha* – its contribution to
the formation and development of the post-war liberation movement – would
involve us in the consideration of issues which lie outside the scope of this work.
Certain aspects of this contribution have already been suggested in the course of
the narrative, in particular the theoretical debate which started in the 1930s
provided the basis for the discussions of the post-war period. Some former
Suiheisha leaders expected that the democratic revolution superintended by the
occupation forces would remove the basis of discrimination and that a liberation
movement would only serve to perpetuate status consciousness. Many others
recognised that the deep roots of prejudice against them could not be removed by
reforms introduced by outsiders who knew little of the nature of the problem.
How this debate was resolved need not concern us here, but there can be little
doubt that it was a relatively easy task to revive the liberation movement in the
post-war world.

Appendix

The declaration adopted by the Suiheisha movement at its Inaugural Conference

Tokushu Burakumin throughout the country, unite! Long-suffering brothers: In the past half century, the undertakings on our behalf by so many people and in such varied ways have failed to yield any favourable results. This failure was a divine punishment we incurred for permitting others as well as ourselves to debase our own human dignity. Previous movements, though seemingly motivated by compassion, actually corrupted many of our brothers. In the light of this, it is necessary for us to organise a new group movement by which we shall emancipate ourselves through promoting respect for human dignity.

Brothers! Our ancestors sought after and practised liberty and equality. But they became the victims of a base, contemptible system developed by the ruling class. They became the manly martyrs of industry. As a recompense for tearing out the hearts of animals, their own warm, human hearts were ripped out. They were spat upon with the spittle of ridicule. Yet all through these cursed nightmares, their blood, still proud to be human, did not dry up. Yes! Now we have come to the age when man, pulsing with this blood, is trying to become divine. The time has come for the victims of discrimination to hurl back labels of derision. The time has come when the martyr's crown of thorns will be blessed. The time has come when we can be proud of being *Eta*.

We must never again insult our ancestors and profane our humanity by slavish words and cowardly acts. Knowing well the coldness and contempt of ordinary human society, we seek and will be profoundly thankful for the warmth and light of true humanity.

From this the Levellers' Society is born. Let there now be warmth and light among men!

Quoted by deVos and Wagatsuma, p 44.

Glossary

Terms

Ainu The indigenous population of Hokkaido and northern Japan. They suffered from attempts to exert Japanese control over the island of Hokkaido both in late Tokugawa and in the second half of the nineteenth century, and by 1900 only 17,500 remained. Despite the Ainu Protection Law of 1899, the Ainu population was unable to maintain its numbers because of medical problems and dire poverty. There now remain less than 17,000 of them of whom only a few hundred are pure-blooded.

Aoya A group of dyers based in Kyoto who specialised in producing purple coloured clothing. Until 1715 they were treated as outcasts similar to *eta:hinin*, but after this time they seem to have been absorbed into the artisan class.

Ashiarai Process by which an individual or family could be declared cleansed of their polluted status and readmitted to mainstream society. This was theoretically possible for *eta:hinin* prior to around 1715, but thereafter it became virtually impossible for all *eta* and all but a few *hinin*.

Bakufu See Tokugawa Bakufu

Bisaku Heiminkai Organisation formed in Okayama prefecture in 1902 to co-ordinate the activities of the *kaizen* groups there.

Burakumin Literally 'hamlet person', term used in this and most Western language texts to refer to the descendants of the *eta:hinin* of the Tokugawa period or those who are assumed to be so and therefore experience discrimination.

Chasen Makers of bamboo goods especially the whisk used in the tea ceremony (*chasen*), regarded in some areas of Japan in the Tokugawa period as of low status, equivalent to *eta:hinin*.

Chori Term of abuse used to indicate the individual is of *eta:hinin* origin.

Chugai Nippo Daily newspaper founded in 1897 and published in Kyoto. It concentrated mainly on religious issues but also covered social problems outside the religious field.

Chuo Yuwa Jigyo Kyokai Literally Central Conciliation Project Council established in 1925 within the Home Ministry's Social Affairs division and by 1928 the sole government body initiating and co-ordinating the application of the *Yuwa* projects.

Comintern Acronym for the Communist International, the Soviet dominated international organisation of communist parties founded in 1917 by Lenin. Through the ruthless discipline of the member parties it served as a tool of Soviet foreign policy especially under Stalin's control. The national parties were regarded as branch establishments of the international communist movement whose headquarters were in Moscow. Formally dissolved in 1943.

Dai Nippon Doho Yuwakai Literally Greater Japan Fraternal Conciliation Society. Name of the first organisation which attempted to organise *Burakumin* on a national scale. It was formed at a meeting held in Osaka in July 1903 attracting representatives from across the country, but it did not develop into a sustained movement.

Edo Seat of the Tokugawa shogunate, renamed Tokyo (eastern capital) in September 1868.

Eta Literally 'filth abundant', said to be a corruption of the word '*etori*' a group which butchered animals to feed the hawks and dogs of the Imperial household prior to the ninth century. By the thirteenth century it was used to refer to those on the margins of society who carried out functions considered to be polluting.

Fukken Domei Literally 'Restoration of Rights League'. Founded in 1881 in Kyushu, it was probably the first organisation founded by and for *Burakumin*. Branches were established in Hakata, Kumamoto, Kurume and Hita, but it had disappeared by the late 1880s.

Genro Group of senior statesmen who advised the Emperor on all major political decisions, including the appointment of a new prime minister, from the 1890s to the 1930s. The group had no constitutional status but acted as a link between the emperor and formal government apparatus. All of them were former Satsuma or Choshu men who had dominated the administration in the period 1870-1890.

Han The semi-autonomous domains ruled over by the feudal lords in the Tokugawa period.

Heimin Common people. Following the abolition of the status structure after the *Meiji* restoration the population was classified for registration purposes into *kazoku*, descendants of the court nobility or a feudal lord, *shizoku*, descendants of former samurai, and *heimin*. See also *shin-heimin*.

Himmin Kenkyukai Poor Peoples Research Council formed in 1900 by government officers to advise on policy towards the poor.

Hinin Non-people. Name given to those outcasts of the *Tokugawa* period and before who were not associated with a defiling occupation. They would include beggars and street entertainers in such cities as Edo as well as jailers and executioners in most castle towns.

Honganji See Jodo Shinshu

Hyogikai Leftist elements in the Japan Federation of Labour (*Sodomei*) were expelled in 1925 and they formed their own labour organisation, the *Nihon Rodo Kumiai Hyogikai* (Japan Labour Unions Council). By 1926 it boasted 32,000 members and played a leading role in labour disputes and anti-government agitation. It was strongly influenced by the Communist Party but was weakened by internal factional conflict and government oppression. In April 1928 it was forcibly dissolved by the government.

Jinshin Koseki The first family register produced after the *Meiji* restoration in 1873. Although the former outcasts had been formally emancipated, many of the local officials who compiled these registers ensured that it would be possible to identify their descendants.

Jiyuto The Liberal Party, was one of the leading parties of the 1880s which called for the extension of popular rights and the establishment of constitutional government. It won support not only among the urban and rural middle classes but also among the peasants and tenant farmers even among the *Burakumin*. It dissolved in 1884, but in 1891 the name was revived and used by one of the parties active in the Diet until 1898.

Jodo Shinshu Pure Land Sect. A Buddhist sect which derives its doctrine from the ideas expounded by Shinran (1173-1262) who taught that all could achieve salvation provided that they have sincerely invoked the grace of the Amida Buddha by pronouncing his name. Based on the notion that all men are to some extent impure, its teaching held a particular attraction for those in outcast communities. When in the early eighteenth century the government ordered separate registers for *eta:hinin* to be established, for the sake of administrative convenience all their temples were ordered to become affiliated to the *Jodo Shinshu* organisation. Its main temples are the *Honganji* (temples of the original vow).

Kaizen undo Improvement movement. Name given to the network of groups which emerged in the early part of the twentieth century to work for the improvement of conditions in the *Buraku* communities to enable their acceptance by the majority community.

Kanto The seven prefectures including and adjacent to Tokyo, i.e., Ibaragi, Tochigi, Gumma, Saitama, Tokyo, Kanagawa and Chiba.

Kansai The Osaka-Kyoto area.

Kawaramono Riverside folk. Term used particularly before the *Tokugawa* period to refer to those beyond the pale of civilised society. Unable because of poverty or social custom to acquire land on high ground they lived on river banks which were liable to be flooded after heavy rainfall.

Kawata Term used in some areas, e.g., Hiroshima, to refer to leather workers.

Kazoku Titled person of the period 1873-1945, usually a descendant of either a court noble or a feudal lord.

Kinki The seven prefectures of the area around Osaka, i.e., Shiga, Kyoto, Osaka, Nara, Wakayama, Mie, Hyogo.

Kogisho Deliberative body composed of representatives of each of the Han authorities which was set up in April 1869 to advise the new government on policies. It does not appear to have had much influence on the government though it did discuss the issue of the status of *eta:hinin* several times.

Kokuhonsha Founded in 1924 with Hiranuma Kiichiro as its president, it stressed the unique religious character of Japan and Japan's mission in Asia. At its peak it had 170 branches and a membership of 200,000 which included many leading politicians, bureaucrats, soldiers and businessmen. It was a stronghold of traditional conservative ideas and regarded by those on the left as a Japanese equivalent of the Italian fascist or German Nazi parties. It was dissolved in June 1936.

Kokusuikai The *Dainippon Kokusuikai* was founded in 1919, its main sponsor being Tokonami Takejiro, Home Minister in the Hara Kei Cabinet. Its main purpose was to oppose the spread of radical thought and the development of the labour and tenant movements. One estimate of its size suggests that in the early 1920s it had 120,000 members most of whom were temporary or seasonal workers who were dependent on foremen or contractors. It was frequently involved in incidents with members of the *Suiheisha* and used to break strikes of workers or tenants through the use of force.

Kokutai Literally national polity. A somewhat nebulous concept used in pre-war Japan to refer to the fundamental character of the Japanese state. It embraced the idea that the Emperor was the highest power of the state and that the nation was an organic whole united by the morality of filial piety and loyalty to the Emperor.

Kyochokai Harmonisation Society. A government backed association for the promotion of industrial harmony founded in 1919, it had branches in factories grouped into regional federations and controlled by a central co-ordinating organisation. Its attempts at mediation were rarely successful but it did extensive research on labour and social problems. It was disbanded in 1926.

Kyoho Kaikaku Name given to the series of reforms carried out in the period 1716-1735, the main aim of which was to deal with the economic problems of the central administration, but they included a variety of detailed sumptuary regulations for all classes. New administrative programmes were also devised such as the five year census which began in 1721. As far as *eta:hinin* were concerned, these measures had the effect of formalising customary discrimination.

Kyudan Censure or denunciation of an individual or group. In the present text used to describe the protest of *Burakumin* against instances of insult or discrimination.

Meiji Name given to the period 1868 to 1912 when Japan was formally ruled over by the *Meiji* emperor (b.1852)

Musan Seinen Domei Proletarian Youth League founded in December 1925 to co-ordinate the activities of all the Communist Party oriented youth groups in the country in their campaign against the militarisation of education. It was forced to disband after the mass arrests of 1928.

Nara The capital of Japan 710-784 AD, which period of history is known as the Nara period.

Profintern The 'Red International of Labour Unions' formed in 1921 to seek 'revolutionary unity' between the red labour unions and Communist parties. The organisation worked closely with the Comintern, and indeed was largely under its control. From 1935 it urged the adoption of a Popular Front strategy and it was disbanded in 1937.

Rodo Nominto Labour Farmer Party. Formed on March 5 1926, with support from a wide range of those involved in social democratic groups, but soon became dominated by the 'legal left' as distinguished from the illegal Communist Party. Two of its members were elected to the Diet in 1928, but later that year, following the arrest of many of its members, it was dissolved.

Ryo Silver coin in use in the *Tokugawa* period.

Ryomin The 'good' citizenry as opposed to the *senmin* the 'base'. A distinction that originated in the eighth or ninth century.

Sanka People who led a migratory way of life in the mountains of Japan living in tents and making a living selling fish or baskets. Their number dropped rapidly before and after the Pacific War. The origins of the group are unknown but they were treated as outcasts, their lifestyle being regarded as strange by a society which saw the settled pursuit of agriculture as the norm.

Sen One hundredth of a yen, part of the coinage in use before 1945

Senmin See ryomin

Shinto The national religion of Japan. A rather confused mixture of ancestor veneration and nature worship which, especially following the *Meiji* restoration, was elevated to a state religion at the centre of which was the Emperor.

Shinheimin New commoner. Neologism used to refer to the descendants of *eta:hinin* during the *Meiji* period. It was originally intended to be a neutral term but soon acquired pejorative connotations.

Showa The era name given to the period of rule of the Showa emperor (b1901) who succeeded his father (the Taisho emperor) to the throne in December 1926.

Taisho Name given to the reign of the third son of the *Meiji* emperor (b1879) who succeeded to the throne in 1912 and reigned until 1926.

Tan Area of land equal to 0.245 acre.

Teikoku Kodokai Imperial Path of Justice Association. Founded in June 1912 by a Buddhist priest from Yamaguchi prefecture, it very soon came under the control of Oe Taku. It held its first national conference two years later and between 1914 and 1917 it produced a journal, *Kodo*, which was distributed throughout the country. Its main theme was that since the emperor had liberated the *Burakumin* it was now up to the people to change their ideas and stop discrimination. However, Oe and others recognised that unless central government provided more money to alleviate the poverty which was rife inside the *Buraku* communities public opinion was unlikely to change and there was a possibility that *Burakumin* would be attracted to the radical movements. The organisation became increasingly active in the wake of the Rice Riots, holding conferences in 1919 and 1922 which were attended by many who were later to become leading members of the *Suiheisha*. However, on Oe's death in September 1921, the organisation seems to have lost its driving force and declined quite rapidly over the next few years. In 1927, along with other groups, it merged with *Chuo Yuwa Jigyo Kyokai*.

Tempo Name given to the era 1830-1844 when a series of reforms were implemented to remedy the political, economic and social problems which beset the Tokugawa régime.

Tenko Conversion. Used to refer to the conversion of communists and other anti-government radicals from their anti-establishment views to support of the ideological position promoted by the state and especially the war on the Chinese mainland.

Tokugawa Bakufu In 1603 Tokugawa Ieyasu was awarded the title of shogun and his descendants remained the governors of Japan until 1868 during which period the imperial in Kyoto was virtually powerless. The name *Bakufu* was given to a military government headed by a shogun.

Tsubamekai The Swallow Association. The name given to the group formed in Kasuyabara, Nara prefecture, by Sakamoto Seiichiro, Kiyohara Kazutake and Komai Keisaku in 1919. The original plan was for the members of the group to 'fly away' from discrimination by migrating to the Celebes islands. This plan was, however, abandoned and it developed into a discussion group which examined other ways in which they might avoid discrimination. It was the members of this group who formulated the proposal to establish the *Suiheisha*.

Yuwa Harmony, reconciliation. Name given to the groups founded in the early years of the twentieth century to promote closer relations between *Buraku* and non-*Buraku* communities. Later adopted by the government for the organisations it sponsored as part of the effort to reduce the influence of the *Suiheisha*. In 1941 the projects were renamed *Dowa* projects and this is the term which has been adopted by the post-war governments.

Names

Arima Yoriyasu (1884-1957) Eldest son of the Arima family who formerly had ruled the feudal fief of Kurume in Kyushu. He studied agricultural chemistry at Tokyo University and then joined the Ministry of Agriculture, but he left his post there in 1918 to each at university. He assisted with the formation of the *Nihon Nomin Kumiai* (Japan Peasants Union) and in 1921 was instrumental in the founding of the Doaikai, a group which, it was hoped, would co-ordinate the activities of the *kaizen* groups. He was elected to the House of Representatives in 1924 and for the next few years raised the issue of *Yuwa* policy in the Diet. When the Doaikai merged with the *Chuo Yuwa Jigyo Kyokai* in 1927 Arima became its deputy chairman. He succeeded to the family title of count in 1927 and took a seat in the Upper House. He served as Minister of Agriculture under Konoe in 1937 and was appointed as the first director of the Imperial Rule Assistance Association in 1940, but was forced to resign due to pressure from the right. He was detained after the war as a war criminal, but was not prosecuted.

Asada Zennosuke (1902-1983) Active within the *Suiheisha* groups and labour union movement in Kyoto during the 1920s at which time he was associated with the anarchist tendency. However, he came to prominence within the *Suiheisha* during the 'dissolution controversy' of the early 1930s and edited the movement's newspaper, the *Suihei Shimbun*, between 1933 and 1937, remaining a central figure in the movement in its years of decline. He was instrumental in the revival of the movement after the war and continued to be active until the time of his death.

Danzaemon The title of the successive outcast leaders in Edo from the Tokugawa to the Meiji period. For most of the Tokugawa era he had control over most of the *eta:hinin* households in the Kanto area and lived the life of a lesser feudal lord. His income derived from the sale of leather goods of which he had a monopoly in the region. He had the powers to arbitrate in disputes between outcasts under his control and organised tax collection and the enforcement of monopolies.

Hirano Shoken (1891-1940) Born in Fukushima but moved to Tokyo in search of work and perhaps to escape discrimination. He was active in the Print workers union, the *Shinyukai*, but became interested in the *Teikoku Kodokai* though he was critical of its nationalism. Attended the first conference of the *Suiheisha* and was an influential figure in the development of the movement in the Kanto area. He was expelled from the movement in 1924 following the 'Spy incident', but he continued to be active in trying to shift the movement away from its Marxist orientation. In 1927 he established the *Nippon Suiheisha* to try to combat this leftward trend, but his efforts were largely in vain. During the 1930s he became more closely involved with patriotic right wing organisations though he retained contacts with some of those in the *Yuwa* and *Suiheisha* groups in the Kanto region.

Hiranuma Kiichiro (1867-1952) Graduate of the Law School at Tokyo Imperial University, Hiranuma became a leading figure in both legal and political worlds. He was vice-chairman of the Privy Council 1925-36 and its chairman 1936-9 and served as Prime Minister for a few months in 1939. He was the leading figure in the *Kokuhonsha* which made him one of the most influential of the respectable right-wing politicians. When the *Chuo Yuwa Jigyo Kyokai* was formed in 1925 he was appointed as its chairman, a position he was to keep until the end of the war. After the war, he was sentenced to life imprisonment as a class A war criminal and he died in prison.

Imoto Rinshi (1905-1984) active in the trade union movement in Fukuoka city from the early 1920s, he began to take an active part in the *Suiheisha* movement from 1924 when he joined a local *Suiheisha* youth group. His activities became a focus of attention in 1927 in the course of the Fukuoka Regiment campaign and when he left the army he became a member of the central committee. In the 1930s he played a central role in several Kyudan campaigns, in particular the Takamatsu Court Campaign of 1933. He was close to Matsumoto Jiichiro and acted as his secretary both before and after the war. Following the liberation movement's post-war relaunch he remained active in it until shortly before his death.

Katayama Sen (1860-1933) Active in the labour movement from the late 1890s and a prime mover in many of the attempts to launch socialist organisations in the first decade of the twentieth century. He went to the USA in 1914, continued with his involvement in the left wing movement and after the Russian revolution worked for the Comintern first in Mexico then from 1921 until his death in Moscow.

Kimura Kyotaro (1902-) Born into a poor *Buraku* family in Nara prefecture, he first became active in a *Suiheisha* group in 1922 and indeed was arrested in December of that year following his involvement in a *kyudan* protest at a school in his home village. Thereafter he was close to the centre of *Suiheisha* and instrumental in encouraging it to adopt a more left-wing approach. Strongly influenced by Marxist literature, he became a member of the Communist Party in 1927 and was the leader of the party cell within the *Suiheisha*. He was implicated in the bomb plot at the time of the Fukuoka Regiment incident and sentenced to three years imprisonment in May 1927. While waiting for the result of an appeal against this sentence he was once more arrested on charges which derived from the Public Peace Police Act and this time sentenced to five years imprisonment. He was finally released from prison on parole in October 1935. Thereafter he took part in some of the activities of groups which sought to launch a nationalist *Buraku* movement. After the war he resumed his left-wing activity and remains associated with the sector of the movement which allies itself with the Communist Party.

Kitahara Daisaku (1906-1981) Born in Gifu prefecture and joined the *Suiheisha* there in 1924. He was a supporter of the anarchist faction at the time of the Anarchist-Bolshevik struggle and was a founding member of the Liberation League. Conscripted in 1927, he continued to oppose discrimination from within the army. In November of that year at a parade of his regiment which was held before the Emperor he made a Direct Appeal to him on behalf of those who had been arrested in connection with the Fukuoka Regiment incident. For this he was sentenced to a year in prison and given a hard time in his remaining period in the army. On his release he moved to Tokyo where he took a course in social studies for a time at Japan University, meanwhile becoming interested in the Communist Party. He was one of those who supported the dissolution of the *Suiheisha* movement in 1932, and when this strategy was abandoned formulated the *Buraku Iinkai* principles. In April 1933 he joined the Communist Party and began to organise a party cell within the *Suiheisha* movement, but was arrested in January of the following year. He was kept in prison for 500 days, being released after having produced a *tenko* statement in which he renounced his support for communism. However, he continued to play an active part in the *Suiheisha* movement, until it was dissolved. After the war he took part in the debate on the theory and practice of the *Buraku* liberation movement, usually supporting the position taken by the faction linked to the Communist Party.

Kiyohara Kazutaka (1895-1970) also known by his pen name of Saiko Bankichi. His father was a priest who took some trouble to try to educate his son by sending him to a school in Kyoto which was specifically for the sons of priests. But even here he came across discrimination when his status background was discovered. In 1914 he moved to Tokyo to study Western painting where he was able to mix freely with other students by concealing his family background. He was strongly influenced by the wave of liberal and socialist ideas which swept into Japan after 1918 and became a member of the short-lived Socialist League. While in Tokyo he never lost touch with his home village in Nara and in 1921 he returned to help form the *Tsubamekai*. Then, encouraged by the ideas of Sano Manabu, with his colleagues, he formulated the proposal to launch the *Suiheisha*. Active in the peasant movement as well as the *Suiheisha*, he became more and more radical until he joined the Communist Party in October 1927. He stood unsuccessfully in the Lower House elections in February 1928 and was arrested soon afterwards. He served most of his five year prison sentence and on his release began to try to organise a nationalist peasant movement in Nara prefecture. After the war he devoted most of his energy to his writing of plays and stories and did not play a role in the revival of the movement.

Komai Keisaku (1897-1945) With Saiko and Sakamoto, he was one of the three founding members of the *Suiheisha*. His father was a wood dealer and fairly prosperous, so he received a good education. He visited Saiko in Tokyo where he became interested in radical ideas, particularly the thought of such socialists as Osugi Sakae and Sakai Toshihiko. He was arrested after the Koku-Sui incident though not charged and from the mid 1920s does not seem to have played a key role in the organisation.

Konoe Fumimaro (1891-1945) Scion of the noble Fujiwara family, he took his seat in the House of Peers in 1916, became its president in 1933 and was frequently asked to become Prime Minister in the late 1930s because of his good relations with both the military and civil service. He served as Prime Minister twice, June 1937 – January 1939 and July 1940 – July 1941. On the second occasion he founded the Imperial Rule Assistance Association which he hoped could counter the influence of the army, but it remained politically weak. From 1944 he worked for an end to the war but this did not prevent him from being designated a class A war criminal and he took his own life.

Kotoku Shusui (1871-1911) A participant in left-wing activity from the late 1880s he wrote for many of the leading radical newspapers and journals. He turned to anarchism during a visit to America in 1904-5 and on his return was an advocate of direct action in opposition to the parliamentarians. He both translated much European anarchist material and made important contributions of his own to the debate within socialist circles in Japan. In 1910 he was arrested on charges of having plotted the assassination of the Emperor, found guilty and executed.

Matsuda Kiichi (1899-1965) Organised the Nishihama *Suiheisha* in April 1923 and thereafter was active in the liberation movement throughout his life. From the start he associated with radicals such as Kimura Kyotaro, was a member of the *Suiheisha* Youth League in 1924 and became a member of the *Suiheisha* central committee in May 1925. In 1927 he joined the Communist Party and set about forming a 'faction bureau' to ensure the *Suiheisha* would develop in accordance with party policy. He was arrested more than ten times, but never charged until 1928 when he was captured along with most of the other active members of the party. Following torture, he admitted membership of the Communist Party and was sentenced to four years in prison. On his release, he became involved with the leather producers' union. After the war he took an active part in reviving the movement.

Matsumoto Jiichiro (1887-1966) Known as 'Father of the Liberation Movement', he exercised a dominant influence on the movement from the time he became involved until his death. Having experienced discrimination both at the school near his home and at schools in Kyoto and Tokyo he left Japan in 1907 to work in a Post Office in Dairen. Dismissed from this post, he survived for three years by selling pharmaceutical preparations. He returned to Fukuoka in 1911 and founded a construction company which he was to see grow into a prosperous organisation. Even before the founding of the *Suiheisha*, he took part in demonstrations against discrimination and was only prevented from attending the first meeting of the Kyushu *Suiheisha* because he was arrested by police and held on a phoney charge for some time before and three days after the conference. At the third national conference he criticised the rewards given by the Meiji government to the Tokugawa family and demanded that Prince Tokugawa be deprived of his title. Soon afterwards, he was arrested with two others on charges of having conspired to assassinate Prince Tokugawa and following a trial he was sent to prison for four months. At the fourth conference he was elected chairman and thereafter both provided most of the movement's money and guided its policies. He played a leading role in the anti-militarist struggle in Fukuoka in 1927 and was once

again arrested on charges of having conspired to bomb the headquarters of the Fukuoka Regiment. This time he was sentenced to three
and a half years imprisonment. As a radical social democrat he never
seems to have been attracted to the Communist Party. In 1928 he stood
for election to the Diet in the Fukuoka constituency for the first time
but did not succeed, then in 1936 when he stood as a member of the
Social Masses Party he was successful. He remained a Diet member
until the end of the war. Matsumoto invested a large amount of his time
and money in the *Suiheisha* movement so that he was reluctant to see it
dissolved despite the pressure from within and without the movement
to do so. After the war he was purged twice. The first time in 1946
because he was suspected of right-wing associations as he had been a
member of the war-time Diet; the second time in 1949 because of his
left-wing sympathies. When the purge order was finally lifted he stood
for election to the newly formed Upper House and served there until
his death. Needless to say, he played a key role in the reformation of the
liberation movement in the late 1940s and oversaw its growth in the
1950s.

While a young man he was well known for his fondness for wine and
women, but he made a public vow not to drink alcohol, get married or
wear a tie until the liberation of *Burakumin* was complete. As far as is
known he never did any of these things.

Minami Umekichi (1877-1947) Son of a *geta* (wooden sandal) maker who
moved to Kyoto from Shiga while he was of primary school age. He had
been involved with the *kaizen* youth groups in Kyoto for more than ten
years before being contacted by the founders of the *Suiheisha*. He
played a crucial role in launching the movement in its early years but
was forced to resign from the movement following the 'Spy Scandal'.
At this stage he seems to have moved to Tokyo, where he received
support from Arima. He was not influenced by the rise of socialist ideas
which came to dominate the movement. Indeed, he sought to oppose
the rise of left-wing ideas in the late 1920s by the formation of the
Nippon Suiheisha. In the 1930s he devoted his energies to the *Yuwa*
movement.

Nakae Chomin (1847-1901) Leading Meiji liberal who had studied Chinese
and Western learning in Nagasaki and then French thought in France
1871-74. He was in the forefront of the opposition movement of the
1880s which demanded recognition of human rights. His most lasting
influence was by his translation of Rousseau's *Social Contract* and his
work as a journalist. Shortly before his death he wrote one of the first
articles sympathetic to the plight of the '*Shinheimin*'.

Oe Taku (1847-1921) Born in Tosa han, Oe had studied Western learning in
Nagasaki and according to some reports had been to Shanghai. He
returned to Kobe at the time of the restoration when he became aware
of the large *eta:hinin* communities there. Appalled by this dire poverty
and concerned that Westerners would be shocked to see such scenes, he
petitioned the new government not only to remove the restrictive
regulations but also to provide the new citizens with some assistance to
enable them to escape from poverty. In 1872 he joined the civil service
first of all in the *Minbusho* (Ministry of Popular Affairs) and then as

Governor of Kanagawa, but he was imprisoned in 1877 for his involvement with the Satsuma rebellion. After serving seven years of his ten year sentence, he was released and once again became active in politics, ultimately sitting as a member of the Jiyuto in the Diet 1890-1892. On losing his seat he entered the business world and was a leading figure in a railway company and a stockbroking company. Eventually he became President of the Stock Exchange until he retired a wealthy man in 1909. Thereafter, he once more took an interest in the *Buraku* problem and from 1911 until his death was the central figure in the *Teikoku Kodokai*.

Osugi Sakae (1885-1923) Strongly influenced by Kotoku Shusui, he became a leading advocate of direct action in the early years of this century. He was arrested and imprisoned for a total of three years 1906-11, the final period of time in jail probably saving him from arrest with 22 other anarchists including Kotoku in 1910. After World War I, he became active within the labour movement which was dominated by the anarcho-syndicalist unions. In the immediate aftermath of the Kanto earthquake of 1923 he was murdered by the police.

Ozaki Yukio (1859-1954) Elected to the Diet in 1890, he was subsequently re-elected 24 times in succession, remaining a member until the time of his death. For a brief period in 1898 he was Minister for Education and between 1914-16 he served as Justice minister. Throughout his career he was a trenchant critic of oligarchic government and later the militarist tendencies within Japanese politics. During the war he continued his criticisms and in 1942 was charged with *lèse majesté*.

Saiko Bankichi See Kiyohara Kazutaka

Sakai Toshihiko (1871-1933) Journalist who worked on such newspapers as *Yorozu Choho* and *Heimin Shimbun*. He was a member of the short-lived *Nihon Shakaito* 1906-7 in which he was close to Kotoku. After 1917 he became influenced by Marxism, and was the first chairman of the JCP when it was formed in 1922. His views were criticised by the Comintern and he did not join the party when it was reformed in 1926. He was involved with the legal left-wing parties and was an unsuccessful Diet candidate in 1930.

Sakamoto Seiichiro (1892-) Born into a fairly wealthy and prominent family in the *Buraku* of Kasuyabara, he was brought up in a sheltered environment. He only came across discrimination at middle school. At the age of 18 he left Japan to find work in Manchuria where he stayed for two years until his brother's illness prompted his father to ask him to return home to help look after the family business. In the late 1910s, he studied in Tokyo at a technical school during which period he lodged with Saiko and was influenced by the influx of Western ideas. These two, along with Komai initiated the proposal to form the *Suiheisha*. Once the movement was launched Sakamoto remained identified with the moderate faction and does not appear to have played a major role in the movement at the national level.

Sano Manabu (1892-1953) A graduate of Tokyo University law department in 1917, he taught at Waseda University where he became interested in socialism. From 1921 he was active in the labour movement and produced a number of pamphlets, one of which, 'On the Emancipation

of *Tokushu Burakumin*', inspired those in the Tsubamekai to launch a
national movement. He was a member of the first Communist Party
and escaped arrest in 1923 by fleeing to Moscow. On his return to Japan
in 1925 he served ten months in prison but nevertheless was on the
party's central committee from 1927. He escaped the 1928 arrests again
by fleeing to Moscow, but was captured in Shanghai in 1929 and
brought back to Japan. In 1932 he was sentenced to life imprisonment
but early the next year he issued a *tenko* statement disavowing the aims
of the party. He was released from prison in 1943 and served with the
Japanese authorities in Peking. After 1945, he took up an appointment
at Waseda University.

Shinran See Jodo Shinshu

Takahashi Sadaki (1905-1935) Born in Oita prefecture, his family background
is a matter of some controversy, his father was from an ex-samurai
family but Takahashi always claimed that his true mother was a
Burakumin. In 1921 he went to Tokyo to study economics, but became
an active member of the *Suiyokai*, a group which was one of the
forerunners of the Communist Party. He was active in the *Suiheisha*
Youth League 1923-5, then, shortly before being expelled from the
movement for not being of *Buraku* origin, he left Japan to study at the
Lenin Institute in Moscow 1926-8. He cut short his studies in order to
return to Japan to rebuild the party in late 1928, but was arrested in
April 1929 and later sentenced to 15 years in prison. In 1935 he became
critically ill, was released from prison, and died soon after.

Yamagata Aritomo (1838-1922) He was a member of a lower samurai family
from Choshu and rose quickly after the restoration to a position in the
early 1870s which enabled him to become the architect of the new
military system. He was Prime Minister 1889-90 during which time the
new local government system was introduced and was Prime Minister
again 1898-1900. As a *genro* from 1891 he was a major influence on
Japanese politics until his death and, in particular, was strongly
opposed to party activity.

Yamakawa Hitoshi (1880-1958) Initially interested in Christianity he
participated in the formation of the Socialist party in 1906 when he gave
his support to the anarchist cause. Arrested four times over the next few
years he retired from political activism in 1910 until 1916 when he
returned from the countryside to Tokyo, where he began to propagate
socialist ideas. With Sakai Tohihiko he was a leading Marxist and was a
founder member of the first Communist Party. However, he sought to
build a united popular front party rather than a vanguard party of the
kind favoured by the Comintern. In 1928 he severed all links with the
JCP and devoted himself to the study of history and Marxist theory. He
was arrested in 1937 and his case was still under appeal in 1945. After
the war, though not affiliated to any party, he was a strong influence on
the Japan Socialist Party.

Yoneda Tomi (1901-) Son of a cobbler who died when he was only fifteen.
From 1917 he was a member of various groups which were set up in
Nara prefecture to keep an eye on the *Buraku* youth so that when he
came into contact with Saiko and others he already had considerable
experience at organising meetings. Yoneda was a member of the central

committee in the movement's early years, but he was implicated in the 'Spy Incident' after which he confined his activities to Nara prefecture. Following Saiko's release from prison they formed a movement which sought to establish a form of state socialism centred on the Emperor. After the war he was active in the revival of the *Buraku* liberation movement and the right-wing of the socialist party.

Bibliography

i *Primary Sources*

Watanabe Toru and Akisada Yoshikazu (eds), *Buraku Mondai Suihei Undo Shiryo Shusei* (Compilation of Documents about the *Suiheisha* Movement). Tokyo, Sanichi Shobo. Vol I, 1973, vol II 1974, vol III, 1974. Supplementary vol I, 1978, Supplementary vol II, 1978.

Ueda Onshi et al. (ed) *Mie-ken Buraku Shiryoshu-Kindaihen* (Collection of documents on the Mie prefecture Buraku – the modern period). Tokyo, Sanichi Shobo, 1974.

Suihei No 1 & 2, First published 1922, reprinted 1969. Sekai Bunko, Tokyo.

Suihei Shimbun (The Suihei Newspaper) Reproduction of all the editions from 1924 to 1939, Tokyo, Sekai Bunko, 1972.

Nishida Hideaki and Akisada Yoshikazu, *Suiheisha Undo* (The *Suiheisha* movement – a compilation of documents), Kobe Buraku Kaiho Kenkyukai, 1970.

Fujitani Toshio, Mahara Tetsuo et al (ed) *Suihei Undoshi no Kenkyu* (Research on the History of the *Suihei* movement). A collection of documents and essays. Published by the Buraku Mondai Kenkyujo, Kyoto. Vol I, 1971, vol II 1971, vol III, 1972, vol IV, 1972, vol V, 1972, vol VI, 1973.

Ogushi Natsumi, *Tokyo Suiheisha Kankei Shiryo Shusei*, no 1 (Compilation of Historical Material relating to the Tokyo *Suiheisha*). Photocopied small edition produced by Ogushi, 1976.

Yuwa Jigyo Kenkyu (Research on the Yuwa Project). Bi-monthly and later quarterly journal produced by the Home Ministry for circulation to *Yuwa* project group leaders and administrators between 1926 and 1941. Republished by Sekai Bunko, Tokyo, 1974, for the Buraku Mondai Kenkyujo in Kyoto.

Yuwa Jigyo Nenkan (*Yuwa* Project Yearbook). Review of the state of the *Yuwa* project, its budgets and activities in each area of the country produced yearly between 1926 and 1941. Republished by Sekai Bunko, Tokyo, 1970, for the Buraku Kaiho Kenkyujo in Osaka.

Yuwa Undo Ronso (Collection of Essays on the *Yuwa* movement). Selected from various sources, each essay first published between 1913 and 1941. Republished by Sekai Bunko, Tokyo, 1972. *Zenkoku Buraku Chosa* (National *Buraku* Society) compiled from reports made by branches of the *Chuo Yuwa Jigyo Kyokai* in 1934 and 1935. Published in Tokyo by the Chuo Jigyo Kyokai, in 1936.

Zenkoku Buraku Chosa (National Buraku Survey) compiled from reports made by branches of the Chuo Yuwa Kyogikai in 1934 and 1935. Published in Tokyo by the Chuo Yuwa Tigyo Kyokai, 1936.

Zenkoku Minji Kanrei Ruishi (A Handbook of Japanese Customs and Folkways), (Shihosho, 1880).

ii *Books and Articles Referred to in the text – in Japanese*

Akisada Yoshikazu: '1930 nendai Zengo ni okeru Toshi Buraku no Jotai to Dowa Jigyo ni tsuite' (Conditions in the Kyoto *Buraku* around 1930 and the *Dowa* Project). *Buraku Kaiho Kenkyu*, no 1 (October 1972), pp 52-75.
'Buraku Kaiho Undo to Kyosanshugi' (The *Buraku* Liberation Movement and Communism) in *Nihon Shakaishugi Undoshiron* (Essays on the History of the Japanese Socialist Movement), Watanabe Toru (ed), (Tokyo, Sanichi Shobo, 1973).
'Shoki Suiheisha Undo Shiryo no Danpen' (A Fragment of Material on the early *Suiheisha* Movement), *Buraku Kaiho Kenkyu*, no 4 (March 1975), pp 113-133.
'Hisabetsu Buraku to Kindai' (Discriminated *Buraku* in the Meiji period), *Dento to Gendai*, no 40 (July 1976), pp 103-111.
'1916-1922 nen no Yuwa Zaisei ni tsuite' (*Yuwa* Finance, 1916-1922), *Ikenobo Tanki Daigaku Kiyo*, no 7 (1976), pp 47-70.
'Suihei Shiso no Seiritsu' (The Formation of *Suiheisha* Ideas), *Rekishi Koron*, no 6 (June 1977), pp 106-113.
Amano Takuro, 'Buraku Kaiho to Yuwa Undo' (*Buraku* Liberation and the *Yuwa* movement), part I, *Geibi Chihoshi Kenkyu*, no 60, pp 1-13. Part II, *Geigi Chihoshi Kenkyu*, no 61, pp 10-20.
Arai Kojiro, 'Edojidai ni okeru Senmin Shihai no Ikkosatsu' (A Consideration of the Control of *Senmin* in the Edo Period), *Tokyo Buraku Kaiho Kenkyu*, no 3 (November 1974), pp 94-113.
Asada Zennosuke, *Sabetsu to Tatakai Tsuzukete* (The Continuing Struggle against Discrimination), (Tokyo, Asahi Shimbunsha, 1969).
Buraku Kaiho Kenkyujo – Nara-ken (ed), *Buraku Kaiho Undo to Yoneda Tomi* (The *Buraku* Liberation Movement and Yoneda Tomi), (Nara Buraku Kaiho Kenkyujo, 1977).
Buraku Mondai Kenkyujo (ed) *Buraku no Seitai: I Toshi Buraku* (*Buraku* Conditions 1 – a town *Buraku*; Matsuzaka, Mie Prefecture), (Kyoto, Buraku Mondai Kenkyujo, 1964).
Buraku Mondai Kenkyujo (ed), *Buraku Mondai Seminar IV* (Kyoto, Sekibunsha, 1969).
Buraku Kaiho Domei Chuo Hombu, *Zenkoku Suiheisha: Gojunenshi* (National *Suiheisha*: Fifty Years' History), (Osaka, Buraku Kaiho Shuppansha, 1971).
Fuchu-shi Yakusho, *Buraku no Jittai* (The Actual Conditions in the *Buraku*), (Hiroshima-ken, Fuchushi, Town Hall, 1969).
Fujitani Toshio, '*Yuwa Seisaku: Yuwa Undo no Rekishiteki Tokushitsu*' (Historical Characteristics of the *Yuwa* policy and *Yuwa* movement), Buraku Mondai Kenkyu, no 37 (May 1973), pp 2-13. Buraku Mondai no Rekishiteki Kenkyu (Historical Research on the *Buraku* Problem), (Kyoto, Buraku Mondai Kenkyujo, 1973).
Goto Masato, '*Bakuhan horei ni arawareta Senmin Shihai no Shoso to Tenkai*', (Various Aspects of and Developments in the Control of *Senmin* as shown in the Various Statutes of the Bakufu and Han Administrations), *Hoseishi Kenkyu*, no 23 (1973), pp 153-178.

Haraguchi Eiyu, *Buraku Mondai ni tsuite* (On the *Buraku* Problem), (Fukuoka, 1970).

Hayashi Hisayoshi, 'Suihei Honganji to Kokui Domei' (The *Suihei* Honganji and the Black Vestment League), *Buraku Kaihoshi*, no 8 (July 1977), pp 86-111.

Higashi Yoshikazu, 'Yamato no Hisabetsu Buraku' (The *Buraku* of the Yamato area), *Buraku Kaiho Kenkyu*, no 4 (March 1975), pp 2-29.

Hiranuma Kiichi, 'Chuo Yuwa Kikan to Chuo Yuwa Jigyo Kyokai Shimei' (The Role of the Central *Yuwa* Agency and the Central *Yuwa* Project Association), *Yuwa Jiho*, vol 2, no 8 (October 1927), pp 2-29.

Ikeda Takamasa, 'Kaihorei Zengo' (Circumstances surrounding the Emancipation Declaration), in *Kindai Nihon to Buraku Mondai*, (Kyoto, Buraku Mondai Kenkyujo, 1974).

Inoue Kiyoshi and Watanabe Toru (eds), *Kome Sodo no Kenkyu* (Research on the Rice Riots), (Tokyo, Yuhikaku, 6 volumes published between 1959 and 1962).

Iwamura Toshio, *Zainichi Chosenjin to Nihon Rodosha Kaikyu* (Koreans Resident in Japan and the Japanese Working Class), (Tokyo, Azekura Shobo, 1972).

Kadota Hideo (ed), *Hiroshima ken: Hisabetsu Buraku no Rekishi* (Hiroshima Prefecture: a History of the *Buraku*), (Tokyo, Akishobo, 1975).

Kikuchi Sanya, *Etazoku ni Kansuru Kenkyu* (Research Concerning the *Eta* Race), (Tokyo, Sanseisha, 1923).

Kimura Kyotaro, *Suiheisha Undo no Omoide* (Memories of the *Suiheisha* movement), Part One (Kyoto, Buraku Mondai Shinsho, 1972), Part Two (Kyoto, Buraku Mondai Shinsho, 1973).

Kinoshita Hanji, *Nihon Fashisumushi I* (Japanese Fascism), (Tokyo, Iwasaki Shoten, 1950).

Kinoshita Hiroshi, 'Hirano Jukichi (Shoken) ni tsuite' (About Hirano Jukichi (Shoken)), *Buraku Mondai Kenkyu*, no 31 (November 1971), pp 116-120.

Kita Teikichi, 'Tokushu Buraku Kenkyugo' (Special Edition about Research on the Special *Buraku*), *Minzoku to Rekishi*, vol II, no 1 (July 1919).

Kitahara Daisaku, *Senmin no Koei* (Descendant of a *senmin*), (Tokyo, Chikuma Shobo, 1974).

Kitagara Tetsuo, *Saiko Bankichi to Buraku Mondai* (Saiko Bankichi and the *Buraku* Problem), (Tokyo, Toshobo, 1975).

Kobayashi Shigeru, 'Kinsei ni okeru Buraku Kaiho Toso' (The Struggle for *Buraku* Liberation in the Edo Period), *Rekishi Koron*, no 6 (June 1977), pp 88-95.

Koga Seizaburo, *Tokyo Suiheisha to Hikaku Sangyo Rodosha* (The Tokyo *Suiheisha* and the Workers in the Leather Industry), (Tokyo Buraku Kaiho Kenkyukai, 1977).

Koga Seizaburo, *Tokyo Suiheisha Kankei Shiryoshu* (Collection of Material Relating to the Tokyo *Suiheisha*), Tokyo Buraku Kaiho Kenkyukai, 1977).

Mahara Tetsuo, *Nihon Shihonshugi to Buraku Mondai* (Japanese Capitalism and the *Buraku* Problem), (Kyoto, Buraku Mondai Kenkyujo, 1973).

Mahara Tetsuo, *Suihei Undo no Rekishi* (A History of the *Suihei* Movement), (Kyoto, Buraku Mondai Kenkyujo, 1973).

Matsumoto Jiichiro, *Buraku Kaiho e no Sanjunen* (Thirty Years towards *Buraku* Liberation), (Tokyo, Kindai Shisosha, 1948).

Matsuzaki Taketoshi, 'Iwayuru Yoritomo Gyohanbutsu' (A review of the Yoritomo Gyohanbutsu), *Buraku Kaihoshi Fukuoka*, no 2 (October 1975), pp 12-19.

'Edo jidai ni okeru Fukuoka Chiho no Buraku to Nogyo' (*Buraku* and Agriculture in the Fukuoka area during the Edo period), Part One, *Buraku Kaihoshi Fukuoka*, no 6 (January 1977), pp 24-43. Part Two, *Buraku Kaihoshi Fukuoka*, no 7 (March 1977), pp 13-21.

Miyazaki Akira, *Sabetsu to Anakizumu* (Discrimination and Anarchism), (Gummaken, Isezakishi, Kokushoku sensensha, 1975).

Moriyama Senichi et al 'Fukken Domei no Kaimei' (A clarification about the Restoration of Rights League), *Buraku Kaihoshi Fukuoka*, no 1 (March 1975), pp 133-141.

Moroka Sukeyuki, 'Suiheisha: Takamatsu Chiho Sabetsu Saiban Kyudan Toso' (*Suiheisha*: the Takamatsu Court Discrimination Censure Struggle), *Gendai no Me*, vol 14, no 2, pp 118-129.

Murakoshi Sueo, 'Kome Sodo ni okeru Mikaiho Buraku no Kenkyu' (Research on Unliberated *Buraku* in the Rice Riots), *Buraku Mondai Kenkyu*, no 3 (1958), pp 72-108.

Nakamura Masao and Matsuzaki Taketoshi, 'Chikuzen Kokurahan no Buraku Seisaku'. (The *Buraku* Policies of the Chikuzen Kokura Daimiate), *Buraku Kaihoshi Fukuoka*, no 2 (October 1975), pp 30-55).

Nakamura Fukuji, 'Takahashi Sadaki to Suihei Undo' (Takahashi Sadaki and the *Suihei* Movement), *Buraku Mondai Kenkyu*, no 51, pp 2-39.

Nakanishi Yoshio, 'Kome Sodo Gojunen to Buraku Mondai', (The Fiftieth Anniversary of the Rice Riots and the *Buraku* Problem), *Buraku Mondai Kenkyu*, no 24, pp 35-47.

Nakano Shigeru, *Hiroshima ken: Suihei Undoshi* (Hiroshima Prefecture: a History of the *Suihei* Movement), (First published 1930, republished by the Hiroshimaken Buraku Kaiho Domei, 1971).

Narisawa Eichi, 'Yuwa Undo to Seisaku' (The *Yuwa* Movement and Policy), Chapter Six, *Suihei Undoshi no Kenkyu*, vol VI (Kyoto, Buraku Mondai Kenkyujo, 1973).

Ohara Tsunehiko, Matsui Koshiro et al, *Matsumoto Jiichiro to Kaiho Undo* (Matsumoto Jiichiro and the Liberation Movement), (Osaka, Buraku Kaiho Kenkyujo, 1973).

Okuyama Tetsuo, 'Dai Kyoko Zengo no Toshi Buraku no Jotai to Suihei Undo' (Conditions in the Kyoto *Buraku* at the time of the Great Depression and the *Suihei* Movement). *Buraku Mondai Kenkyu*, no 41 (March 1974), pp 64-78.

Okiura Kazuteru, 'Nihon Marukusushugi no hitotsu no Riteihyo – Takahashi Sadaki no Shisoteki Kiseki' (A Milestone in Japanese Marxism – the Tracks of Takahashi's ideas), *Shiso* (December 1976), pp 80-100.

Oyama Shumpei, *Mieken Suiheisha Rono Undoshi* (The *Suiheisha* and the Worker/Peasant Movement in Mie Prefecture), (Tokyo, Sanichi Shobo, 1977).

Saiko Bankichi, *Saiko Bankichi Sakushu* (The Selected Works of Saiko Bankichi), (Published in four volumes between 1971 and 1974, Tokyo, Toshobo).

Shibata Michiko, *Hisabetsu Buraku no Densho to Seikatsu* (*Buraku* Folk Lore and Life), (Tokyo, Sanichi Shobo, 1972).

Shindo Toyo, *Fukuoka Rentai Jiken* (The Fukuoka Regiment Incident), (Tokyo, Gendaishi Shuppan kai, 1974).

Shiraishi Masaaki, '*Buraku Kaizen to Shoki Yuwa Seisaku*' (*Buraku* Improvement and Early *Yuwa* Policy), *Buraku Mondai Gaisetsu* (Osaka, Kaiho Shuppansha, 1977), pp 143-160.

Shiraishi Masaaki, 'Tennosei Kokka Kakuritsuki no Buraku Kaizen Undo', (The *Buraku* Improvement Movement at the Time of the Formation of the Emperor Centred State), *Rekishi Koron*, no 6 (June 1977), pp 96-105.

Shiso no Kagaku Kenkyukai (Committee for the Scientific Research of Ideas), *Tenko* (Conversion), Three volumes (Tokyo, Heibonsha, 1959).

Tada Michitaro, *Osugi Sakae* (Nihon no Meicho no 46), (Tokyo, Chuo Koronsha, 1969).

Teraki Nobuaki, 'Edojidai ni okeru Hisabetsu Buraku no Nominso no Bunkai' (An Analysis of the *Buraku* Peasant Classes in the Edo period), *Buraku Kaiho Kenkyu*, no 4 (March 1975), pp 38-53.

Watanabe Toru, 'Taisho Demokurashii to Guntai' (Taisho Democracy and the Army), *Buraku Kaihoshi Fukuoka*, no 10 (February 1978), pp 10-20.

Yagi Kosuke, *Sabetsu Kyudan* (Discrimination Censure), (Tokyo, Shakai Hyoronsha, 1976).

Yamagi Shigeru, 'Taishoki no Hiroshimaken Shakai Undoshi Gaiyo' (An Outline of the History of Social Movements in Hiroshima Prefecture in the Taisho Period), *Geibi Chihoshi Kenkyu*, vol 74, no 5 (November 1968), pp 7-12.

Yamagi Shigeru, *Hiroshimaken Shakai Undoshi* (A History of Social Movements in Hiroshima Prefecture), (Tokyo, Rodo Jumposha, 1970).

iii *Books and Articles referred to in the text – in English*

Ayusawa Iwao, *A History of Labour in Modern Japan* (First published 1966, reprinted by Greenwood Press, 1976).

J A Banks, *The Sociology of Social Movements* (Macmillan, 1972).

G M Beckman and G Okubo, *The Japanese Communist Party, 1922-1945* (Stanford University Press, 1969).

G M Berger, *The Search for a New Political Order: Konoe Fumimaro, the Political Parties and the Japanese Politics during the Early Showa Era* (Yale University, PhD, 1972).

G M Berger, *Parties out of Power in Japan, 1931-1941* (Princeton University Press, 1977).

D M Brown, *Nationalism in Japan* (University of California, 1955).

Cho Yukio, 'From Showa Economy to Military Economy', *The Developing Economies*, vol V, no 4 (December 1967), pp 568-596.

J D Cornell, 'From Caste Patron to Entrepreneur and Political Ideologue', in *Modern Japanese Leadership*, B S Silberman (ed), (University of Arizona Press, 1966).

G deVos and H Wagatsuma (eds), *Japan's Invisible Race* (University of California Press, 1973, Second Edition).

R P Dore, *Land Reform in Japan* (Oxford University Press, 1959).

M Douglas, *Purity and Danger* (Pelican Books, 1970).

L Dumont, *Homo Hierarchicus* (Paladin, 1970).

J Freeman, 'The Origins of the Women's Liberation Movement', *American Journal of Sociology*, vol 78, no 4, pp 792-811.

W M Fridell, 'Government Ethics Textbooks in Late Meiji Japan', *Journal of Asian Studies*, vol XXIX, pp 823-833.

A H Gleason, 'Economic Growth and Consumption in Japan', *The State and Economic Enterprise in Japan*, ed W W Lockwood (Princeton University Press, 1965).

E G Griffin, *The Adoption of Universal Suffrage in Japan* (Columbia University, PhD, 1965).

G Haessler, 'Japan's Untouchables', *The Nation*, vol 117, no 3035 (5 September 1923).

J Halliday, *A Political History of Japanese Capitalism* (Pantheon Books, 1975).

T R H Havens, *Valley of Darkness: the Japanese People and World War II* (New York, W W Norton, 1978).

C Johnson, *An Instance of Treason* (Tokyo, C E Tuttle, 1977).

P Lloyd, *Slums of Hope?* (Pelican Books, 1979).

W W Lockwood, *The Economic Development of Japan: Growth and Structural Change, 1868-1938* (Princeton University Press, 1968).

Ninomiya Shigeaki, 'An Enquiry concerning the Development and Present Situation of the *Eta* in Relation to the History of the Social Classes in Japan', *Transactions of the Asiatic Society of Japan*, vol 10 (1933), pp 47-154.

R H Mitchell, *Thought Control in Pre-War Japan* (Cornell University Press, 1976).

B Moore Jnr, *Injustice: the Social Bases of Obedience and Revolt* (Macmillan, 1978).

G Myrdal, *An American Dilemma* (New York, Harper Bros, 1944).

Ouchi Tsutomu, 'Agricultural Depression in Japanese Villages', *The Developing Economies*, vol V (December, 1967), pp 597-627.

Ozeki Hiroshi and Boris Badinoff (pseud?), 'Anarchism in Japan', *Anarchy*, Second Series, vol 1, no 5, pp 2-7, 24-31.

J A Price, 'The Economic Organisation of the Outcasts of Feudal Tokyo', *Anthropological Quarterly*, no 47 (October 1968), pp 209-217.

K B Pyle, 'The Technology of Japanese Nationalism: the Local Improvement Movement, 1900-1918', *Journal of Asian Studies*, vol XXXIII, no 1, pp 51-65.

Ryoke Minoru, 'The Nature of the Distribution of Outcasts Communities', *Kwansai Gakuin University Annual Studies*, no 14 (1965), pp 93-105.

Shimazaki Toson, *Hakai* (The Broken Commandment), trans K Strong (University of Tokyo Press, 1974).

Shiota Shobei, 'The Rice Riots and the Social Problems', *The Developing Economies*, vol IV (December 1966), pp 516-534.

R J Smethurst, 'The Creation of the Imperial Military Reserve Association', *Journal of Asian Studies*, vol XXX, pp 815-828.

R J Smethurst, *A Social Basis for Pre-War Japanese Militarism* (University of California Press, 1974).

A D Smith, *The Concept of Social Change* (Routledge and Kegan Paul, 1973).

A D Smith, 'Social Change and Diffusionist Theories', *Philosophy of Social Science*, no 5 (1975), pp 273-287.

E Steinhilber-Oberlin, *The Buddhist Sects of Japan* (Allen and Unwin, 1938).
P G Steinhoff, *Tenko* – Ideology and Societal Integration in Pre-War Japan (Harvard University, PhD, 1969).
I Taeuber, *The Population of Japan* (Princeton University Press, 1958).
Taira Koji, 'Urban Poverty, Ragpickers and the Ants' Villa in Tokyo', *Economic Development and Cultural Change*, vol 17, no 2 (January 1969), pp 155-177.
Takahashi Makoto, 'The Development of Wartime Economic Controls', *The Developing Economies*, vol V, no 4 (December 1967), pp 648-665.
Takeuchi Yoshitomo, 'The Role of Marxism in Japan', *The Developing Economies*, vol V, no 4 (December 1967), pp 727-747.
Tanin and Yohan, *Militarism and Fascism in Japan* (First published 1934, republished by Greenwood Press, 1975).
B Traven, *The Treasure of the Sierra Madre* (Panther Books, 1974).
Tsurumi Kazuko, *Social Change and the Individual* (Princeton University Press, 1970).
R H Turner and L M Killian, *Collective Behaviour* (New York, Prentice Hall, 1972).
B A Waswo, *Landlords and Social Change in Pre-War Japan* (Stanford University, PhD, 1969).
B A Waswo, 'Origins of Tenant Unrest' in *Japan in Crisis: Essays on Taisho Democracy*, B S Silberman and H D Harootumian (ed), (Princeton University Press, 1974).
J T Winkler, 'Corporatism', *Archive Europeene Sociologie* (1976), pp 101-136.
W D Wray, 'Aso Hisashi and the Search for Reform in the 1930s', *Papers on Japan*, vol 5 (Harvard University Press, 1970), pp 55-97.
W D Wray, 'The Japanese Popular Front Movement, July 1936–February 1938', *Papers on Japan*, vol 6 (Harvard University Press, 1972).
Yamaoka Masaki, 'Coastal Life of *Buraku* along the Tosa Coast in Japan', *Proceedings of the Faculty of Liberal Arts and Education* (Yamanashi University, 1962).

Formal Interviews

Asada Zennosuke, 30 January 1978, Kyoto.
Fukugawa Fujio (son of Fukugawa Takeshi), 1 December 1978, Tokyo.
Imoto Rinshi, 14 November 1977, Fukuoka.
Kimura Kyotaro, 31 January 1978, Kyoto.

Index